North Carolina
Civil War Obituaries,
Regiments 1 through 46

North Carolina Civil War Obituaries, Regiments 1 through 46

A Collection of Tributes to the War Dead and Veterans

Compiled and edited by
E.B. MUNSON

McFarland & Company, Inc., Publishers
Jefferson, North Carolina

LIBRARY OF CONGRESS CATALOGUING-IN-PUBLICATION DATA

North Carolina Civil War obituaries, Regiments 1 through 46 : a collection of tributes to the war dead and veterans / compiled and edited by E.B. Munson.
    p.   cm.
Includes bibliographical references and index.

ISBN 978-1-4766-6222-0 (softcover : acid free paper) ∞
ISBN 978-1-4766-2239-2 (ebook)

1. North Carolina—Genealogy. 2. North Carolina—History—Civil War, 1861–1865—Registers. 3. Soldiers—North Carolina—Registers. 4. Veterans—North Carolina—Registers. 5. United States—History—Civil War, 1861–1865—Registers. 6. Obituaries—North Carolina. I. Munson, E.B., compiler, editor.

F253.N877 2015   929.3756—dc23   2015027522

BRITISH LIBRARY CATALOGUING DATA ARE AVAILABLE

© 2015 E.B. Munson. All rights reserved

No part of this book may be reproduced or transmitted in any form or by any means, electronic or mechanical, including photocopying or recording, or by any information storage and retrieval system, without permission in writing from the publisher.

On the cover: Wheeled cannon Civil War memorial (Chris Boswell/Thinkstock)

Printed in the United States of America

*McFarland & Company, Inc., Publishers
Box 611, Jefferson, North Carolina 28640
www.mcfarlandpub.com*

To my wife, Jane,
for 55 great years.

And to our sons and their families:
John and Diana and
grandson Samuel Booker;
Paul and Anne-Marie and
granddaughters Megan and Sara;
Will and Jessica and granddaughters
Alexis, Madison, and Samantha.

Acknowledgments

I acknowledge my grateful thanks to the following individuals: John R. M. Lawrence, North Carolina librarian, Joyner Library, East Carolina University, for suggesting this project; Mr. Michael Hill, research office supervisor, N.C. Department of Cultural Resources, Office of Archives and History, Division of Historical Resources/Research Branch, for granting permission to use information from Louis A. Manarin and Weymouth T. Jordan, Jr., comps., *North Carolina Troops, 1861–1865: A Roster* to verify soldier information in the manuscript; and to my great wife, Jane, who is used to this sort of thing by now.

Table of Contents

Acknowledgments vi

Introduction 1

1st Regiment North Carolina Troops	7
2nd Regiment North Carolina Troops	12
3rd Regiment North Carolina Troops	15
4th Regiment North Carolina Troops	20
5th Regiment North Carolina Troops	28
6th Regiment North Carolina Troops	32
7th Regiment North Carolina Troops	39
8th Regiment North Carolina Troops	44
9th Regiment North Carolina Troops (1st Regiment North Carolina Cavalry)	48
10th Regiment North Carolina Troops (1st Regiment North Carolina Artillery)	52
11th Regiment North Carolina Troops	56
12th Regiment North Carolina Troops	60
13th Regiment North Carolina Troops	65
14th Regiment North Carolina Troops	71
15th Regiment North Carolina Troops	80
16th Regiment North Carolina Troops	84
17th Regiment North Carolina Troops	87
18th Regiment North Carolina Troops	88
19th Regiment North Carolina Troops (2nd Regiment North Carolina Cavalry)	96
20th Regiment North Carolina Troops	99

21st Regiment North Carolina Troops	107
22nd Regiment North Carolina Troops	110
23rd Regiment North Carolina Troops	114
24th Regiment North Carolina Troops	121
25th Regiment North Carolina Troops	125
26th Regiment North Carolina Troops	127
27th Regiment North Carolina Troops	140
28th Regiment North Carolina Troops	149
29th Regiment North Carolina Troops	152
30th Regiment North Carolina Troops	153
31st Regiment North Carolina Troops	157
32nd Regiment North Carolina Troops	163
33rd Regiment North Carolina Troops	166
34th Regiment North Carolina Troops	170
35th Regiment North Carolina Troops	173
36th Regiment North Carolina Troops (2nd Regiment North Carolina Artillery)	177
37th Regiment North Carolina Troops	179
38th Regiment North Carolina Troops	185
39th Regiment North Carolina Troops	191
40th Regiment North Carolina Troops (3rd Regiment North Carolina Artillery)	192
41st Regiment North Carolina Troops (3rd Regiment North Carolina Cavalry)	195
43rd Regiment North Carolina Troops	197
44th Regiment North Carolina Troops	203
45th Regiment North Carolina Troops	206
46th Regiment North Carolina Troops	210

Notes 217

Bibliography 229

Index 231

INTRODUCTION

Wounded and Killed

It takes but little space in the columns of the daily papers; but O! what long household stories and biographies are every one of those strange names that we read over and forget!
"Wounded and killed!" Some eye reads the name to whom it is dear as life, and some heart is struck or broken with the blow made by that name among the list.
"It's our Henry, it's our John, or our James, or our Thomas that lies with his poor broken limbs at the hospital, or white, still, and with ghastly face on the battlefield. Alas! for the eyes that read!—Alas! for the hearts that feel!
"He was my pretty boy that I've sung to sleep so many times in my arms!" says the poor mother, bowing her head in anguish that cannot be uttered. "He was my brave, noble husband, the father of my little orphan children!" sobs the stricken wife. "He was my darling brother, that I loved so, that I was so proud of," murmurs the sister amid her tears as the terrible stroke falls on each home throughout the land.
"Killed and wounded!" Every name in that list is a lightning stroke to some heart, and breaks like thunder over some house, and falls a long black shadow upon some hearthstone.
—Published in the *Spirit of the Age*, Raleigh, North Carolina, November 24, 1862

Only the names of our wars change through the centuries—Revolutionary War to the current Iraq and Afghanistan—but the hardships and sufferings and sacrifices of the men and women who fight them remain constant and this news article is as true today as it was 150 years ago during our Civil War.

No one could conceive at the beginning when the first shots were fired at Fort Sumter, South Carolina, the extent to which death and destruction would consume the following four years. It brought the specter of death into a new reality for the American people. Before the war, death was more of a private matter. Burial rites had often taken place in the home of the deceased or in a nearby house in the town or village—sometimes in the church. There were family members either in the home or close enough that they could assemble in time to give comfort to the dying or give the deceased a final viewing. Burial could be in a familiar place. Sometimes the dead were buried in the churchyard or in a site selected years before by the family for their burials. In these the deceased members would stretch back over several generations.

Americans had experienced death in war before, but it was not on the grand scale that the Civil War was about to take. The Revolutionary War lasted from 1775 to 1783, and the estimate for battlefield death is about 8,000. But that is over an eight-year period. The War of 1812 brought about 2,000 combat casualties. In the two years the United States fought the Mexican War our forces lost about 1,800. However, on September 17, 1862, at the Battle of Sharpsburg, called Antietam by the North, casualties were almost 4,000 soldiers killed. It was a staggering number for the American people to grasp—all those deaths in a single day! The old perceptions of death that existed in pre-war days were gone. What would happen to the bodies of their loved ones—fathers, husbands, sons, brothers, and other relatives so far away from home?

In some instances it depended on what side controlled the battlefield at the end of the fighting. Nat Raymer, a soldier in Company C, 4th Regiment North Carolina Troops, recorded what he saw on a visit to the battlefield of 1st Manassas, called Bull Run by the North. His letter was published in the Salisbury, N.C., *Carolina Watchman*, August 15, 1861.

> *The next day after our arrival here, many of us visited the scene of the late battle. The field, of course, did not present as shocking an appearance as it did immediately after the fight, yet we saw enough to give us a real idea of the horrors of a bloody battle. Dead horses filled the air with a sickening odor, rendering it almost unbearable to go near the points where the hardest fighting had taken place. Numerous graves—or rather imitations, for they could scarcely bear the name of graves—were scattered over the field. In many places limbs lay exposed, and in several instances, the naked skull was visible, so shallow was the covering of the body.—Those thus buried, however, were Northerners, to whom a decent burial was refused by their own friends, and they were left to the care of their more humane enemies. The Southerners, of course, attended to their own dead first, and consequently, by the time they came to the Yankees, they were much decayed. It was, therefore, impossible to remove them or remain long enough to give them a decent burial. The ground around the graves was blackened by the life blood of the occupant, and in many instances, showed marks of the death struggle. Despite our hatred towards those invaders of our soil, we could but pity the fate of those who lay around us. To a person of refined feelings, there is something very repulsive in the thought of being thus buried, out of the reach and knowledge of relatives and friends.* (1)

Raymer's last statement compares the traditional view of death in pre-war America to Civil War America—it's repulsive—to be killed or to die of disease away from home—no relative to soothe the dying family member—or dying alone on the battlefield—no regular home place for burial—no traditional stone, just a board with a name or perhaps nothing to mark the grave. There were exceptions to this, of course. The declaration of a truce at the end of the fighting allowed both sides to collect their dead and wounded and give them a proper burial and give care to the wounded. Word of a dying soldier could also reach home and a father, mother or both parents would come to comfort their son in his last moments. The saddest times would be the parents' arrival just after their son died. Parents would also come to the battlefields or burial sites to bring their sons' bodies home if possible. A letter to the soldier's family might carry directions to the grave along with condolences, as in this letter from S. P. Collins to the father of Colonel Henry King Burgwyn, 26th Regiment North Carolina Troops, who was killed at Gettysburg. The letter was published in the *Raleigh Register*, July 22, 1863. *"It was my painful privilege to assist Captain Young to inter his body under a walnut tree about one mile west of the town on the North side of the turn-pike road, 75 yards N. E. of a medium sized stone farm house, which has a yellow barn on the opposite side of the road leading from Gettysburg to Chambersburg. There are several graves under the tree, but his is directly east of the tree, with the head straight towards it. I have given this description that in case none of us should ever return, and this reaches you, you might still recover his remains. I cannot attempt to offer consolation to friends so bereaved, but can only mourn with them the loss of one of my most cherished friends."* Burgwyn's body was recovered and buried in Wilmington in the early summer of 1867.

Deaths on both sides would total over 600,000 for the four years; indeed, some recent estimates place the toll at 800,000. Again, a staggering total for a war fought on the home soil and not some foreign country. Compare that to the World War II total of over 400,000, a war that was fought all over the world.

An advance in weaponry and the use of old Napoleonic mass charges were large contributors to battlefield deaths. Cannon shells, mortars, and canister shot cruelly ripped men apart. Long-range sharpshooters picked soldiers off. A massed charge, such as Malvern Hill and Gettysburg, struck down hundreds of troops. More sinister were diseases and infections occurring because of wounds, contaminated water, inadequate shelters, and poor food. Large numbers of men living together brought typhoid fever, pneumonia, measles, and smallpox. Diseases, in fact, brought more deaths on both sides than death on the battlefields.

Think about current American wars. The wounded, as well as the dead, can be flown off the battlefields to a waiting MASH unit. Seriously wounded can be further evacuated to a hospital, perhaps in Germany, and as soon as possible, flown back to the United States. Flag-draped caskets also bring the honored dead home. Compare this to the following letter:

I am sorry to announce the death of one of our company. Private L. M. Franklin has left these shores of affliction and wars and gone to a world of spirits. His complaint originated from cold which settled on his bowels; he lived but a few days after being taken sick. I had just returned from picket and was very tired, but I went and helped to dig his grave and lay his body therein. I sang the following hymn while the clods were falling on his body and the floods of rain were descending from the heavens:

> *Why do we mourn departing friends,*
> *Or shake at death's alarm;*
> *'Tis but the voice that Jesus sends,*
> *To call them to his arms.*

Farewell, fellow soldier, we deplore thy loss, but thou art at rest and we soon may follow thy steps. Our friend never faced the mouth of the cannon, but we can say he died the death of a soldier. Oh, reader, can you form no idea how I felt when I saw my fellow soldier laid in his grave, far away from friends and home.

> *Far away from friends and his native shore,*
> *He sleeps in death and hears of war no more.*

—From a letter by T. C. C., thought to be Thomas C. Christenbury, published in the Raleigh, North Carolina, *Spirit of the Age*, September 4, 1861.

Like the above, thousands and thousands of bodies never reached home and their burial sites in fields and valleys across Virginia and other states have long vanished into the landscapes. Identifying bodies and sending word of their passing home was also a problem. The modern soldier has a dog tag to identify him. Civil War soldiers would write their names on a piece of paper and pin it to their uniforms in case of their deaths. Unless there was a designated person in the Company to send word of a death home, that death could go unrecorded. Consequently every soldier did not have an obituary in the home or nearby newspaper reporting his death. Many that were sent to newspapers began with the words "Killed," or "Died," devastating words to family and friends at home awaiting word of loved ones. Some were written by those who were there when a boyhood friend or comrade-in-arms or brother fell in battle, creating a sense of immediacy that conventional narrative cannot duplicate. Others are written by family members, pastors, and friends, or communicated to newspapers by unknown individuals. In this collection a large number of obituaries are anonymous. By far the largest number of obituaries in the collection appeared in the *Fayetteville Observer*, possibly because it's North Carolina's oldest and still published newspaper and therefore would be well-known; it also republished obituaries from other newspapers. Besides obituaries, it would publish long lists of killed and wounded after major battles. Each publication of a local newspaper could bring a notice of the loss of an individual who grew up in the community the paper served.

Publication of an obituary after the paper received it could be anywhere from a week to several weeks—even months. Many demands were placed on newspapers for space, and a war report or an advertisement would compete with obituaries for that space. As the war went on, especially in the South, materials, like paper and ink to print, became scarce, and editors were forced to make choices on what to publish. Not only could there be a time lag from battlefield or hospital to an obituary's being published in the civilian world, the military side could also have difficulty in learning of a soldier's death. The *Fayetteville Observer* of June 29, 1863, in a short paragraph titled "Neglect," speaks to this.

> *Neglect*—*An officer in the army sending us for publication the death of one of his men, which had occurred in a Hospital a month ago, asks us to call attention to an evil existing in most Hospitals. The Surgeons generally, he says, never notify Captains of deaths of their men in a Hospital. A soldier in his company died in a Petersburg Hospital some time ago, and not for two months did his officers know anything of it; and then they ascertained it by going to the Hospital and searching the books to ascertain his whereabouts.*

In finding obituaries for this collection, I was fortunate that so many North Carolina papers from the war period survived over the past 150 years, either in long press runs or in bits and pieces of a year or in just nine issues. Many fell to the war's destruction; others were lost over time. The following newspapers, which were microfilmed, provided obituaries:

Alamance Gleaner, Burlington
Asheville News
Beaufort News
Carolina Watchman, Salisbury
Creedmoor Times-News
Daily Bulletin, Charlotte
Daily Reflector, Greenville
Eastern Reflector, Greenville
Elizabeth City Independent
Fayetteville Observer
The Gold Leaf, Henderson
Greensborough Patriot
North Carolina Argus, Wadesboro
North Carolina Presbyterian, Fayetteville
North Carolina Standard, Raleigh
Peoples' Press, Salem
Raleigh Confederate
Raleigh Register
Raleigh State Journal
Way of the World, Greensborough
Wilmington Daily Journal
Wilmington Journal

In the above list, some papers have the city of publication in the title. For those that don't, the city follows afterward. The *Confederate Veteran* magazine, published 1893–1932, provided some obituaries for soldiers who survived the war, as well as papers that published into the 20th century.

In the compilation, I started with the First Regiment and went straight through to the 46th—Infantry, Cavalry and Artillery. The obituaries for the 1st Regiment North Carolina Volunteers (six months) and the 1st Regiment North Carolina State Troops are combined, and the soldiers identified by type of regiment. Some regiments, like the 26th, have a large number, others just a few. No obituaries were found for the 42nd Regiment North Carolina State Troops. For the most part the obituaries appear as they were published; however, certain ones, like tributes of respect and eulogies, had to be edited because of repetitious language, insubstantial prose that contributed nothing to the soldier's obituary but might have been the style of the day, flowery language, and being too overly religious and praiseworthy (as those found in a religious publication, such as the *North Carolina Presbyterian*).

The return of the bodies of loved ones to their families in the North and the South was highly important. Unfortunately, it could not always be done. Many bodies had been savaged beyond recognition. Many were unidentified. Embalming was in its infancy. Bodies began to smell after a few days and wooden coffins couldn't contain the odor. Some trains would refuse to carry them. So, to this day, thousands lie in unknown graves. Still being able to say a farewell to a loved one and see him properly buried was desirous to both sides—especially among Southerners. The following obituary closing, written by an unknown author, captures the need for Southerners to see the body properly at rest, particularly after the war ended:

> *Notwithstanding that the weather was gloomy and inclement, the attendance was large; for it is the only sad privilege now left us to honor those who surrendered their lives in behalf of a cause in which our best interests, our dearest hopes, and our most holy affections were enlisted—a cause now, alas! crushed and broken, oppressed and insulted, but honorable to us still.*
>
> —*Wilmington Journal,* March 22, 1867

1st Regiment North Carolina Troops

Julius Sadler of this town, a member of the Company B, "Hornet's Nest Riflemen," was killed Friday night last between Richmond and Yorktown, by falling from the cars. On that night the 1st Regiment North Carolina Volunteers (6 months) left Richmond for Yorktown in platform cars, and as all men had been without sleep most of the two preceding nights, it is supposed that Mr. Sadler dropped to sleep and fell from the car on which he was riding. His remains were brought home on Sunday night in charge of *Mr. Richard Tiddy*, (2) also a member of Company B. He was about 22 years old. His corpse was followed to the grave on Monday morning by a large concourse of citizens, escorted by a company of Fisher's Regiment.

—Originally published in the *Charlotte Democrat*, reprinted as "Sad Accident," *Carolina Watchman*, Salisbury, N.C., May 30, 1861

Mr. Benjamin F. Britt, of the 1st Regiment North Carolina Volunteers (6 months), Company I, a native of Edgecombe was accidentally shot at Yorktown, and his remains were brought home for interment.

—*North Carolina Standard*, June 29, 1861

Marcus Allsbrook, of the "Enfield Blues," Company I, died at Yorktown on the 24th, and **John J. Coker** and **Samuel L. Arrington**, of the same company, on the 26th. All were members of the 1st Regiment North Carolina Volunteers (6 months), and all died of pneumonia. **Private Joseph A. Johnson**, of Edgecombe, died at Yorktown on the 23d. He was a member of Company A, 1st Regiment North Carolina Volunteers (6 months) and had participated in the battle of Bethel.

—*Fayetteville Observer*, August 5, 1861

Died at Yorktown, Virginia, on the 7th of August, **Henry Harrison Avery**, youngest son of James Avery, Esq., of Burke County, North Carolina, a private of the "Burke Rifles," Company G, First Regiment of North Carolina Volunteers (6 months).

When too unwell for exertion, he [asked] to be permitted to accompany his Regiment in the rapid march to Bethel, where he participated in the fatigues and perils of the conflict, and returned with his victorious companions. His constitution had received an exhausting shock; it could not rally. Lingering sickness and death ensued.

—*Raleigh Register*, August 24, 1861

Until now this community had been spared the loss of any one of the hundreds of volunteers. But yesterday the sad spectacle of the funeral of one of them, **James Wemyss**, a private in the "Fayetteville Independent Light Infantry," Company H, took place from the

Presbyterian Church. He was but 17 years and 4 months of age, the youngest of three brothers in the same First Regiment North Carolina Volunteers (6 months). He died at Yorktown on the 6th inst., of typhoid fever and his body was brought here to his home and sorrowing parents, Davis and Ellen Wemyss, and relatives for interment. The "Clarendon Guards" and a large congregation united in the affecting services.
—*Fayetteville Observer,* **September 12, 1861**

Evan L. Miller, Esq., of the Lillington Rifle Guards, Company C, 1st Regiment North Carolina State Troops, departed this life at the residence of his grandfather, Isaac Lamb, Esq., in New Hanover County, on the 6th day of August, of a disease contracted while in camp with the Company at Warrenton, N.C.
—*North Carolina Presbyterian,* **September 14, 1861**

The last issue of the Observer announced the death of a member of the Independent Company, and it was then written here that the Lafayette Company was the only one in the 1st Regiment which had sustained no loss. Since that time, we have learned of the death, at Yorktown, of **John B. Clark**, a Private in Co. F—the Lafayette. He died on the 10th inst., aged 22 years, 9 months and 15 days. The body was brought here on Saturday and was interred with military honors by the Clarendon Guards.
—*Fayetteville Observer,* **September 16, 1861**

Died, at Chimborazo Hospital, Richmond, Va., of typhoid pneumonia, on the 11th day of September 1862, Private **Lemuel G. Barker,** of Wake County, N.C., aged 25 years, 1 month and 25 days. He was a member of Company G, 1st Regiment N.C. Troops. He fell not on the battle field, yet he sacrificed his life on the altar of his country. He has left an aged mother, brothers, and sisters. He had been a consistent member of the Baptist Church for seven years. His remains were sent home to the family burial ground, accompanied by his brother, John W. Barker.
—*North Carolina Standard,* **October 14, 1861**

Died near Yorktown, Va., Oct. 16th, 1861, **Jonas Gallant Rudisill**, a soldier in Company K, 1st Regt. of N.C. Volunteers (6 months) of Typhoid fever, aged 24 years, 5 months and four days.

He was a son of Dr. J. C. & C. A. Rudisill, and was raised near Tuckasaga Ford in Gaston County, N.C. On the 18th of May 1859, he was married to Miss J. O. Simonton, of Iredell Co., and settled in Lincolnton, N.C., where he followed merchandise for a livelihood. When the war broke out in April, he volunteered and met the enemy in that celebrated engagement and victory at Bethel Church. He was a member of New-Hope Church in Gaston County. He came home a few weeks before his death to see his wife, child, and friends. On his return to camp he contracted disease and died.
—*North Carolina Presbyterian,* **November 30, 1861**

Died, in Fredericksburg, Va., on the 27th of November, of typhoid fever, **Private Albert Pleasants**, son of Mr. Robert Pleasants of this place. He was a member of Captain Edward M. Scott's Company D, 1st Regiment of N.C. State Troops. During his illness, he received all of the attention that medical skill and the kindness of friends could afford; nothing could arrest the hand of death. Before their departure from Fredericksburg, Captain Scott, with deep feeling, at the midnight hour, assembled a number of his company around the lifeless form of their departed brother, and with uncovered heads, with the enemy's guns sounding in the distance, so touchingly addressed them, that tears coursed their way down each manly cheek, of which even a soldier need not be ashamed. His remains were then sent to Hillsborough for burial.

—*Hillsborough Recorder,* **December 11, 1861**

Died on Thursday, the 26th ult., on the battle field near Richmond, **James Allan Wright**, Captain Co. E, 1st Regiment N.C. State Troops, and son of the late Dr. Thomas H. Wright, of this town, aged 26 years. There is scarcely a family circle in the South from which death has not stricken some gem since this unholy war began; scarcely a community which does not mourn the loss of some valued member, who has sacrificed his life for his country. While leading his Company in a charge upon a battery which nearly decimated the regiment to which he belonged, Capt. Wright received a ball in his forehead, and died instantly.

—*Wilmington Daily Journal,* **July 1, 1862**

John W. Heartsfield, son of Dr. W. Heartsfield, of Wake County, was slain in battle while charging a battery near Richmond on Thursday night the 26th of June. He was First Sergeant of Co. I, 1st Reg't North Carolina State Troops, under Col. Stokes. He discharged the duties of his office with perfection—was loved by all his company, and leaves many relatives and friends to mourn his early death. His remains were interred at his father's residence.

—*Raleigh Register,* **July 9, 1862**

Died, on the field of battle before Richmond, Thursday, June 26, 1862, **Major Tristram Lowther Skinner**, of Chowan County, N.C. In May 1861, he was chosen Captain of Company A from his own county, and soon won their affectionate esteem by his devotion to the cause and to them. His services, in due time, secured him promotion to the rank of Major in the 1st Regiment North Carolina Troops. He fell whilst leading a charge against one of the enemy's heavy batteries.

—*Raleigh Register*, **July 12, 1862**

Col. Montfort Sidney Stokes, commander of the 1st Regiment N.C. Troops, died in Richmond a few days since, from a wound received in the battle of the 1st July at Malvern Hill. Col. Stokes had one of his legs shattered, and amputation was necessary. Soon after this mortification set in, and all efforts to save his life were unavailing. Colonel Stokes was a son of Gen. Montfort Stokes, who was at one time Governor of this State and a member of the United States Senate. He had been in the war from its commencement. He possessed considerable military knowledge, and had seen service before this war, having been a Major of the regiment from this State in the war with Mexico. He was a good officer and a worthy man, and his death will be deplored by our people generally.

—**Originally published in the** *Raleigh Standard* **and reprinted in the** *Fayetteville Observer*, **July 14, 1862**

Died near Richmond, Va., on the evening of the 6th July, **Corporal James Montague**, son of P. Montague, New Hanover County, N.C., aged 19 years. The deceased was a member of Co. C, 1st Regiment N.C. Troops. A youth more brave and true than James has never found a resting place beneath the blood-stained hills of Virginia. In the hard contested fight on Thursday, the 26th, at Mechanicsville, he bore the Flag off the field, and though sick then and prior to the fight, he kept with his Regiment until Monday morning following,

when the Regiment moved and he was taken to the residence of the Rev. J. Gibson, where he breathed his last on the 6th July. How much more intense must be the agony of an aged father after days and nights of travel and toil, in search of a sick or wounded son, to find him (as in this case) in the home of a kind stranger, in the agonies of death.—When he clasped the cold motionless hand and gazed into the once bright eyes of his son, no word was spoken, no look of recognition, a slight pressure of the hand and all was soon over.
Lillington, N.C., Aug. 9th, 1862.

—*Wilmington Daily Journal,* **August 16, 1862**

It becomes my painful and melancholy duty to record the death of my friend, **Orderly Sergeant Dr. John Wesley Heartsfield** of Wake County, who was killed, on the battlefield at Ellison's Mills, Thursday, the 26th of June. He matriculated at Randolph Macon College in 1855, in the eighteenth year of his age, where he graduated after four years. In 1860, he entered the Medical College in Richmond. At the commencement of the war, he enlisted as a private in Company I, of the 1st N.C. Troops, to serve during the war, and was immediately promoted to the rank of Orderly Sergeant; the difficult duties of which office he discharged with marked ability. He had such a buoyancy and fondness for military life that whether on the tented field, or on the long and tedious marches, amid snows of winter campaigns on the Potomac, or through the mud and swamps of the Chickahominy—in heat or cold—around the camp fires at night—he was ever the same cheerful happy companion, ready to inspire courage to those failing on the march, and never leaving his post. He fell at the head of his company, being pierced through the neck by a minie ball, and died without a struggle, after charging the enemy at the point of the bayonet for over one mile.

—J. H. Foote, *Raleigh Register,* **August 27, 1862**

Died, of typhoid fever, at Camp Winder, Richmond, on the 27th of July, **William H. Watson**, aged twenty-six years, a member of Company D, 1st. Reg. of N.C. Troops. He was from Orange County, N.C., where his widowed mother and family still live to mourn their sad loss. He was a good soldier, and was in the terrible conflicts before Richmond until his company was well nigh cut to pieces. Though he escaped from the battle-field untouched, the hardships to which he was subjected were too great for a body naturally feeble, and he fell beneath the power of disease. He was a member of the Methodist Episcopal Church. All honor to the memory of our brave defenders, whose lives are given for their country.

—*Hillsboro Recorder,* **October 23, 1862**

Died, on the 11th of May 1863, in the hospital at Richmond, Va., of wounds received in the recent battles near Fredericksburg, **Lieut. Jno. P. Lack**. He was a citizen of Raleigh, and at the beginning of hostilities volunteered as a soldier in Company D, 1st Regiment N.C. Troops, and was made Orderly Sergeant of that company, in which capacity he distinguished himself in many hard fought battles, and was promoted to 2d Lieutenant for his gallantry in the great battle of Sharpsburg. The writer of this little notice has witnessed on various occasions the coolness and efficiency of this brave young man in times of great danger. While Sergeant, he commanded his company alone in several battles in the absence of the commissioned officers. It is thus the good old State is being bereft of her brave sons. Lieut. Lack leaves a young wife and child in this city to mourn over their loss as widow and orphan only know. His body we learn was buried in the cemetery in Richmond.

—*North Carolina Standard,* **May 26, 1863**

Killed in action at Berryville, Va., on the 15th of June, **Corp'l. Charles R. Christmas**, of Company D, 1st Regiment, North Carolina Troops, eldest son of Mr. John R. Christmas, of this town, aged 33 years. He enlisted in the company in the Spring of '61, and since the commencement of this bloody and unchristian struggle the Southern Confederacy has lost no more efficient or heroic soldier. With his gallant regiment he participated in all of the principal battles of Virginia and was taken prisoner at Sharpsburg, Maryland, in September, '62. He returned from captivity in time to fill his place in those terrible engagements on the Rappahannock and to start, buoyant with hope, with his companions in arms on their glorious march of invasion. But he has fallen, and now sleeps in a soldier's grave. May no rude hand disturb his resting place.

—*Hillsboro Recorder,* **July 29, 1863**

Died after being captured near Gettysburg, Penn., on the 24th of July, from the effects of a wound received during the battle, **William C. Paul**, of Company D, 1st Reg. N.C.T., in the 20th year of his age. The deceased was a son of the late Thomas P. Paul, of Orange County. From the effects of ill health, occasioned by heavy marches and hardships incident to camp life, he lingered at home some months, but inspired by patriotism and a love for his comrades in arms, he returned before he had entirely recovered. Although he died in the hands of the enemy, we are told that he had every possible attention during his suffering to render him comfortable, yet nothing in his condition could save his life.

—*Hillsboro Recorder,* **September 9, 1863**

Died, in this place, on the evening of the 28th ult., after a short but painful illness, **Dr. Edward M. Scott**, in the thirty-third year of his age. In the same month, and only twelve days before, he led his bride to the altar, full of youthful joy and promised happiness, of a long and unclouded life. Truly in the midst of life we are in death!

Having early espoused the cause of Southern independence, Dr. Scott cast aside his professional duties and took up the sword to battle for his beloved South. By his energy, skill and indomitable perseverance, he succeeded in raising three large companies of infantry for the period of the war, and was immediately commissioned as Captain of Company D, 1st Regiment, N.C. State troops, with which company he remained until after the memorable battle of Seven Pines and those around Richmond, willingly enduring all the dangers and hardships. He was in the desperate assault at Gaines' Mill, where he received a stun which for a short time disabled him. In this desperate assault he lost nine of his men killed and a number wounded. Being a physician he was then assigned to duty to attend to the numerous wounded. In this capacity he acted a noble part, having combined a warm and tender feeling and sympathizing nature with a well-stored knowledge of his profession, he was enabled to do much good among his comrades, and to-day there are many maimed and emaciated sufferers who can testify and well remember the many acts of generosity and kindness received from his hands, after he resumed command of his company. Having passed through the dangers of many a battle-field and the hardships incident to camp life, his health giving way, he comes to his childhood home to die. His spirit is gone to that "God who gave it."

—*Hillsboro Recorder,* **January 13, 1864**

Died on the 6th October 1863, the **Rev. J. D. Clark**, a member of Company B, 1st Regiment N.C. Troops, of Buncombe County, N.C.

At Gordonsville, Va., Oct. 23d, 1863, in the 23d year of his age, **Wm. H. Profitt**, Serg't Company B, 1st N.C. Reg't. He had been in the army since May 1861.

Killed in the battle at Payne's Farm, Va., on 27th Nov 1863, **Corp'l Lynson M. Welborn**, Company B, 1st N.C. Reg't, while gallantly discharging the duties of a brave soldier.
—*Fayetteville Observer*, **January 14, 1864**

Durham, N.C., July 4.—Ex-Congressman **John Wilbur Atwater**, December 27, 1840—July 4, 1910, of Farrington, Chatham County, dropped dead late this afternoon while plowing on his farm. The news of his death came here by the Durham and South Carolina road and only the bare facts could be gathered. He had not been previously ill, so far as known. When found, he was dead. He lived with his son and worked on the farm. His wife and four children survive him, one of these being a prominent physician. Mr. Atwater was elected Congressman from the Raleigh district in 1894. Though he went off with the populist movement, he served as an independent and, while doing nothing brilliant, was much liked and he was a good man. He was about sixty-nine years of age. During the late war, he served in Company D, 1st Regiment North Carolina Volunteers (6 months).
—*News and Observer*, **July 5, 1910**

Mr. George Clayborn Guthrie died Tuesday in his home in Newlin Township, aged 76 years. He had been in declining health for some time. He was a Confederate soldier and a sergeant in Company E, First Regiment North Carolina Troops. Mr. Guthrie was an excellent citizen. He is survived by his widow and several children. Mrs. Jas. P. Harden near here is a daughter of deceased.
—*Alamance Gleaner*, **August 1, 1912**

2nd Regiment North Carolina Troops

Killed in a fight with the enemy, on the 21st of June, between Richmond and the Chickahominy, **Henry Clay Gorrell**, Captain of 2nd Company E. in the 2nd Regiment N.C. State Troops, in the 23rd year of his age An officer who saw him when he fell, remarked to a friend upon the spot where he was killed, that "no man could have fallen in the regiment whose death would have been more lamented,—no man could have fallen who was better prepared to go."

At the start of the war, he was attached to the "Guilford Grays," and with that company went to Fort Macon, where he remained for several months. But supposing that his company would be confined entirely to garrison duty, and panting for more active service in the field, he withdrew from the Grays, and attached himself to a Volunteer company of State Troops raised in his county; he was elected first Lieutenant, and afterwards was promoted to the rank of Captain. On the 21st of June his regiment was ordered out to storm and carry at the point of the bayonet, a strong redoubt of the enemy, flanked by two other strong works on the north and south. Whilst on this perilous duty he fell, pierced entirely through the head with a minnie ball, and instantly died.

The following extract of a letter from *Lieut. James M. Hobson*, (3) also of Company E, to a friend in this place, describes the manner of his death, and records the estimation in which he was held in his regiment:

> But nothing during the war has so much affected me, as Capt. Gorrell's death. It would not have been so bad if there had been any necessity for the sacrifice. Four companies charged

two batteries supported by a brigade of infantry. Our company and Capt. Howard's led the charge. The men acted handsomely. Capt. Gorrell was among the foremost of his men. He fell in the thickest of the fight, only a few feet from me. He was standing perfectly cool, encouraging his men. One of his men rose up beside him; he told him to take good aim, and had scarcely uttered the words when he was pierced through the head with a ball, and fell, groaned and died without a struggle. Soon after he fell, we were ordered to retreat, and it was impossible to recover his body. I tell you, Joe, he fell like a brave man, and the death of no man in the regiment would be regretted as much as his. He was universally popular with officers and men. I was very sorry to hear that his father failed to recover his remains. The day after he left, his grave was found by the Orderly Sergeant of company B. His hat was found at the grave with the hole through it, and is preserved.

—*Greensborough Patriot,* July 24, 1862

A brave and patriotic youth, **Private Owen C. Philips**, of Company K, 2nd N.C. State Troops, sick and excused by the Medical Surgeon, got up during the late battle at Richmond and went with musket in hand, as he said, to drive or help drive the invading foe from our soil, contrary to the wishes of his officers, and took his gun and rushed into battle, and whilst in the thickest of the fight, was stricken down by a grape shot. His comrades insisted on taking him off the field, but he refused, saying no, you can do more good here where you are—go on—which we did, and in an hour returned and found him dead of his wounds. He would not permit a man to stop to attend to his own sufferings, but urged them to go on and drive the wretches back. He leaves broken hearted mother, sisters and brothers to mourn his loss.

—**One who fought at his side**, *Carolina Watchman,*
July 24, 1862

The following is from the army correspondent of the New York Tribune. The "rebel poetry" alluded to is "North Carolina's Call to Arms," by "*Laola*" which has been published in the Patriot.

I saw a melancholy sight a day or two since. It was that of a young Confederate officer, **Capt. Henry C. Gorrell**, from Greensboro, N.C. and Captain of Company E, 2d North Carolina Reg't who fell in an attack, which he had led on our batteries, Saturday evening, 14th inst. In his hand he held his sword. It was one of the old regulation swords, manufactured by Ames, at Springfield, Mass. It is marked "U.S." Alas, that it was ever drawn against our country's cause. The scabbard and belt were gone, flung impetuously away in that gallant but vain charge. In his pocket were a watch, his pocket book, a lock of hair, tied with a piece of white satin ribbon, and a sprig of cedar, carefully tied, and enclosed in the same way as a memento. His commission was also in his pocket and a note for $500, &c. I trust the money will be given to his heirs by those who found it, but the sword whose use was so perverted, that should remain in loyal hands forever! I send you a little poem, which was also found in his pocket, and given me by those who found it, and which shows the state of feeling and the argument used to induce enlistment and warfare against the Union and its Government. It may be worth publishing as a curiosity, and is better than most Rebel poetry.

—**A. B. F.**, *Greensborough Patriot,* July 31, 1862

George H. Raney, of Company B, 2d regiment N.C. volunteers, son of Mr. Thomas H. Raney, was born in Granville county, N.C., April 6th, 1843, and died of typhoid fever, at the residence of his father, July 2d, 1862. Soon after his regiment left Norfolk, upon the evacuation of that city by our troops, he was taken sick; and the constant travel and great

destitution that he suffered, prevented him being restored to health. After the battle at Hanover Courthouse, he, with his brother, both sick, came home. He lingered on for several weeks before succumbing to the fever.
—*North Carolina Standard*, **August 6, 1862**

Departed this life in Davie County, N.C., on the 8th of July 1862, **Henderson E. Livengood**, aged 26 years, 2 months and 6 days. The deceased was a member of Co. E, 2d Regiment N.C. Troops. He had been pursuing his studies with a view of entering the ministry, but like hundreds of our noble-hearted young men, he laid aside his studies, parted with his beloved parents, sisters and brothers and joined the army. A few weeks ago, sick and unable to do duty, he left his company, and returned home, but died a few days after reaching there.
—*Carolina Watchman*, **September 1, 1862**

At Boonesville, Md., 4th Oct., **Capt. John Howard**, of Wilson, N.C., 2d Reg't. He was wounded and taken prisoner at Sharpsburg, but died of pneumonia, in the 29th year of his age. He was promoted to Major of the Regiment on the day of the battle.
—*Fayetteville Observer*, **November 10, 1862**

Milas J. Fraley, of Davie County, N.C., died in camp at Fredericksburg, Va., on the 17th March last, after an illness of three days of typhoid pneumonia. He often expressed his desire to be in the service of his Country previous to his enlistment, but was advised otherwise from his physical disqualification, until sometime during the past year, he determined to enter the service, and volunteered in Company E, 2d Regiment N.C.T., but was in camp only a short time before he was discharged and returned home, but volunteered again in the next call for troops in the same Company & Regiment, was accepted and discharged his duty faithfully to his Country, and yielded up his life in her service.
—*Carolina Watchman*, **May 4, 1863**

At Chimborazo Hospital Richmond, Va., on the 1st instant, **William Anderson Thompson**, in the 22nd year of his age, a member of Company E, 2nd Regiment N.C. State Troops. He had been about two years in the army. Up to the battle near Fredericksburg on the 13th of December 1862, where he received his mortal wound, he had enjoyed good health, with the exception of a slight wound received in his hand June 1862, at Ellerson's Mill, Virginia.
—*Greensborough Patriot*, **July 2, 1863**

Died at the residence of Mr. Buchanan, in Martinsburg, Va., on the 14th inst., of wounds received on the 3d at Gettysburg, **Nicholas Collin Hughes**, Assistant Adjutant General to Gen. Pettigrew, aged 23 years. He was 1st Lieutenant Company I, 2nd Regiment North Carolina State Troops and transferred to General Pettigrew's Staff October 1862.
—*Fayetteville Observer*, **August 3, 1863**

Died in Rowan County, at Mr. P. Holland's, on the 12th instant, of small pox, **Capt. Sylvester Taylor**, Company I, of Newbern. Capt. S. volunteered as a private. His good conduct and worthiness as a soldier secured his subsequent promotion. He was one of the first to respond to the call of Gov. Ellis, in April 1861, and was wounded at Chancellorsville.
—*Carolina Watchman*, **February 2, 1864**

Died, on the 15th of May 1864, from wounds received on the 12th, at the Battle of Spotsylvania Court House, **Lieut. John T. Fraley**, of Company E, in the 23d year of his age. He volunteered as a private at the beginning of this fatal strife, but was soon promoted to

a Lieutenancy. He had been with his Regiment in all its engagements, borne a conspicuous part (unhurt) until he received his death wound. With many others near the borders of the Wilderness "he sleeps his last sleep."
—*Carolina Watchman,* **September 19, 1864**

After a short illness **Lemuel S. Wood**, of New Bern, N.C., died at his home there in his eighty-first year. He is survived by his wife, three daughters and three sons. He was a native of Craven County, born May 8, 1842, and, with the exception of service in the Confederate army, spent his entire life there. At the age of eighteen, in 1861, he enlisted in Company K, 2nd North Carolina Regiment, and served with his unit until it was captured by Northern troops at Kelly's Ford, Va., November 6, 1863. His war record was as brilliant as that of any soldier who fought in the War Between the States. Enlisting as a private, he was promoted to sergeant on May 5, 1863, after having gone through severe service. He was with his Regiment in every skirmish and battle in which it was engaged up to November 1863, including the seven days fighting around Richmond, first Maryland campaign, Fredericksburg, Chancellorsville, and Gettysburg. He was at Chancellorsville with Stonewall Jackson when the latter was mortally wounded. After the war he became a lieutenant in Company C, of the State Guard, and held that commission until that organization disbanded.
—*Confederate Veteran* **Volume 31, Number 7, July and Number 10, October 1923**

3rd Regiment North Carolina Troops

Died of pneumonia at Camp Price, Va., on Thursday evening the 16th inst., **Capt. Robert H. Drysdale**, aged 29 years, of the 3d Regiment N.C. State Troops, Company A. He is from Greene County, but was born in Scotland, where he leaves a mother and other relatives. He came to this country when quite a youth. His remains were brought to Goldsboro last Saturday night, and were buried here on Sunday last. The ceremonials of his funeral were held in the Protestant Episcopal Church, the Rev. Mr. Hunter officiating, and the members of the Masonic Lodge at this place, paid the usual token of respect to their departed brother.
—*North Carolina Standard,* **January 25, 1862**

Died in this town, at 3 o'clock this morning, of pneumonia, **Lieut. John W. Runciman**, in the 28th year of his age. The deceased was born in Charleston, S.C., but for the last 18 or 20 years had been a resident of this town. He entered the service in the latter part of May 1861, and was appointed to a Lieutenancy in the Cape Fear Riflemen (now Co. F., 3d Reg't N.C. Troops), and since the organization of the regiment, has been in service on the Potomac. For a few months previous to his death, his health had been declining, and he had but recently returned to camp from a sick furlough.

The friends and acquaintances of the family are invited to attend the funeral services at the residence of Mr. Thos. R. Lawrence, corner of Fifth and Mulberry streets, tomorrow (Friday) morning at 9½ o'clock.
—*Wilmington Daily Journal,* **April 3, 1862**

Gaston Meares, the 3d son of our distinguished townsman, the late Wm. B. Meares, was born March 1821. From Mr. Bingham's school in Orange County, he went to West Point in '38, where he remained as a cadet until his resignation in August 1840.

He read law first with Gov. Swain at Chapel Hill, and afterwards with Judge Pearson, at Mocksville; he was admitted to the bar, Dec. '42, and obtained his Superior Court license the subsequent December. In the spring of '44 he emigrated to south western Arkansas, where he opened his office as attorney.

The war with Mexico in '46 invited him to an unexpected career. He became Adjutant of Col. Yell's regiment, and was by the side of that gallant gentleman when he fell upon the field of Buena Vista. The term for which his regiment enlisted soon expiring, Col. Meares returned to his profession, but not before he received from his comrades the compliment of election to the rank of Lt. Colonel. He returned to North Carolina in 1848.

When the current war began, he served first upon the Potomac, in Walker's Brigade, and then in North Carolina; he was recently ordered again to Virginia with the 3rd Regiment. Constituting a part of Ripley's Brigade, he soon engaged in the series of battles which have illustrated the strategy of Lee and the prowess of our troops. In the attack upon Ellison's Mill his regiment suffered severely.—Tuesday, July 1st, 1862, in the evening, he was slain, being struck by a fragment of a shell in the forehead at Malvern Hill.

Col. M's wife and several children survive.

—*Wilmington Daily Journal*, **July 5, 1862**

The remains of **Col. Gaston Meares**, 3d Regiment N.C.T., who fell at the head of his command cheering on his men in the fight of last Tuesday night, and also the remains of A. D. Moore, Sergeant Major, and W. A. Wooster, 1st Lieut. Co. I, 18th Regiment N.C. Troops (the two latter having fallen in the defense of their country on the 27th ult.) all reached here yesterday forenoon, and were escorted to their respective residences by Col. Leventhorpe's Regiment and the Independent Guard of the town, Capt. Burr.

The remains of the two latter were interred yesterday afternoon at 4 o'clock in Oakdale Cemetery with military honors. Col. Meares body was kept until this morning, owing to the absence of his family from town, when they were interred in Oakdale Cemetery with military honors.

—*Wilmington Daily Journal*, **July 5, 1862**

Died on the 28th of July, at the Camp of the 3rd N.C. Troops near Richmond, after an illness of five days of Typhoid Fever, **Private John Jones**, of Co. "K" 3d Regiment N.C. Troops, aged 19 years.

The deceased had been in the service of the Confederate States since the first day of June 1861; and in the recent battles in front of Richmond, he did valuable service for his country. On the 1st of July, at the battle of Malvern Hill, while the missiles of death were mowing down his comrades by his side, he rushed forward cheering his comrades worthy of one in high ranks. During the battle he fired more than thirty rounds at the enemy, and came off the battle field unhurt.

—*Wilmington Daily Journal*, **August 1, 1862**

Died on the night of the 18th ult., at the residence of his brother, R. C. Johnson, Esq., in Duplin County, from the effects of his wounds and secondary hemorrhage, **Milton H. Johnson**, aged about 36 years. He enlisted in June of last year (for the war) in *Capt. Stephen D. Thurston*'s (4) company (B, 3d regiment), and though rejected as being physically disqualified for the military service, he urged a re-examination by a different surgeon, and was finally passed into the service with his company. He was wounded severely in the arm during the desperate charge of his regiment upon the enemy on Tuesday evening at Malvern Hill. He reached his brother's a few days afterward, when he was attacked, first by erysipelas fever, and then secondary hemorrhage, and died. Sometimes in the delirium of fever he would express a desire to be with his company, and during his more rational moments he said repeatedly that his most ardent wish for recovery was to be able to rejoin his company, to share their trials and toils, and finally with them enjoy the blessings of a dearly blood-purchased, but glorious peace.

—*Wilmington Daily Journal*, August 7, 1862

Died at the St. Charles Hospital, Richmond, Va., on the 28th of June last, from the effects of a wound in the left breast by a piece of shell, done the 26th of June, at the Battle of Ellison's Mill, Virginia, **Private James A. Hall**, of *Capt. Henry W. Horne's* (5) (formerly *Capt. Peter Mallett's*) (6) Co. C, 3d Reg't N.C.T. Early at his country's call he left a widowed mother and little sisters to go to defend his home and all that was near and dear to him. He was stationed at one of the batteries at Acquia Creek on the Potomac River from July 1861 till the fall of Newbern, thence he returned back to N.C., under the command of Maj. Gen. T. H. Holmes; then was ordered to meet the enemy below Richmond, and in the first fight he received the fatal blow. He was a member of the Baptist Church at Magnolia, Cumberland County.

—*Fayetteville Observer*, September 29, 1862

Lieut. Arthur W. Speight was born in Greene County, North Carolina, on the 2nd day of May 1841. Immediately upon the outbreak of war, he enlisted as a private in Capt. Drysdale's Company A—was afterwards appointed 3rd Sergeant. The company was attached to the 3rd Regiment N.C. Troops. Arthur remained with the regiment from its organization to the time of his death. He was soon promoted to the position of Orderly Sergeant of his company, which position he filled with great credit to himself and the entire satisfaction of all the officers of the regiment. A vacancy having afterwards occurred in the position of Junior 2nd Lieutenant, he was unanimously elected by his company to fill that position. He led the company in one of the severest engagements that occurred before the city of Richmond, and escaped unhurt, but was afterwards slain in the battle of Sharpsburg, on the 17th of September, while gallantly cheering his men on to the conflict, and pointing them to their reward when victory should be won.

—*Wilmington Daily Journal*, October 6, 1862

On January 21, 1907, the *Eastern Reflector*, Greenville, North Carolina, published an account of the finding of Speight's body which had been buried on the Sharpsburg battlefield. The article was originally published in the Snow Hill, Greene County, *Standard Laconic*.

Last week a farmer near Sharpsburg, on Antietam Creek in Maryland, while plowing in his field plowed up human bones, upon further investigation the entire skeleton of a man was unearthed and with it a sword bearing the inscription "Arch W. Speight, Co. A, 3rd N.C. Reg. C.S.A." This find was on the battle field known as Sharpsburg, or Antietam, where Lee and McClellan fought one of the great battles of the Civil War, Sept. 17, 1862.

Lieutenant Arch W. Speight, a son of Abner Speight, of Speights Bridge Township, this county, was killed in this battle, and buried upon the battle field, receiving a soldier's burial, being rolled in a blanket with his sword and thrown in a hole. He was a member of Co. A, 3rd N.C. Regiment which holds its reunion here every 10th of April. We understand that some of his relatives are talking of having his remains removed to some cemetery. His request when he left for the war, if slain on the battle field, was that his remains be allowed to remain where first interred.

—Originally published in the Snow Hill *Standard Laconic* and reprinted as "A Member of Co. A, 3rd N.C. Regiment Plowed Up in Maryland," *Eastern Reflector,* June 21, 1907

Died in Washington D.C., on Sunday 21st Sept., 1862, **Lieut. Thomas Cowan**, Co. B, 3d Reg't N.C. State Troops, of a wound received at the battle of Sharpsburg, on the 17th Sept., aged 23 years, 5 months and a half.

Born April 8th, 1839, Lieut. Cowan graduated from the University of North Carolina, in the class of 1858, read law with Judge Pearson for two years, was admitted to the bar in 1860; and while attending the Superior Court in Brunswick County in April 1861, received information of the order of Gov. Ellis to seize Fort Caswell. He returned at once to his home and volunteered as a private in the ranks of the Wilmington Light Infantry. Afterwards he was tendered a commission as 2d Lieut., in the original appointment for the N.C. State Troops—ranking from May 16th, 1861. He served for a long time in Gen. Walker's celebrated brigade, but at the period of his death, his regiment was under the command of Gen. Ripley. In all the history of the glorious Third, Lieut. Cowan was thoroughly identified. After the battle at Richmond, he was promoted to a 1st Lieutenancy, and was in the command of his company, at the battle of Boonsboro,' and on the bloody day of September 17. Wounded in the head, he was captured and removed by the Federal authorities to Washington on Thursday, the day succeeding the battle, and lingered in suffering until the Sabbath morning. Consigned at first to the rude grave of the prisoner, he was afterward committed to consecrated ground, with the solemn service of the church, and the tears of the noble women who had ministered to him. Such is the record of his life—simple, indeed, but to those who knew Tom Cowan, eloquent beyond the expression of words.

—*Fayetteville Observer,* January 12, 1863

Again is old Cumberland called upon to mourn the loss of one of her sons who was as true a patriot as she contained—**David T. Hollingsworth**, of Company C, 3rd Regiment who was killed at Chancellorsville. As proof of his patriotism he volunteered when the business that he was engaged in cleared him from service. His conduct as a soldier I cannot better describe than by an extract from a letter from a comrade:

> On the first of May our regiment left camp for the battle-field. David was with us, well and in fine spirits. We reached the place of destination Saturday evening 2d, went into the engagement about three hours by sun, fought until night. Sunday morning 3d, we renewed the engagement; David went with us; we charged their breastworks and went over; David was among those that went over loading and firing. A ball struck him above the left eye, killing him instantly. It is not worth my while to try to describe to you his bravery, for he had but few superiors in that respect.

—*Fayetteville Observer,* May 25, 1863

Captain Thomas E. Armstrong, Company K, 3rd Regiment of N.C. Troops, fell at the head of his company while urging them on to victory in the hotly contested action at Chancellorsville.—His country owes him gratitude for much hard and dangerous service rendered in our national struggle. *All* the contests in which he was engaged are not known to the writer, but he bore himself gallantly and honorably through four of the famous actions "around Richmond," through the second fearful struggle on the Plains of Manassas, through the trying scenes of the battle of Sharpsburg, through the first battle of Fredericksburg, and finally met his fate on the 3d of May on the field of Chancellorsville. All honor to the gallant dead who perish for our defense.

—*Wilmington Daily Journal,* **July 1, 1863**

Died, in Richmond, June 22d, of Bibulous Fever, **Captain John F. S. Van Bokkelen**, Company D, of 3d N.C. Regiment. He entered the service at the first organization of the 3d N.C. Regiment, as 2d Lieut., and by subsequent promotions was made Captain of his Company, which position he held until his death. He was in every battle and skirmish in which his Regiment was engaged, and escaped unhurt until the battle of Chancellorsville, when he received a painful wound in the side. From this, however, he shortly recovered, but afterwards was stricken down with bibulous fever, which soon terminated his life. For some years past, he had been an active member of the Episcopal Church at this place.

—*Wilmington Daily Journal,* **July 13, 1863**

Serg't. Stephen S. Carroll, of Company B, 3d Regiment, N.C. Troops, fell July 2d, 1863, in a gallant charge on the enemy at Gettysburg, Penn. He entered the army in his 17th year (Jan. 1862), and went soon after to Virginia. He followed his Regiment under Gen. Lee, through Virginia and Maryland, and was wounded in the foot at Sharpsburg. Though compelled to go on one foot, he re-crossed the Potomac, carrying his gun and knapsack, and remained in the Regiment Hospital until able for duty. He was next in the battle of Fredericksburg. At Chancellorsville he was again wounded—flesh wound—ball through the arm. Placed in Hospital, he nursed those worse wounded than himself, until again able for duty. Soon after this he went to his *last battle field.*

Serg't. Carroll was a consistent member of the Baptist Church, at Mount Gilead, for four years, and a citizen of Sampson County, N.C. He leaves an aged father, step-mother, brothers, and sisters, to mourn an irreparable loss.

—*Wilmington Daily Journal,* **August 12, 1863**

Dr. Thomas J. Kelly, of Kenansville, Duplin County was wounded July 2nd in the battle of Gettysburg, while in command and gallantly leading his company (B) 3rd N.C. Regiment on to the bloody charge. He was captured on July 4th and died a prisoner in the hospital there July 9th.

—*Wilmington Daily Journal,* **September 29, 1863**

Died of wounds received at Gettysburg, Pa., July 3, 1863, **John T. Williams**, Co. H, 3d N.C. Infantry, and son of Joel and Pearcy Williams of Randolph, N.C. At the beginning of the war he joined, in the 20th year of his age, the Bladen Rifles, then being organized. For two long and trying years he underwent the hardships of the camp and fatigues of hard marches, and went through ten hard battles; and at last, while charging the enemy at Gettysburg, he fell mortally wounded and survived only one day.

—*Fayetteville Observer,* **March 10, 1864**

Died, on the 23d ult., near Spotsylvania Court House, Va., of a would received in the battle of the 10th ult., **Sergeant Major Robert Cowan McRee**, 3d Regiment N.C.T., in the 19th year of his age. He was the oldest son of James F. McRee, Jr., Surgeon C.S.A., attached to Lane's Brigade. Although urged, on account of his feeble health, to accept a different position, a sense of what he owed to his country constrained him to remain in the field as long as his physical ability would permit. He was determined to emulate those of his blood who had won distinction in the Revolution, the war of 1812-14, the invasion of Mexico, and the present sanguinary struggle.

From the nature of his wound, it was impossible to remove him; he had to be left in the enemy's lines. It is some consolation to be assured that he received every attention that could be given, and that every respect was paid to his remains.

—*Wilmington Daily Journal*, July 17, 1864

On the 9th inst., at Mount Pleasant, Spotsylvania County, Va., of a wound received at Spotsylvania C. H., on the 10th of May, **Lieut. Cicero H. Craige**, of Wilmington, aged 22 years and 8 months. When the war began, he was living in Georgia, and he joined the 1st Georgia Regiment—Co. D., Oglethorpe Infantry—with which he served twelve months. After disbanding he came home and remained thirty days and then left here for Virginia, to unite himself with Co. I, 3d Regiment N.C. Troops, where he performed his duty faithfully until he received his last but fatal wound; and after much suffering breathed his last among friends, though strangers.

—*Wilmington Daily Journal*, July 20, 1864

Departed this life on the 6th of June, of wounds received on the 13th of May, in the engagement near Spotsylvania C. H., **Capt. Edward Hall Armstrong**, of the 3rd Regiment N.C. Troops, Company G, aged 23 years and 26 days. In the Summer of 1860 he espoused his country's cause by active service in the field; and from that time until the fatal 12th of May 1864, he with comrades in arms have been ever in the thickest of the fray.

Both the campaigns in Maryland witnessed his heroic bearing, his exposure amidst danger and death, and his fortunate escape unharmed. But after wearing an apparently charmed life amidst the missiles of death for three years, he was destined, in the mysterious providence of God, to receive his "last furlough" amidst the disasters of the 12th of May.

—*Wilmington Daily Journal*, July 23, 1864

Ayden [Pitt County] Items.... **Arnold T. Baldree**, an old veteran of the late war, died near here last Friday and was buried Saturday. He was 75 years old. He was a member of Company D, 3rd Regiment. At the Battle of Sharpsburg, September 17, 1862, he was wounded in the thigh and captured. He was held prisoner at Fort McHenry and exchanged in February 1863.

—*Eastern Reflector*, July 10, 1904

4th Regiment North Carolina Troops

On the 28th of January 1862, at the General Hospital near Manassas, of pneumonia, **Jonas Johnston Atkinson**, son of John A. and Esther Atkinson, grandson of Samuel Ruffin, and great grandson of Col. Jonas Johnston, of Revolutionary memory, who was wounded at the battle of Camden, and died on his return home. He entered the service of his Country as a private in *Capt. Jesse S. Barnes'* (7) Company, and was stationed at Fort Macon about two months. He afterwards volunteered for the war in the same Company (F) 4th Regiment

North Carolina State Troops, went to Virginia, and was located near Manassas Junction. Deceased was a native of Edgecombe County, N.C. There are, at the present time, three more brothers in the Confederate army, two (privates) in Virginia, and one, Lieut. R. W. Atkinson, in the 19th Regiment of State Troops (2d cavalry).
—*North Carolina Standard,* **February 12, 1862**

A land slide on the Western Extension, six miles from here (Salisbury), caused a sad accident last Thursday morning, by which **James Briggs** (a member of *Capt. J. H. Wood's* (8) Company B, of the 4th Regt. N.S.T.) lost his life. He was standing on the platform when the train struck the slide, and was caught between the cars. Both his legs were broken, and he was otherwise badly injured. He died in about one hour after the accident.
—*Carolina Watchman,* "Sad Accident on the Western Railroad," **March 24, 1862**

Killed, at the battle of Seven Pines on Saturday 31st of May, **George S. Winters**, a member of Co. K, 4th Reg. N.C. Troops. He was a native of New York; enlisted in the C. S. army more than twelve months ago, and by his services and death proved his devotion to the Southern cause, and that true worth and bravery had not entirely deserted every man of Northern birth.
—*Western Democrat,* **June 8, 1862**

Killed on the 31st of May, in the Battle of Seven Pines, near Richmond, **Lieut. Thomas L. Perry**, of Beaufort County, N.C., Adjutant of the 4th Regiment N.C. State Troops. One of the first to volunteer for the war, he was elected 1st Lieutenant of Company E, *Capt. D. M. Carter,* (9) and was appointed Adjutant by its distinguished Colonel. The valor and discipline of the regiment are attested by the terrible carnage of the battlefield, and by the company by the fact that of the 55 men who went into action, 44 were killed or wounded. The regiment was full of talent and courage, but there was no brave or more gallant man upon that field than Lieut. Perry.
—*Fayetteville Observer,* **June 9, 1862**

Fell in the Battle of the Chickahominy (Seven Pines), **Seth Brinn**, a Private of Company E, 4th Reg't., N.C. State Troops. He was 21 years old and a resident of Hyde County, N.C.
—*Raleigh Register,* **June 16, 1862**

Died recently: **Earnest A. Morrison**, Iredell County Co. A, killed at Seven Pines. He had enlisted in October 1861 as a substitute; **Robert M. Gray**, Iredell County, Co. A, in Richmond hospital, in May or June, of typhoid; **Wiley E. Cox**, Co. B, was born in Randolph County. He was farming in Rowan County and enlisted at age 36 in 1861. He was wounded at Seven Pines and died a few days later on June 5, 1862; **Robert A. Hall**, Iredell County, Co. C, age 22, died in Richmond but cause not reported; **Freeman J. Fisher,** Iredell County, Co. C, age 29, place and cause not reported; and **Nelson P. Hooper**, Iredell County, Co. C, died near Richmond June 14, 1862, but cause not reported, **Francis M. Current**, Iredell County, age 22, Co. H, was wounded at Seven Pines and died the next day, June 1, 1862; and **Joseph A. Dobson**, Iredell County, Co. C, "Saltillo Boys," aged 19, in Richmond of bronchitis, May 19, 1862.
—*Fayetteville Observer,* **June 30, 1862**

Died at Richmond, Va., of wounds received at the battle of "Seven Pines," **Samuel A. Jones**, of Company G, son of the late Gen. Charles R. Jones, of Iredell County, N.C. He was born in Fayetteville, and was at the time of his death, aged 16 years, 3 mos. and 11 days.
—*Fayetteville Observer,* **July 14, 1862**

Died at his father's residence in this Rowan County, June 28th, **Stephen A. Brown**, of Company K, son of Alexander Brown, from the effects of a wound in the foot, received 31st of May in the Battle of Seven Pines, near Richmond. Aged 22 years and 9 months.

—*Carolina Watchman*, **July 14, 1862**

Killed on the 27th June, in the Battle of Gaines Mill, near the Chickahominy, in Va., **David Calvin Brandon**, son of Matthew H. & Elizabeth M. Brandon, of Iredell County, N.C., aged 28 years on the 6th of March last. He was a soldier in Co. B, Capt. Wood, 4th Regt. N.C.T., now in command of Col. Bryan Grimes. He was among the bravest of this gallant Regiment, and well sustained the reputation of Revolutionary ancestors from whom he had descended on both sides of his family.

—*North Carolina Presbyterian*, **July 19, 1862**

Killed on the battle-field of Seven Pines near Richmond, May 31st, 1862, **Nehemiah John Sloop**, Company B, of Rowan County, N.C., aged 22 years, 4 months and 6 days. While bearing the flag of our Confederacy on the battle-field of the 31st, he fell pierced with many balls (besides him, seven other flag-bearers fell)—he was a good, brave and noble-hearted soldier. At the age of seventeen, he made a public profession of religion and connected himself with the Evangelical Lutheran Church, at Luther's Chapel, Rowan County.

—*Carolina Watchman*, **July 21, 1862**

Died, on the 3d of Aug., at the residence of his uncle, John C. Palmer, Esq., in Raleigh, **Dr. William M. McKenzie**, aged 25 years and two months. At the period of his death he had been a member of the Methodist Church for seven years. He was in Company B, 4th regiment of N.C. Troops, and later promoted to Hospital Steward. He was earnestly devoted to his duties, and even after disease was destroying the very foundations of life in his own constitution, he dragged himself to the couch of his suffering fellow soldiers to minister to their wants. He had a younger brother, M. Stokes Mckenzie, stricken down in the battle of Seven Pines, and now he also has passed away.

—*North Carolina Standard*, **August 6, 1862**

M. Stokes McKenzie was a member of Co. B, 4th Reg. N.C.S. Troops and was killed at Seven Pines. He endured the hardships, and privations of a long and arduous campaign, until on the 31st of May, he sealed his devotion to his country with his blood. He died a hero—and although shot, shell and minnie ball, were rained around him thick as hail, his comrades falling on every side, yet on he went, until a ball struck him, terminating his life suddenly.

—*Carolina Watchman*, **August 11, 1862**

Fallen on the 27th of June, in the battle of Gaines Mill, before Richmond, **Paul Barger** of Company K, youngest son of John Barger, in the 20th year of his age. He volunteered near the commencement of the war, when a student of North Carolina College, promising his chums to meet them on the field of battle. He left home the 12th of May 1861, went to Fort Johnson, and joined the Rowan Rifle Guard.—On the 19th of July they were ordered to Manassas, where they arrived at the close of the battle. They remained there until the evacuation, when they retreated to Yorktown; thence they marched to camp near Richmond. Paul was actively engaged with the enemy in the battle of Seven Pines, came out unhurt, though a number of shells dropped within a few feet of him, one passing over his saddle just as he dismounted. At the early dawn, on the morning of the 27th of June, the din of war was again heard, and he marched forth into the field. Having pursued the enemy until about one o'clock p.m. a shell struck him just above the hip, killing him instantly. His remains were subsequently conveyed to his father's and deposited in the burial ground at Salem Church.

—*Carolina Watchman*, **August 11, 1862**

Capt. John Barr Andrews was a native of Rowan County, North Carolina. He graduated with distinction, at the University of our State in May 1854. He then engaged in teaching with Mr. Bingham in Alamance County; and subsequently was partly in charge of the male classical and military academy in Wilmington, 1856. Later he was elected to, and accepted a Professorship in Concord Female College, located in Statesville, Iredell County, N.C. He resigned after a year and in connection with his elder brother—Capt. C. M. Andrews, 2d N.C. Cavalry—opened a classical and military school in the same village. At the breaking out of the war he closed his school, raised a company of Infantry, composed largely of his own pupils, joined the gallant 4th Regt., as Company C, shared all its hardships, trials and triumphs from Carolina to Manassas, from Manassas to Yorktown, Williamsburg and the "Seven Pines," and was never again seen at his home. In the series of recent battles around Richmond, while in the gallant discharge of duty at Gaines Mill, a ball wounded his hand and lodged in his breast. While convalescing from these wounds and when about to leave Richmond, on furlough, he was taken with fever, erysipelas of his wound ensued, and about 2 o'clock, a.m., on the 23rd of July, in the 30th year of his age, he died. His remains were brought home and interred in Statesville. Three days afterwards his venerable mother was laid by his side.

—*North Carolina Presbyterian*, **August 16, 1862**

Killed, on the 31st of May, in the battle of Seven Pines, near Richmond, **Thomas C. Deaton**, a member of Co. I, 4th Regt. N.C.T. He was a son of James Deaton, a resident of Iredell County. He left his home at the age of twenty, and entered the battlefield where he now sweetly sleeps in peace.

—*North Carolina Presbyterian*, **August 23, 1862**

We are ill prepared to record now the fate of this distinguished officer, kinsman and friend, **General George Burgwin Anderson**, but we must address oneself to the task with what heart we may. The country has lost much, his native State more, and his family and friends most of all. He was wounded at Sharpsburg in the foot. His wound, though painful, was not considered dangerous until his arrival at Raleigh, where, at the residence of his brother, Col. W. E. Anderson, his wound was examined by Surgeons of great distinction and skill, and amputation was deemed necessary. A Minnie ball had been previously extracted by Dr. Chas. E. Johnson, which was found imbedded among the tendons, nerves and muscles, and which had produced mortification or gangrene. The amputation of the foot was made on Wednesday last, as the last hope of saving his valuable life. But his time had come. He had fought his last battle and he sleeps the last sleep. God Almighty help his poor widow and child! We cannot speak of *them* now. He died at his brother's residence on Thursday morning, between 8 and 9 o'clock, surrounded by his kindred and friends, whose love of their friend and grief for his loss knew no bounds.

He was the eldest son of the late Colonel W. E. Anderson, and was born in the town of Hillsboro, N.C., in the year 1831. From his earliest years he was equally distinguished for mental capacity and great docility of temper. Gen. A. was educated at West Point Military Academy, and was graduated with distinction. Upon leaving West Point he entered the U.S. Army as Lieutenant in the 2d Cavalry. In the beginning of our present troubles he resigned his position in the Federal army, and we believe he was the very first man who tendered his services to his native State through the lamented Governor Ellis. He was appointed Colonel of the 4th Regiment N.C. State Troops, which Regiment, as is well known, greatly distinguished itself at the battle of Seven Pines. On that occasion he commanded the Brigade to which his regiment was attached. Subsequently he was promoted to the office of Brigadier General, as the country knows, and was in all the battles around Richmond, and wounded in the hand at Malvern Hill. His Brigade was left on the South bank of the Potomac to act as scouts, while the main body of the army crossed into Maryland. That movement having been accomplished, his Brigade joined the Division to which it belonged, that of Gen. D. H. Hill, and aided at Boonsboro in keeping at bay the overwhelming odds with which Gen. Hill had to contend until reinforced by Gen. Longstreet's division. Then came the battle of Sharpsburg, in which after fighting with great valor in the Bloody Lane, he received the wound which has so unexpectedly terminated his brilliant career. The youngest brother of Gen. Anderson, acting as his Aid in this bloody battle, also received a serious wound, but Capt. Walker Anderson still lives, and long may he live to serve his country and his native State, which these two brothers have loved and served so well, and or which they have so severely suffered.

On the night before his death, Gen. Anderson was delirious, and fancied himself in battle. Such expressions as the following, and many others of kindred spirit, escaped him. "Sergeant! Attend to it, that these men do their duty." "I most decidedly disapprove of that line falling back." "It must be done. It is the order of Gen. Hill." Raising himself up on this arm, he exclaimed, vehemently: "Here they are," and seemed ready to dash at the foe, of which he was evidently dreaming.

But his battle was with his last enemy, and for the first time he was conquered.

His funeral will take place to-day, at 11 o'clock, at the Capitol.

—*Raleigh Register,* **October 18, 1862**

Died of typhoid fever at Staunton, Va., on the morning of Tuesday, Oct. 14th, 1862, **Lieut. Ashbel S. Fraley**, of Co. A, 4th Regiment, N.C.S. Troops, aged about 28 years. He contracted the fever in the long march from Richmond to Maryland and was taken sick at the battle of Boonsboro, Maryland, and thence removed to the hospital at Staunton Lieut. Fraley was a native of Rowan County, but for several years previous to the out-break of war, resided at Statesville and studied law under Hon Anderson Mitchell. He was one of that part of the "Iredell Blues" who first responded to the call of Gov. Ellis for volunteers to take and hold the forts in the State. He is not known to have been off duty since the organization of the regiment. He was with the regiment in all its trials and dangers; its long, hard marches and bloody and hotly contested battles.

Sometime previous to the evacuation of Manassas he became Orderly Sergeant of the company. In this most difficult, vexatious, and laborious office he served up to the time he was taken sick with satisfaction to all concerned and with credit to himself. After the death of Capt. Simonton he was almost unanimously elected 2d Lieut., a position to which his company had long desired to raise him. By some means or other, none of the commissions of the newly elected officers of the regiment have been forwarded; consequently Lieut. F. never acted in his new position.

—*Carolina Watchman,* **November 10, 1862**

Drowned on the 23d February 1863, in the South Yadkin River, near Renshaw's Ford, Davie County, **James W. Neely**, aged 21 years, 8 months, and 18 days, formerly a member of the Rowan Rifle Guard, Company K. At the first call of his State for troops, to meet the vandal foe of the North, he entered her service, and discharged the duties of a soldier to the time of the battles around Richmond, at which time he received a wound in the face at the Battle of Seven Pines which rendered him unable for the duty of a soldier. He leaves a bereaved mother and three sisters.

—*Carolina Watchman,* **March 16, 1863**

At Baker's Mills Rowan County, N.C. on the 14th Inst. **Dr. James W. Shinn, Orderly. Sergeant**, Co. B, 4th Regt. N.C. Troops, in the 29th year of his age. Dr. Shinn volunteered, as a private, among the first troops that left Rowan, *for the war.* He resigned a good practice and a fine prospect of usefulness and distinction, in his profession. He participated in all the hardships incident to the war but was often confined to the hospital, owing to great feebleness of constitution. At the Battle of Seven Pines, where all the superior officers of the company were wounded, he led the company most gallantly through the fight; and on that and other occasions was honorably mentioned for gallant conduct. After passing safely through his last battle at Sharpsburg he was taken to the Hospital at Richmond. He was promoted to 1st Lieutenant shortly before he died. About the first of January he worked his way home, literally *worn out* to die. He was a consistent member of the Methodist Episcopal church.

—*Carolina Watchman,* **March 23, 1863**

Captain William T. Marsh, Company I, was a resident of Beaufort County, and enlisted at age 30. This gallant officer fell mortally wounded, in the bloody battle of Sharpsburg, on the 17th of September 1862, and died September 24, 1862. He was in command of the 4th Regiment N.C. State Troops near the end of this sanguinary fight. No part of the army during this terrible battle was more exposed than Gen. G. B. Anderson's brigade in the Bloody Lane, to which Capt. Marsh's regiment belonged. What it suffered in this unequal contest may be learned from the significant fact that every commissioned officer present was killed or wounded. He was a member of the Legislature of North-Carolina when Lincoln declared war on the seceded States. He promptly raised a company of volunteers, and soon after joined the regiment of Col. George B. Anderson, who was later promoted to brigade command.

—*North Carolina Standard,* **March 29, 1863**

Private William Henry Gaither, son of Ephraim and S. H. Gaither, of Mocksville, N.C., and member of Company G. 4th North Carolina Regiment, was killed on the 3d of May 1863, in the battle of Chancellorsville, Va. This sad intelligence reached his family just three short weeks, after they bid him farewell on the day of his departure for his Regiment, after a furlough of seventy days.—He had been in the service over 18 months and received his first furlough in January, and while home was laid low on a bed of suffering, but his life was spared, and he fell on the field of strife, bravely defending the home of his loved ones.

—*Carolina Watchman,* **June 15, 1863**

Hugh Francis Pridgen, of Bladen County was a student at the Military Academy at Wilson, under the charge of Col. Radcliffe and me. When war came, he quickly laid aside his books at the call of his country and volunteered his services in her defense as member of Company F, 4th N.C. Regiment. In the battles around Richmond he was wounded in the foot and came home a short time. He returned to his post before he was entirely healed, and on the 3d June, in the battle of Chancellorsville, he perished, in the 25th year of his age.

—*Charles F. Deems, Wilmington Daily Journal,* **July 29, 1863**

Lieut. James P. Cowan, of Co. A, 4th N.C., was born in Rowan county, N.C., Oct. 17th, 1840, and was killed in the battle at Chancellorsville, May 3rd, 1863. Lieut. Cowan was at Davidson College prosecuting his Literary course, but when the tocsin of war sounded, he was among the first to volunteer to defend his country's rights. He was captured at Frederick, Maryland, in September 1862, and exchanged in October. He bore a conspicuous part in all the long marches, and in the many hard fought battles which the "gallant 4th" has participated, but came out unhurt until the recent bloody battle of Chancellorsville, when he received a ball and expired in a moment.

—*North Carolina Presbyterian,* **August 1, 1863**

Deaths of North Carolina Prisoners

The *Richmond Sentinel* has been furnished with a list of deaths among Confederate prisoners at the Hammond General Hospital, Point Lookout, Md., from the 4th day of October to the 30th day of November 1863, including the following from the 4th Regiment North Carolina Troops:

Sgt. J. W. Simpson,
L. Morris,
H. R. Reeves,
J. R. Tyler,
E. Avery.

—*Fayetteville Observer,* **December 21, 1863**

The following is significant. We have never doubted the patriotism of the old North State, and we have frequently taken occasion to commend her gallantry and steadiness. The following letter affords a melancholy example of the effect of bad teaching. We hope such examples will be rare: [*Exchange paper*]

PROVOST MARSHAL'S OFFICE, Rodes' Division, Feb. 9, 1864.

Col. Bryan Grimes, Com'g 4th N.C. Regiment—Colonel: I deem it my duty to make known to you the last words of **Private James King**, Company B, of your regiment, who was executed for desertion on the 30th January, ult. After bandaging his eyes I told him he had but two more minutes to live, and asked if he had any message to send to his relations or friends. He replied, "I have no message. I only wish that my body may be sent to my friends, but I wish to say to you, Lieutenant, though others persuaded me to do what I did, the reading of Holden's paper has brought me to this, but thank God I shall soon be at peace."

As it may be the wish of his friends or relatives to know in what spirit he died, I make this statement, and if you think proper you may convey it to them.

Very respectfully, Colonel,
Your obedient servant,
J. M. GOFF,
1st Lt. Co. I., 5th Alabama Regiment, and Provost Marshal, Rodes' Division.

—*Wilmington Daily Journal,* **March 3, 1864**

The Official Roster of the North Carolina Troops, Volume 4, Page 61 contradicts this information, stating that the Federal Provost Marshal records indicate that he was taken prisoner at Strasburg, Virginia, October 19, 1864, while a member of Company E, 4th Regiment. He was a prisoner of war at Camp Lookout, Maryland, and was released in June 1865, after taking the Oath of Allegiance. There were no further records.—Editor

Jacob L. Fraley, aged 30, a member of Co. K, 4th N.C.S. Troops, was killed at the battle of Spotsylvania C. H., on the 12th of May 1864. Previous to the war he resided in Texas, but as soon as hostilities broke out, he hastened to his native county, joined the "Rowan Rifle Guard" and served on the coast of North Carolina, below Wilmington. With a majority of his Company he enlisted for the war. The "R. R. Guard" then went to Garysburg and became Co. K of the 4th Regiment N.C.S.T., which was then being organized by the lamented Brig. Gen. G. B. Anderson. This regiment was soon sent to Virginia. His gallantry was conspicuously displayed on the day of his death. The division, to which his regiment belonged, made one of the most gallant charges of the war and retook some works and artillery we had lost. In the absence of regular artillerists, he volunteered his services and worked one of the re-captured guns with great effect. In a subsequent part of the engagement he was killed.

—**[October 31, 1864]** *Carolina Watchman*

Died, at Winchester, Va., of wounds received in battle there, of September 19, **Lieut. James E. M. Howard**, Adjutant of the 4th Reg't N.C.T., aged 22 years. Lieut. Howard was a native of the town of Washington, N.C., and was among the first to rally to the flag of his country. Entering the army as a private, he was an active participant in many of the bloodiest battles of this sanguine war. In the seven days battle before Richmond, he was severely wounded. Barely recovering from the effects of his wound, he hastened back to the army, and was promoted to a Lieutenancy. Accompanying Gen. Early's command to the Shenandoah Valley, throughout that arduous campaign, he bore himself with the soldierly spirit characteristic of the true gentleman and brave man.

—*Daily Confederate*, **February 9, 1865**

The remains of **Capt. Wm. T. Marsh** passed through our place on Tuesday, accompanied by his brother *Maj. Ed. S. Marsh*. (10) Capt. M. was wounded at the battle of Antietam, [Sharpsburg], on Sept. 17th. 1863, while in command of his Co., "I" 4th N.C., and died eight days after from its effects. It will be a melancholy satisfaction to his friends to learn that he now sleeps his last sleep peacefully in the family burial ground in Bath.—Another martyr to our "Lost Cause."

—**Originally published in the** *Tarboro' Southerner* **and reprinted in the** *Wilmington Journal*, **February 1, 1867**

Francis M. Mills died at his home here last Friday afternoon about 5 o'clock, aged 68 years. He was a brave Confederate soldier and entered service from Virginia. He served in Company K and was paroled at Appomattox Court House. Prior to his death he had been in feeble health for several years and for nearly a year past he had been confined to his home. He leaves a widow, four sons and two or three daughters to mourn his death. His remains were laid to rest in the town cemetery Saturday.

—*Alamance Gleaner*, **August 4, 1904**

William P. Wootten, born in Wayne County, N.C., March 14, 1844, removed to Wilson, N.C., with his widowed mother when he was thirteen years old. From that place he volunteered for the Confederate army, joining Company F, of the 4th Regiment North Carolina State Troops, and he served through the four years of war. He was wounded twice, having been shot through the thigh at the battle of Chancellorsville, and through the arm at the battle of Seven Pines, though neither shot broke the bone. He was in the battle of Gettysburg and was captured at the Battle of Winchester September 19, 1864, and exchanged two months later. He was at the surrender at Appomattox. He died at his home in Wilson, N.C., September 12, 1916.

—*Confederate Veteran* **Volume 25, No. 6, June 1917**

5th Regiment North Carolina Troops

Died at Charlottesville, Va., on the 3rd inst., of Measles, in the 25th year of his age, 4th **Sergeant William H. Matthews**, Company A., 5th Regiment N.C. State Troops, of Harnett County. William, who will be better remembered as Smith in his native county, was a true and gallant soldier. Although unable to do service on the memorable 21st of July, the Battle of Manassas, he would not consent to leave the ranks, although often requested to do so by his commander, but begged to be permitted to do his share of the fighting. When the Regiment retired in the evening from the field, he was so debilitated that he was scarcely able to walk. He was carried to Charlottesville, Va., thence in a few days to his last resting place. He leaves a mother to mourn his loss.

—*North Carolina Presbyterian,* **September 7, 1861**

Died in Fayetteville, N.C., on the evening of the 22nd of October 1861, **Edward Moneghan, Jr.**, of Company A, 5th Regiment, in the 24th year of his age. He was on the battle fields of Manassas. After having gone through the many privations of a soldier's life at various points in Virginia, he returned home to his parents, where in a few days he closed his eyes to the world.

—*North Carolina Presbyterian,* **November 9, 1861**

We learn from the *Baltimore Republican* of May 21, that **Thomas Jones**, Co. H, 5th N.C. Reg't, who was wounded at the battle of Williamsburg, and taken prisoner, died at Baltimore, May 20.

—*Wilmington Daily Journal,* **June 6, 1862**

Died, at the residence of Mrs. Elmira Lee, on Jackson Street, Richmond, on the 14th ult., of wounds received at Gaines' Mill in defense of our National Capital, **Hardy W. Parker, Esq., Orderly Sergeant** of *Capt. Garrett's* (11) Company F, 5th N.C. Regiment. He was a native of Gates County and was a farmer prior to enlisting at age 35.

—*North Carolina Standard,* **August 6, 1862**

Died in this town, yesterday morning, after a long and painful illness, **Sergeant Henry D. Huske**, Co. A 5th N.C. Troops. Sergeant Huske served as a private in the Independent Company of this place during its Peninsular Campaign last year, and at the expiration of 1st Regiment's term of service, became a Sergeant in *Capt. Robinson's* (12) company of Col. McRae's 5th Reg't. With that gallant regiment he shared in the battle of "Seven Pines" and other conflicts near Richmond, escaping the dangers of battle only to die by disease. He was a native of Wake County and a printer by trade.

—*Fayetteville Observer,* **November 10, 1862**

Died at Farmville, Va., on the 25th of March, **Rufus Allen Rose**, son of Allen Rose, Esq., of Rowan County. Thus two brothers have gone to eternity in so short a time, there being only 20 days between the death of each other. They were members of the 5th Regiment, Company K, N.C. Troops. They were consistent members of the Presbyterian Church. **John A. Rose**, (13) aged 23, died at home on March 5th of disease.

—*Carolina Watchman,* **April 20, 1863**

Killed at the battle of Gettysburg, on 1st day of July, **Henry Roland Starnes**, aged about 30, a member of Co. H, 5th Regiment, N.C.T. He was a farmer and not possessed of the world's goods, but like a pure patriot, he gave his life freely for the independence of his Country. He never murmured at the hard-ships of the soldier's life, and obeyed the commands of his superiors.—Peace to his ashes—honor to his name. He left a wife and two children, mother, three sisters and four brothers to lament his loss.

—*Carolina Watchman,* **September 21, 1863**

Died on the 17th inst., at Gettysburg, **Lt. Theodore DeSausure Deems**, son of the Rev. Dr. Deems, of the 5th Reg't, Company G. He had passed through many battles unharmed, but died of a severe wound received at Gettysburg. He was captured after the battle and died in a Yankee hospital.

—*Fayetteville Observer,* **September 28, 1863**

Died of chronic diarrhea on the 19th Dec, 1862, in Richmond in the 25th year of his age, **N.C. Williams**, youngest son of Richard and Nancy Williams of Rowan County. The deceased was a member of Company H, 5th N.C. Reg't His remains were brought home and after an appropriate funeral discourse, they were interred at Jerusalem Church in Davis.

—*Carolina Watchman,* **November 2, 1863**

Departed this life, on the night of the 23d July, at Petersburg, Va., of typhoid fever combined with gangrenous poison, **Samuel C. Hackney**, in the 31st year of his age. Deceased was a member of Co. A, 5th Regiment, N.C.T. He went with the army into Maryland, September 1862, was wounded and taken prisoner at South Mountain and sent to Philadelphia, where he remained until December; he was then exchanged and sent to Petersburg, was there appointed Steward in the Fair Ground Hospital, where he remained until the time of his death. It was not the privilege of his parents, brothers or sisters to witness his last moments or administer to his necessities, but it is gratifying to them to know that through the kindness of his many friends he received every attention. The writer can barely realize that Samuel is no more. He was the loved one among his brothers and sisters, the pride of a father and the idol of a fond mother's heart.

—Sister, *Fayetteville Observer,* **November 9, 1863**

Died in West Hospital, Baltimore, July 11th, of wounds received in the battle of Gettysburg, **Hugh Torrence Powe**, Company K, of Rowan County, aged 32 He was shot through the left lung, and afterwards taken prisoner.

—*Fayetteville Observer,* **December 21, 1863**

Died of chronic diarrhea, at his own residence in Randolph County, 26th Sept. 1863, **Wilbern Russell**, aged 27 years, of Company I, 5th Reg't, N.C.T. For twelve months he had been in the service of his once happy country, and nobly discharged his duties. After a short stay in the army he was sent home on a sick furlough; after resting a while he returned to camp and participated in the battles of Sharpsburg, Boonsboro' and Chancellorsville, at which time he was stricken down with disease and taken to the hospital at Richmond where he remained a few weeks and obtained a furlough and returned home. After lingering 2 months and 11 days he died. He was a member of the M. E. Church South—holding his membership at Eleazer. He has joined his little angel child who had gone before and left a wife, 8 children, parents, 3 sisters, 1 brother—(a prisoner of war) to mourn his untimely death.

—Lassiter's Mill, N.C., *Fayetteville Observer,* February 25, 1864

Newitt D. Bridgers volunteered in Co. C, 5th Reg't N.C. State Troops, on the 30th of May 1861. From that time forward, he participated in every fight in which his regiment was engaged, except the First Manassas (he being sick at that time). After the battle of Chancellorsville, he was chosen, by the voice of his company, as the one most worthy among them to wear the Badge of Honor and Merit. On the 1st of July 1863, at Gettysburg, he was killed. No inscription marks the humble mound beneath which he reposes, but by his fortitude on the march and noble bearing, coolness and intrepidity in the hour of battle, he is remembered.

—A Messmate, *Daily Confederate,* March 19, 1864

Died, in Pennsylvania, 11th July 1863, **Thomas J. Hancock**, youngest son of Elisha and Anna Hancock, aged 19 years and 2 months. He was a member of Co. I, 5 N.C.T., and was mortally wounded in the thigh the first day of the battle of Gettysburg, from which he suffered the most intense pain for ten days, and died while the physicians were amputating the broken and shattered limb. Thomas had been in service twelve months, during which time he had been a prisoner of war for six months, after being captured at Paris, Virginia. After having been paroled, he returned to his home in Randolph County, and there remained until exchanged, at which time he returned to his company. His *Captain, John E. Bailey*, (14) said, after his death, he had done his duty and done it nobly. Thomas was a member of the M. E. Church, and although he died far from home (in an old barn), with no kind mother or sister near to smooth his aching brow; he said it was hard to die away there and be buried as he would have to be, but said he was no better than many others that had to share the same fate; said he was ready and willing to die. He told his father when last they parted that if he died or got killed that he wanted to be brought home to be buried. How many a noble soldier has uttered the same words when last they said farewell, never to return even when dead! He has left parents, sisters, and two brothers away in the army.

—Parthenia, *Fayetteville Observer,* May 12, 1864

Among the many deaths recorded in the *Washington Chronicle* of the 2d is **William L. Smith**, Co. I, 5th N.C. He was wounded and captured at Spotsylvania Court House and died May 31, 1864, at Washington D.C., after the amputation of his leg.

—*North Carolina Argus,* June 16, 1864

Died July 29, 1864, at York Hospital, Winchester, Va., **First Lieut. James C. Goodman**, of the 5th N.C. Troops, Company H, of a wound in the neck received July 24th while gallantly leading a company of skirmishers in the battle of Kernstown. He was wounded at Williamsburg and at the battle of Seven Pines, and again in the leg on July 7, 1863, at Hagerstown, Maryland. He was a native of Gates County.

—*Wilmington Daily Journal,* **August 11, 1864**

Died, at the hospital at Louisa Court House, Va., on the 28th of May last, of a wound received in the battle of Spotsylvania Court House, **Corporal William T. Baity**, of Co. G, 5th N.C.T., aged 35 years and 18 days. On the 18th of July 1862, he left his home and went forth to meet the enemies of his country. He was with Lee's army all through Maryland and Pennsylvania, and he fought bravely in the great battles at Gettysburg and Chancellorsville. While lying wounded, he often expressed great desire to see his wife and little children which were dear to him. He leaves a father, mother, three sisters, three brothers, and a wife and three little children to mourn his untimely loss.

—*Hillsboro Recorder,* **September 21, 1864**

The remains of this brave young officer, **Lieutenant Edward S. Smedes,** who was killed at Spotsylvania C. H., on the 12th day of May 1864, while acting as Adjutant as the 5th N.C. Troops, were received in this city on Friday afternoon last.

On yesterday afternoon the funeral obsequies took place, and there was a very large and general turn-out of our citizens, of both sexes, to do honor to the memory of the noble and lamented youth. The funeral cortege, as it moved from St. Mary's School (the residence of his father), presented a strikingly impressive appearance. The hearse containing the remains was preceded by quite a large body of ex-Confederate soldiers, some of them his former immediate comrades, and following it were perhaps a hundred or more young ladies of St. Mary's School and the city, each bearing a chaplet with which to crown the young soldier's sepulture. Arrived at the Episcopal Church, which was filled to its utmost capacity, the solemn burial service was read by the Rev. Dr. Mason, when the procession, increased by the accession of hundreds of citizens, moved in the same order to the City Cemetery, where the final rites were performed. After closing the grave, it was literally covered with flowers by fair hands, as was that of a younger and equally gallant brother, Ives Smedes, Adjutant of the 7th Regiment North Carolina Troops, slain at Chancellorsville, by whose side he rests. The whole scene was beautiful and touching.

On the afternoon of the 14th of May 1864, the writer of this assisted in committing all that was mortal of Edward Smedes to a rude soldier's grave on the field where he fell. His then sole requiem was the roar of musketry along the still contending lines. Yesterday, how different! The peaceful Sabbath—the ritual of the Church he loved—the solemn swell of the organ—the grateful offices of friends and the mourning presence of the family—the floral coronation and the dear soil of *home!*

—*Wilmington Journal,* **November 6, 1866**

Our people have recently been called upon to consign to the grave the remains of one of those martyrs in peace: **William Tillinghurst Anderson** died in Wilmington (where he has been for some time residing), on the 27th of October, at the early age of 27 years. It is well known that his firm and robust constitution had been injured and broken by the afflictions which he suffered, and which were consequences of his services in the Confederate army, which he entered at the beginning of the great civil war, and in which he served bravely and faithfully to the end, both as a private and as an officer. While gallantly leading his men at the bloody and disastrous battle at Williamsburg, he was shot through the head by a minnie ball, and was borne, as dead, from the field. Strangely, he recovered from the wound, though he always bore the broad scar full upon his brow, and it was destined to cut short his life. He rejoined Company A of his Regiment and was later captured at Spotsylvania Court House. He was held at Fort Delaware and released from there in June 1865. After the close of the war, rheumatism, contracted through privation and exposure, seized him, torturing him cruelly, and rendering him a cripple and an invalid. No remedies, in his case, seemed to bring relief; no panacea seemed to assuage constant, unsparing pain, only death.

—*Fayetteville Eagle,* **November 11, 1869**

The loss of a veteran of Lawson Ball Camp of Confederate Veterans has been reported by Mrs. L. G. Connollee, of Bertrand, Va., Historian of the Lancaster County Chapter. U.D.C.

Dr. R. C. Smith, an appreciated member of the Lawson Ball Camp, passed away in May. He was a resident of White Stone, in Lancaster County, having located at that place twelve years ago, and since that time he had been a member of the Camp. He was popular with the young people as well as with the "boys of the sixties," possessing a bright, genial disposition which carried cheer and happiness wherever he went. Dr. Smith was born and reared in Gates County, N.C., and from 1861 to 1865 he served in Company B, 5th Regiment North Carolina Infantry, taking part in all the battles of his regiment. His war record, like that of his after life, was filled with brave and kindly deeds.

—*Confederate Veteran* **Volume 28, Number 8, August 1920**

6th Regiment North Carolina Troops

Col. Charles F. Fisher fell at the head of his regiment, gloriously fighting for his native land in the Battle of Manassas. We have various accounts of the manner of his death; but our correspondent at Manassas, Capt. York, states that he fell at the head of a ravine, near Sherman's battery, while leading, it is presumed, the two right flank companies into the hottest of the fire. He is said to have given his watch and sword to his servant before entering the ravine. He was instantly killed, the ball entering his forehead and coming out at the back of his head. His hat shows the mark of the ball, the rim having been split in front, and the band out behind. His remains reached this place [Raleigh] on Wednesday morning last, *via* Goldsborough, on their way to Salisbury, his native town. The cars were draped in mourning, and his body was attended by some of the officers of the regiment, and several of the officers of the Road, who were much attached to him. Capt. Cole's company, Col. Pettigrew's regiment, by the order of the Governor, accompanied the remains from this place to Salisbury.

No man ever loved his men more than he, and none labored for them as he. There was nothing that he would not do for his men, even the lowest private in the ranks. While others might pride themselves upon their rank, he felt as a man, though he acted as a soldier. He never was with the Regiment until at Raleigh, and on our way to Virginia his labors were incessant for the soldiers. On the march from Strasburg to Winchester he walked all the way, giving both his horses to sick soldiers, and when we were thrown into the line of battle, hungry and thirsty, on foot he went with the men, his hands full of canteens, to show them where the water was—then went back to Winchester, helped to cook our supper himself, and then did the same thing again at breakfast. These things riveted the affection of the men, and death itself can never eradicate from their hearts the memory of our gallant Colonel.

It is now pretty well authenticated (says the Richmond *Examiner*), that the first charge on Sherman's Battery was made by the lamented Col. Charles Fisher, who commanded the Sixth North Carolina Regiment of regulars. As he filed his Regiment around an adjacent hill, he found himself suddenly fronted by the bristling array of this battery, not two hundred yards off. Retreat was out of the question. To go forward was not only his inclination, but his only recourse. Calling on his troops to follow him, and going himself some paces ahead, he charged it, and was last seen standing on one of the guns, waving a sword in the air. It was here that he fell mortally wounded. The loss of his Regiment was seventeen killed and fifty-odd wounded—a loss chiefly experienced in this charge. Nearly all the horses attached to the battery were killed by the murderous fire of Fisher's musketry. Hon. Mr. Clingman and other gentleman, spectators of the scene, bear testimony to the correctness of this statement.
—*North Carolina Standard and Carolina Watchman,*
July and August 1861, respectively

Sad news comes up today of the death of **Lieut. William Preston Mangum, Jr.**, who was wounded severely in the action at Manassas. He had a Bible in his breast-pocket, and was struck on it by a Minnie ball, tearing the book, and severely injuring his lungs. He was the only son of Hon. W. P. Mangum, of N.C. He enlisted as a private in the Flat River Guards, but was promoted to a 2nd Lieutenancy. He was much loved by his comrades.
—*North Carolina Standard,* August 7, 1861

Died at Charlottesville, Va., **John W. Wilder**, aged 26 years. The deceased was a volunteer in Capt. York's Company I, of N.C. State Troops, and received a wound in the lower region of the spine, which proved fatal after two weeks suffering. He was wounded early in the engagement which took Sherman's battery at Manassas; and though unable to go forward himself, called upon his comrades to press forward and bear off the victory. He lived to hear the glorious news of the victory of the Confederates; and now he is gone to sleep in the patriot's grave.

Died at Manassas Junction, Va., **Joseph T. Morris**, aged 24 years. The deceased was a volunteer in *Capt. York's* (15) Company I, of the Sixth N.C. State Troops, and received a wound near his left breast which proved fatal after five weeks suffering. He was in the engagement at Manassas when Sherman's battery was taken, and was in the act of loading his gun when he received the fatal wound.
—*North Carolina Standard,* September 7, 1861

Died, of typhoid fever, near the famous battle ground of Manassas, on Friday, September 27th, **Joseph Armstrong Leathers**, son of John B. and Parthenia Leathers, of Orange County. The deceased was only 22 years of age. He was a very worthy member of *Capt. William K. Parrish's* (16) Company B. He was at the battle of Manassas under the gallant Col. Fisher. A few weeks later he died of pneumonia and was brought home for interment.
—*Hillsboro Recorder,* October 9, 1861

Died of disease at Ashland, Va., on the 14th of April 1862, **Silas J. Holeman**, in the 17th year of his age. He was the youngest son of Edwin Holeman, and leaves a father, mother, brothers and sisters to mourn his early death. He had been a consistent member of the Baptist Church at Shady Grove for more than 12 months. He volunteered about the last of February, and at the time of his death was a private in Capt. York's Company I, 6th regiment N.C. troops.

—A Brother, *North Carolina Standard,* May 3, 1862

Died, in the Ligon hospital at Richmond, Va., on Saturday the 17th instant, **John T. Wedding**, aged 19 years, 3 months and 24 days. He was a young man of good talents; joined the Flat River Guards, Company B, in May last; conducted himself well in all his soldier life; fought bravely and unhurt in the Manassas battle. He was seriously wounded in the left thigh and leg by a shell in the battle of Williamsburg, Va., and in consequence of the great confusion he lay for sometime without much attention. But as soon as it could be done his wounds were attended to, and he was sent in a wagon over the rough road to Ligon Hospital. By this time a fever had risen in his leg, and so increased that his wound had to be opened; after which he seemed to mend, until Saturday morning, when he appeared very sad, and expressed a conviction that he should die during the day, and requested all to pray for him. From this time he rapidly sank, and died between twelve and one o'clock. His remains rest among the dead at Richmond, but he and his doings will long be remembered by his parents and friends whom he has left behind.

—*Hillsboro Recorder,* May 28, 1862

Capt. William Johnson Freeland, Company C, of Orange County, was among the first to volunteer for the defense of Southern rights. He fell wounded in the leg on the 31st May, at the battle of Seven Pines, was taken prisoner and carried to Fortress Monroe, where he died on 21st June.—His nurse treated him with marked attention, on account of his private worth, and he was buried with Masonic and military honors.

—*North Carolina Standard,* July 26, 1862

John W. Coletrane, a private in Company A, fell, mortally wounded in the chest, while bravely fighting for his country, at Malvern Hill, Tuesday July 1st, and has since died from his wounds, July 7th. He responded to the call of the late lamented Col. Charles F. Fisher; and was in the battle of Manassas, and has been with his company in all the engagements before Richmond, and has always conducted himself in a soldierly and orderly manner. He was a consistent member of the Methodist Episcopal Church from early youth.

—*Greensborough Patriot,* August 7, 1862

Died, in Greenwood Hospital, Virginia, on the 16th day of July 1862, **Thomas Scott**, and on the 14th of the same month at the same place, and of the same disease, typhoid pneumonia, **William R. Scott**, both sons of John Scott, of this county, Orange. They were both members of Company K, 6th Regiment, N.C. State Troops. They were respected members of the Christian Church.

—*Hillsboro Recorder*, October 8, 1862

Wm. E. McManning was 2d Lieutenant of Company B, from Orange County, that was attached to the 6th Regiment of State Troops under Col. Fisher. Lieut. McManning, who had enlisted for the war, proved himself a faithful and efficient officer during the time the Regiment was in Camp of Instruction. About the 10th of July 1861, they were hurried to Virginia to reinforce Gen. Johnston at Winchester. The trials of the regiment in that march were very severe. Before they had time to rest from their fatigue, the forced march to Manassas

was begun. From Winchester to Piedmont there was an awful amount of suffering, as the men were then unused to such privations and such exhausting marches. Through all this Lieut. McManning bore a brave and cheerful heart. On the 21st he entered his first battle with determination and courage. In that sanguinary shock, in which his devoted Colonel fell, he braved the leaden storm and manfully rallied his men to the charge. In the evening, when the impetuous attack was made on the enemy's right, he with a fragment of his Regiment joined in the victorious advance; and when their columns broke and fled, he, with the young soldier's enthusiasm, followed in the pursuit, until his exhausted frame sank down for repose on the field of his triumph. Exposed as he was that night and the day following, his constitution was assailed by a disease which baffled all the skills of his physicians, gradually withered his hopeful prospect, and prepared him for a soldier's rest in the tomb. For a long while he could not resign, hoping to be restored. But in the last of October he bid adieu to his comrades of the glorious old 6th, on the banks of the Potomac, and sought the comforts and rest of home. There his health having improved some, he was made Colonel of the 45th Regiment of Militia, with directions to superintend the draft. In attending to this duty he contracted fresh cold, and from that time rapidly gave way to the ravages of consumption. In the month of July he repaired to the Rockbridge Alum Springs, but it appeared that his days were numbered. There, among friends though strangers, he closed his brief career on the 14th of August 1862, in the 22d year of his age.
—*Hillsboro Recorder,* October 22, 1862

All who have been acquainted with **Lieut. Jacob Sheppard,** youngest son of Hon. A. H. Sheppard, will be pained to learn that he fell in the battle of Fredericksburg, on the 13th inst., aged 21 years. We have been intimately acquainted with him and can fully attest to his gentlemanly deportment and moral worth. Lieut. Sheppard entered the service as a private, in Company F and was severely wounded in the battle of "Seven Pines," near Richmond, after which Gen. Pender gave him the appointment of Aide-de-Camp, and he entered upon his duties about the 1st of October last. We have no particulars of his death;—all we know is that Gen. Pender telegraphed, "Poor Jacob fell gallantly yesterday,"—Saturday the 13th.
—*People's Press,* December 19, 1862

Philo D. Wilson, son of John and Jeanette Wilson, of Orange County, was killed on the 4th inst., in the battle of Chancellorsville near Fredericksburg, Va. Philo was 22 years old when he answered his country's call. He was an original member of Capt. Parrish's Company B, 6th Regiment, N.C. Troops. He was present at every fight it participated in, and evinced much bravery and determination in all of them, from the first Manassas to the last glorious victory for which he died struggling. No fatiguing march nor hardships of any character has been shunned by him, but he was always at his post, executing orders.
—*Hillsboro Recorder,* May 27, 1863

Died, at Camp Fisher, in Virginia, on the 19th of January 1863, of typhoid pneumonia, **Wesley P. Shaw,** 22 years old. Wesley was an orphan boy, having lost his parents when quite young. He volunteered in the 6th N.C. Regiment, Company F, where he so conducted himself as to gain the esteem of all his company. His remains were sent to his home in North Carolina, Alamance County, and now lie in the Churchyard at Hawfields.
—*North Carolina Standard,* June 5, 1863

Killed in battle, at Gettysburg, July 1st, 1863. **Sergeant William G. Ray,** Orange County, of Co. B, aged about 22 years. At the commencement of hostilities he volunteered his services.

At the first Manassas battle, he was slightly wounded and the wound detained him from service but a short time. At the battle before Richmond he was again wounded, on a retreat from a charge from the enemy's breast-works. From the effects of this wound he lingered at home for some months, but inspired by patriotism and a love for his comrades in arms, he returned to his command before he was entirely recovered. He was in all the battles up to the time of his fall, fought by the memorable Sixth N.C. Regiment. He fought with firmness, bravery and determination, never faltering from duty, in camp, on a march, or the battle field, ever ready to bear his portion of the burdens of warfare. He was a consistent member of the Presbyterian Church at Little River. He leaves an aged and afflicted mother, five brothers (three of whom are in Illinois and two in the Confederate service), and five sisters (two of whom are in Illinois and three in North Carolina), to mourn their irreparable loss.

—Hillsboro Recorder, **August 26, 1863**

Died of disease, in Orange County, on the 15th of January last, at the residence of his father, **Private Allen C. Parrish**, Company B, 6th N.C.T. He was among the first to respond to the call of our Governor to drive back the hostile foe. He met them upon the bloody plains of Manassas, Sharpsburg, Chancellorsville, Richmond, and almost in every major engagement in Virginia. He was ever willing to discharge the duties of a soldier, and when the tattoo shall beat to summon his companions to arms, they will feel sad when they take a view of their line and see that there is a place vacated by the untimely death of one of their brave soldiers.

—Hillsboro Recorder, **February 24, 1864**

Sergeant James Brown McNeely fell wounded at Winchester, Virginia, the 19th day of September 1864, and afterwards was taken to the Hospital at Winchester, where he died. He was from Rowan County and was a student before enlisting. He left a mother, brother, and sisters to mourn his loss. His body is laid in the Southern graveyard at Winchester, Va., with a distinctly-marked head-board inscribed with his name, Regiment, and Company. He was 21.

—Carolina Watchman, **November 21, 1864**

Died, **Sergt. J. H. Upchurch**, Co. I, 6th N.C. Regt., at Charlottesville, Va., Nov. 13th, 1864, from a wound in the left arm, received at the battle of Cedar Creek, Va., 19th October 1864, in the 26th year of his age. He was the eldest son of Sims Upchurch, Esq., of Chatham County, who has given five sons and four sons-in-law to the army. He married Delia, daughter of M. D. Williams, Esq., who, with one child, mourns an irreparable loss. His gallantry had been witnessed upon Virginia's fields, where he had been wounded at the Battle of Sharpsburg, and at Gettysburg. He was captured at Rappahannock Station, Virginia in November 1863, but got away from his captors. In the long and dreary march, in the hour of defeat and amid the shouts of triumph, he was the same—cool, calm and collected.

—Daily Confederate, **December 6, 1864**

Thomas L. Cooley died in Brooklyn last week, and his remains reached here for interment on Sunday last. They were escorted to the grave by the Orange Guards, of which under the old organization, 6th Regiment North Carolina Troops, he was 1st Lieutenant of Company B and also by the Masonic fraternity and a large concourse of citizens. Mr. Cooley was a native of this place, a printer by trade, and a gallant soldier of both the Mexican and the late Civil War; he was wounded in the Battle of Second Manassas, Virginia, in August. 1862. He was captured at Rappahannock Station, Virginia, in November 1863, and held prisoner at Johnson's Island, Ohio, until paroled in June 1865. He was a little upwards of fifty years of age.

—*Daily Bulletin,* **July 3, 1878**

Died, near Mebane, N.C., on Saturday the 10th day of Dec., 1887, after an illness of some months, **Mr. Levi Faucette**. He was a member of the Presbyterian Church at Hawfields, from his early boyhood. He was fifty-five years of age. He was a farmer at the outbreak of the late civil war, and was among the first to take up arms in defense of our homes and enlisted at the beginning "for the war" in company F, 6th N.C.S.T., and all his comrades will bear testimony to his faithfulness and promptness to perform every duty. He was never known to miss "roll call" if able to be there. He was captured at Sharpsburg, Maryland, and held at Fort Delaware before being sent to Point Lookout. He was paroled at Greensboro in May 1865. He has left a widow and several children to mourn his loss.

—*Alamance Gleaner,* **December 15, 1887**

John Hutcheson died at his home in Bellemont on the 25th of July 1899. He was about 62 years old. He had been critically ill for a long time and his death had been expected almost daily for several weeks. He joined the Confederate army in 1861 and was in the Second Manassas Battle and lost his left arm. He was reported absent wounded through December 1864. He was paroled at Greensboro in May 1865. He married the daughter of Capt. Mitchell, of Caswell County, a sister of Mrs. P. A. Mitchell, of Graham. He was a citizen of Graham for a number of years and while living there he and his wife both joined the Presbyterian Church of which he was a member at his death. He was also a member of the Masonic Lodge at Graham. He leaves a wife and one son to mourn his loss.

—*Alamance Gleaner,* **July 27, 1899**

After an illness extending over several weeks, **Thomas Graham White** died at his home in Burlington on the morning of August 3rd, 1901, aged 56 years. He was conscious up to twelve hours before his death, when he was stricken with paralysis. He was a brother of Mr. Jas. I. White, of this place, who is the only one of his family now living. He was a member of the Presbyterian Church. He leaves a widow and three children, one of whom resides in Raleigh and two in Durham. At the age of seventeen he joined the 6th North Carolina Regiment, Company F, in 1863, was a brave soldier, and was wounded in Virginia a few days before the surrender. He suffered from his wound more or less the remainder of his life.

—*Alamance Gleaner,* **March 8, 1901**

Mr. James Jefferson Younger died suddenly at his home at Burlington last Thursday. He was the keeper of Pine Hill Cemetery. He was in the city talking with friends, and after reaching home he passed through the house, got a drink of water, went back to the front porch and sat down and in a few moments fell over dead. He married a daughter of the late James R. Fonville, who preceded him to the grave. He was ex–Confederate soldier, and was about 65 years of age. He joined the 6th Regiment, Company F, "for the war," in May 1861 and was a mechanic prior to enlisting. He was discharged in Richmond in December 1862, for chronic rheumatism. His remains were buried at Burlington.

—*Alamance Gleaner,* **July 17, 1902**

Mr. John T. Vincent, a native and a former citizen of Alamance County, died at his home at Locust Hill, Caswell County, July 17, 1903, after a brief illness. The remains were brought to Alamance and buried in the burying ground at Cross Roads Church on July 18th. His only brother, Mr. G. D. Vincent, former Clerk to Court, survives him. He was a brave Confederate soldier, joined the 6th North Carolina Regiment, Company K, in 1861, and was wounded in the shoulder at Gettysburg on the second day of the battle. He remained in service and was discharged in Virginia in February 1865, because of his wound. He had been a farmer.

—*Alamance Gleaner,* July 23, 1903

Mr. John Q. Allison, an inmate of the county home, died in the early part of last night. He was close to 70 years of age and had been quite feeble for several years. Mr. Allison was a brave Confederate soldier and joined the 6th Regiment, Company K in March 1862 at age 37. He was captured during the fighting around Petersburg in March 1865, and held prisoner at Point Lookout, Maryland until the war was over. He received a small pension and had laid by a portion of it to meet his funeral expenses and to pay for a tombstone. He had requested Mr. J. H. Tarpley, Supt. of the Home to look after burying him. The remains will be buried at Cross Roads tomorrow. The old soldiers are fast answering the last roll call.

—*Alamance Gleaner,* February 23, 1905

Mr. James A. Dixon was stricken with paralysis at his home here the latter part of last week and passed away yesterday evening, aged about 70 years. The remains were buried at Hawfields yesterday. He is survived by his widow and three or four children. Mr. Dixon served in Company F, 6th North Carolina Regiment. He was wounded in the leg in the fighting around Richmond in July 1862, and was wounded again at Gettysburg. He was paroled at Appomattox Court House and has answered his last roll call.

—*Alamance Gleaner,* November 10, 1910

Capt. James T. Rosborough, Confederate veteran, lumberman, planter, and highly respected citizen of Texarkana, Tex., died May 28, 1918, in his seventy-sixth year. Captain Rosborough was born July 21, 1842, in Ridgeway, N.C., his father Dr. James T. Rosborough, dying on August 15, following his birth. Going to Texas with his widowed mother and sister when it was a republic, his entire life was passed in Bowie and Marion Counties, except when at school in North Carolina and in the Confederate army.

It was from the Hillsboro Military Academy as a cadet of eighteen years of age that he volunteered his services "for the war" to the State and was commissioned by Governor Ellis as lieutenant in Company G, 6th North Carolina State Troops, under *Capt. J. A. Craige,* (17) in May 1861. He took part in all of the principal battles of the Army of Northern Virginia; his first participation being at Manassas in July 1861, and he commanded his company in almost every engagement. He was in every battle of the Seven Days' fight before Richmond, and was wounded at Malvern Hill and again very severely at Sharpsburg in the noted cornfield, which necessitated an absence of weeks from the army; but returning to his command, he was the following morning in line of battle at Fredericksburg, commanding his company, with his head still bandaged, so anxious was he to do his full duty.

The gallant Col. Pender, commanding the 6th North Carolina Regiment, being advanced to general, chose Lieutenant Rosborough for his marked bravery as a member of his staff with the rank of captain. After four years of constant and faithful service, the war being ended, he was mustered out of the army and took up the work of rehabilitating a devastated land.

During his business career, Captain Rosborough was extensively engaged in the manufacture of yellow pine lumber, the operation of large plantations in the Red River valley and in various other enterprises. A devoted husband and father, a member of the Episcopal Church, an active member of the A. P. Hill Camp, U.C.V., he leaves to his beloved family the heritage of an honorable life well spent.

—*Confederate Veteran* **Volume 26, Number 9, September 1918**

After an illness of several weeks, **George Nicholas Albright** died at his home in Stanton, Tenn., on September 6, 1918, at the age of seventy-nine years. He was born in Alamance County, N.C., and received his education at the old Bingham School, of that State. When the war came on in 1861, he enlisted with the 6th North Carolina Regiment, Company F. He was 2nd Lieutenant and took part in some of the important battles the first two years of the war, including Fredericksburg where he was wounded. He was captured at Rappahannock Station, Virginia in November 1863 and held prisoner at Fort Delaware, Delaware until his release in June 1865. Three daughters and three sons survive him.

—*Confederate Veteran* **Volume 26, Number 12, December 1918**

Sergeant William J. Kerr, one of the most honored and respected citizens of Alvin, Tex., passed away on February 25, 1922, aged eighty-one years. He was laid to rest in the city cemetery with full Masonic honors.

He was born in North Carolina, May 7, 1841, and went to Texas in early life. At twenty-six years of age he went to Alvin from Lockhart, Tex., settling upon his farm four miles south of Alvin, in the Mustang neighborhood, where he resided until the time of his death.

He enlisted in Company F, 6th North Carolina Infantry, and went to Virginia in 1861, and was with the Army of Northern Virginia from Manassas to Appomattox. He was wounded at Chancellorsville and Gettysburg, both times in the knee. He was orderly sergeant of his company, and up to the time of his death could call the roll from memory.

He was a member of John A. Wharton Camp No. 286, U.C.V., of Alvin; also a member of Alvin Lodge No. 762, A. F. & A. M. He was proud that he was one of the charter members of the original Ku Klux Klan of the sixties, and served as chief of one of the local organizations of North Carolina.

Two daughters survive him.

—*Confederate Veteran* **Volume 30, Number 10, October 1922**

7th Regiment North Carolina Troops

At Camp Argyle, Carolina City, N.C. on the morning of the 9th instant, **Mr. William Hampton Beaver,** in the 25th year of his age. He was a native of Mecklenburg County, N.C., a farmer there, and was a member of Company H, 7th Regiment, N.C. State Troops. He died of camp fever in the Hospital. A cousin and other members of the same company watched over him in his last illness.

—*North Carolina Presbyterian,* **November 30, 1861**

Deaths in the Seventh Regiment

We have been furnished with the following authentic account of the deaths in that portion of the 7th North Carolina regiment, captured at Fort Hatteras, from the office of the Adjutant General in this city:

List of privates belonging to the 7th Regiment North Carolina Volunteers, who died at Governor's Island, New York Harbor, and at Fort Warren, Boston Harbor.

At Governor's Island:
1. **J. C. Midyett**, Sept. 23, Co. D., Capt. Lamb.
2. **W. B. Griffin**, Sept. 28, Co. E, Capt. Gilliam.
3. **Hosea Blount**, Sept. 29, Co. E, Capt. Gilliam.
4. **Thomas Carter**, Sept. 29, Co. K, Capt. Sharp.
5. **A. Modlin**, Oct. 4, Co. D, Capt. Lamb.
6. **David Swain**, Oct. 4, Co. E, Capt. Gilliam.
7. **John R. Harrell**, Oct. 7, Co. I, Capt. Clements.
8. **J. B. Collins**, Oct. 7, Capt. Duke.
9. **John B. Scott**, Oct. 8, Co. I, Capt. Clements.
10. **W. A. Philpot**, Oct. 8, Co. I, Capt. Clements.
11. **D. Rogerson**, Oct. 9, Co. D, Capt. Lamb.
12. **James G. Harrell**, Oct. 10, Co. E, Capt. Gilliam.
13. **M. Roberson**, Oct. 11, Co. D, Capt. Lamb.
14. **James Whitehurst**, Oct. 11, Capt. Duke.
15. **H. Tyson**, Oct. 16, Co. G, Capt. Johnston.
16. **Wilson G. Gregory**, Oct. 17, Capt. Duke.
17. **Stanton Roberson**, Oct. 24, Co. D, Capt. Lamb.
18. **W. H. Brown**, Oct. 27, Capt. Duke.
19. **Stephen Kite**, Oct. 28, Co. I, Capt. Clements.
20. **Samuel Tetterton**, Oct. 30, Capt. Lamb.
21. **Frederick Jolly**, Nov. 6, Co. D, Capt. Lamb.

—*North Carolina Standard*, **November 30, 1861**

Please notice in your paper the death of **Sidney J. Sorrell**, a farmer in Wake County, age 21, a member of my company, who died at Carolina City (as I understand), on Thursday, the 9th inst., and was brought home to be buried. This is the first death that has occurred in my company since we entered the service in June last.

Hiram Weatherspoon, Capt., Company G., 7th Reg., N.C. State Troops.

—**Cedar Fork, Jan. 16, 1862,** *North Carolina Standard*, **January 22, 1862**

Died in Cabarrus County, N.C., at the residence of his father, Mr. N. T. White, on Sunday the 22nd of Jan'y, 1862, **Mr. Daniel Cornelius White**, aged 25. In July previous, he had enlisted for the war as a soldier of the Confederate army. He belonged to Company H, Capt. J. G. Harris (18) 7th Reg't. N.C.S. Troops. Whilst at Camp Argyle, near Carolina City, he took the measles which was followed by typhoid fever. This brought on the consumption which soon completed the work of destruction. On May 7th, 1854, he had joined Rocky River Church, remaining a member till his death. He was a farmer before enlisting.

—*North Carolina Presbyterian*, **January 25, 1862**

Duncan Cameron Haywood, son of the late Hon. Wm. H. Haywood, of this city, was slain in battle on Friday morning last, June 27th, at Gaines' Mill the vicinity of Richmond. He was Captain of Company E in Col. Campbell's 7th Regiment in which his elder brother, *Edward Graham Haywood*, (19) is Lieut. Col.

In the charge which the Regiment was making, the bearer of the flag was shot down; when the Colonel, seizing the colors, called on his men to follow him, he, in a few moments was himself killed. Capt. Haywood then raised the flag-staff and waving it over his head, exclaimed, "Now, Boys, this is our chance, follow me!" He was soon pierced by a large ball and died instantly.

Capt. Haywood was 22 years of age, a brave youth and a general favorite. His body was brought here by a younger brother who participated in the same fight, and was interred Monday in the city cemetery.
—*Raleigh Register*, July 2, 1862

The fall of this able officer in the battle before Richmond on Friday last, will awaken the deepest regret in the minds of thousands in this State. The 7th N.C. State Troops, on that bloody field, was completely decimated. It is rumored, but we cannot vouch for its truth, that no company in the regiment was left with more than fifteen men unhurt—It exhibited a gallantry which has covered the living and the dead in glory.

Col. Reuben P. Campbell fell leading on his men with the coolness, skill and intrepidity for which he was distinguished. His regiment was devoted to him and reposed entire confidence in his ability and gallantry. Col. C was a native of Iredell County, a graduate of West Point, and occupied a high position in the old U.S. Army. We have heard him spoken of by officers of the old army with much affection, and of his high character as an officer and a gentleman. The remains of Col. Campbell and Lt. Miller passed through this city on Monday morning, to be conveyed to their homes for interment.
—**Originally published in the** *Raleigh Standard* **and reprinted in the** *Carolina Watchman*, July 14, 1862

Died on the 8th day of July 1862, in the Hospital near Richmond, Va., **Albert B. McClellan**.

He was born on the 12th day of November 1839, in the County of Cabarrus, N.C. Soon after North Carolina seceded, he enlisted as a private for the war, in Company H., 7th Regiment of State Troops, and went forth to meet the insolent invader and help to drive him from our soil. He endured the fatigues of camp life for nearly one year; was in that hard fought battle near Newbern on the 13th and 14th of last March, where the Confederate forces, having encountered the enemy vastly superior in numbers, were compelled to retreat to Kinston. From Kinston his regiment went to Virginia, where Typhoid Fever soon laid hold on him. He died far from home, with no kind parental hand to smooth his pillow or even give him a cup of cold water to cool his parched tongue; nothing but the rude, though kind hand, of a fellow soldier to administer to him in his dying hours. He was a consistent member of the Presbyterian Church of Rocky River for several years.
—*North Carolina Presbyterian*, December 6, 1862

Died at the Hospital in Staunton, Va., on the 7th December last, **Alexander C. McMillan,** of Robeson County, aged about 27, a member of Co. C, 7th Reg't. He had been ill for near three months at Winchester and Staunton, of fever, erysipelas and chronic diarrhea. The physician who attended him in his last moments writes to his afflicted family, that "he was conscious that life was fast ebbing out, but as a follower of the meek and lowly Savior he bore his afflictions with much fortitude." He leaves a wife and two small children to mourn their irreparable loss.

—*Fayetteville Observer,* **February 16, 1863**

Died in the city of Richmond, on Sunday, the 10th of May, of wounds received the previous Sunday in the battle at Chancellorsville, **Ives Smedes**, a son of the Rev. Dr. Smedes, aged 20 years and 2 months. He was Adjutant (1st Lieutenant) of the 7th N.C. Regiment and had served in the 3rd Regiment North Carolina Cavalry before his transfer. His remains reached here on Monday night, and, after appropriate funeral services, were interred with military honors on Tuesday.

—*North Carolina Standard,* **May 15, 1863**

Lt. Col. Junius L. Hill was a native of Iredell County. At the war's commencement he raised a fine company of young men in the county, and was commissioned as Captain by Governor Clark. This company became Company A, 7th Regiment N.C. State Troops. He bore an honorable part in nearly all the great battles his regiment participated in, beginning with the Battle of Newbern. Upon the promotion of Maj. Hall in another regiment, Capt. Hill took his place as Major, being the Senior Captain.

When the 7th lost its noble commander (Reuben Campbell) in a desperate charge at the battle of Gaines' Mills, Major Hill was promoted to Lieut. Colonel. Col. Hill had, at Chancellorsville, on the 3d of May, about 8 o'clock in the morning, while in command of his regiment, routed the enemy from their works, and was encouraging his men to hold the place until reinforcements might arrive, when he fell pierced through the neck by a minnie ball, and died without a struggle. I have known him from his youth up, as a model of exemplary character. He was a member of the Presbyterian Church, and leaves behind him pious parents, brothers and sisters, to lament his sudden death.

—*North Carolina Standard,* **May 19, 1863**

Fell mortally wounded May 3, in the battle of Chancellorsville, **Lieut. James W. Emack**, of Company F, North Carolina 7th Regiment. Lieut. Emack was a native of Maryland—descended from a soldier of American Revolution—one of the Maryland Line. He and his youthful brother, Serg't George Emack, left their home and all its endearments, to assist their brethren of the South, in driving back to their dens the Northern demons. In his last moments he was attended by a minister of the Gospel. The surviving officers of his noble regiment stood by his side affording every comfort and consolation in their power, but he died the following day.

—*Carolina Watchman,* **June 8, 1863**

Died of pneumonia, at the way-side hospital, in Salisbury, N.C., Oct. 26th, 1863, **James Patrick Query,** a Cabarrus County farmer, Co. H, 7th Regt., N.C.T., in the 26th year of his age. He was wounded in battle at Frayser's Farm, Virginia, June 30, 1862, and disqualified for active service, but detailed for duty as a guard in Salisbury. His death made another young widow, with neither father nor mother, with a fatherless twin infant. He was a beloved member of Rocky River Church.

Died at his residence in Cabarrus Co., N.C., Nov. 17th, 1863, **Hugh James Smith**, in the 30th year of his age. He was a member of Co. H, 7th Reg. N.C.T.; had been in service 12 months; had fought 12 battles, was wounded at Sharpsburg; and was at home for the first time on furlough when a violent attack of pneumonia hastily terminated his life. On reaching his home, he was the veriest picture of health, and in a few days he was gone. He left an aged and a very infirm father (who had already lost two sons by the war), a loving wife and three children and numerous relatives and friends to mourn his death. He was a consistent member of Rocky River Church.

—*North Carolina Presbyterian,* **December 5, 1863**

Died of pneumonia, in Camp near Orange C. H., Va., Dec'r 20, 1863, **Thomas Bullard**, of Bladen Co., in the 26th year of his age. He volunteered in *Capt. R. B. McRae's* (20) Co. C, 7th Reg't N.C.T. in June 1861; was in the fights around Newbern, and discharged his duty faithfully in all the fights before Richmond, Fredericksburg and many others; was wounded in the battle at Gaines' Mill, Virginia, but not confined. He was a member of the First Baptist Church about 4 years. He leaves a father, mother, brothers and sisters.

—*Fayetteville Observer,* **February 11, 1864**

1st Sergeant Thomas M. Erwin, a member of Rocky River Church, Cabarrus County, N.C., volunteered as a member of Company H, 7th Regt., N.C.T., for three years or the war, in August 1861. He fought without ever faltering in 15 battles, including those around Richmond, where he was wounded, at Fredericksburg, Harper's Ferry, Sharpsburg, Chancellorsville and Gettysburg. Since then, he has barely been heard from. A wounded member of his own regiment, who was left on the field and captured by the enemy, reports that he saw him dead on the bloody field. A father, two brothers (one of them in the army) several sisters survive him. He was indeed killed on the 3d of the Gettysburg fight, in the 37th year.

—*North Carolina Presbyterian,* **June 1, 1864**

Died, at Verdiersville, Orange County, Va., on the 6th day of May 1864, from wounds received in the battle of the Wilderness, on the 5th, **William H. Haywood, 2d Lieut.**, Company K, 7th Regiment of N.C. Troops, aged 23. Lieut. Haywood, the youngest son of the late Hon. Wm. H. Haywood, was born on the 21st of December 1841, and joined as a private the 7th Regiment N.C. Troops, at the time of its first organization, in the summer of 1861, and has served ever since in its numerous battles and exhausting campaigns. He was in bloody battles around Richmond, and at the battle of Cold Harbor narrowly escaped death—a musket ball passing through his cartridge box, grazing but not injuring his body. On the 1st of September 1862, at the battle of Ox Hill, Lieutenant, then Private Haywood, received a wound which compelled him to leave the field, but he did so reluctantly, and before doing so, reported to Brig. Gen. L. O'B. Branch, to whom he tendered his services as a messenger during the rest of the battle. Gen. Branch, seeing his wounded condition, declined the service tendered, but afterwards complimented Lieut. Haywood highly for his conduct, and recommended him for promotion.

On the 13th of December 1862, at the battle of Fredericksburg, while the fight was raging hottest, a volunteer was called for by the gallant and lamented Lieut. Col. Junius L. Hill of the 7th, to perform the dangerous service of carrying a message to Brig. Gen. Lane, in full view and under the deadly fire of the enemy's sharpshooters. Lieut. Haywood promptly undertook and successfully performed this duty; and being commended for his conduct by Col. Hill, was promoted a Lieutenant from this date, for his gallantry; and he continued in this position until he rendered up his life. On the memorable 5th of May 1864, at the bloody battle of the Wilderness, when the Northern hordes were so gallantly and successfully repulsed, Lieut. Haywood received the death wound, and on the 6th of May, the day following, he expired. Not two years since, an elder brother fell, at the same age, on the bloody field of Cold Harbor, staining with his life's blood the battle flag of the same regiment which he was bearing forward in the charge; *now* his widowed and bereaved mother mourns her youngest son.

—*Daily Confederate,* **June 7, 1864**

Died, in hospital, in Richmond, Va., of disease contracted in the service, on the 25th day of October 1864, **Bushrod W. Vick, 2nd Lieut.** of Co. E, 7th Reg't., N.C.T. Lieut. Vick was born in Nash County, N.C., on the 27th day of January 1827. At the breaking out of the war, in 1861, he was a resident of Baltimore, and citizen of Maryland; but he immediately returned to his native State, leaving his family behind him, to cast his fortunes with us. He entered service in Company E, of the 7th Reg't, N.C.T., of which his brother, *Joshua Washington Vick*, (21) was Captain, as a private, and was soon designated a Sergeant in said company; his efficiency procured him the responsible position of Sergeant of the Provost Guard at Maj. Gen. Cadmus M. Wilcox's Head Quarters. While holding said position, he was promoted to 2nd Lieutenant in Company C, 7th Reg't N.C.T., during his last sickness, and never lived to take charge of his command in the line. Thus, away from his immediate family circle, amidst all the discomforts of a military hospital, has perished another martyr in our holy cause.

—*Daily Confederate,* **February 3, 1865**

The remains of the late **Lt. Col. John McLeod Turner** will reach Raleigh on the night of the 8th instant, under escort of a detail from the Raleigh Light Infantry, sent to Georgia for that purpose. The casket will remain at the N.C. depot, guarded by a detail of the R. L. I., until the morning of the 9th, when the entire company will escort the remains to the Confederate Cemetery, where all that is left of the gallant dead soldier will be laid at rest in the soil of his native State. The funeral procession will be joined at the capitol square by the Society of the Ex-Confederate Soldiers and Sailors, by the Ladies Memorial Association, and by citizens. He was Lt. Colonel of the 7th Regiment. At Gettysburg he was terribly wounded and lay for dead for a whole day on the field. He was captured and sent to Fort McHenry and later Fort Delaware. He was exchanged in September 1864. He survived, however, only to be a great sufferer the remainder of his life, during the last three years of which he was kept alive on morphine. His place occupies a prominent place in the medical history of the war, and it is generally conceded that he was the worse wounded man to survive his injuries of any man on the Southern side. After the war he was made Superintendent of the capitol at Raleigh, N.C. He will be given a State funeral, at which the Governor and State officials will be present.

—*News and Observer,* **March 8, 1883**

8th Regiment North Carolina Troops

Killed on the battle field at the Neuse River Bridge near Goldsboro,' on the 17th ult., **Corporal John A. Johnson.** He was a member of Co E, 8th Reg't N.C.T. He was captured at Roanoke Island in February 1862, and exchanged later in the year. He was a native of Harnett County, son of Archibald and Nancy Johnson, in his 25th year.

—*Fayetteville Observer,* **January 19, 1863**

The most melancholy incident connected with our late move upon Newbern, was the death of this useful and meritorious officer, **Colonel Henry M. Shaw**. He fell a victim to a shot from the enemy's skirmishers fired at very long range and evidently purely at random. He was struck in the throat, the ball severing the artery and producing death almost in the instant. He was a valuable officer, and his death is sincerely deplored. We met his remains at Kinston. They were wrapped in his martial cloak, and we were struck with the peculiar expression of his countenance. His last thought seemed to be a pleasant one, and there was upon his lips a smile of satisfaction.

He was in command at Roanoke Island when it fell, and he was taken prisoner. When exchanged, he immediately re-entered the service, his devotion to which he has sealed with his life's blood.

—*Daily Confederate,* **February 6, 1864**

Died on the 1st inst., of wounds received at Batchelder's Creek near Newbern, **David M. Barringer**, Company K, of Rowan County. He was captured at Roanoke Island in February 1862, and exchanged later in the year.

—*Fayetteville Observer,* **February 29, 1864**

The following letter in relation to Lieut. McKethan, of this county, who fell at Plymouth, has been handed to us for publication:—

CARVER'S CREEK, May 4th, 1864.

James McKethan, Esq., My Dear sir: With a painful heart I received the sad intelligence of the death of your noble son, the brave and gallant **Lt. James K. McKethan** of the 8th N.C. Reg't., Company E. Having been associated with him since the beginning of this unhappy strife, I can testify to his high personal worth as a brave and gallant soldier, and his noble and manly virtues. He was beloved by both officers and men of his command, and though his body be committed to the alien grave, he still lives—he lives within our hearts who were with him so long and knew him so well; long will we cherish his memory with freshness there, and his noble and shining examples will have their efficacy.

Amidst your sorrows for the loss of so noble and worthy a son, it will doubtless prove a balm to your bereaved and bleeding heart to reflect that it was while in the faithful discharge of his duty, leading his Company at the Battle of Plymouth, that he fell mortally wounded, with his "sword by his side and his face to the invader."

I regret very much that I cannot be with you at this time; duty imperative demands my return to the army.

With [deepest] sympathy, my dear sir, I am, respectfully, yours
    L. R. BREECE, (22)
    Capt. Co. E, 8th N.C. Reg't.

—*Fayetteville Observer,* **May 16, 1864**

Departed this life May 11th, 1864, of wounds received at the battle of Plymouth, **Private John F. Skipper**, Co. F, 8th Reg't, N.C. Troops, aged 22 years. He received the Sacrament of Baptism just before his death. He had been captured during the battle for Roanoke Island in February 1862, and released later that year.

—*Fayetteville Observer,* **June 2, 1864**

On the 1st day of June, AD 1864, **Capt. Leonard A. Henderson** fell mortally wounded in the right side by a minnie ball, about six o'clock in the evening, and breathed his last two hours afterwards. At the time of his death he was Captain of Co. F, 8th Regiment N.C. Troops, attached to General Clingman's Brigade. The battle, which to him proved so fatal, was fought at Cold Harbor, a point which will ever be remembered in the history of that grand series of victories which have been achieved by our troops in defense of the Confederate Capitol.

I know full well that the writer of brief obituaries can have no balm to heal the afflicted hearts of a [family] scourged by war; that he has no arts to fill the void seats in the family circle; no power to stay grief and mourning with their sable robes, for the lost ones.

Leonard A. Henderson was the eldest son of Archibald and Mary Steel Henderson, of this vicinity. On the maternal line he is a descendant of Gen. John Steele, Comptroller General during the administration of Gen. Washington, and the intimate friend and confidential adviser of that illustrious man. He is also the descendant of that Mrs. Elizabeth Steele, the pious and patriotic lady so beautifully and touchingly connected with the Revolutionary history, by the manner in which she relieved Gen. Green, who, fleeing before Cornwallis, had come to her house weary, hungry, alone and without money. On the paternal line, he traces through those of his name whose lives have formed a part of the history of North Carolina from its colonial existence. He was born on the 14th day of November 1841, and was in his 23d year when killed.

When the war began he was nineteen, and student at the University of Virginia. Without consultation, or even the knowledge of his parents, he volunteered as a private on the 14th of April 1861, in a company formed by the students of that institution to assist in the first capture of Harper's Ferry. His company arrived at the scene of action just in time to see our soldiers marching in after the evacuation of the enemy. He informed his brother of his intentions, but enjoined secrecy, lest it might distress his mother. Shortly after the evacuation, the students were disbanded in order that they might resume their studies. He, however, did not avail himself of this privilege, but without returning home repaired to Fort Johnson, below Wilmington, where he again volunteered as a private and worked in the trenches six weeks. At this point he wrote to his father, urging him to make no request from Gov. Ellis of an appointment for him, stating that he did not leave the "University to get office, but to defend the Old North State." Gov. Ellis, had awaited no solicitation, but had already given him that of 2d Lieutenant, which had not been received on account of some accidental misdirection.

Captain Henderson's first appearance on the field of battle was at the fall of Roanoke Island, where though 2d Lieut. he was in command of his Company. The request being made that the men should lie down, he alone kept his position standing, marching backward and forth in front of his company and regarding only their safety. This was done while the unseen missiles of death came hissing from the enemy and filled the air as a hail storm, not in recklessness, but with a solemn conviction that the first duty and most sacred obligations of an officer are to protect those whom he commands; for his life is a unit, but upon theirs depends the success of the cause. His sword had by some means gotten into the possession of an officer who was killed. One of the Rowan boys took it from his body and threw it into the sound with the determination that *Leon's sword* should never be surrendered. He was taken prisoner with the whole garrison and very shortly paroled and returned home.

Upon his exchange he was made Captain of his company and the Regiment was attached to Gen. Clingman's Brigade, the fortunes of which he followed without any particular incident or opportunity of distinction up to the storming of Plymouth at which he was present, and again conspicuous for coolness and intrepidity. He came out of that battle unscathed, as he himself expressed it, "under the protection of a divine providence," though his clothes were fairly riddled with balls.

Gen. Hoke's Division of which Gen. Clingman's Brigade formed a part, being ordered to Virginia for the protection of Petersburg, he participated in the battles about Drury's Bluff, and between Petersburg and Richmond, in one of which he was wounded painfully in the thigh. For this he declined to be relieved from duty, but appeared the next day at the head of his men.

An officer in a letter to a brother officer, speaking of him says:

> He was at all times in the thickest of the fray, urging his men on by his example in the fights around Drury's Bluff. He was always to be found at his post, acting in his cool, undaunted style.
>
> During the engagement of the 20th May, he was in command of the skirmishers of our regiment, fifty in number. The whole skirmish line was ordered to advance; but through some mistake *he only* received the order; but without hesitation he ordered forward his men, and without any support *led* them to the charge of the enemy's rifle pits under a heavy fire from the front and both flanks—gained his position and held it until the regiment came to his support.

Instances of this kind doubtless occurring more frequently than those at home had any opportunity of learning, had won the confidence and esteem and commanded the admiration of every officer and soldier in the Regiment. In another letter he is spoken of as "the best soldier I ever knew. He was the pride of the regiment. Every soldier gloried to emulate him." And his love for them too was as unbounded as theirs for him. He was proud of their gallantry and jealous of the reputation of each individual. Being told by his Colonel on one occasion at Charleston when about to go upon some dangerous charge "to leave the least reliable man behind to take care of the camp," he replied promptly, "I have not an unreliable man in my company." Nor had he, nor did he or any man of his company or his regiment ever blanch in the face of the foe during this war.

Capt. Henderson's next appearance on the battle field was that final one at Coal Harbor. Who commanded the enemy has not been learned. They had been three times repulsed, each time with scarcely any loss on our side—"all were jubilant of victory" writes a gentleman and officer in the regiment, "when the Brigade on the left gave way thereby allowing the enemy to get on our flank and rear." The Colonel at this time was supposed to have been killed, the Major was sick, and Capt. Henderson being called upon by the officers and men, took charge of the regiment. Their numbers were reduced to seventy, but says another gentleman, writing to his parents, "when the order came to charge they were a legion." And though the charge is described as "almost certain death," he threw himself at the front of his men, his eye quailed not nor did his voice falter. He cast aside his sword and fought with a musket, man to man and hand to hand. The fatal bullet was sped, and he was borne bleeding and dying from the field—still the soldier—still the patriot—still brave and noble, even in death.

—*Carolina Watchman*, [June 20, 1864]

It is with deep sorrow, we announce the death of **Lt. Col. John Reed Murchison**, who died in the hospital at the White House, Va., June 7th, from a wound received in the head near Cold Harbor, June 1st. At the time the fatal shot was received, he was in command of his Regiment—the 8th N.C.T.—was cheering his men on to deeds of noble valor. He was in his 38th. His skill and bravery were fully attested on Roanoke Island, the siege at Charleston, and the battles at Plymouth and around Petersburg. Being in command of his Regiment, in several of the last engagements in which he participated, he acted with such

conspicuous gallantry, as to attract the attention of his superior officers, and to draw from them the highest commendation. The deceased has left a widow and five children.
—*North Carolina Presbyterian,* **August 10, 1864**

Andrew W. McKinnon, born in Cumberland County and a member of Co F, 8th N.C.T., Clingman's Brigade, was shot through the body and both legs in the charge on Ft. Harrison on the 30th Sept 1864; he was there taken prisoner and after much suffering died on the 26th of Oct at the U.S. Hospital, Hampton, Va., lacking 5 days of being 28 years old. The meager details of a chaplain's letter are all that his family has of his death. He was for several years a member of the Lumber Bridge Presbyterian Church.
—*Fayetteville Observer,* **December 8, 1864**

Dr. Gaston B. Cobb, a prominent citizen of this county, died at his home in the western part of the county last Saturday morning, the 11th, and was buried in the burying ground at Providence on Sunday afternoon. He had been rapidly declining in health for the past two years or more, getting feebler and feebler, until a week or so before his death he was prostrated, at the same time suffering a slight stroke of paralysis. Dr. Cobb was born in Caswell County Jan'y 18, 1821, and was in his 62nd year. He served in the Mexican War and was promoted. He also served in the late War Between the States as a Captain of Company I, 8th Regiment. He was captured at Roanoke Island and released two weeks later at Elizabeth City. In the fighting at Morris Island in Charleston Harbor in 1863, he was wounded in both eyes and had to resign in January 1864. He was followed to his last resting place by a large number of his neighbors, friends and relatives who sincerely sympathize with the widow and the eight fatherless children in their sad bereavement.
—*Alamance Gleaner,* **December 8, 1864**

9th Regiment North Carolina Troops (1st Regiment North Carolina Cavalry)

We are pained to announce the death of **Mr. Jonathan Berry White**, son of Mr. John White of this country, and a member of the "Buncombe Rangers," Company H, First Regiment N.C. Cavalry. He died in the hospital at Richmond, on the 17th ult., of typhoid fever. He was a young man greatly esteemed by his acquaintances, and his death will be much lamented.

—*Asheville News,* **April, 12, 1862**

Maj. Thomas Newton Crumpler, of Ashe County, died near Richmond a few days since, of a wound received in a conflict with the enemy below Richmond. He was struck by a minnie ball, which passed through his lungs and came out near his shoulder blade. Maj. Crumpler belonged to *Col. Baker*'s (23) (formerly Ransom's) cavalry. He entered the service as a Captain, and was promoted to Major of the regiment. He was among the foremost in the charge in which he lost his life.

We had the pleasure of conversing with him at length, a few days before his death. He was on his way to Richmond, and spoke in the most animated terms of his regiment, and of the opportunity which would soon be presented of meeting the enemy. A braver or a nobler spirit than his never animated a human body. He was a young gentleman of education and fine abilities, and had already taken a respectable position among the leading public men of the State. He opposed the dissolution of the Union up to Lincoln's proclamation; and when told, in the House of Commons, of which he was a member, that he was tardy in the work of revolution, he replied that he would cling to the old government as long as he honorably could, but that if any attempt should be made to coerce the South he would resist it, and that when the day of battle arrived, he and his friends would be found as far in front, among the broken columns of the enemy, as those who appeared to be so anxious for the war. Most nobly has he redeemed his pledge.

The whole country mourns. "Red battle stamps his foot," and his victims fall on every hand. Our best and most useful men disappear forever as rapidly as snowflakes on the river. Every family laments some victim of battle or camp disease. But they sleep in honored graves, and the day-star of independence will soon shine over the turf that covers their remains.

—*North Carolina Standard,* July 26, 1862

On the fourth day of the fight before Richmond, Va., on the battlefield, 27th June last, **Marshall Lindley White**, in the 21st year of his age. He was a member of *Capt. Rufus Barringer*'s (24) company F in the 1st N.C. Reg't of Cavalry. He fell just after a gallant charge upon one of the batteries of the enemy, at Willis Church, Va., just below Richmond. From early youth he had been a consistent member of Rocky River Church, Cabarrus Co., N.C. He is another of our numerous martyrs to constitutional liberty. Poor Marshall! He lies in an unknown grave. But his memory is embalmed in the hearts of relatives, friends, and comrades.

—*North Carolina Presbyterian,* **October 4, 1862**

Died, near Hanover Courthouse, Va., on the 19th of Aug., 1862, **Marcemas O'Brien**, son of Dr. John and Elizabeth O'Brien, of Franklin County, N.C., aged 18 years and 7 months. He promptly volunteered with two other brothers, in company E, 1st N.C. Cavalry. He was an affectionate and doting son, whose loss will be deeply felt by his fond parents.

—*North Carolina Standard,* **October 10, 1862**

Lieut. Jesse W. Siler, of Company K, 1st N.C. Cavalry, was killed in a skirmish with the enemy on the 7th inst. He was gallantly leading a squad of his men on a position of the enemy at Gaines' Cross Roads, Va., when he was shot and instantly killed. Lieut. S. was a truly brave soldier and a gallant officer. We had the pleasure of making his acquaintance when he first entered the service, and can truly say that a nobler and more gallant young man has not fallen in defense of the cause of humanity and liberty. The county of Macon has lost one of its most promising young men; but the blood of our martyrs is the seed of future liberty.—*Raleigh Standard*

—*Wilmington Daily Journal,* **December 2, 1862, originally published in the** *Raleigh Standard*

Corporal John M. Pharr, Co. F (Capt. Barringer's), 1st N.C. Cavalry, died Sept. 3rd. 1862, of a wound received in action near Fairfax Court House, Va., aged 33 years. Kind friends stood by him—bore him from the field, soothed his dying moments, and bear witness to the heroic courage and Christian resignation with which he met his sad and untimely end. His remains rest in the burial-ground near Fairfax C. H. He is mourned by a lone and

aged mother and by many friends and relatives; but by none more than those who shared with him the privations and hardships of a soldier's life and best knew his many virtues.
—*North Carolina Presbyterian,* **February 21, 1863**

At Three Springs, Va., on the 27th March 1863, **Serg't Benajah C. Merritt**, aged 26 years, of Sampson County, N.C., and a member of *Captain W. J. Houston's* (25) Company I, 1st Regiment N.C. Cavalry. The death of Serg't Merritt, so sudden and unexpected, in the midst of high hopes, bright prospects and blooming youth, was indeed appalling. In one of the battles before Richmond, when his regiment made a brilliant but fearful and disastrous charge against the enemy's lines of infantry and artillery in position, he was assigned by his Commander to the post of danger and honor, as leader of the advanced guard. He fired the first gun upon the enemy and brought down his man, but he narrowly escaped with his life—having received a Sharpe's rifle ball in the lock of his own Carbine as it hung by his side. Afterwards, on 7th August, in a skirmish at Malvern Hill, he was again in the hottest fire, but this time less fortunate; He was slightly wounded on the head—his horse was killed under him and his leg broken. He fell into the hands of the enemy for several hours, but being unable to ride on horse-back, they left him by the road side, where he was re-captured by a portion of his Company, who went in hot pursuit. His wound was slight, but his broken limb resulted in hopeless lameness for life, and his usefulness as a soldier was at an end.

He had recently been at home, but had returned to the regiment to procure a discharge, which he was entitled to, but owing to some unknown cause, the Surgical Board of Gen. Hampton's brigade, could not be gotten together.—Eight weeks of marching and exposure, in his crippled condition, to the most inclement weather of winter, brought upon him severe cold, followed by congestion and death. Serg't Merritt was a man of mark. His loss will be no less severely felt in the community in which he was an active. enterprising, intelligent citizen, than in the regiment to which he belonged, and in which he had won, by his gallantry and honorable soldierly bearing, the respect and special confidence of all, from Col. commanding, to the humblest private in the ranks. It will even be a source of consolation to his bereaved friends to know that he received the kindest attention of the hospitable family of Mr. Kyger, at whose house he died, as well as of sympathizing friend and comrades. Peace to his ashes.
—*Wilmington Daily Journal,* **May 28, 1863**

William Marcellus Potts, of Mecklenburg County, a private of Capt. Barringer's Co. F, 1st Reg't N.C. Cavalry, was killed on the 21st June in a gallant charge on the enemy near Middleburg, Va.

—*Fayetteville Observer,* **July 20, 1863**

Died, at Grace Church Hospital, Alexandria, Va., on Saturday night, 17th inst., **Col. Thos. Ruffin**, 1st. N.C. Cavalry. The letter which conveys this intelligence says he received every attention from the surgeon in charge and his assistants. His remains were deposited in a vault in the burial ground of the Methodist Protestant Church, subject to the order of his family in North Carolina. Col. Ruffin was never married, but he leaves a mother and brothers and sisters to mourn his fall. It will be recollected that Col. Ruffin was wounded in the recent fight at Bristow Station, and fell into the hands of the enemy. A correspondent of the New York Commercial *Advertiser*, writing from Washington, Tuesday last, October 20, says; Col. Ruffin, who was wounded at the Bristow fight, died and was buried at Alexandria Sunday.
—*North Carolina Argus,* **November 5, 1863**

Near Concord Church, Sussex county, Va., on the 29th June, **John R. Stirewalt**, a member of Co. F, 1st N.C. Cavalry, received a shot through the breast just above the heart; he departed almost instantly, aged 28 years and 5 months. His body having lain in the enemy's possession all night was reclaimed the next morning by his sorrowing companions. He had been wounded in a fight at Barbee's Cross Roads, Va., in November 1862. For three years has this young soldier been bravely battling for his country's rights; three years have passed since he went out from a quiet town, fearless and determined; feeling, as expressed in his own words, that he who fears his God has nothing else to fear. In 1856, he, by public profession, connected himself with the Presbyterian Church at Poplar Tent, Cabarrus County, N.C.

—*North Carolina Presbyterian,* July 27, 1864

The community was shocked Saturday afternoon at the announcement of **General William H. Cheek**'s death. The summons came suddenly, while he was yet apparently in the possession of his usual strength and vigor. For a week or more Gen. Cheek had complained of something like indigestion. He had been taking some simple remedy for this but did not seem to be relieved of the trouble. About half past five o'clock Saturday afternoon he went to Dr. Bass's office to have him prescribe for him. Finding the Doctor engaged, he walked up and down the hall several times until the patient was dismissed. He appeared to be in good spirits and nothing about his looks or manner indicated that the vital spark of life was soon to be extinguished. Taking a seat, he and Dr. Bass talked a few minutes when he suddenly threw his head back, a gurgling sound escaped his lips, the face blanched and the spirit of one of North Carolina's most distinguished citizens and illustrious warriors, whose brilliant achievements added to her fame and glory, returned to the God who gave it.

Gen. Cheek was 66 years old. He was born in Warren County, with the exception of the four years during the war, until he came to Henderson about eighteen years ago. He married Miss Alice Jones of Warren, and she and three daughters and two sons survive him. The funeral was held from the Church of the Holy Innocents at 5 o'clock Monday afternoon.

In 1861, at the commencement of the Interstate War, he raised Cavalry Co. E, First Regiment, N.C. Cavalry, and was elected Captain of the same at its organization. The First North Carolina Regiment was commanded by Col. Robert Ransom. From this regiment there were promoted five Generals: Ransom, Baker, Gordon, Barringer, and Cheek. Capt. Cheek was promoted to Lieutenant Colonel, Colonel, and General. He was appointed Brigadier-General just before the fall of Petersburg, but owing to the retreat of General Lee's small army, he never received his commission.

He was engaged in the Seven Day's fight around Richmond, second Malvern Hill, two battles at Brandy Station, Gettysburg, Chancellorsville, and campaigns in Maryland, Pennsylvania, and many other fights. He was always at the head of his command, urging his men not to go, but to follow him. At the Battle of Jacks Shops, near Petersburg, his horse was shot from under him. Bugler Duke brought him another horse that he soon caught afterwards without a rider. While dismounted, Col. Cheek formed his men in a line and stood under fire while he sent a courier to Gen. Stuart for orders. The arrival of heavy reinforcements of the enemy compelled his men to retire. Col. Cheek, if we recollect rightly, was the hero of the splendid charge of the Confederate soldiers at Chamberlain's Run, in Virginia, where the men had first to cross a stream, then get through an abates of felled trees, all under fire, which they successfully accomplished, driving the enemy before them. General Lee, as we remember the story, stood upon an eminence watching the attack, and, when its success was assured, turned to General Rufus Barringer, who was at his side, and exclaimed: "General, the world has never seen such fighting!"

The snow that never melts has fallen on the heads of most of the brave men who followed Lee in the War Between the States, and one by one, they are called to join their great commander in the Better Land. Col. W. H. Cheek, who died here last Saturday, was one of the bravest of the brave and his death will be widely mourned by his comrades in arms and citizens alike.

—*Gold Leaf,* **Thursday, March 28, 1901**

10th Regiment North Carolina Troops (1st Regiment North Carolina Artillery)

Suddenly of disease, on the 29th ult., in the 25th year of his age in Richmond, Va., **Nathaniel A. Dunn**, of Wake County. He belonged to the Ellis Artillery, Company A, under Capt. *** and was in the Williamsburg battle.

—*Fayetteville Observer,* **January 23, 1862**

Lieut. Walter H. Pender of Carteret County, Co. G, 10th N.C.T. (artillery), was accidentally shot and almost instantly killed last Friday morning, by Private *Stephen B. Holland* (26) of the same company. Pender was playfully brandishing his sword at Holland, the latter playfully at a "charge" against Pender, but whilst backing from Pender, Holland's musket stock came in contact with a fence, and the concussion exploded the piece, shooting Pender through the centre of his body. He survived some three hours. He had been captured at Fort Macon in April of this year and exchanged in August.—*Raleigh State Journal*

—**Originally published in the** *Raleigh State Journal* **and reprinted in the** *Fayetteville Observer,* **November 3, 1862**

As Company F, 10th Regiment N.C. Troops, forming garrison of this place, was falling in for dress parade yesterday evening, April 3, a rifle in the hands of one of the men was accidentally discharged, and the ball went through the head of **Edwin Walker**, the man on the right of the company, killing him almost instantly. The affair was purely accidental. He was captured at Fort Macon in April 1862 and exchanged in August. He was 39. He was a native of Currituck County and was a seaman before enlisting in 1861.

—**Originally published in the** *Wilmington Journal* **and reprinted in the** *North Carolina Argus,* **"Soldier Accidentally Killed," April 6, 1863**

Died, in the Hospital at Wilmington, Jan'y 3d, 1864, **Johnston Fry**, in the 41st year of his age. He was a member of the Wilmington Artillery, Company K, and only served seven weeks before his death. He lived a consistent member of the church for the past 19 years. He was a good and obliging neighbor, a kind and affectionate father, and a true and devoted husband. He leaves a wife and five children to mourn their irreparable loss.

—*Fayetteville Observer,* **March 14, 1864**

Died in General Hospital, Raleigh, April 26th, 1864, of wounds received in the battle of Plymouth, **Corporal John W. I. McKeithan**, Company E, aged 26 years, 3 months and 4 days.

He was a member of *Capt. A. D. Moore*'s (27) light artillery, and a native of Brunswick County. Prompted by the spirit of patriotism at the commencement of hostilities he rallied around his country's standard and went forth to battle in defense of the rights and liberties of the Southern cause. He endured the hardships of camp life without a murmur, and passed through all the campaigns in Eastern N.C., and participated in every engagement up to the battle of Plymouth, in which he received a shell wound in the leg which soon terminated in death. His remains, far from relatives and friends, sleep quietly in the soldiers' large cemetery at Raleigh. He leaves two brothers in the army (one in the same company of which he was a member), a father and several sisters at home to mourn his death.
—**A friend, Burgaw Depot, N.C. May 12, 1864,**
Wilmington Daily Journal, May 16, 1864

At the residence of F. M. Harper, in Lenoir County, July 13th, 1864, of typhoid pneumonia, **Mr. Lott A. Croom**, aged 23 years. When the war broke out he was ready, at the first call of his country. He entered service June 1861, Company B, 10th Regiment, North Carolina troops. He was captured at Fort Macon in April 1862 and released in August of the same year. He leaves an affectionate mother, wife and one child, and sisters to mourn their irreparable loss.
—**A friend, Clayton, N.C., Daily Confederate, August 18, 1864**

In Petersburg, Va., on the 19th Sept., from a wound in the breast by a minie ball, **Sergeant William Wallace**, a member of Miller's Battery, Company E, aged 38 years. He was from New Hanover County and worked as a mason before enlisting. He leaves a bereaved wife and two devoted children. He was a brave and patriotic soldier, and was beloved by all his fellow soldiers with whom he fought, bled and died.
—*Wilmington Daily Journal,* **October 3, 1864**

Died, at Wilmington, N.C., on the eve of the 13th inst., of yellow fever, **Charles Cornelius Southerland**, aged about 17 years, a member of *T. J. Southerland*'s (28) Light Battery, Co. "I," 10th N.C. Regiment. He enlisted in April 1864 and died six months later. He voluntarily enrolled himself among the *patriotic band*, but alas! the fell hand of disease has cut him off, ere his youthful hopes and expectations could be realized—that of seeing his country *free and independent*.
—*Wilmington Daily Journal,* **October 17, 1864**

Below we give the names of some of the troops, belonging to the 10th N.C. Regt., of Artillery, captured at Fort Fisher, who have died in prison at Elmira, New York. They all belonged to Co. K., of that Regiment.

Levi B. Kennedy enlisted in April 1864 and died April 6th, 1865. He was buried in Woodlawn National Cemetery, Elmira.

John F. Bond enlisted for the war in April 1861 and was captured at Fort Hatteras on August 29th. He returned to his regiment after his exchange in February 1862. He died of chronic diarrhea in prison February 18, 1865.

William Lawson was captured January 15, 1865, and died at Elmira February 20. He is also buried at Woodlawn.

William. T. Gainor enlisted in Pitt County in May 1862 for the war. He was captured January 15, 1865, and died a prisoner March 4, 1865, of chronic diarrhea. He is buried in Woodlawn.

John. B. Furr enlisted in New Hanover County in March 1864. He was captured January 15, 1865, and died of variola March 3. Burial was at Woodlawn.

Harrison Roberson enlisted in 1862 in Company 7, 17th Regiment N.C.T. and transferred to the 10th Regiment in April 1864. He died at Elmira of pneumonia March 7, 1865, and was buried in Woodlawn.

Slade R. Stallings joined the 10th in April 1861 and was captured at Fort Hatteras, in August of that year. Confined at Fort Warren, Massachusetts, he was exchanged in February 1862. He returned to his regiment and served until captured at Fort Fisher. He died at Elmira of pneumonia March 10, 1865, and was buried at Woodlawn.

Owen Congleton enlisted at age 17 in May 1864. Captured at Fort Fisher, he died of pneumonia at Elmira February 24, 1865, and was buried in Woodlawn.

—*Daily Confederate,* **March 23, 1865**

Thos. Thomas was found dead yesterday within a short distance of Moses Peelers' with whom he was boarding. Mr. Thomas was an Englishman, in the last stage of consumption, and had walked out a short distance from his boarding house, was attacked with hemorrhage, and, it is thought, soon expired. He was a member of the Rowan Artillery, Company D, 10th Regiment North Carolina Troops during the war, having joined in March 1862. He was paroled at Salisbury in May 1865. He leaves no family.

—**Originally published in the** *Salisbury Banner,* **15th inst. and reprinted in the** *Wilmington Journal,* **"Found Dead," September 20, 1866**

Died.—On Thursday, Aug. 6, very suddenly, of cholera, **Richard Washington Evans** of Wayne County, son of the late Dr. Augustine C. Evans, of Goldsboro,' N.C. Thus has fallen a young man of most exemplary life, who, in the words of his companion, who communicates the intelligence of his death to his afflicted mother, "bore about him in the most evident manner, principle, fairness, good breeding, and all the qualities that are creditable and correct." Lieut. Evans was a cadet in Gen. D. H. Hill's Military School at Charlotte when the war broke out. He was appointed a Lieutenant in Co. F, 10th N.C. Regiment in June 1861, and served faithfully to the time of the surrender, proving gallant in action, and faithful in the performance of every duty. He was captured at Fort Macon in April 1862 and exchanged in the following August. His loss deprives his family of one to whom they trustfully looked for support.

—*Wilmington Journal,* **August 16, 1867**

Ayden, Pitt County, Items.... On Saturday morning at five o'clock at his home in Coxville, the soul of **Mr. William S. Roach** took its flight to God, who gave it. Mr. Roach had been in feeble health for some time and his death was no surprise to his friends. He was buried Sunday with Masonic honors at St. John's Episcopal Church, where he has long held his membership. He was a farmer and merchant and was one among the most upright and pious men of our acquaintance. He was a loyal ex–Confederate soldier, a Private in Company I, 10th Regiment North Carolina Troops, filling his full time in the Civil War and laid down the musket with the satisfaction of duty well done. He was a charter member of the old Roundtree Masonic Lodge, and when that lodge suspended he moved his membership to Grimesland, and it remained there until his death. We have never heard ought spoken against his good and spotless career.

—*Daily Reflector,* **January 3, 1911**

Mr. James S. Norman died Friday afternoon at his home in Beaver Dam Township. He was a Confederate veteran and one of the heroes of Fort Fisher, serving as Corporal in Company K, 10th Regiment North Carolina Troops. He was captured at the fort, held prisoner at Elmira, New York, and released there in July 1865. He was a native of Beaufort County but moved to Pitt just after the war, and was among our best citizens. Mr. Norman was 80 years of age and is survived by four sons and a daughter.

—*Daily Reflector,* **May 6, 1911**

An old and highly esteemed citizen of the county was lost last Sunday night when **Mr. Isaiah C. Leffers** of Straits passed away. Mr. Leffers had been sick for several weeks having had an attack of apoplexy from which he never rallied. At the time of his death Mr. Leffers although he was 76 years old was County Surveyor. He was one of the few Confederate veterans still living in Carteret County, having served in Company G, 10th Regiment North Carolina Troops. Mr. Leffers wife died a good many years ago but he had a son Robert Leffers living in Norfolk and two daughters, Mrs. Maude Willis of Straits and Mrs. Lucy Willis who lives in Florida.

—*Beaufort News,* **April 15, 1920**

One of Beaufort's oldest and most respected citizens passed away when **David S. Liddon** died Tuesday morning at about half past four o'clock. Mr. Liddon had gone to an outhouse in the yard and when he failed to return after some time search was made for him and he was found dead. It is supposed that he died from heart failure. Mr. Liddon was not a native of Beaufort having come here some fifteen years ago from Washington, N.C. He made his home with Captain J. T. Beveridge who married Mr. Liddon's daughter. Mr. Liddon was eighty years of age and for his years seemed to be right strong. He was a boat builder by trade and until about two years ago was usually engaged in that work. During the war he had charge of building some large barges for the late W. B. Blades. Mr. Liddon's nearest surviving relatives are several nieces and nephews. He was a Confederate veteran, serving in Company K, 10th Regiment North Carolina Troops, and was captured at Fort Hatteras in April 1861 and held at Fort Warren, Massachusetts. He was exchanged in February 1862 and returned to his regiment. He was again captured at Fort Fisher in January 1865, held a prisoner at Elmira, New York, and paroled in May 1865, after taking the Oath. He was a member of the Methodist Church. His body was taken to Washington Wednesday morning for interment in that city.

—*Beaufort News,* **March 17, 1921**

One of the most highly regarded citizens of Carteret County passed away last Saturday morning when **Dr. John W. Sanders** died at his home near Ocean. Dr. Sanders was born at Grace Point in Onslow County on March 15th, 1842 and therefore lacked only about two months of being 80 years of age. He married early in life to Miss Sally J. Koonce and lived happily with her until about a year ago when she departed this life. Of their union two children were born both of whom died in infancy. An adopted daughter Mrs. Daisy Koonce of Richlands two brothers, B. F. and S. J. Sanders survive him and a number of nieces and nephews.

Dr. Sanders enlisted for the war in the Confederate army, Company H. 10th N.C. Regiment in 1861. He was captured at Fort Macon during Burnside's invasion in February 1862 and exchanged in August 1862. He served to the close of the war with distinction. He started in as a private and was promoted to 1st Lieutenant. Dr. Sanders was elected and served a member in the State Senate in 1888. He was also for a time a director in the State Hospital for the Insane. He was a devout member of the Methodist Episcopal Church. He was a Mason and members of that organization conducted his funeral. Dr. Sanders was a practicing physician for a half a century or more and did a great deal of good in his community. He did not leave much of this world's goods but died rich in affection and regard of those who knew his best.

—*Beaufort News,* **January 19, 1922**

J. W. Gaskill of Sea Level, died Saturday March 16th. He was 84 years old. Services were held Sunday at the home of his son. Mr. Gaskill enlisted in the War Between the States in 1862, Co. K 10th N.C. Regiment, later he was transferred to Latham's Battery 5th N.C. Regiment where he served until the close of the war. A large number of friends from his home and Beaufort attended the funeral. The Rev. W. Styron of the Primitive Baptist church conducted the funeral services. A daughter Mrs. Floreida Hamilton and two sons William and Washington Gaskill and several grandchildren survive the deceased. The Daughters of the Confederacy U.D.C. attended the funeral; a laurel wreath was placed on the casket by the President. A wreath of flowers by Children of Confederacy, also a Confederate Marker were also placed. Mr. Gaskill was dearly loved by this organization.

—**A friend,** *Beaufort News,* **March 21, 1929**

In the presence of a large crowd of friends the body of **Winfield Scott Chadwick** was laid to rest Saturday evening shortly after five o'clock in the Chadwick plot in old Live Oak cemetery. A simple service according to the ritual of the Methodist Church on Ann Street, conducted by the pastor Reverend Leland L. Smith, preceded the burial. He was born in Beaufort on March 18th 1848 in the home now occupied by Mrs. Walter Chadwick on Front Street. He was the son of Capt. Barnabas and Mary A. Chadwick. On November 1st 1863, while 15 years of age, he enlisted in Co. G Tenth Regiment, North Carolina Troops, and served until the end of the war.

—*Beaufort News,* "Carteret County's Most Successful Businessman Died Last Thursday," **August 8, 1929**

11th Regiment North Carolina Troops

At the Hospital, Camp Mangum, Raleigh, on the 8th April, of typhoid fever, **Private George Patton**, aged fifteen, of *Capt. Mark Armfield's* (29) Company (B), Bethel Regiment. Also, **Private John Patton** (George's senior brother), aged eighteen, of the same company, died on the following day, of the same disease.

—*Fayetteville Observer,* **April 21, 1861**

In the hospital at Wilmington with Typhoid fever, on the 1st inst., **Seaborn McQuay**, of Mecklenburg in the 28th year of his age, leaving an aged mother, and many relatives and friends to mourn his loss. He was a member of *Captain John S. A. Nichols'* (30) company, 11th Bethel Regt., Co. E.

—*Daily Bulletin,* **July 14, 1862**

In Wilmington, N.C., on the 12th July 1862, of congestive fever, **Capt. P. J. Lowrie, Commissary** of the 11th Reg't N.C. Troops. Capt. Lowrie was a native of Mecklenburg County, a most excellent officer, a courteous gentleman. His body was sent to Ansonville, [Anson County] where his wife now resides.
—*Wilmington Daily Journal,* **July 14, 1862**

The news had arrived suddenly, and had fallen like a thunder stroke upon the hearts of those that loved him. In the course of the night his body was brought up from the Railroad Depot in a hastily constructed coffin, and carried at once to the graveyard to await burial (it being reported that he had died of yellow fever), and there were assembled next morning his old neighbors and friends to pay the last offices of respect to one who had given his life to the common cause. A group stood round the open grave, into which a light wind was whirling a few yellowing leaves—some were gathered near the wagon containing his body—and others loitered through the tall grass and weeds, among the graves, recalling the faces of those that lay below—but all were thinking of the broken-hearted mother, and wife and little one, whose arrival we were awaiting.—"The only son of his mother, and she was a widow." And when we saw his childless mother and his widow bowed in wild and bitter lamentation together over the coffin that held their hope and stay in life, while his blue-eyed, fair-haired baby girl stood by unconscious, looking down into her father's grave, there was no eye in the assemblage that refused to weep with them. The soft September sunlight shone on no sadder scene that morning. The kind hands of those who had known him since childhood gently lowered the dead soldier into his last resting place close to the grave of two of his children—kind hands adjusted the closely fitting planks above him, and showered on them the heavy clods of clay—ashes to ashes and dust to dust.

And thus was buried, in the 34th year of his age, **Captain James R. Jennings**, of Co. G, 11th Regiment. He was among the first to volunteer for the defense of his country, and was 1st Lieutenant of the Chapel Hill "Light Infantry," in the famous 1st "Bethel" Regiment which took part in the Battle of Bethel Church fought June 10, 1861, in Virginia. In that eventful campaign he bore himself so well and bravely as made it an easy matter for him, on his return home at its close, to raise a company of his own. He had served also in the Mexican War, though only 18 years old—and then, as on all occasions as a soldier, had done his work manfully.—And now he has died in the service of his country, and though that country has many another gallant son to stand up for her in her hour of need, yet who shall supply his place to his mother, his wife, or his child. And this is the story of thousands.
—*North Carolina Standard,* **October 3, 1862**

DIED—At Wilson Hospital, on the 24th of Sept., **Thomas Smith**, a member of Co K, 11th Reg't N.C. Troops. He was the son of Mr. Burton Smith, of this county [Buncombe] who has several sons in the army, who have shown a gallantry in defense of their country surpassed by none. We had no personal acquaintance with the deceased, but he has given his life to his country, and his memory, along with thousands of other gallant young men, will be fondly cherished by a grateful country. His disease was Typhoid fever. He was 20.
—*Asheville News,* **October 9, 1862**

Lieut. John Henderson McDade, Co. G, 11th N.C. Infantry, fell in the front of his company at Gettysburg, Pa., July 1st, 1863, in the 33d year of his age. He was a native of Orange County, N.C., the eldest son of Jas. B. McDade, Esq., who for many years has held the office of Post Master at Chapel Hill. Lieut. McDade was a graduate of the University, class of 1852, where he sustained a reputation for classical knowledge and modest demeanor. He entered the military service at the very outset of the war as a private in Capt. Ashe's company from Chapel Hill, and was at the Battle of Bethel, in Company D, 1st N.C. Vols. After the time of service of the regiment had expired, he assisted in raising another company, Co. G, 11th N.C., and was elected 2d Lieut. thereof, and afterwards becoming 1st Lieut. at the death of Capt. Jennings.

—*Fayetteville Observer,* **September 7, 1863**

We make the following extract from a letter relating the circumstances of the death of **Lieut. Henderson C. Lucas**, of Charlotte, Adjutant of the 11th N.C. Troops, and a family well known here where his mother was born and his ancestors lived.

He was wounded in the first day's fight at Gettysburg and was taken immediately to Martinsburg, traveling three days and nights without a mouthful to eat or having his wounds dressed. There he was taken care of by kind strangers. It seemed so hard to die away from those that loved him so much that he sent many messages and when he could not live he replied that he was ready, that he was not afraid to die, that his full trust was in God. He died about July 25th.

He was shot down while bearing the colors of the 11th. When Col. Leventhorpe was wounded the regiment was thrown into some confusion; he seized the colors (the color-bearers having all been shot down),—and led the charge through a murderous fire until,—twenty paces in from of the line, calling on the men to follow their flag,—he was shot down, but rose again, waving the colors and urging on the men. He was again brought down, but still supported the old Bethel colors with his left arm until that arm was shot through, and the colors were once more down. He then exclaimed—"Boys I have played out, go on to victory." The colors were received by another, who was instantly shot down, and a soldier who stopped to examine his comrade also fell dead.

—*Fayetteville Observer,* **September 7, 1863**

Fell at Gettysburg, on the battle-field, 1st July, **William V. Morrison**. He was the son of a Presbyterian minister, the Rev. W. N. Morrison, of Buncombe, N.C., and at the time of his death was about 18 years old. He was a member of Co. K, 11th N.C. Regt. Though of a delicate frame he never shrunk from a single duty, either in camp, along the march, or on the field. The writer heard one of the officers, whose own life-blood was ebbing fast away speak of him in terms of high commendation.

—*North Carolina Presbyterian,* **October 3, 1863**

Died a prisoner of the enemy, on 6th July, from the effects of a wound received at the Battle of Gettysburg, on the first of July, **Wm. H. McQuay**, aged 19, of Co. E, 11th Reg't., from Mecklenburg County.

—*Fayetteville Observer,* **January 14, 1864**

Died a prisoner at David's Island, New York Harbor, 26th July, **James C. Darnold**, of Buncombe County, a member of Co. K, 11th Reg't N.C., after being wounded and captured on the first day of the Battle of Gettysburg.

—*Fayetteville Observer,* **February 1, 1864**

Killed on the first day of the battle at Gettysburg, **Daniel H. Haynes**, of Lincoln County, aged 19, Company I.

—*Fayetteville Observer,* **February 1, 1864**

Lieut. Samuel M. Young, of Company K, 11th N.C. Reg't died in a field hospital, 7th July 1863, after being wounded and captured by the enemy during the first day's fight at Gettysburg.

—[February 11, 1864] *Fayetteville Observer*

Killed on the battle-field of Gettysburg, Penn., on the first day, in his 21st year, **Major Egbert A. Ross**, of the 11th N.C. (Bethel) Regiment, and eldest son of Dr. Francis M. and Dorcas Ross, of Charlotte, N.C. Though only in his eighteenth year and previous to the call for soldiers being issued, he had raised a company of his young fellow-townsmen, drilled and had them prepared for active service. His training during the two years preceding, in the Charlotte and Hillsboro' Military Institutes eminently qualified him to be a skillful and competent officer. The "Charlotte Grays" Company C formed part of the 1st Regiment then raised and commanded in the State, under the command of Lt. Gen. (then Col.) D. H. Hill, and with their youthful Captain, greatly distinguished themselves in the Battle of Bethel. After the disbanding of that Regiment, Capt. Ross immediately raised a new Company A, joined the 11th N.C. (Bethel) Regiment, and upon an election of Field Officers, was chosen Major, being then in his nineteenth year. With the regiment in all its perilous campaigns through North Carolina and Virginia, Major Ross continued, faithfully executing his duties, until that fatal day, when he fell fighting bravely on the bloody heights of Gettysburg. He lived but two short hours after receiving his mortal wound. He called upon a friend to kneel down and pray beside him that he might make good use of the little space left him to prepare for the exchange of worlds.

—*North Carolina Presbyterian,* **February 17, 1864**

Died from the effects of a wound received at Gettysburg, July 1st, 1863, **George Pinckney Keever**, Co. I, 11th "Bethel" N.C.T. He was captured by the enemy and passed away in their hands, July 7th.

—*Fayetteville Observer,* **June 25, 1864**

Among the noble lives that were sacrificed on the altar of their noble country at Bristoe Station, Va., on the fatal 14th of October last, was that of **Lieutenant Paul Barringer Grier**, of Co. E, 11th (Bethel) Regiment N.C.T. He was twenty-five years old, a brave and patriotic youth, the third son of Andrew Grier, deceased, and Mrs. Margaret Grier, a widowed lady of Mecklenburg County, who had lost another gallant son in the service of his country. A few days before his death, in reply to his mother requesting him to come home on furlough he wrote: "Dear mother—I desire greatly to visit my dear home and see you all once more; but I cannot ask a furlough now, when the call of our bleeding country requires every man who can raise an arm in her defence to be at his post.—Important movements are going on, and soon we will be called on to strike one more blow for our homes and our firesides." Again he says: "Nothing but the narrow stream separates the two armies—and even now the distant roar of cannon tells me the contest has begun. If I be so fortunate as to escape unhurt and safe you shall hear from me again, *but it is very uncertain.*"

These were his last words to his devoted mother. Seven days later he fell gallantly, a noble martyr to his country's cause.—*Raleigh Confederate.*

—**Originally published in the *Raleigh Confederate* and reprinted in *Way of the World,* March 24, 1864**

Died in hospital at Gettysburg, 25th August last, of wounds received at Gettysburg, **Hugh A. Tate**, of Morganton, of Company D, 11th Reg't. He was severely wounded in right leg on the 3rd day and captured. His leg was later amputated and he died on the above date after a second amputation. He had served in Company C, 1st "Bethel" Regiment, and was at the Battle of Bethel Church, June 10, 1861.

—*Fayetteville Observer,* March 31, 1864

One of the last three surviving Confederate Veterans in this city has died. **Capt. Edward Ralph Outlaw**, of this city, died at Nags Head last Friday night. He was 81 years old and had been ill for two years. He was Captain of Company C of the Eleventh N.C. Regiment and served with Lee in the Army of Virginia for four years, taking part in every important battle of that memorable struggle. He was paroled at Appomattox Court House on April 9, 1865. Captain Outlaw was born in Bertie County, near Windsor, and lived in that county until fifteen years ago, when he moved to Elizabeth City, where he had lived ever since. He leaves four sons and five daughters. The sons are Edward R., Jr., John R. and David Outlaw of this city, and Alex B. Outlaw, of Windsor. The daughters are Mrs. W. H. Huff, of Oxford; Mrs. S. W. Worthington, of Wilson; Mrs. William McQueen, of Elizabeth City; Mrs. D. M. Conner, of Durham, and Mrs. T. Gilliam, of Windsor. The remains were carried to the old home at Windsor for interment.

—*Elizabeth City Independent,* August 26, 1921

Sergeant James Monroe Sims was born November 6, 1840, in Cabarrus County, N.C., and in early manhood located at Charlotte. At the first call for volunteers, he joined the Charlotte Grays, Company A. This command was soon at the front, and took part in the first battle of the war, Big Bethel, and was near where the lamented Henry Wyatt fell, the first soldier martyr to Southern Independence. In the battle of Gettysburg he was wounded in the right hand, and a gunshot passed through his hat. He was captured at Falling Waters, Maryland during the retreat on July 14, and held prisoner in Baltimore until exchanged in late summer. He was afterwards made quartermaster sergeant and was in charge of the regimental wagon train until he and his train were captured near Petersburg on April 3, 1865. He was confined in the Hart's Island Prison, New York Harbor until his release in June. In 1869 Comrade Sims was wedded to Miss Fannie Moody, and to them were born four daughters and a son, the latter dying in youth. His life companion was also taken by death, and he lived in bereavement for the last ten years. He conducted a successful grocery business until the weight of years bore too heavily, and he retired.

Our comrade took a commendable pride in Confederate memories, and served for many years as treasurer of Mecklenburg Camp No. 382, U.C.V., holding that office at his death on July 13, 1922. He was quiet and unassuming, but was keenly interested in matters pertaining to civic, political, and religious affairs. He was a deacon in the Presbyterian Church for more than an average lifetime.

—*Confederate Veteran* Volume 30, Number 11, November 1922

12th Regiment North Carolina Troops

MR. EDITOR: I am pained to record the death of **James W. Elixson** of our company (the Granville Grays), 2nd Company D, 2nd Regiment North Carolina Volunteers [later

12th Regiment North Carolina Troops]. He died yesterday morning, of typhoid fever. He was a most estimable young man; and our company has sustained a most grievous loss. This is the first death that has occurred in our company, and has cast a gloom over all; it being that of such a *worthy young* man.

—*North Carolina Standard,* September 4, 1861

Dr. W. J. T. Miller, of Cleveland, passed through this place on Sunday last, with the body of his son, **Lt. David M. Miller**, of the 12th regiment of State Troops, Company E, who was slain in the battle of Tuesday at Malvern Hill. Dr. M. has two others sons in the army near Richmond.

—*North Carolina Standard,* July 9, 1862

George M. Fleming was killed in the long to be remembered battles fought before Richmond. He died at Malvern Hill on the 1st of July. He first enrolled his name on the list with *Captain Thomas L. Jones'* (31) noble band, the "Warren Riflemen," that later became 2nd Company C in the 12th Regiment N.C. Troops. George bade adieu to home, parents, brothers, sister, all that he held dear on earth, and took his place upon the tented field.— For several days preceding the battle, he had been lying ill in the hospital; but that eventful morning found him at his post, and almost instantly after the firing commenced, he fell, pierced through the heart by a Minnie ball. He had been a farmer and was 20 years old.

—*Raleigh Register,* July 23, 1862

Captain John Tillinghast Taylor, of the Townesville Guards, Company B, fell a martyr to the cause of Southern Independence at Gaines' Mill, on Friday 27th June last. While gallantly leading his Spartan Band he was shot through the head and immediately expired. Capt. Taylor was the eldest son of John C. Taylor, Esq., of Granville County, N.C., and was in his 28th year. He was an Alumnus of the University of N.C.; was a young man of fine literary taste and culture; and in enlisting recruits in the service of the Confederacy, early in the contest, exhibited oratorical talents of his order. He was a communicant of St. John's Church, Williamsboro, N.C.; and as a vestryman was active and eminently useful in the parish.

—*North Carolina Standard,* August 6, 1862

Died, of typhoid fever, in Richmond, on the 25th of June 1862, **Peter Evans Spruill**, Company F, in the 27th year of his age. He leaves a widowed mother and sisters. Graduating from the University of North Carolina with honor, he was appointed and accepted the position of tutor, where he discharged his duties with credit and fidelity. Having made choice of the law as his profession, and obtained license to practice, he visited Europe for the purpose of completing his studies. He learned of the rupture between the North and the South, and hastening home, he joined as a private one of the volunteer companies of his native county. His regiment was soon ordered into service, and for twelve months, through heat and cold, sunshine and tempest, he faithfully discharged his duty, until stricken down by disease.

—*North Carolina Standard,* August 13, 1862

Died, at Bird Island Hospital, Richmond, Va., July 12th, 1862, of wounds received at the battle of Malvern Hill, on the 1st of July **George W. Harper** of Halifax County, N.C., a member of Company I, aged exactly 22 years on the day of the battle. He had previously volunteered and served out his term in the immortal first, or Bethel Regiment, having quitted College to join the Enfield Blues, belonging to that regiment, and after the disbanding of it, he joined the company above named, which he was bravely leading in a charge upon the enemy—(the first officers of the company being all sick, wounded, or missing)—when he received the wound that terminated his young and promising career. He leaves a mother, sisters, and numerous relatives and friends to mourn his death.

—*North Carolina Standard,* September 3, 1862

Edward Jones of Warren County, N.C., died August 23rd, aged 30. He joined a company for the defense of our beloved land soon after the John Brown raid, and since that time, without regard to health, fortune or life, has faithfully devoted his all to her. The writer of this has known him most intimately and never remembers to have seen him angry, or to have heard him speak a cross word to anyone. He belonged to Co. F, 12th Reg. N.C.T. In the battle of "Slash Church," [also known as the Battle of Hanover Court House—Ed.] he fought till completely cut off from his men and surrounded by the enemy, and though within a few feet of them, he was not taken prisoner; and there in the swamps of Hanover, he was lost three nights and two days, without food, shelter, and almost without raiment, for when Norfolk was evacuated, his regiment lost all their baggage. A negro piloted him out of the swamps, and on foot he found his way to camp in Richmond, hungry, weary, naked and sick. His brothers brought him home, to linger awhile with us, and then yield up his life as a sacrifice to this unholy war. He never boasted of his achievements or sufferings but always evaded the subject if possible. But in the delirium of the disease, he thought himself in battle, spoke of "McClellan's orders," "shooting our pickets," begged the bystanders to "help the poor soldiers," and to "wash and dress his wound, it is a deep one, and he is a good fellow." He spoke of the war, and wept with distress, saying that it was forced on us, and that our little boys had to fight and be butchered by the Yankees. O, God! the blood of our slain calls for vengeance from on high; I pray Thee avenge them a thousand-fold. A short time before his death, he said, "There is health up there." We know that he is at rest, peace and glory, but believe that his life was a sacrifice, and could we go into battle our shout should be, "no quarter to the Yankees."

—A Sister, *Raleigh Register,* September 10, 1862

Junius Cullen Battle, member of 2nd Company D, a son of Judge Battle, died at Middletown in Maryland in the early morning of the 2d day of October last. His left ankle had been shattered by a minnie ball in the fight at South Mountain upon Sunday, the 14th of September. Having been taken prisoner, he was carried into Middletown in the evening of the same day. The wound rendered amputation necessary. After it had been undergone, the young soldier seemed to be recovering, but unfavorable symptoms came on, and having lingered for several days, he died. His parents have the consolation of knowing that he was kindly and skillfully attended during his decline and that he was tenderly nursed by the ladies of Maryland. Two brief notes have been received by Judge Battle from ladies who watched and tended his son. They afford glimpses of scenes around his couch which are extremely grateful and refreshing.

Young Battle had been reared in the quiet village of Chapel Hill. He had been privileged to obtain the whole of his education under the eye of a devoted Mother,—and thus it was that his personal gallantry and good intellect were graced even to manhood by a rare and admirable candor and modesty. The war found him teaching in Oxford, and a sense of duty to North Carolina carried him into the army. Like many of his class in society he held no commission in the service, and died a private. His frequent letters exhibit him in a very amiable light. The hardships which he was called to endure wrung no complaint from him,—he found no fault with his superiors of any grade,—and for a long time he made no allusion even to the ill-health which followed him so generally during the year and a half of his connexion with the Army, and which at last prevented him from rallying from under the effects of his wound. An officer in an Alabama regiment, personally a stranger to him, who had been confined in a house near that in which Junius Battle lay wounded, returning towards home, conveyed to his family the earliest news of his death. This gentleman had been impressed by hearing that a young man, named Battle, had very greatly attracted the esteem and love of the strangers who were attending him; and that he was passing such time as he could redeem from the distress of his wound, and the weariness of exhausted nature, in reading to the crowd of Confederate and Federal wounded around him. After some days he was told that the young man was dead. We can easily imagine how eloquent that reading was to such an audience.

—*Fayetteville Observer*, **November 17, 1862**

Major David Pinkney Rowe fell mortally wounded at the battle of Chancellorsville, May 2d, while acting as Colonel of the 12th N.C. Reg't., and died May 3d. He previously was Captain of Company A, had been wounded at the battle of Gaines' Mill.

—*Fayetteville Observer*, **June 15, 1863**

Died at the residence of his father, B. E. Cook, Esq. in Warrenton, on Tuesday the 16th inst., **Sergeant Major John Thomas Cook**, in the 26th year of his age. He received a dangerous wound in the leg in the bloody battle of Chancellorsville, May 2, which terminated his life on the 16th inst., about 6 o'clock p.m. His sufferings were severe, but were borne with serene patience and fortitude. He was also wounded in the battle of Gaines' Mill, June 27, 1862. Mr. Cook was a member of the Episcopal Church.

—*Raleigh Register*, **June 24, 1863**

Died at Gettysburg, 17th July, after being wounded and captured on the 1st, **Corpl. Daniel Allen**, of the 12th Reg't, Company F, from Warren County, aged 24. His brother **Turner** died of a wound received at Malvern Hill, 1st July 1862, precisely a year before. David was also wounded at Malvern Hill.

—*Fayetteville Observer*, **August 31, 1863**

Killed, instantaneously, on the battle-field at Chancellorsville, May 2d, **Willoughby H. Hicks**, of Warren County, in the 22d year of his age. Died, 30th July, at the residence of his father, **John W. Hicks**, in the 21st year of his age, of chronic diarrhea, contracted by exposure in Maryland. These brothers voluntarily joined the Warren Rifles, 2nd Company C, 12th Reg., in the beginning of the war.

—*Fayetteville Observer*, **September 14, 1863**

Killed in action, on the 19th day of May 1864, at the Battle of Spotsylvania Court House, **Private Amasa J. Newman**, in the thirty-ninth year of his age, a member of Company B, 12th N.C.T.

He joined the army on the 1st of June 1861. Impelled by the strongest impulses of patriotism, he quit his happy home, amid the tears of a loving wife and an innocent little boy of just seven summers, to share in his country's weal or woe. He participated in the campaigns of '63, attending his command on every march, however arduous, and always to be found amongst the first and foremost in death's drear array. Conspicuous for his gallantry on the memorable fields of Chancellorsville and Gettysburg, unmoved by the din and roar

of battle, he was always prepared to give a word of cheer and a smile of comfort to the fainthearted and sick. He bore himself with that same Christian courage that had characterized him in all the engagements of the present bloody campaign, up to the date of his death.
—A friend, Aug. 25, 1864, *Daily Confederate*, August 30, 1864

The remains of **Junius C.**, 12th Regiment, and **W. L. Battle**, 37th Regiment, sons of the Hon. William H. Battle, who fell at Sharpsburg and Gettysburg respectively, will be removed to Chapel Hill, for re-interment in a few days.

Thus, one by one, North Carolina is gathering her jewels to her bosom.
—*Wilmington Journal*, April 26, 1866

Private Junius C. Battle, 12th Regiment N.C.T., Companies B and D, and **Lieut. Wesley Lewis Battle,** 37th Regiment N.C.T., Company D, youngest sons of Judge Battle, volunteers in the late Confederate army, were buried in Chapel Hill, on the 16th inst.

Junius Battle, 12 Regiment, Companies D & B, died at Middletown, Md., on the 2nd October 1862, from the effects of a shattered ankle at the battle of South Mountain. Lewis Battle, 37th Regiment, Company D, died at Gettysburg, Penn., August 22nd, 1863, having been mortally wounded in the disastrous charge on Cemetery Hill, July 3rd.

We learn that their brother R. H. Battle, Jr., who went on for their remains, on his mission of love met with the same sympathy from the kind strangers who had soothed with tender nursing the dying soldiers.

Their remains were met at Chapel Hill by many of their surviving comrades. The companions of their happy college days, with weeping eyes sang a requiem to their memory, in the Village Church, where they so long worshipped; and spread flowers over the mound, under which they who in life loved one another so well now peacefully repose, to be parted nevermore.—*Sentinel*
—*Wilmington Journal*, April 26, 1866

A brave, true, manly man has "passed over the river." The death of **Capt. Benjamin M. Collins** at his home near Ridgeway, N.C., on March 8, 1913, removed from earthly scenes one of Warren County's truest citizens. Born about seventy-two years ago near the place of his death, he grew to manhood and lived to an old age, honored and beloved by his associates. Entering the Confederate army as a young man, he endeared himself to his countrymen by his valor and patriotism. He was wounded at the Battle of South Mountain on September 14, 1862, and was wounded at Gettysburg on the first day of the battle. He was later promoted to Acting Adjutant of the Regiment. He was ever faithful, surrendering at Appomattox as Captain of Company C, 12th North Carolina Regiment. It was said of him that no braver man served in Lee's army. His remains were followed to the grave at Warrenton Place, by a host of old companion in arms, headed by Capt. J. M. B. Hunt, of the Townsville Grays. There were present from four hundred to five hundred friends, and many flowers decorated the grave. A few years after his return from the army Captain Collins married Miss Mollie Plummer, a sister of Messrs. Thomas and Blount Plummer, and reared a charming family, who ministered to his every wish. A military company, under Captain Rose, turned out in full force as an escort of honor and fired three volleys over his grave.
—*Confederate Veteran* **Volume 22, Number 3, March 1914**

James Henry Gordon, born at Oxford, Granville County, N.C., on the 28th of January 1844, was a descendant of Archie Gordon, a Revolutionary soldier. He enlisted in the Con-

federate army in April 1861, at the age of seventeen years as a member of a company from Granville County, N.C., under Capt. Henry Coleman's (32) Company B and served throughout the four years faithfully, never failing to perform any duty assigned him and was paroled at Appomattox Court House, April 9, 1865. After the war he was connected with the Parker News Company, of Jacksonville, Fla., for twenty-five years. He died at his residence, in that city, after a short illness, in the summer of 1916. He is survived by his devoted wife and three daughters: Mrs. W. E. Pritchard, of Savannah, Ga.; Mrs. F. D. Terry, of Atlanta, Ga. Mrs. E. O. Rehm, of Jacksonville, Fla. Also, three brothers: W. L. Gordon, of Jacksonville, Fla., and F. P. and John Gordon, of Earlington, Ky., and one sister, Mrs. John Masoncup, of Madisonville, Ky. He was laid to rest in Evergreen cemetery, at Jacksonville.
—*Confederate Veteran* **Volume 24, Number 11, November 1916**

Judge Walter Alexander Montgomery died at his home in Raleigh, N.C., on November 26, in the seventy-seventh year of his age. He was born February 17, 1845, in Warrenton, N.C., the son of Thomas A. Montgomery, for many years a merchant of that town, and his first wife Darien Cheek, member of one of the largest family connections of that section of the State.

While in preparation for his university course, young Montgomery volunteered for cavalry service in the Confederate army; being rejected because of physical disability, he reenlisted as a private in Company F, of the Second North Carolina Infantry, known after May 1862, as the Twelfth North Carolina. As private, sergeant, lieutenant, he participated in all the great battles of the Army of Northern Virginia, in which his command was engaged, from Hanover Courthouse, in May 1862, to the surrender at Appomattox, where he was paroled. He was twice wounded, at Chancellorsville and the first day's fight at Gettysburg.

Returning to Warrenton, he resumed his studies, devoting himself daily to the classics, English literature, and history, as preparation for his legal studies. After securing his license in 1867, he practiced that profession until his appointment in 1895, as Associate Justice of the Supreme Court of North Carolina. He retired from the bench in 1905 and was appointed Standing Master of the Eastern District of the United States Court; and he also devoted himself to literary study and historical research. He was especially interested in the causes leading up to its civil and military policies, the formation of the Southern Confederacy, and the part taken therein by his native State. As an active member of the State Literary and Historical Association, his contributions were marked by strict accuracy, clear reasoning, and scholarly style. He was noted as an orator, and especially in demand on Confederate memorial occasions, while his memory of men and events of more than sixty years of the State's history was remarkable and rendered him one of the most interesting of his day. Judge Montgomery held the honorary degree of Doctor of Laws from the University of North Carolina.
—*Confederate Veteran* **Volume 30, Number 3, March 1922**

13th Regiment North Carolina Troops

Died in a hospital at Washington City, [D.C.] on the 12th inst., **Rufus Walston**, a farmer from Edgecombe County, Co. G, 13th N.C.T. He was wounded and captured at Williamsburg and died of his wounds. He was about 18.
—*Fayetteville Observer,* **June 23, 1862**

Died of disease in a Richmond, Va., hospital May 21st, **Mr. Samuel P. Moore**, of Rockingham County, N.C., in the 19th year of his age, a soldier in the 13th (Col. Scales') Regiment, Company H.

—*Fayetteville Observer,* June 30, 1862

Died in Richmond, Va., on the 17th of June, **Sergeant Daniel M. Roney**, aged 21 years and 11 months. He volunteered in the first company raised in Alamance County, and as a member of the Alamance Regulators, Company E, 13th Regiment North Carolina Troops, he discharged faithfully his duties as a soldier. He was in the battle of Seven Pines, near Richmond, and acquitted himself with a firmness and courage worthy of his native State. Typhoid fever, with the fatigue and exhaustion occasioned by the battle, terminated his life.

—*North Carolina Standard,* July 5, 1862

Died at Fortress Monroe, on the 25th May, **Sergeant Wm. Peel, Jr.**, Co. G, 13th N.C.T. He was wounded in the leg and captured at the Battle of Williamsburg, May 5, 1862.

—*Fayetteville Observer,* July 21, 1862

Lieut. Wiley P. Robertson, of the Yanceyville Greys, Com. A., 13th Regt. N.C. Vol., fell at Gaines' Mill on the evening of the 27th of June. It is with true patriotic Southern pride that we record his brave, his noble bearing, in the hour of danger. Only 20 years of age, yet amidst the deadliest fire, exhorting his men to keep cool that he would die with them, or by them. When the flag-bearer fell, Col. Scales and Willie were two of the first to seize the colors; Willie exclaiming to his Company whilst waving the flag, to come on, he would lead them to the mouths of the cannon if necessary. Thus they fought, and thus they conquered, till exhausted, they were ordered to retire and give place to fresh troops, and then it was the fatal missile did its work, and the buoyant, sanguine boy fell and never moved or spoke.

—*North Carolina Presbyterian,* August 2, 1862

Died, from wounds received on the battle field, near Gaines' Mill, on the 27th of June 1862, in the 21st year of his age, **Mr. Henry A. Weddon**, a member of the Leasburg Grays (Company D). Private Weddon was a citizen of Raleigh, N.C., and being on a visit to his relatives in Caswell County at the time the call was made for volunteers for the defense of our sunny South, he enlisted in the gallant corps who were among the first to respond to the call made by his noble State.—The deceased leaves a fond mother, two brothers, and one sister. His death was instant at receiving the wound. His remains were interred upon that memorable battle field near Richmond, Va., by his comrades in arms.

—*North Carolina Presbyterian,* August 16, 1862

Died at the hospital in Richmond, 23d July, **Joseph W. Dupree**, in the 36th year of his age. He was wounded in the great battle before Richmond, Gaines' Mill, while carrying the colors. He belonged to the Yanceyville Grays, 13th Regiment, Company A. He was from Caswell County.

—*Fayetteville Observer,* August 18, 1862

Nathaniel R. Kerr, aged 19, youngest son of Judge Kerr, and a private in the Yanceyville Greys (Company A), was accidentally shot and instantly killed by one of his own men, in the midst of a recent battle near South Mountain. Being in a front line as he raised his head

to shoot, a rifle ball from the rear ranks passed through it. He was an estimable and promising young man.
—**Originally published in the** *Milton Chronicle* **and reprinted in the** *People's Press,* **October 10, 1862.**

One of the most distressing features of the present war is that our country is fast being bereaved of her hope and her pride. Our young men are passing away. Our noblest spirits are first to hear our country's call—first to rush to posts of danger, and first to fall in her defense, while thousands of mean spirited, craven hearted wretches, of whom the country would be well rid of, remain behind to speculate, extort, and grow rich on the country's misfortunes. Among those who deserve a place in the hearts of their countrymen, few deserve it more richly than the subject of this notice, **Lt. William Speight McLean Hart**, of Pleasant Hill, N.C. He had just passed his 25th year when he fell a victim to Typhoid Fever, contracted in the camp near Richmond, Va. He was among the first to enlist in his country's defense. He was a member of the company called the Randlesburg Riflemen, Company B, and, boldly assuming the post of greatest danger, became its standard bearer; but his courageous bearing and affable deportment soon secured for him the office of 3rd Lieutenant, which he held at the time of his lamented death. Amid all the hardships and privations of camp he preserved a cheerfulness and equanimity of temper which made him the object of universal esteem, and assisted to keep up the flagging spirits of his companions. In the memorable and bloody affair of Williamsburg he was in the thickest of the fight, and after his company was almost cut to pieces, his Capt. and 2nd Lieut. wounded, his first Lieut. killed and himself thrice grazed by bullets, his daring and dauntless spirit gathered the fragments of his company, and led them to the last desperate, but unsuccessful charge. But he escaped the perils of the field only to become the victim of disease. In early life he connected himself with the church at Steel Creek, under the preaching of Dr. Baker. Peace be to his ashes.
—**A friend,** *North Carolina Presbyterian,* **October 18, 1862**

James Monroe Herbin of Rockingham County fell wounded, in the 25th year of his age, in the battle of Gaines' Mill, Virginia, June 27th, before Richmond. He was a member of Company H and died July 17th.
—*North Carolina Presbyterian,* **October 25, 1862**

Died at the residence of his father in Caswell County, N.C., on Tuesday evening, October, 14th, **Mr. Joshua H. Butler**, in the 28th year of his age. Mr. Butler was a member of the Leasburg Greys, Company D. He was a brave soldier and attended manfully to his duties until he was prostrated by a severe attack of disease which finally terminated his life. He was in the battle of Seven Pines, also in the fight of Tuesday near Richmond. But from both of these he came out unhurt. He left a widow and two small children to mourn their loss. He was a member of the Presbyterian Church of Bethesda in Caswell County, in which church his father has been a ruling elder for many years.
—*North Carolina Presbyterian,* **[November 22, 1862]**

A touching romance in real life is afforded by the deaths of **Captain Chalmers Glenn**, Company I, of Rockingham County, N.C., and his faithful servant, Mat. Reared together from childhood, Mat had shared in all his boyish pranks and frolics of his master, and, in later life, had been his constant attendant and faithful servant. On the morning of the battle of South Mountain, Captain Glenn called Mat to him and said: "Mat, I will be killed in this

battle; see me buried; then, go home, and be to your mistress and my children all you have ever been to me." From behind the rock the faithful fellow watched all day the form of his beloved master, as the tide of battle ebbed and flowed over that eventful field. At last he missed him, and, rushing forward, found the prediction too truly verified—life was already extinct. Assisted by two members of his company, a grave was dug with bayonets, and soon the cold and silent earth held all that was dearest in life to Mat. Slowly and sadly he turned his face homeward, and there delivered all the messages and valuables which his master had entrusted him; from that time it seemed as if his mission on earth was accomplished. Though constantly attending his master's children, and promptly obedient to the slightest word of his mistress, he visibly declined. Finally he was taken sick, and despite the best medical attention and the kindest nursing, he died February 4, 1863.—*Richmond Whig*
—**Originally published in the *Richmond Whig* and reprinted in the *People's Press*, February 27, 1863**

On the 15th September 1862, of wounds received the 14th in the battle of South Mountain, **Nicholas H. Dalton**, Co. H, 13th Reg't., N.C.T., in the 25th year of his age. The deceased was the son of Euel and Sarah Dalton, of Rockingham County, N.C. He fell mortally wounded at the close of that memorable day on South Mountain, bearing himself like a hero and a patriot. The sad news that he was seriously wounded and left upon the battlefield reached his friends shortly after the engagement, and it was only a short time since, that their anxiety and suspense were relieved by the still sadder news of his death.
—*North Carolina Presbyterian*, **May 2, 1863**

Lieutenant Henry Barksdale Fowler, of Company A, fell in that terrible battle of Sharpsburg, on the 17th September, while gallantly leading his men, sword in hand. While he was being borne from the field by three of his men, two of them were severely wounded. Such was their devotion, however, that they did not leave him until he breathed his last. A message from one of the regimental officers to his father "that few fathers ever had such a son to love," conveyed a just estimate of his standing with his comrades-in-arms.
—*Carolina Watchman*, **April 18, 1863**

Robert Lee Swann, a member of Co. B, 13th Regiment N.C.T., fell a martyr to his country's cause in the memorable and bloody battle of Chancellorsville, May 3d, 1863. North Carolina has sacrificed thousands of her noble sons and many a hill and valley has been made red with her best blood in this our second struggle for freedom; but she never presented one more willing to do his duty than the subject of this sketch. He was with the old 3d, now the 13th, in her first and among the bloodiest battles of the war, at Williamsburg, where he fell into the hands of the enemy, seriously wounded. After lying in a Northern prison undergoing intense suffering, he exchanged in the July following. First of January 1863, he rejoined his company, hardly sufficiently recovered from his wounds, for duty, yet eager to be with his comrades to aid in keeping back the insolent foe. He bore, without murmuring the fatigue of camp life, during the severe snow storms that fell in the latter part of the winter, which those who experienced them will never forget. In the hard contested battle of Chancellorsville he stood firmly with his company while charging the enemy's breast works, when early in the morning he received the fatal stroke which caused his death on the following morning (Sunday). He was a citizen of Mecklenburg County, N.C., and leaves a father, brothers, sisters and a large circle of friends to mourn his loss.
—**Member Co. B, 13th N.C.T.**, *Daily Bulletin*, **June 5, 1863**

Died of typhoid fever, at a Hospital in Richmond of wounds received at Fredericksburg (Chancellorsville), **Mr. William E. King**, of Co. E, 13th Reg't, in the 21st year of his age. He was also wounded during the Battle at Seven Pines.

—*Fayetteville Observer,* **June 5, 1863**

Died near Gettysburg, Pa., on July 6th (his 25th birthday) **William W. Rainey**, Capt. of Co. C, 13th Reg. N.C.T., of a wound received on the 3rd. His funeral was preached at Red House, in Caswell County, on 1st Sabbath, Oct, seven years to a day, from the time he became a communicant. He was a true soldier, and example of excellence in every particular. In his death there is nothing to regret except the loss which his family, his country and the church have sustained.

—*North Carolina Presbyterian,* **December 5, 1863**

Killed at the battle of Sharpsburg, Md., **Peyton Chambers**, Company K, 13th Regiment N.C.T., in the 28th year of his age. Deceased was born in Rockingham County, N.C.; was in all the battles that his Reg't had ever been up to that time except the battle of Williamsburg, when he was absent on detail. He leaves one brother (now fighting in defense of his country), and aged parents to mourn his untimely loss. Such is a soldier's fate. He always bore the reputation of being a good soldier—ever ready to discharge his duty when called on.

—*Fayetteville Observer,* **April 11, 1864**

Died, on the 24th day of February, AD 1864, in camp near Orange C. H., Va., of typhoid fever, **Capt. Thomas T. Lawson** of Company H, 13th Regiment, N.C.T., in the 24th year of his age. A native of Rockingham County, N.C., and influenced by patriotic zeal and love of country, he quit college in 1861, soon after the war broke out, and entered the service of his country as a private, although of feeble and delicate constitution and contrary to the advice of his friends, who did not believe he could undergo the hardships of camp life. Upon the organization of his company he was elected first Lieutenant. While the regiment was at Yorktown he was taken sick and fell into the hands of the enemy, and was kept a prisoner for some time. Upon his release, his relations fearing for his health, advised him to resign and employ a substitute, but noble and patriotic, he declined, saying his country needed his services, and faithfully and valiantly did he devote himself to her cause until silenced by the cold hand of death. Such was his gallantry and noble-bearing that on the very first vacancy he was promoted to captaincy, which position he filled when death claimed him. In September 1863, he married a young and lovely wife, who is left to mourn her irreparable loss, with his two sisters, the only surviving members of his family.

—*Daily Confederate,* **May 12, 1864**

It is rare that husband and wife die so near together. Mrs. Julia F. Ireland was a native of Kentucky and her maiden name was Ireland, though of no akin to her husband. She had a stroke of paralysis Thursday afternoon and died that night. At the time of her death her husband, **John Rich Ireland**, was at Winterville at a sanatorium for the treatment of cancer and was in a precarious condition. He was brought home and died Monday night in the 69th year of his age. Mr. Ireland was one of the best citizens of the county and highly esteemed. He was a brave Confederate soldier and had a most honorable war record. He was 3rd Lieutenant of Company E, 13th Regiment and was wounded in the leg at Gettysburg on the third day of the battle. Mr. Ireland was a member of the County Pension Board. They leave surviving four children—two sons and two daughters.

—*Alamance Gleaner,* **March 18, 1909**

On the 25th day of July 1911, there passed away **Private James J. Foster**, of Company E, 13th North Carolina State Troops, at his home in Wilmington, N.C. He enlisted in the above named Company and Regiment in the spring of 1861, and he served as a private soldier throughout the entire struggle for Southern independence, being captured on the 1st day of April, near Petersburg, when the lines of Lee were broken in that last fierce struggle for the capture of Richmond. He was held prisoner at Point Lookout, Maryland and released in June. No braver or better soldier served in that great war. Always at his post of duty, and always in the forefront of every fight his command was engaged in, he exemplified the true man and true soldier in all things. The writer served with him and knows whereof he speaks when he says that such was his record as a soldier. After the war was over, he, with all other true Southern soldiers, accepted the results and went to work to build up the South, and he was a good citizen, and did his duties as such in every way, rendering due obedience to all the laws of the land.

The writer visited him often during his last days, and he expressed his confidence in the religion of Jesus Christ, and his acceptance of the Savior as his hope for salvation, and also that he was, he said, fully prepared to answer his last roll call. To the family of my deceased friend and comrade I extend my heartfelt sympathy in this, to them, great bereavement.
—William H. Andrews, 1st Lieut. Co. H, 13th C. S. Army, Burlington, N.C., Aug. 12, '11, *Alamance Gleaner,* August 24, 1911

On Dec. 30, 1911, **Henderson Herring**, Co. E, 13th Reg., died at his home in Newlin Township, aged about 86 years. He was wounded at the Battle of Chancellorsville.
—*Alamance Gleaner,* January 4, 1912

Mr. Bryant B. Martindale, a well-known old Confederate Soldier of Company E, 13th Regiment, and a citizen of this place, died yesterday at the home of his daughter at Altamaha, aged about 69 years. At 2 o'clock this afternoon the remains were buried at New Providence. His widow survives him. Mr. Martindale saw hard service in the war and ever since has been a great sufferer from wounds received at Chancellorsville. He was in many of the severest engagements of that great conflict.
—*Alamance Gleaner,* February 15, 1912

On Monday, 19th inst., **Mr. James A. Dickey** passed away at his home in Pleasant Grove township, near Long's Chapel, aged 70 years and five months. He was taken suddenly ill Friday night and declined till the end came. He was one of the county's best citizens— quiet, unassuming and attentive to his own affairs. For four years he filled the office of County Treasurer. He was a soldier, Company E, 13th Regiment, in the civil war and lost his right arm at Gettysburg. Captured, he was held on David's Island in New York Harbor and exchanged in October 1863. He was a member of the church at Long's Chapel. On Tuesday his remains were interred at Union Bridge. His widow, who was Miss Permelia Maydard, one son almost grown, and one brother, Mr. Allen S. Dickey, survive him.
—*Alamance Gleaner,* February 22, 1912

The news of the death of **Capt. William Murphy Andrews** will be learned with regret throughout the county. He had not been well for two months or more, but his condition did not become critical until he took to his bed two weeks ago. He died about 3 o'clock this morning at his home in Burlington aged about 70 years. He was a member of Co. E, 13th Reg., a company composed almost wholly of Alamance boys, and he was as brave a Confederate soldier as ever shouldered a musket. He was promoted to 2nd Lieut. from the

ranks and was paroled at Appomattox Court House at war's end. For a number of years Capt. Andrews has been a member of the Pension Board for Alamance County. He was a faithful and consistent member of the New Providence Christian Church where his burial will take place at 3 o'clock tomorrow afternoon. He is survived by two sons and two daughters.
—*Alamance Gleaner,* **May 9, 1912**

Mr. Henry Harrison Cape, an aged Confederate veteran, died at his home near this place on Saturday morning, April 12, 1913. He was born Dec. 28, 1841, and was 71 yrs., 3 mos., and 14 days old at the time of his death. He is survived by his widow, Mrs. Bettie Cape, two sons—Buck Cape of Burlington and Samuel Cape of Haw River, and three daughters—Mrs. J. W. Boggs of Haw River, Mrs. Reesie Squires and Miss Mattie Cape of Carolina. He was married on May 1*, 1861, and on May 30, 1861, volunteered and went to the war under *Capt. Giles P. Bailey,* (33) Co. K, 13th Regiment, Gen. Pender's Brigade later Gen. A. M. Scales', Gen. A. P. Hill's corps. He was wounded at Chancellorsville in 1863 and was captured while in a Richmond hospital April 3, 1865. The remains were buried at McCray and the funeral was conducted by Elder W. C. Jones of the Primitive Baptist Church.
—*Alamance Gleaner,* **April 17, 1913**

G. H. Denison, Adjutant Jeff Davis Camp, No. 117, U.C.V., of Goldthwaite, Tex., reports the following deaths during the past year:

David G. Womack, Company A, 13th North Carolina Infantry, died February 12, 1917. He was captured at Williamsport, Maryland in September 1862, held prisoner at Fort Delaware, and released in October.
—*Confederate Veteran* **Volume 25, Number 10, October 1917**

14th Regiment North Carolina Troops

On Tuesday night last, **Mr. Elbert J. Shearin**, aged 26, a private in the Roanoke Minute Men, Company A, [4th Regiment North Carolina Volunteers, later 14th Regiment North Carolina Troops] commanded by *Capt. William A. Johnston,* (34) died at Camp Ellis, Virginia. He had been sick of measles for several days, but was not supposed to be in a dangerous condition, until a few hours before his death. Private Shearin was from Warren County, where he has a widowed mother and two sisters living. He has also 4 brothers, one of who is also in Capt. Johnston's company. It may be some consolation to his widowed mother and sisters to know that several ladies visited him during the last two days of his life, and tenderly ministered to his wants.

The remains were sent home for interment in charge of his brother and a commander, the whole company following the corpse to the Railroad where appropriate funeral services were performed by the Rev. Mr. Cobb, (35) the Chaplain.
—*Raleigh Register,* **July 17, 1861**

Henry Ball, Private in *Capt. Jesse Hargraves's* (36) Company of Lexington (N.C.) Wild Cats, Company I, 14th Regiment, died at Camp Ellis, Suffolk, Va., on the 27th. His remains were to be sent home.
—*Fayetteville Observer,* **August 1, 1861**

Since the date of my last there have been two more deaths in Camp Ellis, or rather members of the 4th Regiment North Carolina Volunteers [later 14th Regiment N.C.T.]. **Geo. T. Lewis**, Company I, a young man about 20 years old, member of Capt. Hargrave's company, from Lexington, died on Thursday last, and to-day, **Mr. Robert B. Patterson**, Company D, of Cleveland County, a private in *Capt. Edward Dixon's* (37) company, died. Both these young men had barely recovered from measles, when they were attacked with Typhoid fever.

—*North Carolina Standard*, "Suffolk, Va., Aug. 6th, 1861," **August 10, 1861**

Letters received here state that *Serg't. Hamilton* (38) and *Bailey Yarborough* (39) of this city belonging to the Oak City Guards were wounded in the battle at Williamsburg, and that **Lewis H. Powers,** Company E, son of David Powers of this County, was killed. We also learn that two sons of Walter R. Moore of Johnston County, were also wounded, and it is feared that one of them has since died or fallen into the hands of the enemy.

—*North Carolina Standard*, "Killed and Wounded," **May 17, 1862**

Died in Richmond, Va., at Winder Hospital, on the 16th inst., **Sergeant Charles W. Robertson**, of the "Raleigh Rifles," Company K, of Camp Fever, in the 19 year of his age. Sergeant R. is spoken of highly by his Captain as a brave soldier, who bore himself well and courageously in the battle of Williamsburg, Va. He was taken sick a few days after, and died lamented by his comrades in arms, and his relations and friends at home.

—*North Carolina Standard,* **May 31, 1862**

MR. EDITOR:—Please say through your paper to our friends at home, that **Thomas Leverett**, one of the "Rough and Ready Guards," Company F, *Captain James M. Gudger's*, (40) died after a painful illness of several days, at the "Winder Hospital," Richmond, on the 27th ult. He became ill at "Burnt Ordinance," on the Peninsula, on the 7th of May, and was sent to the Hospital on the 17th of that month. There he received good medical attention, but he continued to grow worse until he died of Typhoid Pneumonia.

Mr. Leverett enlisted in our company on the 3d of May 1861. He was a brave man, a first rate soldier, and won and deserved the confidence and esteem of all our officers and his immediate comrades in arms. He was decently buried in such manner as will enable his friends at some future and appropriate time to remove his remains to a final resting place in some "sweet valley" among our own blue mountains. Peace to his honored ashes!

Say further, that **James R. Deboard** of our company died of Pneumonia on the 10th inst. He grew sick on the 1st, and was sent to "Chimborazo Hospital," Richmond, on the 3d or 4th, where he died.

Mr. Deboard joined our company at Suffolk, Va., on the 6th of August 1861. He was a warm hearted companion, a good soldier, and possessed the esteem of the whole company. The loss of him is much lamented, and our officers and all his comrades in arms, warmly condole with his stricken parents and friends.

Being almost in the presence of the enemy, we had no opportunity to be present to attend to his interment, and pay a last act of solemn respect to a worthy comrade in arms. Thus two more of our band are gone to the hills of the dead. They will join us no more in the struggle for liberty, home, and independence! Their work is done!

—**Bivouac, near Richmond, June 13, 1862,** *Asheville News,* **June 26, 1862**

Died of disease in Richmond, Va., on Friday, the 27th ult., **Charles R. Eaton,** of Warren County, N.C., in the 42nd year of his age. The deceased was a private in Company A, of the 14th Regiment of North Carolina, having joined in March 1861. He was discharged in June 1862 due to failing health and died one month later. He was an amiable and honorable man.
—*Raleigh Register,* **July 12, 1862**

Died at Winder Hospital, Richmond, Va., of brain fever, **Jacob M. Rogers,** the first born son and child of James W. & Mary Adeline Rogers, in the 19th year of his age. He was a Private in company K (Raleigh Rifles), 14th Regt. N.C. Troops. He entered the service as a volunteer in May 1861. His last hours were cheered by the presence of his father. His remains were brought to this city for interment.
—*North Carolina Standard,* **July 19, 1862**

Colonel Philetus W. Roberts was born in Franklin, Macon County, N.C., but when five years old his parents, Joshua and Lucinda Roberts, removed to Buncombe County, where Col. Roberts was raised, and where his widow and five children still reside. He was a member of the Methodist Episcopal Church. At Emory and Henry College he had the foundation of thorough scholarship. On reaching majority he chose the law as his profession, as his father had done before him. He was for years a trustee of the Female College and Steward of the Methodist Church in Asheville.

After the celebrated proclamation of Mr. Lincoln, he abandoned all hope of a peaceful solution of difficulties pending between the North and the South. He volunteered as a private in the Confederate Army. He was at once made first Lieutenant of Company F, and upon the promotion of the Captain, Hon. Z. B. Vance, he was chosen Captain. When the regiment was reorganized he was elected Colonel. He commanded in several skirmishes and two regular pitched battles, viz: the battles of Williamsburg and Seven Pines. In both he displayed a coolness and valor that elicited the admiration of all. But his exposure at the latter battle cost him his life. Perfectly exhausted and drenched with rain, he threw himself upon the wet ground to rest after the battle was over. Disease at once set in, he was removed to Richmond and placed under the care of a physician of ability, but all in vain. He died of typhoid fever on the 5th July, in the 38th year of his age, at the residence of Mr. H. W. Tyler, Richmond.

The mortal remains of this gallant soldier and accomplished gentleman reached his late home near this place on Thursday last and on Friday afternoon were deposited amid the sleeping dust of kindred and friends at Newton Academy burying ground. Appropriate religious services were held at the Methodist Church by the Rev. Mr. Stewart, the pastor. A large concourse of citizens followed his remains to the grave, the business houses all being closed as a feeble testimonial of the universal esteem in which the deceased was held.
—*Asheville News,* **July 24, 1862**

Lieut. William Marcellus Thompson, of this County, son of George W. Thompson, Esq., fell in battle at Gaines' Mill, on Friday the 27th June, while leading the Oak-City Guards, Company E, 14th regiment. He was in command of the company when our regiment was ordered in conjunction with the other regiments of the brigade to charge the enemy. All through this glorious charge, his voice could be heard animating and cheering his command onward to victory, until a fatal bullet struck him and cut short his valuable life.

The day after our glorious victory, we occupied the ground we had won from the enemy, and wishing to bury his body as well as circumstances would admit of, I asked permission to go and find it and consign it to the dust. I found his body and we buried it in the old field, near the spot where he fell. As I looked upon his noble and truly handsome features, and the sad thought and reality came across my mind that he was lost to us forever, the tears, hot and scalding, started from my eyes, and I resolved then and there never to quit the field until the last Yankee scoundrel is driven from our beloved soil and I have avenged his untimely death.

—*North Carolina Standard,* **July 26, 1862**

Killed on the field of battle at Malvern Hill on Tuesday, the 1st of July 1862, in the 22d year of his age, **Serg't Marion Smith**, company K, 14th N.C. Troops. At the battle of Williamsburg, he sustained himself nobly and bravely, and also at the Seven Pines, and at the different battles up to Tuesday, when he fell a martyr to his country's cause. His friends and relatives may rest assured that he was attended to as well as circumstances would admit. His comrades buried him, placed a board at the head of his grave, with his name inscribed upon it, also a rail fence around his grave.

—*North Carolina Standard,* **July 30, 1862**

J. C. Fulton Weaver, son of the Rev. M. M. and Mrs. Jane Weaver, of this county, was born May 9th, 1837. He had already gathered around him a comfortable property; was established in a good home, and had commenced business for himself. When the war began, Mr. Weaver, with many other gallant sons of the mountains, organized that noble company, the "Rough and Ready Guards," under the leadership of the intrepid VANCE, and threw themselves into the breach between the invaders and the loved ones at home. They marched from Asheville on the 3d May 1861—the second company from the *volunteer county*.—From that time to the day of his death he was engaged, with his company, in defending the coast of his own State and Virginia. His company was attached to the 14th Regiment, of which the late gallant and lamented P. W. Roberts, from being Captain of the "R & R Guards," was elected Colonel. In his proper place amidst his comrades in arms, Mr. Weaver faced the foe at the Battle of Williamsburg and assisted to repulse them from the bloody field. He was also among the daring spirits of the "Seven Pines," who hurled death into the face of the insolent invaders and in those actions, right nobly no doubt, did he and his company sustain the high renown of his own "Old North State." For a considerable time he had been chilling, but still, was able to do his whole duty as a soldier up to the 18th ult., when he was removed from camp to the Chimborazo Hospital, Richmond, Va. On the evening of the same day he was taken violently ill with typhoid fever and on the 20th June, a little after 12 o'clock noon, he departed peacefully and calmly as the sleeping of an infant. His remains were brought home, and with appropriate ceremonies, and in the presence of many of his old friends and neighbors, were interred in the family burying ground near his father's residence.

—**French Broad, N.C., July 1862,** *Asheville News,* **July 31, 1862**

Died, in this City, on the 19th of July, **John B. Perkinson**, of the "Raleigh Rifles," Company K, 14th Regiment, aged 25 years.—The deceased acquitted himself as a good soldier, performing all his duties and submitting cheerfully to all the hardships of the service. He was wounded in the fight of Tuesday the 1st of July, at Malvern Hill, near Richmond, and was able to return home where he died.

—*North Carolina Standard,* **August 6, 1862**

DIED—In Richmond, Va., July 29th, after an illness of some days, **Capt. William C. Brown, Assistant Quartermaster**, in the 14th Regt. N.C. Troops, in the 31st year of his age. He was a native of Dayton, Ohio, but most of his life was spent in Buncombe County, N.C., where he was highly respected and much beloved. He was a member of Mocksville Masonic Lodge, No. 134. He relinquished his profession (the law), at the call of his country, and in the faithful discharge of his onerous duties, he fell as truly and as bravely his country's friend, as if on the battle field. His body was brought home, and on Sabbath last after appropriate services by the Rev. Peck, deposited in the Presbyterian grave yard, Asheville, N.C., beside his brother **2nd Lieut. Samuel S. Brown**, Company F, aged 24 whose remains were placed there a short time ago, after his death in February of this year, both victims of this cruel savage war.

—*Asheville News*, **August 14, 1862**

Sergeant Charles Z. Candler died on the 16th July 1862, at Richmond, Va., of Typhoid fever contracted in the army before that city. He joined the "Rough & Ready Guards," Company F, the day after Lincoln's Proclamation calling for troops to subjugate the South reached Asheville. From that day to the day of his death he ceased not to join in the struggle. He was in two or three engagements with the enemy, and no one acquitted himself more gallantly then did he. His premature death hurried a devoted father to the grave, who followed him within six days. He was born on the 29th day of July 1843. He was not quite twenty years old.

—*Asheville News*, **August 28, 1862**

Thomas D. Simons, a member of the "Anson Guard," Company C, was born in Montgomery County, N.C., on the 13th of Sept. 1842, and died on 14th of July 1862 of wounds received in the battle of Malvern Hill before Richmond. Amid the privations of the camp, the toils of the march and the conflicts of the field, he was the same unmurmuring, unfaltering, unflinching patriot. He was a private in the ranks and aspired to go to no higher position. He felt that the post of duty was always the post of honor, hence he was ever ready to stand as sentinel by his weary comrades while they slept or to follow his leaders to victory or death. During the twelve long, burning, wearisome days which intervened between the time when he was stricken down by the enemy's missile and the hour of his death, he bore his sufferings with all the fortitude of a christian soldier.

—*North Carolina Argus*, **September 25, 1862**

DIED—At the residence of his father-in-law, on the 17th Nov. 1862, of Typhoid fever, **Charles R. P. Byers**, in the 31st year of his age. He was a member of Capt. James M. Gudger's company, R & R Guards, Company F, 14th Reg't N.C.T., and formerly Editor and Proprietor of the Asheville Spectator.—He was taken ill before starting on the march to Maryland, but notwithstanding his illness, he marched with the company all day, and stacked arms with his comrades at night. When near Hagerstown, Md., he was taken prisoner and sent north to Fort Delaware where he remained two days, was paroled and sent back to Richmond where he remained three weeks in Winder Hospital, suffering greatly all the time. He at length procured a furlough and came home to his family and friends—*but to die*. He lingered four weeks after his return home bearing his sufferings with great patience and fortitude.—He was quite cheerful at times and gave us great hope of his recovery; but alas death tore him from our hearts and crushed our hopes.

—*Asheville News*, **December 18, 1862**

Simeon D. Ferrell was a native of Wake County and a member of the "Oak City Guards," Company E. 14th Regt. He was captured at the battle of Sharpsburg, September 17, 1862, and held prisoner at Fort Delaware. He died there on December 10.

—*North Carolina Standard*, **January 16, 1863**

Died in Richmond, Va., on the morning of the 7th Dec., 1862, **Jeremiah B. Sibley**, of the Anson Guards, Company C, in the 24th year of his age. He was wounded at the battle of Malvern Hill on the 1st of July. He was the Color Bearer of his Regiment, the 14th North Carolina—as brave a man as ever has faced the enemy, and true to honor and friendship. When wounded, he was some twenty-five paces in advance, bearing proudly aloft the battle-flag of his Regiment. He fell—but in the act of falling struck his flag-staff into the ground, thus flaunting defiance in the face of his enemies. He fell—but the battle-flag still waved. Jerry lay beside it—not dead, but fearfully wounded—his arm shattered to the shoulder. While he thus lay, a cowardly Yankee rushed forth from his ranks to bayonet him and secure the flag. Jerry raised himself up, and drawing his revolver, presented it at his advancing foe in so threatening a manner that he hesitated—stopped, and backing to a safe distance, took deliberate aim, and fired at him, as he lay wounded and helpless, the ball taking effect in his already wounded limb. He had now five balls in his arm and shoulder, yet there was still the light of battle in his eyes, and unconquerable determination in his heart. He thought as little about surrendering, as when, far in advance of his regiment, he proudly bore his country's flag, and charged up to the very muzzles of the guns of the enemy. Alas, poor Jerry! a braver or better soldier never marched to battle. He was sent to Chimborazo Hospital, Richmond, where for six, long weary months, he suffered untold agony until his death.

—*North Carolina Argus,* **January 29, 1863**

Died at the residence of his kinsman, P. F. Pescud, on the morning of the 21st inst., after a lingering illness, contracted while in the service of his country, **Thomas P. Chrisman, Jr.**, in the 24th year of his age. He was a son of the late Thomas. P. Chrisman, late of Hampton, Va., and for three years prior to the war, a resident of this city, and employed in Pescud's Drug Store. He has left many relations, including a sister and seven brothers to mourn his early death. Six of his brothers are now in the army of the Confederacy. Thomas volunteered in the Oak City Guards, Company E, 14th Regiment N.C. Troops.

—*Raleigh Register,* **January 31, 1863**

Died, Nov. 9th 1862, on a march near Strasburg, Va., **Hartwell S. Pool**, of Co. H, 14th Reg't N.C.T., son of John S. and Nancy Pool, of Montgomery County, N.C. In this death the parents are bereaved of an only son and three little babes are left fatherless with a young widowed mother.

—*Fayetteville Observer,* **February 9, 1863**

Died in Montgomery County, 29th April, **Samuel Yarborough**, aged 29 years, 3 months and 21 days. He was a consistent member of the M. E. Church for 10 years, had been in the army the last nine months and contracted the disease that caused his death; he got home to his family only one week before he died. He leaves a wife and one child. He was a member of Company A, 14th Regiment.

—*Fayetteville Observer,* **June 8, 1863**

Killed in the battle of Chancellorsville, May 2d, 1863, **Sergeant William Waddell Lanier**, Co. H, 14th N.C. Reg't, aged 21 years, leaving a desolate, father, mother, sisters and brothers to mourn for him.

—*Fayetteville Observer,* **July 20, 1863**

William A. Long, Company D, "Cleveland Blues," 14th N.C. Troops was wounded in the arm at Chancellorsville, May 3rd. His arm was amputated, and he died later in a Richmond hospital, July 27th.

—*Daily Bulletin,* **November 18, 1863**

Died at Camp Winder Hospital, Richmond, 7th August, **J. P. Randall**, aged 23, of Co. D, 14th N.C.T., of wounds received in a skirmish at Hagerstown, Md., in July, during the return from Gettysburg. He was previously wounded at Malvern Hill, July 1, 1862.

—*Fayetteville Observer,* **January 7, 1864**

Died at his father's residence in Montgomery County, N.C., June 12th, 1863, in the 23d year of his age, **John Milton Cranford**, a member of Co. G, 14th N.C. Reg't. He served his country for nearly ten months; was captured by the enemy at Frederick City, Md.,, and remained with them at Fort Delaware more than three months, during which time he suffered much from sickness; he was exchanged in December and before he finally recovered he hastened to rejoin his companions. In the memorable battle of Chancellorsville he received a severe wound in the right arm; it was amputated and he was conveyed to Richmond. He contracted the typhoid fever; he bore it all with much patience. His father on hearing the sad fate of his son went immediately after him and brought him home, where he survived only a few days.

—**Cousin M.,** *Fayetteville Observer,* **February 1, 1864**

Killed in the battle along the line of Totopotomy Creek, Hanover County, Virginia, June 2d, 1864, **William Calvin Little**, Co. C, 14th N.C.T., aged about 25 years. He entered the service during August '62, and participated in most of the engagements which occurred in the department of Northern Va., after his enlistment. He was captured at Sharpsburg and held prisoner at Fort Delaware before being exchanged. Especially eminent were his services in the series of engagements which culminated with the advance of Grant south of the James. For months he was a member of the sharp-shooting corps of Ramseur's' brigade, the feats of which elicited the applause of the correspondent of the London Herald. On the fatal afternoon of June 2d, the commanding officer of the brigade entrusted to him a reconnaissance on which the safety of the command depended; scarcely had the report of that advance been communicated when Little joined his line and the pitiless bullet crushed through his person. He died that day near Bethesda Church, Va. It is much regretted that he did not survive long enough to commit his dying thoughts to his fellows' ears.

—*North Carolina Argus,* **June 30, 1864**

Killed in action, near Bethesda Church, Hanover County, Virginia, on the evening of the 30th of May, **Eli Freeman**, Captain commanding Co. C, 14th N, C, Troops. He was born in Ohio but came to Anson County years ago. He was wounded and captured at Sharpsburg and held prisoner at Fort Delaware until exchanged. He had been in service since the commencement of the war, and by his conspicuous gallantry, had distinguished himself on several hard fought fields one of which was Spotsylvania where nearly all the cannoneers had been killed from a gun, the use of which was very essential to the dislodgement of the enemy from a strong position which they occupied. The undertaking was a very perilous one; but he, as ever ready to place himself where most needed, regardless of his life, volunteered his services and under a most murderous fire assisted in getting the gun into position by the aid of which the enemy was eventually expelled. He entered the service as a Sergeant in the Company of which he was Captain when killed.

—*North Carolina Argus,* **July 7, 1864**

William H. Kirby, of Anson County, a member of Co. C, 14th N.C.T., aged 28 years, enlisted in April 1861. He was captured at Hanover Junction, Virginia, May 22, and held prisoner at Point Lookout, Maryland before being sent to the prison camp at Elmira, N.Y. He died there on August 7, of chronic diarrhea.

—*North Carolina Argus,* **October 4, 1864**

Lt. James M. Watkins, member of Co. C, 14th N.C. Troops, died from disease in the Yankee prison at Elmira, New York, during the month of August last. He joined at age 17 in March 1863. He was captured at Mechanicsville, Virginia in May 1864, sent to the prison at Point Lookout, Maryland, then to Elmira.

—*North Carolina Argus,* **October 6, 1864**

Littleton, N.C., Nov. 4.—(Special.)—**Lt. Col. William A. Johnston** died at his residence here last night at 2 o'clock, from a stroke of paralysis. His death was not unexpected, as he had been a constant sufferer several months from the same cause. He served with distinction throughout the Civil War, going out in May 1861, as captain of a crack company of this section, the "Roanoke Minute Men," Company A; was twice wounded in battle, once at Malvern Hill and again at Chancellorsville, where his right arm was broken. In the latter fight he was promoted for special gallantry to the colonelcy of the Fourteenth North Carolina Regiment. He was also wounded at Petersburg, and was paroled at Appomattox. No braver man ever breathed the breath of a Christian and a soldier then W. A. Johnston.

For twenty-five years since the close of the war he has lived among his people, and has been their leader even as he had lead many of them over the hills and through the valleys of Virginia. He was a devoted member of the Methodist church, and a Mason of high standing. He leaves seven children who have the sympathy and prayers of our community.

—**Originally published in the *Raleigh* News *and Observer* and reprinted in the *Gold Leaf,* November 10, 1898**

Wadesboro, Sept. 16.—**Benjamin K. Threadgill** died at his home in Ansonville Wednesday, aged about 68 years. Mr. Threadgill, who had been feeble for some time, lived alone. Tuesday night his friend and neighbor, Col. J. J. Colson, sat up with him. Not long before day, Col. Colson says, Mr. Threadgill got up and went out into the yard and stayed a short time. He then returned to the house and sat in a chair beside the door a short time, after which he went to bed. Mr. Threadgill did not get up at his usual time yesterday morning, but Col. Colson, thinking he was asleep, would not disturb him for some time, but, finally, he went to the bed and found that he was dead.

Mr. Threadgill was a veteran of the War Between the States and was a gallant soldier in Company C, 14th Regiment North Carolina Troops. He was captured during the battle at Sharpsburg, and released a few days later. He was wounded at Fredericksburg, December 13, 1862, and again at the battle of Chancellorsville. He was captured at Petersburg a week before Lee surrendered and held prisoner on an island in New York Harbor until his release in the summer. In the black days of Reconstruction he took an active part in ousting the rascals who then held sway in Anson and in restoring white rule. The burial was at Pleasant Grove yesterday afternoon at one o'clock.

—*Raleigh News and Observer,* **September 17, 1910**

The recent death of **Judge Risden Tyler Bennett**, of Wadesboro, N.C., brings back to mind some stirring memories of the war. I shall never forget him. It was under him as commander of the brigade that my regiment, the 4th North Carolina, was attached, and I heard the first Yankee bullets whiz by my head. I was a boy in my teens, fresh from a military school, and I freely confess that I was badly frightened and wished that I was somewhere else.

We were marching at a double-quick through a long lane with nail fences on each side, attempting to flank two divisions of the enemy that were firing on us from a large body of woods to our left; and the firing became so hot that Colonel Bennett sprang upon the rail fence, facing the enemy, and gave the command to change direction, left wheel, double-quick, march. We were marching in fours. We wheeled to the left, struck the fence with vim, and it went down, and so did we. Colonel Bennett then gave the command to dress on the center colors, and you could hear his clear voice from one end to the other of the brigade.

We had a field and meadow to cross before reaching the enemy, who were posted in the woods across this meadow; and as we came in full view of them we saw two lines of battle, the first line kneeling, the second standing, and every man with his finger on the gun trigger ready to fire. It was grand but terrible-looking to us. We had not fired a shot, and as we leaped the ditch to ascend the hill every man fell flat on his stomach. As we fell every Yankee soldier pressed his trigger, and there was one long flash of smoke, and the terrible missiles of death passed over our fallen bodies, and the strangest part of it was that not a man was struck. Immediately every man sprang to his feet and with deadly aim we fired, and with a yell that only a Southern soldier knows how to give we were on them. We shot down many, drove the line half a mile, and captured nearly 2,000 of the enemy.

After the fight I asked Colonel Bennett who gave the order to lie down as we crossed the ditch. I said no man heard any order. He looked at me with a smile and said: "My son, God Almighty gave that order."

In May 1863, Maj. Gen. R. E. Rodes, commanding Hill's Division, mentioned Colonel Bennett, with others, for "great gallantry and efficiency."

General Ramseur reported Colonel Bennett as "conspicuous for his coolness under the hottest fire." Again, under date of August 3, while in command of Early's Division, he states: "in this extremity Colonel Bennett, 14th North Carolina, offered to take his regiment from left to right, under a severe fire, and drive back the growing masses of the enemy on my right. This bold and hazardous offer was accepted as a forlorn hope. It was successfully executed. The enemy was driven from my immediate front and the works were held. For this all honor is due Colonel Bennett and the officers and men of his regiment."

General Rodes reports Colonel Bennett among the wounded at Gettysburg, July 3, and General Ramseur thanks him in a report of that battle "for skill and gallantry displayed." Capt. A. J. Griffith, who commanded the 14th North Carolina, in reporting the engagement at Sharpsburg, gives the casualties in kill, wounded, and missing, as two hundred and thirteen, "including Colonel Bennett, blown up by a shell, severely shocked." Maj. Gen. D. H. Hill in his official report stated: "Colonel Bennett, 14th North Carolina, who had conducted himself most nobly throughout, won my special admiration for the heroism he exhibited at the moment of receiving what he supposed to be a mortal wound." (Series I, Volume XIX, Part I, page 1027.)

Col. R. T. Bennett died at Wadesboro, N.C., July 21, 1913. He was born near there June 28, 1840, his forefathers on the Bennett side having gone to Anson County from the eastern shore of Maryland in 1749. He studied law at Cumberland University, Lebanon, Tenn., graduating there in 1859.

In 1861, he volunteered as a private in the 14th North Carolina Regiment. A few months later he was made quartermaster of the regiment, and in 1862, when the regiment was reorganized, he was made captain. Later he was promoted to lieutenant colonel, and to colonel when twenty-two years old.

In the "Official Records" Colonel Bennett's name appears in no less than eight volumes. His regiment was assigned to Gen. G. T. Anderson's brigade, Jackson's Corps, and participated in all the battles in which his brigade was engaged. At Sharpsburg, while holding the Bloody Lane, General Anderson was severely wounded and Colonel Bennett assumed command of the brigade. He a short time afterwards was wounded. Gen. D. H. Hill in his official report speaks of him in this action in the highest terms. General Stephen D. Ramseur was put in command of this brigade, and at Gettysburg, where Colonel Bennett was again wounded, General Ramseur complimented him highly.

While at home on a furlough from his wounds he was married to Miss Kate Shepherd in August 1863, and is survived by his widow and three married daughters, Mrs. Eugene Little, Mrs. John Leak, and Mrs. John T. Bennett. He was back with his command in the fall of 1863, and participated in the battle of Mine Run and the next spring in the Wilderness Campaign, being wounded for the third time at Spotsylvania. In that battle he volunteered to take his regiment into the Bloody Angle, which offer was accepted by General Ramseur, as he says in his official reports, "As a forlorn hope, and which helped to turn the tide of battle in our favor."

Later in the year his command was with Jubal A. Early in the Valley campaign, fighting the battle of Monocracy on July 9 and a few days later reaching the outskirts of Washington, the nearest to Washington that the Confederates reached during the war. On September 9, in the battle of Winchester, he was captured and sent to prison at Fort Delaware. He was paroled from there late in February 1865, and while at home waiting for exchange came the collapse at Appomattox.

In peace Colonel Bennett was as great as in war. He was one of the most polished scholars in the Carolinas and a lawyer by profession. In 1875 he helped to regain his native State from negro rule, and at the Constitutional Convention of that year was chairman of the Judiciary Committee, and soon after was elected judge of the Superior Court. In 1882 he was elected Congressman at large from North Carolina, and was on the Judiciary Committee, the chairman being the famous lawyer, John Randolph Tucker, who said: "Colonel Bennett's legal knowledge was superior to any other member of the committee." After serving two terms in Congress, he was offered the nomination for Governor of North Carolina, but declined on account of ill health and retired to his home, in Wadesboro, devoting the last years of his life to writing his articles, especially obituaries, being widely quoted.
—*Confederate Veteran,* **Volume 21, Number 11, November 1913, "Judge Risden Tyler Bennett," Sketch by John G. Young, Winston-Salem, N.C.**

15th Regiment North Carolina Troops

Died near Yorktown, on the 2d inst., **Cornelius Haywood Stallings, M. D.,** of typhoid fever, Company L, 5th North Carolina Volunteers [later 15th Regiment N.C.T.] in the 27th year of his age. At the start of war, Dr. Stallings had a profitable and increasing practice in his native county of Franklin. He entered the Army as a private. He performed all the duties of the common soldier, and when the desolating camp fever threatened to decimate the North Carolina 5th Regiment Volunteers, his medical skills were needed and he was transferred to the hospitals. He labored in this department, by night and by day, in sickness and in health, until prostrated by the disease from which he had been the means of rescuing so many of his comrades.

—*North Carolina Standard,* October 26, 1861

Died in this County, on the 5th of October, at the residence of W. J. Holleman, **Henry B. Holland**, of Harnett County, Company F, aged 29 years. He volunteered to defend his country in May 1861, and went to Yorktown, where he was taken sick. He lingered there several months, when he was brought home, and died after about ten days. He had been a member of the Baptist Church for about three years, and the Palmyra Masonic Lodge, 147. He was buried in full uniform as a soldier.

—*North Carolina Standard,* November 13, 1861

Died in hospital at Yorktown, of malignant sore throat on the 10th ult., **James Gallatin Webster**, son of Mr. James Webster, of Chatham County, N.C., in the 23d year of his age. He was of Company M, 5th Regiment of N.C. Vols., [later 15th N.C.T.] and a member of Columbus Lodge No. 102, Pittsborough.

—*Fayetteville Observer,* February 10, 1862

The remains of this gallant young officer, the Colonel of the 15th Regiment N.C.T., were brought to this city yesterday on the City Point train, in charge of a detachment of his late regiment. The dispatch stated that "he fell while gallantly leading his men in a charge at Lee's Mill, April 16." No more honorable tribute could be paid to a noble commander than this. **Colonel Robert M. McKinney** was a native of Lynchburg, where he now leaves an aged and afflicted father, sisters and brothers, to mourn his early death. He was a man of brilliant literary acquirements, and a military genius of the best school. Col. McKinney was a graduate of the Virginia Military Institute, and when war broke out was Professor of Tactics in the North Carolina Military Institute at Charlotte. He had moved to North Carolina two years ago. He volunteered his services to his adopted State, was elected a Captain of Company A, and subsequently Colonel of the 15th N.C. regiment, at the head of which he fell, day before yesterday. His men loved him because he shared their hardships and exposures, and associated freely and affectionately with them. Col. McK. was about twenty-five years of age, and was as brave and fearless as it is possible for a man to be. His remains are to be sent to Lynchburg.

Military honors were shown to the deceased by several of the companies encamped in town, who were in waiting at the depot, on the arrival of the train. The body subsequently exposed to view for a short time, and was visited by a good many of our citizens. *Petersburg Express, 18th.*

—**Originally published in the *Petersburg Express, 18th* and reprinted in the *Fayetteville Observer,* April 21, 1862**

Died in the Hospital at Richmond, Va., from wounds received at Malvern Hill, July 1, **David George Johnson**, of Harnett County. He belonged to company F, 15th Regiment N.C. Troops. He possessed not the advantages of wealth that many do, but a finer spirit never dwelt in man.

—*North Carolina Standard,* July 19, 1862

We have seldom been called upon to perform a more painful duty than to announce the death of our much esteemed friend, **Capt. Willie Perry, Jr.**, of the 15th Regiment of N.C.T., Company E.

At the time of Lincoln's declaration of war against the South, Capt. Perry occupied the position of a farmer in Granville County, enjoying the fruits of his honest industry, and the confidence of his fellow-citizens, by whom he had only a few years before been honored with a seat in the Legislature.

He was among the very first in the community to step forward in defense of his country. When organized, his company without a dissenting voice, elected him as their Captain. We pass by many incidents of his life worthy to be recorded, to notice briefly the memorable charge at Malvern Hill, made July the 1st, upon one of the most powerful Yankee batteries, perhaps, ever exhibited on any battle field.

At the time the order was given to charge the battery, he had but a handful of men able to take their places in the ranks, but with a voice that faltered not, he commanded his men to follow him—to victory or death. With a firm step and a steady eye, he advanced upon the enemy, who were pouring deadly fire upon him and his men. Some were killed, and others wounded, but still he pressed onward, nor did he sheath his sword till his arm was shattered by a ball from the enemy, and he was borne from the scene of carnage where thousands of brave men fell to rise no more. He was removed to Richmond, where every attention was paid him. After suffering a most painful amputation, he lingered a few days, and on the 19th inst., he breathed his last, in the 39th year of his age. He has left a brother and two sisters to mourn his loss.

—R. C. Maynard, *North Carolina Standard,* **August 9, 1862**

Died, on the battle field in front of Richmond, on the 1st day of July, **Lieut. Leonidas J. Merritt.** of the "Chatham Rifles," Company M, 15th Regiment N.C. Vols. Lieut. Merritt was a native of Chatham County, and graduated at the State University, with honor, in the class of 1854. Having studied law, he came to the bar of Chatham with a bright future before him. At the opening of the war, he volunteered and served gallantly until in a most daring charge at Malvern Hill, he received the deadly missile from the enemy. He was a member of Columbus Masonic Lodge, No. 102. He had also been wounded at Lee's Mill, Virginia, in April of this year.

—*North Carolina Standard,* **August 27, 1862**

Died at the residence of his brother in Harnett County, on the 23d Oct., of chronic diarrhea, **Ica Parker,** of Co. F, 15th Reg't N.C.T. He was in the battles around Richmond; afterwards was taken sick and returned home just in time to die. He was 31 years old.

—*Fayetteville Observer,* **December 1, 1862**

> The youth I knew and loved him well,
> And 'twas at Bristow that he fell.

1st Sergeant Eli B. Branson, Jr., son of E. B. and L. Branson, of Co. H, 15th Reg't, N.C. Troops, volunteered in May 1861, and was a faithful member of that command until the ill-fated affair at Bristow Station. He had passed through the ordeal of several previous battles; he was wounded in the leg and captured at the battle of South Mountain, September 14th and held at Fort McHenry until exchanged in October. He fell at his post while facing the hail of shot, shell and ball that thinned the ranks so fast at Bristow. He was a young man of much promise, and had received a liberal education, and when the war broke out was reading medicine. He went as a private in one among the first companies from Alamance. He fills a soldier's grave away among strangers

—A friend, *Fayetteville Observer*, December 28, 1863

Killed in the battle of Fredericksburg, Va., Dec. 13th, 1862, **Private Orren Lamb,** Co. H, 15th Reg't N.C. Troops, aged 20 years. He volunteered in May 1861 for 12 months, and in Dec. '61 re-enlisted for 2 years more. He was an honest, sober and industrious youth, and although he made but little noise in the world, if everyone had done their duty as promptly as he did, our country would now be in a much better condition than it is. He never complained much of hardships and toilsome marches. He was in the fights at Dam No. 1, Yorktown, Malvern Hill, South Mountain or Boonsboro' and Sharpsburg, and finally fell at Fredericksburg. He never straggled but was always at his post. He leaves a mother and brothers and sisters. The writer will never forget him.

—A friend, *Fayetteville Observer*, December 28, 1863 r

At the residence of his mother, in Franklin Co., on Sunday, the 31st inst., of Chronic Diarrhea, **Captain Thomas T. Terrell,** of Company G, 15th Regiment N.C.T., in his twenty-seventh year. Capt. Terrell entered the service in May 1861, as a private, and was promoted by the confidence and respect of his comrades, won by his merits, to the rank which he held at his death. He was hardly ever absent from his Company, although his health was never good since he entered the army, and it was often so bad as to render him unfit to be outside of a hospital. He was captured at Crampton's Pass, Maryland, on September 14, 1862, held prisoner at Fort Delaware, and later exchanged. He came home on sick leave about the middle of December last, since which time he has not left his room, until borne out to his grave.

Louisburg, Feb. 24, 1864.

—*Daily Confederate*, February 27, 1864

Josephus Braddy Company I died on the 20th November 1862, at Gordonsville, Va., of pneumonia. He had entered the service as a substitute in August 1862, at age 37. He was from Edgecombe County and a member of Falkland Masonic Lodge, No. 196.

—*Daily Confederate*, May 5, 1864

Private William J. Douglas, Co. F, 15th N.C.T., fell mortally wounded Oct'r 1, 1864, while on the skirmish line near Jones' Farm, Va. He was enlisted May 18th, 1861, and since that time he has nobly done his duty as a brave, cheerful, Christian soldier.

—*Fayetteville Observer*, December 22, 1864

At Winder Hospital, Richmond, Va., on the 25th of December. 1864, **Corporal Solomon Tesh,** aged 33 years 10 months and 24 days. He was a member of Co. H., 15th Regiment N.C. Troops, Cook's Brigade. The first engagement he was in was at Crampton's Pass, South Mountain in Maryland, where he was wounded in the shoulder. He was in the second battle of Fredericksburg, and in every engagement in which his brigade participated, until about three weeks before his death, when he was sent to the hospital in Richmond where he died of disease. The deceased was a member of the Moravian Church at Friedberg, and both at home and in the army, adorned his profession by his consistent walk and conversation. He enjoyed the confidence and esteem of privates and officers in his regiment, so that he was often excused from duty in order to enable him to participate in the revivals going on in the brigade, and aid the Chaplains in their labors.

—His Pastor, *People's Press,* January 19, 1865

Jasper N. Wood died quite suddenly at his home in Albright Township Monday; aged 70 years, 9 mos., and 29 days. He had not been well for a long time; nevertheless his death came as a surprise. The remains were buried Tuesday at Moore's Chapel and the funeral services were conducted by the Rev. Geo. W. Holmes. Mr. Wood was a Confederate soldier and a member of Capt. John R. Stockard's (41) company—Co. H., 15th Reg. He was a sergeant and was paroled at Appomattox Court House, April 9, 1865. He is survived by his widow and four daughters—Mrs. L. F. Johnston of Mebane, Mrs. John M. Foust of the Southern part of the county, Mrs. Joliette Henley, who lived with her parents, and Miss Daisy Wood, who has been a clerk in Graham post office for a number of years
—*Alamance Gleaner,* **June 12, 1913**

16th Regiment North Carolina Troops

DIED,—At the N.C. Hospital, Petersburg, Va., April 1, 1862, **John A. J. Best**, a member of Co. L, 16th Reg. N.C. Troops. Death has stolen from our ranks another of our boys. He responded to the first call of North Carolina for troops to drive the vandals from the land that gave him birth; but he is no more.
—W. H. Moore, (42) 2d Sergt. Co. L, 16th Reg. N.C.T.,
Asheville News, **May 8, 1862**

We are pained to learn that **Col. Champion Thomas Neal Davis**, of Rutherford, was killed in the late battle near Richmond, at Seven Pines, on Saturday last, the 31st. The following dispatch to his father-in-law, N. N. Nixon, Esq., appears in the Wilmington *Journal* of Tuesday last:

RICHMOND, VA., June 2nd, 1862
Col. C. T. N. Davis, of the 16th Regiment N.C.T., fell on the evening of the 31st ult., in the fight on the Chickahominy, whilst leading his regiment against the enemy's batteries. He was left on the field. He was wounded three times before he fell. His conduct was gallant and glorious beyond all praise. "His conduct was gallant and glorious beyond all praise." Let this be inscribed on his tomb.—wounded three times, he still led his regiment on, until he fell to rise no more.

Col. Davis was a native of Halifax County, Va., and was about 35 years of age. He studied the profession of law, and settled in Burke County, in this State, where he soon obtained a strong hold on the confidence of the people. He represented the Burke district for one term in the State Senate; and, having subsequently removed to the County of Rutherford, he was elected to the House of Commons of the last Legislature from that County.—Soon after this State had separated from the old government, he volunteered as a private in a Rutherford company, and was made Captain. As Captain of Company G, 16th regiment, he encountered all the perils and privations of the campaign in Northwestern Virginia, during the past winter. On the reorganization of this regiment, he was elected Colonel, and it was while leading the regiment in the battle near Richmond, that he lost his life.
—*North Carolina Standard,* **June 7, 1862**

Died June 20th, at Saint Charles Hospital, Richmond, from a wound received in the battle of the 31st May, at Seven Pines, **Jackson R. Mull**, of Buncombe, N.C., in the 21st year of his age, a member of Co L, 16th N.C. Regiment
—*Fayetteville Observer,* **June 23, 1862**

We are pained to hear that **Captains Henry C. Worley** of Company F and **Andrew A. Coleman**, of Company A of the 16th Regiment, are among the slain in the great battles near Richmond. Capt. Worley was killed at Mechanicsville, on June 26, and Capt. Coleman was struck and killed by a shell at Frayser's Farm, June 30. They were noble and gallant men, and the blood of a thousand of the hireling invaders will not atone for their loss.

—*Asheville News,* July 10, 1862]

1st Sergeant Thomas G. Enloe, Company A, was wounded in the fight at Mechanicsville June 26, and died a few days later.

Webster, N.C., July 25, 1862.

—*Asheville News,* July 31, 1862

DIED.—On the 30th day of June on the battle field near Richmond, at Frayser's Farm, **Miles Killian**, in the 20th year of his age. He was a member of Company I, 16th Reg. N.C.T., and fell in the thickest of the fight on that bloody field. He joined the first company that left Henderson County under Capt. W. M. Shipp, and participated in the arduous campaign in western Virginia. In all the trials and hardships of that campaign, he never gave way. He was always at his post, never disobeying orders, and cheerfully performing all his duties. In all subsequent trials, the same fortitude and energy marked his character. At Williamsburg, Seven Pines, &c., he exhibited the valor and coolness of the veteran, and in his last effort, he fell with his armor on and his face to the foe.

—*Asheville News,* August 7, 1862

William Culberson, aged 19, of Buncombe County, left the home of his parents last summer, and went to meet our Northern foes. He was a member of Company F, 16th Regiment and was killed in the late fight at Gaines' Mill near Richmond. He was a member of Hominy Creek Division, No. 289, Sons of Temperance.

—*Asheville News,* August 21, 1862

Ansel Randolph was born in Yancey Co., N.C., April 1st, 1840, and died in a Richmond hospital, July 15, 1862, from wounds received at the battle of Mechanicsville, June 26. He was the son of Wm. and Patsa Randolph, and received from them early religious instructions. He joined the Baptist Church. He was a private in Co. C, 16th Reg. N.C. Vols., under the brave *Capt. J. S. McElroy.* (43) He leaves a father and mother.

—*Asheville News,* September 4, 1862

Caleb A. Rickman and **Marquis Lafayette Rickman**, both of the 16th Regiment N.C.T. Company I, sons of Marvin and Sarah Rickman, were casualties in the recent battles before Richmond. Caleb, aged 22, was killed at Gaines' Mill, June 27, and his brother, aged 20, was wounded at Mechanicsville, June 26, and died in a hospital at Staunton. Both were members of the Baptist Church at Mills' River.

—*Asheville News,* September 4, 1862

David Swain Moore, Company A and Regimental Sergeant Major, son of Capt. Chas. and Lucinda Moore, of this county, fell, mortally wounded in the battles before Richmond, at Mechanicsville, June 26, 1862, while bravely defending the cause of Southern Independence. A friend marked the spot where he fell, and when the rush of war was past, sought him out to minister to his dying wants. His Reg't, the 16th, endured many hardships, and he was with them in their heroic charge at the battles of Seven Pines, and came out unharmed. Capt. Moore had gone to Richmond at the time of his death, to look after his

sons, and sad indeed must have been the heart of that aged father as he sought among the slain on the battle-field for his boy and craved of the citizens a burial place for him; and alone and sorrowful he laid him, not in the tomb of his ancestors, but in a strangers' graveyard, and sad was the news and heavy the blow to the stricken ones at home.
Sept. 29, 1862.

—Carrie, *Asheville News,* October 9, 1862

Killed on the 9th of August, in the evening of the battle of Cedar Mountain, **William Howard**, in his 25th year. He had been in his country's service since the beginning of the present war, except when ill health compelled him to resort to his home for a short season, several times. In the spring of 1861, he joined Co. G of the gallant 1st N.C. Reg't. Though often ill, he passed safely though that six months campaign on the Peninsula. When the 1st Reg't disbanded he joined *Capt. Elijah J. Kirksey's* (44) Co. E of the 16th N.C. Reg't. Sickness compelled him to spend part of last summer at his home in McDowell County, and he had retuned but a few weeks, when he met his sad and early doom at Cedar Run. Brave to a fault, he was in advance of his comrades, when one of the enemy in ambush fired at him and he fell with his face to the foe. His last words were a call to his brother, to whom he was tenderly attached, and whom he thought to be in danger. His brother, having heard that he had fallen, placed three prisoners whom he had taken, under guard, and followed, to find him dead by the road-side. He carried him into the woods, and watched alone over him, throughout the dark hours of a terrible night. When morning dawned he wrapped him up in his oil-cloth and blanket, and hired a servant to assist him in the sad burial. A reader of the Bible, he was killed with that precious volume in his pocket.

—*North Carolina Presbyterian,* November 29, 1862

At his father's in Gaston County, on the 4th Sept., 1862, **William Adolphus Henderson**, son of J. A. and S. P. Henderson, aged 20 years, 6 months and 15 days. He was a volunteer in Co. M., 16th Reg't. N.C.T., and died of chronic diarrhea contracted in camp.

—*North Carolina Presbyterian,* January 17, 1863

At the Marine Hospital in Richmond, July 18, 1862, **Pinkney L. Edwards**, aged 21, and on the 3rd of Sept., **Julius A. Edwards**, aged 24, sons of the Rev. P. W. Edwards, of Haywood County. Both were in Company L. Julius was wounded at Ox Hill, Virginia, September 1. Pinkney had been wounded and hospitalized on June 27.

—*Fayetteville Observer,* July 20, 1863

DIED,—Of Chronic diarrhea, on the 3d of September 1862, at the General Hospital in Danville, Va., **Mathias Meece**, son of Peter Meece of Haywood county. The dec'd was in his 22d year, and a member of the 16th N.C. Reg't., Company L. He made a profession of religion and was baptized on his death-bed.

—*Asheville News,* October 16, 1863

John A. Carpenter, 1st Lieut. and Ensign of the 16th N.C. Reg't, fell mortally wounded and died in a few hours on the 6th of May 1864, at the Battle of the Wilderness. Lieut. Carpenter was born and reared in Lincoln County, N.C. He was Color Sergeant of Company M and was wounded in the head and blinded in the left eye at the battle of Chancellorsville. He was nominated for the Badge of Distinction for his gallantry in that battle. He returned to the Regiment in September and was later appointed Ensign. His elder brother, **Pinkney D. Carpenter**, was a member of a company [G] commanded by the writer, who also fell on the 3d of May 1863, just one year before the subject of this notice. He was wounded and captured at Gettysburg and died in the hands of the enemy.

—M. C. D., *Fayetteville Observer,* December 22, 1864

Maj. John N. Prior, one of the most highly esteemed citizens of Fayetteville, N.C., died in September 1913 in his seventy-sixth year. Major Prior was a son of Warren and Louisa McIntyre Prior and a man of sterling integrity, kindly heart, good business ability, and bright mind. He was a gallant Confederate veteran, volunteering at the outbreak of the Civil War and going to Yorktown in the Lafayette Light Infantry Company, 1st North Carolina Regiment. When the 1st Regiment was mustered out of service, he served as captain in the 16th North Carolina Regiment, and was wounded in 1864. On his recovery he was made major of the 4th Regiment of Senior Reserves (the 73d North Carolina).

After the war Major Prior went to New York City, where he was for years engaged in the dry goods business. About fourteen years ago he returned to Fayetteville to live, succeeding his father in the jewelry business, which he was conducting at the time of his death. He is survived by a daughter and a son.

—*Confederate Veteran* Volume 22, Number 6, June 1914

17th Regiment North Carolina Troops

Died at Camp Mangum, [Raleigh] **Sergeant Aurelius Brett**, aged 28, of Company D, the Hertford Light Infantry. He was captured at Fort Hatteras, August 29, 1861, and held a prisoner at forts in New York and Boston harbors. He was exchanged in February 1862. The company later disbanded and he joined Company C.

—*Fayetteville Observer,* June 16, 1862

Died of typhoid pneumonia in Northampton County, 24th July, **Lieut. Wm. J. Latimer**, of the 17th Reg't. He entered service as a sergeant in Company D and was captured at Fort Hatteras, August 29, 1861, and held a prisoner at forts in New York and Boston harbors. He was exchanged in February 1862. The company later disbanded and he joined Company C as 2nd Lieutenant.

—*Fayetteville Observer,* August 18, 1862

Died at the residence of Mr. Shanks, of the city, on the 18th inst., of typhoid fever, **Serg't. Benjamin W. Turnage,** of Co. K, 17th Reg. N.C. Troops, in the 26th year of his age. He leaves a devoted and amiable wife, who was with him during his last illness; and also pious parents and many friends to mourn their irreparable loss.

Petersburg, Va., August 14th.

—A friend, *Raleigh Register,* August 23, 1862

Corporal James M. Savage entered the service as a member of the Edgecombe Guards, Company A, 1st Regiment N.C. Troops, 6 months. After the disbanding of his regiment he again entered the service as a private in the 17th Regiment, Company I. He died at the Hospital in Wilmington, December 7th, 1863, of acute dysentery.

—*Wilmington Daily Journal,* December 8, 1863

On the 2nd day of February 1864, near the village of Shephardsville, N.C., **Captain James J. Leith**, of Co. B, 17th N.C.T., fell, while bravely and efficiently commanding his Company as skirmishers against the enemy. He was a farmer from Hyde County and was aged 34.

—*Wilmington Daily Journal,* February 18, 1864

Died, on the 27th ult., at the Officers' Hospital, Petersburg, Va., of wounds received in the late battle on the Southside near Bermuda Hundred, **Lieut. Col. John C. Lamb**, of the 17th N.C. Regiment, aged about 28 years. It had scarcely become a stern fact in 1861 that war existed between the two countries before he went to work with his wonted energy, and raised in Martin County a fine company, which was offered to the State and subsequently sent to Hatteras Inlet. During the bombardment of that place he stood manfully to his post, and by his coolness and fearlessness of danger, he won the admiration of both his comrades and the enemy. It was the misfortune of the garrison (the 7th regiment) to be captured and for months Capt. Lamb endured the servitude of confinement in Fort Warren—declining the offer to be allowed to come home on parole—choosing rather to stay and be a partner in the sufferings of his company. After the exchange and reorganization of the 7th (afterwards called the 17th) Capt. Lamb was elected Lt. Colonel, and all who knew him can testify to the fact of his filling the position with credit to himself and regiment. He never dared to lead in any expedition or onset, and from his almost constant study of the subject, became an excellent officer. For years he was an exemplary member of the Church of the Advent (Episcopal) at Williamston.

—*Wilmington Daily Journal,* June 2, 1864

Mr. Joel Tyson died Sunday night at his home about 4 miles above Greenville. He was nearly seventy years of age, a Confederate soldier of Company K, 17th Regiment, an industrious farmer and good citizen. He leaves a wife but no children.

—*Daily Reflector,* June 11, 1906

Ex-Sheriff John F. Hellen died at his home in Swift Creek township last Friday and was buried the day following. He was [an] ex–Confederate soldier and lost a leg during the civil war. He was a member of Company C, 17th Regiment. Captured at Fort Hatteras, August 29, 1861, he was held prisoner at forts in New York and Boston harbors. After exchange, his company disbanded and he joined Company E, 55th Regiment. At the Battle of the Wilderness, May 5, 1864, he was wounded in the left ankle and part of his leg was amputated. He was retired from service in November 1864.

—*Daily Reflector,* August 21, 1906

18th Regiment North Carolina Troops

In this town, at the residence of Mr. W. H. Allen, on the morning of the 19th last, from effects of measles, **William Robeson**, son of W. B. and A. C. Robeson, of Brunswick, in the 17th year of his age. He was a member of the Wilmington Light Infantry, Company G. He was 17.

—*Wilmington Daily Journal,* October 21, 1861

At Camp Stephens, near Coosawhatchie, S.C., of typhoid pneumonia, on the 31st of December 1861, **Frederick J. McKeithan**, of Company B, 18th Regiment N.C. Vols., aged 18 years, 6 months and 25 days. The deceased was a native of Brunswick County, and for seven years a member of the M. E. Church.
—*Wilmington Daily Journal,* January 13, 1862

At Camp Stephens, near Coosawhatchie, S.C., on the 21st inst., of typhoid pneumonia, **Edward N. Johnson**, of Co. I, "Wilmington Rifle Guards," 18th Regiment N.C. Vols., aged 24 years. The funeral of the deceased will take place this afternoon at 3 o'clock from Front Street Methodist E. Church, thence to Oakdale Cemetery.
—*Wilmington Daily Journal,* January 25, 1862

Caleb Sutton, a member of the Robeson Rifle Guards, Co. D, 18th N.C. Regiment, died February 10th, of disease. He had been a farmer and was our elder member; was one among the first to enroll his name on our list; he was 62 years of age. He left his home in defense of his country, with five sons in the service. His friends persuaded him not to volunteer; his reply was that he should go with his boys. He was taken sick in January, with pneumonia; was quite sick in hospital but recovered, when on the morning of the 10th of February, he was found dead. His comrades can never forget him, for his good advice, his cheerful and lively conservation.
—*Wilmington Daily Journal,* March 7, 1862

James. T. Highsmith, of the Moore's Creek Rifle Guards, Co. E, died in the hospital at Camp Stephens, S.C., March 4th, 1862, of brain fever. He was from New Hanover County, North Carolina, and taught school before enlisting. He was 22 years old.
—*Wilmington Daily Journal,* March 7, 1862

The remains of **Alexander Duncan Moore, Sergeant Major** of the Regiment and **William Augustus Wooster, 1st Lieut.** Co. I, from New Hanover County, aged 21 at enlistment, who were killed defending their country on June 30th, at Frayser's Farm, Virginia, reached here yesterday forenoon, and were escorted to their respective residences by Col. Leventhorpe's Regiment and the Independent Guard of the town, under Capt. Burr.

They were interred yesterday afternoon at 4 o'clock in Oakdale Cemetery with military honors.
—*Wilmington Daily Journal,* July 5, 1862

Sergeant William Moore, Jr., of the Robeson Rifle Guards, Co. D, died June 10th, 1862, of disease. He was born in Robeson County, N.C., a son of John Moore, Esq., one of Robeson's most worthy citizens. He volunteered in this company, was with us in the battle of Hanover Court House on the 27th ult., and fought bravely to the last; he was taken sick in a few days after and died in the La. Hospital, Richmond, Va.
—**Capt. Morgan C. T. Lee.**, (45) Captain Company D,
Fayetteville Observer, July 14, 1862

Died on the morning of the 20th July, of wounds received in the recent battles near Richmond, **Thomas M. Simpson**, of Co. E. He fought in the battle of Hanover Court House, but escaped unhurt, to participate in the battles of the 26th and 27th of June at Gaines' Mill. While bravely marching in the very face of the storm of leaden death, he received the fatal ball in his side that took his life, along with thousands of his comrades on those crim-

soned fields. He was carried to a Richmond hospital, and then transferred to Petersburg, where he died. He had been a farmer and was 34.
—*Wilmington Daily Journal,* July 24, 1862

Died three weeks after his return to his father's residence on Topsail Sound, July 25th, from the effects of a wound in the side, received in the battle of Friday evening, June 27th, at Gaines' Mill, Virginia, **James M. Sidbury**, eldest son of Woodman and Nancy Sidbury and a member of Co. G, 18th Regt. N.C.T. He had passed safely through the deadly fire at Hanover Court House but was struck down in his next battle. Slow and mournful the procession wound their way to the last resting place of the brave soldier, escorted by Capt. A. J. Newkirk's Cavalry, where he was committed to the earth with military honors. He had been a farmer and was 19.
—*Wilmington Daily Journal,* July 26, 1862

Died of wounds and typhoid fever, in a hospital near Richmond, Va., on Sunday evening, the 20th inst., **James H. M. Everett**, a farmer, aged 20 years, 11 months and 20 days, a member of Company G. He was a native of New Hanover County. He was in several of the battles near Richmond, but, though passing through some of the hottest fires, came out unhurt, until wounded at Frayser's Farm on June 30. His remains were brought home and interred in the family grave yard.
—*Wilmington Daily Journal,* August 1, 1862

Died at Leesburg, in New Hanover County, on the 2d inst., **Serg't. William H. Alderman**, a farmer, aged 19 years. He was a son of Owen Alderman, Esq., of this county. He was among the first to offer his services to defend the Confederacy he so dearly loved, and was a member of *Col. Robert H. Cowan's* (46) regiment, the glorious 18th, Company E. He bore himself handsomely in all the engagements of that noble regiment, and passed through them all with only a slight wound. Since the close of the recent battles around Richmond, he sickened with typhoid fever. He started from the hospital for his home, but only lived to reach Leesburg in his native county, where he died amidst kind, sympathizing friends.
—*Wilmington Daily Journal,* August 6, 1862

Died at Chimborazo Hospital, Richmond, Va., on the 5th inst., **John Herring**, a farmer, of Company E, 18th Reg't. N.C. Troops, son of James Herring, deceased, and aged 25 years. At the outbreak of war, he gallantly responded, forsaking home with all its endearments, for the defense of our cause. When called upon to test his skill and bravery, he passed through the heavy fire at Hanover, and soon after the great battles before Richmond without receiving a single wound. Soon after, he was taken with Typhoid fever and shortly died, without being surrounded by his relatives and friends. He leaves an affectionate mother and several loving brothers and sisters.
—*Wilmington Daily Journal,* August 20, 1862

Departed this life, in Richmond County, N.C., Aug. 6, 1862, **Duncan McLauchlin**, a farmer, in the 41st year of his age. He entered the service in May 1862, in Co. F (Scotch Boys), 18th Reg. N.C.T., and after passing safely through all the diseases incident to camp life, and after escaping the implements of death that flew so thickly in the late battles near Richmond, receiving only a slight bruise from a spent ball, he returned home two weeks ago, having been honorably discharged under the operation of the conscript law—being over age—only to sicken and die in the embraces of a widowed mother and loving sisters.
—*North Carolina Presbyterian,* August 23, 1862

Died at his residence in Columbus County, on the 1st inst., of putrid sore throat, **Capt. William K. Gore**, of Company C, 18th Regiment N.C.T. He promptly and unhesitatingly responded to his country's call by volunteering and tendering his services in Company C, of which on its first organization, he was chosen 1st Lieutenant, and after its reorganization, he was appointed Captain. He was always regarded as one of the best and most useful officers of the regiment. He was in the battles of Slash Church, Mechanicsville, Gaines' Mills, and Frayser's Farm, in which last he was severely wounded in the thigh, while bravely and gallantly leading his men in the fight. On every battle field his bearing was cool, brave and determined. His memory will long be cherished by his company and regiment, and his place will not be easily filled. As a friend, he was constant and true—to his enemies he was generous and forgiving.

—By one who knew him well, *Wilmington Daily Journal,* September 11, 1862

Died at the Hospital in Fredericksburg, **Daniel Melvin Monroe**, of Co. K (Bladen Guards), 18th Reg. N.C.T., son of John and Jane M. Monroe of Bladen County, aged 20 years, 6 months. At the commencement of this war he quietly gave up home and its joys and entered the service of his country. He went through the campaign in Virginia unhurt, up to the battle at Fredericksburg. On the 12th Dec. he was wounded in the thigh; amputation was resorted to, but on the 27th he died from its effects. His father reached him a few moments after he died, and brought his body to the home of his childhood, where now it rests.

—*Fayetteville Observer,* January 19, 1863

Colonel Thomas James Purdie, a Bladen County merchant, formerly Captain of Company A before his promotion to Colonel of the 18th Regiment, was killed at the battle of Chancellorsville, May 3. He was shot through the centre of his forehead, at a distance of seventy yards, while gallantly leading his Regiment to the charge. He fought and fell under the eye of his Brigadier (Gen. Lane). The vandals occupied our ground and stripped him of his coat. They were repelled in turn, and his body recovered and brought to the beautiful cemetery of his home, to repose by the ashes of them who were nearest and dearest to him. His funeral was largely attended, and every heart seemed deeply to sorrow at his early doom.

—*Wilmington Daily Journal,* May 25, 1863

Manuel Simmons, a native of Lisbon, Portugal, who died in Richmond on the 13th inst., of thigh wounds received in the battle of Chancellorsville, was a member of the Moore's Creek Rifle Guard, Co. E, 18th Regt. N.C. Troops. We mourn with heartfelt sorrow the loss of our fellow soldier, who though a foreigner, with little to defend save the cause of justice, at the first call of his adopted country sprang to arms and shared in every conflict in which the Regt. had been engaged, from Hanover Court House to Chancellorsville, where he fell mortally wounded within a few yards of the enemies entrenchments.

—*Wilmington Daily Journal,* May 28, 1863

Serg't Joseph McRimmon was from Robeson County, North Carolina, and a member of Co. G, 18th Reg't. He volunteered in April 1861 and fought through every fight the Regiment has been engaged in since its organization up to the bloody fight of Chancellorsville, when he was killed by a ball through the head. He was one of a few young men who never sought distinction; he was content with his humble position. Modest and retiring in his

disposition he was little known beyond his immediate neighborhood. After two years duty in camp and field he applied for a furlough for the first time and returned home a few weeks ago on a short visit and hurrying back before his time expired, he met a soldier's death *with his face to the foe.* He now fills a soldier's grave in Virginia.
—*Fayetteville Observer,* June 8, 1863

Died, in this place, on Sunday evening last, in the twenty-first year of his age, **Henry Potter Nash**, the eldest son of the late Frederick K. Nash. He was second Sergeant of Co. G, 18th Regiment N.C. Troops, and was with his regiment in all its marches and battles, including those of Hanover Court House and around Richmond, in all of which he merited and received the approbation of his superiors. The fatigues and exposures of the successive battles around Richmond resulted in an attack of Typhoid Fever, from which he never recovered. He adds another one to the long list of youthful patriots who have yielded up their lives in defense of their country.
—*Hillsboro Recorder,* June 10, 1863

At Chimborazo Hospital, Richmond, Va., on the 22nd May, of wounds received at the late battle of Chancellorsville, **Francis D. Garriss**, of Co. E, 18th Regiment N.C.T., aged 22 years, 4 months and 22 days. He enlisted in the service at the first breaking out of hostilities and passed through all the battles in which the Regiment engaged from Hanover Court House till the late battle of Chancellorsville. He was wounded in his ankle which required amputation of his foot. After great suffering, he died on the 22d May. Peace to his ashes, and may God comfort his aged parents in this their sad bereavement.
—*Wilmington Daily Journal,* June 20, 1863

John D. McDonald, of Bladen County, Company K, 18th Regiment, was killed in the battle of Fredericksburg, Virginia, on the 13th of December 1862, in the 25th year of his age. He was the son of the late Archibald and Sarah McDonald. He was among the first to volunteer and leave a happy home, his beloved mother, five sisters and three brothers to brave the storm of the bloody battle field. Bravely did he fight through 12 or 13 battles; near Richmond and at Sharpsburg, and bravely did he meet his death on the battle field. The fatal ball struck him in the breast and he was conscious that in a short time his body must be laid in the cold ground. He remarked to his companions, "I am not afraid to die; I have put my trust in God and all I have to request of you is to bury me decently."
—*North Carolina Presbyterian,* June 20, 1863

Killed by a minnie ball, at Chancellorsville, on the 3rd May. **Serg't Ollin Munn**, Co. B, 18th N.C.T. He was in the battle at Hanover Court House, in the battles around Richmond, where he was wounded, and the first fight at Fredericksburg. His *Captain, M. W. Buie,* (47) says, "He acted nobly at Chancellorsville, and being the acting Orderly his conduct came under my eye more readily than that of any other, and I feel called upon to say that not a braver, truer or nobler spirit fell on that sanguinary field."
—*North Carolina Presbyterian,* July 4, 1863

1st Lt. Archibald W. McGregor, Co. F, 18th N.C. Troops, in the Spring of 1861, quit a lucrative business and one that would have exempted him from all military duty, and enlisted in the first Company organized in his native county, Richmond. The Company (Scotch Boys) was gotten up by that most efficient officer, *Capt. Charles Malloy.* (48)

Lt. McGregor served the first year as a Corporal, but at the re-organization of his regiment in 1862, his company promoted him to a Lieutenancy. He was in the battle of Hanover Court House and in the seven days' battles around Richmond, on every occasion conducting himself with the utmost coolness and gallantry.

After the battles of Richmond he was prostrated by a violent attack of typhoid fever, from which his recovery was for a long time doubtful even by his attendant physicians, but after a long and painful illness he fully recovered tolerable health, but had never been restored to that buoyancy and elasticity of former days. He rejoined his regiment at Camp Gregg about the middle of May. Soon afterwards the campaign opened. He was with his company throughout to Gettysburg, and when on the 3d July the Light Division under command of Maj. Gen. Trimble was ordered to charge, he sprang forward. When the brigade had come within musket range, and exposed to a terrible fire of small arms and artillery, the line began slightly to falter, Lt. McGregor rushed out in front of his company and waving his sword in the air, exclaimed, "Hurrah for Dixie! Follow me, boys. Let us show them what we can do"; he proceeded thus but a short distance when a minie ball pierced his left breast near the heart, and he fell and shortly afterwards expired.

He fell in a stranger's land. His remains were consigned to their last resting place by stranger hands. No polished slab, no towering shaft, nor even a simple board, mark the last resting-place of our noble Archie, but his memory will ever live green in the minds of those who knew him.

—*Fayetteville Observer,* **August 24, 1863**

In the memorable charge of Lane's Brigade on the bloody heights of Gettysburg, many brave and noble men were lost, none of whom more gallantly discharged their duty than **Lt. John Walter Stewart** of Company F, 18th N.C.T., who fell at the head of his company on July 3d, 1863. He was 23.

He volunteered in the first company from his native county (Richmond). He served as a Corporal and Sergeant twelve months. He passed through several engagements unhurt, but he received a severe wound at Cedar Mountain, April 9, 1862, which disabled him for a short time. Before he recovered from his wound he hastened to rejoin his companions. Soon after his return, he was appointed 2nd Lieutenant. At Gettysburg the fatal missile ended his bright career. Having fallen into the hands of the enemy, he died in their hospital July 19. Two long months passed before his parents and friends received the painful intelligence of his death. He died far away from home, with no kind sister to dress his wounds, and no affectionate parents to minister to his wants in his last hours.

—*Fayetteville Observer,* **October 26, 1863**

Killed on the bloody field of Fredericksburg, on the 13th of December 1862, **Chester Swindall**, a farmer from Bladen County, N.C., and a member of Co. K, 18th Regiment, N.C. Troops, aged about 28 years. He volunteered in April 1861, one among the first to compose the "Bladen Guards." He was in the Regiment's first engagement at Hanover Court House, Va., in May 1862, where he fought with the utmost coolness. He was taken prisoner at said place and did not join us any more until after the battles around Richmond (he being confined in prison at Fort Delaware and Governor's Island, New York, until he was exchanged in August). He participated in many fights and long marches with the Reg't. He had been a member of the Presbyterian Church for about eight years. He fell while making a charge on the enemy and lies near Fredericksburg in some lonely and sacred spot with several of his comrades in the same grave.

—Archie, *Fayetteville Observer,* **November 9, 1863**

Washington Hall, son of James Hall, Esq. of Bladen County, died 20th April 1864, aged 21 years, 8 months and 13 days. He volunteered in June 1861, and was a member of Co A, 18th Reg't N.C.T. He took part in the many battles and hardships of the 18th Reg't and was captured during the battle of Hanover Court House, May 27, 1862. After exchange he was hospitalized a while then returned to duty. On the retreat from Gettysburg, he was taken prisoner at Falling Waters, Md., July 14th 1863, and was carried to Point Lookout; was paroled, and came home March 12th 1864, where he died of disease.

—*Fayetteville Observer,* June 16, 1864

Mortally wounded near Cold Harbor, Va. on Monday June 6th, 1864 and died the next evening in one of the hospitals in Richmond, **Lieut. James Calvin Buchanan**, of Co. F (Scotch Boys), 18th Reg't N.C.T., in the 28th year of his age. He joined one of the first Volunteer companies formed in Richmond County, more than three years ago. Early this spring, and a few weeks before his death, he with his brother William, now a prisoner, were received as members, by letter, of Laurel Hill Church, with which his parents have been long connected. He was kindly nursed by a friend who reports him as calm and peaceful, and ready to die. His friend also had his body brought home, and it now rests in peace in the family burying ground. He was wounded through the bowels, either by a random shot, or by one of the enemy's sharpshooters. He felt he was mortally wounded; but his faith in Christ sustained him. This makes the second son that family has lost during the present war, and a third is now a prisoner in the hands of the enemy at Elmira, New York. May God sustain them under these sad trials.

—*Fayetteville Observer,* July 14, 1864

On the 12th June 1864, at Moore Hospital, Richmond, Va., of wounds in the back and foot received on the 11th June 1864, at Turkey Ridge, Va., **Corporal David J. Stringfield**, a member of the Moore's Creek Riflemen, Co. E, 18th N.C. Regiment. He was born in New Hanover County in 1839. When war began, he immediately left the peaceful haunts of his boyhood and enrolled in a volunteer company. He was captured during the battle of Hanover Court House and held at Fort Columbus in New York Harbor. He returned to duty after exchange and was wounded at Chancellorsville. Fare well! David! We miss you sadly from our midst.

—*Wilmington Daily Journal,* August 6, 1864

We are pained to learn that **Lieut. Camden Lewis**, of Company B, 18th regiment N.C.T., was killed in the fight at Fussell's Mill below Richmond on the 16th instant. Lieut. Lewis was a native of Bladen County, and in command of one of the companies from that county. He was previously wounded in the arm at Cold Harbor in May. We understand that his remains will be sent home for interment.

—*Wilmington Daily Journal,* August 19, 1864

Died near Petersburg, Va., on the 16th inst., **Lieut. Louis Thomas Alderman**, Company E., 18th Regiment, N.C. Troops. At the commencement of the war he volunteered as a private in the Company to which afterwards he was a Lieutenant, and which he commanded in several engagements with credit to himself. On the 16th inst., while in the discharge of his duties, he was struck in the head by the fatal shot and expired. He had connected himself with the Baptist Church for some time previous to his death.

—*Wilmington Daily Journal,* September 22, 1864

Died, on the 1st day of August 1864, at Point Lookout, Maryland, in the 19th year of his age, **Sergt. Frederick Nash**, Company G. second son of the late Rev. Frederick Nash, a well-known Presbyterian minister in the State. His elder brother, Henry, died a year ago, from disease contracted in the army of the Confederacy, but he died at home, surrounded by friends and relatives and family. During the campaign of 1864 he was captured at Spotsylvania Court House and carried as a prisoner to Point Lookout. Here his feeble frame, worn by the hardships of camp and field, and wasted by disease, became the prey of speedy death. Frederick died in the same good cause and after three years service, among strangers, and a prisoner, without one familiar countenance to look upon or one kind hand to smooth his fevered brow in his struggle with the last great enemy. Both of these noble and gallant boys entered the service as volunteers with the full consent and approbation of their father. One of his commanding officers in announcing the death of Frederick Nash, thus speaks of him: "Among the many gallant dead, none did their duty more faithfully than he did; or were held in higher esteem by his associates in arms for soldierly qualities, strict deportment, and gentlemanly bearing." In his last letter to a dear relative, just before the battle in which he was taken prisoner, he writes: "If I fall in the approaching battle and you are called upon to mourn, do not mourn as one without hope; I have made my peace with Jesus, and am prepared, knowing in whom I trust for whatever may befall me." After he died, his body was consigned to the prison burying ground. His relatives, unwilling that his remains should repose among strangers, had them removed to this place. On the twenty third of April amid a concourse of sympathizing friends and sorrowing relations, his precious dust was laid beside the hallowed ashes of his kindred.

—*Hillsboro Recorder*, **October 19, 1864, and** *Hillsboro Recorder,*
May 9, 1866

At the age of eighty-three years, **Lieut. John O'Neill Frink** died at his home in Taylor, Tex., after a short illness. Interment was in Fairmount Cemetery, with Masonic rights.

A native of North Carolina, born July 9, 1843, he went to Texas in 1871, and then in 1906 located in Tom Green County. He was the postmaster at Taylor, Tex., for ten years, and mayor of the town for four years, and for the last six years held the office of justice of the peace. Always interested in politics, he was widely known as a man of honor and activity. He was commander of the Schuyler Sutton Camp of the Mountain Remnant Brigade, U.C.V., and had taken a leading and stimulating part in the work of the organization. In its annual reunion at Christoval, this Confederate organization passed resolutions expressing the sense of loss by its membership in the passing of this valued member and loved commander.

Lieut. Frink served with the 18th North Carolina Regiment, Company H, under Stonewall Jackson, and took part in the famous drives of the "foot cavalry" of that daring leader. He also served as Color Sergeant of the Regiment. It was his misfortune to be captured at Spotsylvania Court House, and he was one of the six hundred officers placed under fire of the Confederate guns at Charleston, S.C. He had been captured at Chancellorsville in May and released in the same month.

He is survived by four sons and one daughter, also numerous grandchildren and great-grandchildren.

—*Confederate Veteran* **Volume 34, Number 10,**
October 1926

19th Regiment North Carolina Troops (2nd Regiment North Carolina Cavalry)

At Kittrell's Springs, October 19th, of bowel consumption, **Mr. Isaiah Mathews**, of Moore County, a member of Capt. Bryan's cavalry, Company I, leaving a mother, two brothers, a sister and a large circle of friends to mourn their loss. At the age of about 22 years he made a profession of religion. His body was brought home on the 28th inst. for interment by *Mr. John Owens* (49) of Capt. Bryan's company, at his own expenses.
—*Fayetteville Observer,* **October 28, 1861**

Died at the Hospital in Kinston, on the 24th April, from the effects of a wound in the jaw, received the night of the 13th in a skirmish with the enemy, at Gillett's Farm, Onslow County, **Private Love Melvin**, of *Capt. Strange's* (50) Company E, 2d Cavalry, 19th Reg't N.C. Troops. He could not willingly stay at home while the invader was approaching. On the 29th of June last he volunteered, not for 6 or 12 months, but for the period of the war. He was ever ready to perform any duty as a soldier, and was esteemed by all his officers and company. He received the fatal blow as a valiant soldier, with his face to the enemy; and after ten days' suffering, he yielded his spirit to God who gave it. He leaves an aged father and mother, three sisters and a brother, to mourn his departure.
—*Fayetteville Observer,* **May 5, 1862**

At the residence of his father, near Ellisville, Bladen County, on the 16th Dec., in the 27th year of his age, **Corporal Lucian H. Hall**, a member of the "Cumberland Cavalry," Co. D (Capt. Strange), 19th Reg't, 2d N.C. Cavalry. He was a young man of promise for usefulness. But he has, with many others, fallen a victim to that dreadful disease Small Pox.
—*Fayetteville Observer,* **January 5, 1863**

We regret to hear that **Col. Sol Williams**, the gallant young officer who commanded the Second Regiment North Carolina Cavalry, was killed in the engagement on the Upper Rappahannock, Tuesday, June 9, at Brandy Station. Col. Williams was, we believe, a native of Warren County, N.C., and, if we mistake not, a graduate of West Point. He entered the service as Colonel of the 12th Regiment of North Carolina Infantry, and was stationed at Norfolk during the first year of the war, before transferring to the Cavalry. His untimely death is rendered doubly melancholy from the fact that only three weeks ago yesterday he was united in marriage to a young lady of rare personal accomplishments and excellencies, on whom this bereavement will fall with crushing and overwhelming effect. In this community, where she is so widely known and greatly beloved, she has the heartfelt sympathies of all. Colonel Williams was we believe, about 29 years of age, and gave unusual promise of usefulness and distinction in the army.
—**Originally published in the** *Petersburg Express* **and reprinted in the** *North Carolina Argus,* **July 25, 1863**

In Camp Winder Hospital, Va., on the 12th of July 1863, of typhoid fever contracted in camp, **Sergeant Jabez Hunt**, of Co. F, 2nd N.C. Cavalry. He left his home, his aged parents and everything that was near and dear to him, and took up arms in defense of his country. His last visit to his home was in February last, although in feeble health, he returned to his company, in accordance with his furlough, and was soon sent to the Hospital where he lingered for five months until death relieved him of his suffering. His remains were brought home by his brother-in-law and sister, Mr. and Mrs. Gardner, and now quietly rest in the Church grave yard at Friendship in sight of his house, while his spirit has taken up its abode in the bright mansions above.

—*Greensborough Patriot,* **August 27, 1863**

Lt. John C. Baker of Moore County, Co I, 2nd N.C. Cavalry fell on the bloody field of battle, gallantly fighting in defense of his country's rights at Culpepper C. H., October 11, 1863.

—*Fayetteville Observer,* **November 9, 1863**

Corpl. Neill A. Wilkes, Company D, 2nd N.C. Cavalry, fell mortally wounded in the breast and abdomen in the engagement near Jack's Shop, Virginia, Sept. 22d, 1863, and died Sept. 24th, 1863.

—*Fayetteville Observer,* **November 9, 1863**

Lt. James A Cole, Company I, 19th Regiment, who volunteered in Capt. Bryan's Cavalry from Moore and fell at Upperville, Va., while gallantly leading his command in a charge the 21st of June last. He was a brave and patriotic man and leaves an aged mother and brother to mourn their loss. He was a member of Crain Creek Lodge, No. 213.

—*Fayetteville Observer,* **November 16, 1863**

At Orange Court House, Va., 30th Nov, from a wound received in the left lung on the battle field on the Rapidan River, **Randall H. Reese, Captain** of Co. H, 2d N.C. Cavalry, 19th N.C.T., of Northampton County, aged 29. He fell mortally wounded while gallantly leading his men in a charge upon the enemy on Sunday 29th of Nov. 1863.

—*Fayetteville Observer,* **December 28, 1863**

The Adjutant of the 2nd N.C. Cav. Reg't, **Shubal G. Worth** of Asheboro, N.C. was killed in a charge made by that Regiment against the enemy at Winston's, 14 miles west of Richmond, on the 11th day of May during the Spotsylvania Campaign. Ad'j. Worth was a brave and accomplished officer. His gallantry on the field was much noticed and his efficiency was marked. At the commencement of the war "Shub Worth's Company" was well known in the troops of our noble old State.

His constitution was frail, and after nearly two years of the most arduous service he was forced to resign his position and go home. Not satisfied with the service he had rendered his country, Capt. Worth went to volunteer aid to Gen'l. Pettigrew, and again gave out in service.

Gov. Vance, knowing this young officer's ability, appointed him Lt. Col. of the Home Guards of Randolph Co, where his efficient service won for him an enviable fame. Having served in this capacity but a few months, he was tendered the position of Adjutant of the 2d N.C. Cav., by the Col. of that Reg't and again did this patriotic man enter the field of strife. A few short months of service and the accomplished Adjutant of the 2d was no more. He was a member of Balfour Lodge, No. 188, in Asheboro.

—*Fayetteville Observer,* **June 22, 1864**

A letter has been received from a member of the 5th N.C. Cavalry, containing the following:

Col. Clinton N. Andrews of the 2d N.C. Calvary was killed in action on June 23, in a fight on the Southside R. Road." Col. Andrews we believe was a native of Iredell County and was about 34. He was Captain of Co. B, when the Reg't was formed in 1861, under *Col. Spruill*, (51) and later promoted to Major.

—*Fayetteville Observer,* July 7, 1864

Killed in the engagement near White's Tavern, Va., 16th inst., **Capt. Geo. Pettigrew Bryan**, Company G, of the 2d Reg't N.C. Cavalry, aged 22 years, 10 months and 7 days. He fell in defense of his country. We mourn our loss. Capt Bryan was the son of Hon. John H. Bryan of this city. He was a distinguished graduate of the University of N.C. in the year 1860, and from that period till his entrance into the army (early in 1861), he held the position of Tutor at the University. He entered the 2d Cavalry Reg't as 2d Lieut.; shortly thereafter, he was promoted to the 1st Lieutenancy, and as such was severely wounded in the head and captured at Upperville, Va., June 21, 1863, and held prisoner at Point Lookout. Only a short time since, he returned from prison. He was a member of the Episcopal Church. He has been laid beneath the soil where rest many of his companions, and I am left to mourn a comrade's loss.

—*Fayetteville Observer,* August 25, 1864

Killed, on the 15th Aug. at White Oak Swamp, Va., **George W. Rowan**, Co. A, 2d Reg't N.C. Cavalry, and a native of Cherokee County. He died at his post, a true patriot and soldier fighting for his country and his last words were, "Never give back." He was ever gay, cheerful, obliging and lively, and strict in the discharge of his duty. Another soldier has gone, another home deprived of its brightest flower and rendered sad and desolate. He leaves a father, mother, sisters, and brother to mourn his fall. Although he fills a soldier's grave far on Virginia's soil, his friends will never cease to remember him.

—Willie, *Fayetteville Observer,* August 29, 1864

Killed, at White's Tavern, near Richmond, on the 16th of August, in a charge on the enemy's lines, **James A. Holmes**, 2d N.C. Cavalry, in the 23d year of his age. He enlisted in *Capt. Turner*'s (52) Company K of Cavalry, from Orange County, at the commencement of the war, and was ever noted for his gentlemanly deportment, his mild and reserved manners, as well as his coolness and courage in the hour of battle, which won for him the esteem and confidence of his officers and comrades in arms. He was buried where he fell, beneath the sod of a strange land. No lingering spirit hovers around his moldering relics to impart information of his present existence. All is as still as the chambers of eternal silence. Yet he will one day be brought to the family cemetery, and there interred to mingle with his ancestral dust.

—J. A. M., *Hillsboro Recorder,* September 7, 1864

Died from the effects of a wound received near Ground Squirrel Church, Va., on the 11th of May 1864, **Gideon Newel**, of Guilford County, a member of Co. F, 2d N.C. Cavalry, aged about 30 years. During his three years' service he was ever prompt and faithful in the performance of every duty assigned him. He was brave as the bravest, and won the affection of his comrades and the respect of his officers by his generous and noble qualities. He leaves a wife and children, father, mother, brothers and sisters.

—David, *Fayetteville Observer,* October 27, 1864

At his home near this place on the 6th inst., after a protracted illness, **Mr. Albert F. Faucett**, of Orange County, aged about 52 years. His wife having died several years ago, he leaves a large family of young children to mourn their loss, and *their loss* is truly great. The deceased was in every sense of the word, a good and true man, a kind and most affectionate father, an open-hearted neighbor and generous friend.

Mr. Faucett was 1st Lieut. of Co. K, 2nd N.C. Cavalry and no truer or braver soldier ever drew blade in his country's cause. He was desperately wounded in the in the left side when struck by a minie ball in a fight on June 21, 1864, and was transferred to the Invalid Corps in February 1865.

—*Hillsboro Recorder,* **March 15, 1888**

20th Regiment North Carolina Troops

The following members of the Independent Blues, Company H, 10th N.C. Volunteers, [later 20th Regiment North Carolina Troops] have died.

At Fort Caswell, on Sunday evening 22d Sept., of Typhoid fever, **William B. Blackman**, **Orderly Sergeant**, aged about 20 years. He was a native of Johnston County.

Also, at Fort Caswell, on Tuesday evening 24th September, of Typhoid Fever, **Matthew M. Giles**, **private**, also of Johnston County, aged 18 years.

In Sampson County, at home, on Saturday the 27th of September, of Typhoid fever, **William H. Jackson**, **private**, aged 23 years. He worked as a laborer.

Lemon H. Lee, also of Sampson was accidentally killed by a sentinel at Fort Caswell, September 11.

—*Fayetteville Observer, "Fort Johnson, Oct. 8, 1861,"* **October 14, 1861**

Junius G. Evans of the Brunswick Guards, Company G, 10th Regiment N.C. Volunteers, died at Fort Johnson on October 2. He received kind attention from Mr. and Mrs. J. Potter, who lived nearby.

—*Wilmington Daily Journal,* **November 13, 1861**

Ryon Giles, of Johnston County, a member of Company H, 10th Regiment, N.C. Volunteers, died at home October 22 of Typhoid Fever. He was a member of the Masonic Fraternity, Mingo Lodge, No. 206, and was buried with Masonic honors.

—*Wilmington Daily Journal,* **December 21, 1861**

Died in the Hospital, near Fort Johnson, of Pneumonia, on the 28th of December last, **Serg't George W. Johnson**, only child of George and Anna Johnson, of Sampson County, N.C., in the 25th year of his age. He was a Sergeant in *Capt. James A. Faison's* (53) Company I of the 10th N.C. Volunteers. His parents are aged people, and this blow is to them worse than death, for he was the hope and stay of their declining years.

—*Wilmington Daily Journal,* **January 27, 1862**

Killed at Gaines' Mill near Richmond, June 27, **William Henry Smith**, aged 28, Capt. Co C, 20 Reg't N.C.T. Capt. Smith, a resident of Columbus County, was among the first to volunteer, his Company having been called to Fort Johnson at the commencement of the war.

—*Wilmington Daily Journal,* **July 5, 1862**

Killed at Gaines' Mill near Richmond, Va., June 27th, 1862, **Thomas Tate McIntire**, son of David and Sarah P. McIntire, of New Hanover County. At the outbreak of war, he attached himself to the "Confederate Greys," Company E, 20th Regiment N.C.T. Whilst gallantly charging a battery of the enemy he met grim death as a soldier should, and died cheering on his comrades to victory.

—*Wilmington Daily Journal,* **July 5, 1862**

Franklin J. Faison was born in Sampson County, and was for a time a student at West Point. He volunteered at the beginning of the war in the first company which left Sampson. Upon the organization of the 20th Regiment he was elected Lt. Col., and was again unanimously re-elected. Lt. Col. Faison was in the charge on the battery of the enemy on the Mechanicsville Road, Gaines' Mill, on Friday last. He led the charge and was foremost in it. Reckless of danger, with an impulsive nature, he first mounted the principal gun of that strong battery, and while his face glowed with satisfaction, mingled with regret at the groans of the wounded and dying of his regiment, and endeavoring to turn the guns of the battery with his own hands against the flying enemy, he was fatally wounded in the head with a Minnie ball, besides receiving two other wounds.

He was able to walk and was led by one of the 20th Regiment—Frank Ireland—(54) a little distance from the battery, where he was laid down. Mr. Ireland did all he could for his comfort, until Col. Faison said to him, "Frank, I am mortally wounded—I do not fear to die, I have fallen in a glorious cause—now go to your Company, you can do more good there—go now, but return again—you will probably find me dead, take my body home for burial. Take charge of my Sword and deliver it to my wife, and tell her that I died in a good cause, and only regret that I could not see her and my children before I died." The scene of action was then changed, and Ireland returned to Col. Faison and found that he was dead. He was then buried on the battle-field, and there rests as noble a specimen of a christian soldier as the world ever saw.

—*Wilmington Daily Journal,* **July 8, 1862**

John D. Shine of Duplin County was a member of Company E, 20th Regiment, until he was promoted to Color Bearer of the Regiment in June 1862. He fell mortally wounded, while bravely, proudly, bearing the flag of his country over the battle field of Gaines' Mill, June 27. He died at home July 21 and was buried with Masonic honors by Belmont Lodge, No. 108, of Duplin County.

—*Wilmington Daily Journal,* **August 2, 1862**

Died at Chimborazo Hospital, July 12th, 1862, **William Augustus Belcher,** a Private in Company C, 20th Reg't N.C.S.T. He was wounded in the thigh on the 27th June, at the taking of the Battery at Gaines' Mill. He fell on the enemy's side of the Battery, near the spot where his Captain, William Henry Smith, his *First Lieutenant, Arthur N. Jones* (55) and the *2nd Serg't., Calvin H. Meares,* (56) and several Privates were killed, all of them having in the charge penetrated the Battery. He was the youngest son of G. A. Belcher, of Columbus County, N.C., and one of the first to volunteer in the service of his country. He was 20 years of age.

—*Wilmington Daily Journal,* **August 21, 1862**

Killed on the 27th June 1862, in the 23rd year of his age, **Warren W. Newell** of Cabarrus County, N.C. He was a member of Co. A, 20th Regt. and 3rd Brigade N.C.S.T. He fell, during the fight at Gaines' Mill near Richmond, Va., a martyr to the liberty of his country.

As far as known, no one was present to witness his death-struggle, or receive a message to his heart-stricken mother. He was a beloved member of M. Creek Church.
—*North Carolina Presbyterian,* **August 23, 1862**

Wounded at Malvern Hill, July 1, and died on the train, between Weldon and Raleigh, on Tuesday last, **George W. Hinson**, 20th N.C.T., Company A. He was of Stanly County. His remains were interred in Raleigh and his effects deposited at the Peace Institute Hospital in that city.
—*Fayetteville Observer,* **September 29, 1862**

William Avery Draughon and **William Roberson Tew**, both from Sampson County and both members of the Independent Blues, Co. H, 20th Reg't N.C.T., were instantly killed in a most fearful charge upon the enemy's batteries before Richmond at Malvern Hill, July 1. Both were members of Mingo Lodge, No. 206.
—*Fayetteville Observer,* **December 1, 1862**

David L. Wilson, a native of Duplin County, Co. E, 20th Reg't N.C.T., in the 22d year of his age, was wounded in Maryland, September 14, 1862, and captured by the enemy. His right arm was amputated and he was held prisoner at Fort McHenry until he was exchanged in October. He returned home and died on November 10.
—*Fayetteville Observer,* **January 12, 1863**

Died at Howard's Grove Hospital, Richmond, Va., on the 8th of July 1862, of a wound received at the battle of Malvern Hill, July 1st, **William R. White**, aged 21 years, son of Wm. White of Cabarrus County, N.C. He was a member of Co. A, 20th N.C. Regiment. Died at Mt. Jackson, Va., on the 11th of October 1862, **Franklin D. White**, from wounds received at Gaines' Mill, June 27. He was aged 16 years, 8 months, also a son of William White. He was a private in Co. A, 20th N.C. Regiment.
—*North Carolina Presbyterian,* **January 24, 1863**

Died in Gordonsville, Va., September 25th, 1862, of chronic diarrhea, **Lieut. William H. Wallace**, Company A, 20th Reg't. N.C. Troops, aged 24 years and eight months, eldest son of J. O. Wallace of Concord, Cabarrus County. He volunteered at the beginning of the war, endured all the hardships of camp for 8 months and never complained, went through the seven days' fighting at Richmond unhurt, started on the march into Maryland, but his strength failed him and he was left behind. He was not a professor of religion but had been sick so long that we believe he has gone to a better world.
—*North Carolina Presbyterian,* **February 21, 1863**

At the request of the family of Nathan Snead, of Johnston County, who was improperly and unjustly published as a deserter, we publish the following letter from Gen. Iverson, to whose brigade his regiment was attached.—Gen. Iverson, it will be seen, speaks in high terms of young Snead:—

DEAR SIR:—Your letter in relation to your brother, **Nathan Snead**, Company H, who was killed at Sharpsburg, has been received. You state that you wished the report of his being a deserter should be contradicted through the same channel by which it had been published. It is necessary to inform you that a list was called for from the Colonels of regiments, reporting all absentees without leave. They in turn called upon their Captains for lists from the companies. These lists being consolidated were copied at my headquarters, one copy furnished to the Governor, and another to the Sheriffs of our different counties. The object of this was to force up men who, without excuse, were remaining away from their posts. The lists were not intended for publication, nor have I seen them in print or known of their being printed. The names amounted to considerably over a thousand from the brigade.—Errors made by Captains could not, of course, be discovered at this office. I have not seen the communication concerning your brother in the Raleigh *Standard,* nor the resolutions of the students of the University, but while Colonel of the 20th N.C., I knew young Snead, and remarked that he was a soldier of fine promise. I know, also, that he was killed at Sharpsburg while fighting gallantly. It is very much to be regretted that through the carelessness of his company commander, his name should have been sent forward on the list of absentees, and you are at liberty to use this letter in any way you think proper to refute the charge of his having deserted.

Yours respectfully.
ALFRED IVERSON, Brigadier General.
Camp near Fredericksburg, Va., April 9, 1863.

—*Mr. E. D. Snead, North Carolina Standard,* "Justice to the Gallant Dead," May 26, 1863

Fell, in the late battle of Chancellorsville, **Lieut. John J. Wilson**, of Sampson County, in the 25th year of his age. He was a member of Co. F, 20th Regiment N.C. Troops. He was a private in the ranks for several months. Then he was elected 2nd Lieut. and soon afterwards promoted to 1st Lieut. He had borne himself in numerous battles, with unexampled bravery and heroism. In the bloody fights near Richmond, Mechanicsville, Cold Harbor, and Malvern Hill, he was seen in each charge, ever ready to strike a blow for his country and share the fate of his comrades. He was in the fights at South Mountain, Sharpsburg and Fredericksburg, where he was endowed with his usual zeal and courage. He scorned the least semblance of cowardice, and the slightest departure from duty's road, however thorny it may sometimes have been. In the last engagement he was as usual; a face full of hope and a heart glowing with enthusiasm as he marched forward to join in the conflict. He commanded his company with usual coolness, skill and bravery. Through the first day, and in the second, while encouraging his men in the last charge which put the enemy to flight and brought victory to our hands, the swift missile of death entered his heart and he expired without a groan. Thus has fallen one, adding another to the band of martyrs who have bled and died for liberty.

Wilmington Daily Journal, **June 2, 1863**

Died in Concord, on the 6th of Aug., 1863, of chronic diarrhea, **David Long Henderson**, a member of Co. A, 20th Regt., N.C.T., aged 26 years. Though of a very delicate constitution, yet, at the breaking out of the great Revolution of 1861, he patriotically buckled on his armor and shouldered his musket to repel the fierce invader from our sunny soil, and was among the first to rush to the defense of our rights. He served for more than a year, until the fights around Richmond, when his strength failed him, on the 2nd or 3d day of those memorable engagements. He was then carried to a Hospital in Richmond, and after a severe illness, through the attention of kind friends, he so far recovered as to be able to return home. He then went into a gradual decline, until death came to his relief.

North Carolina Presbyterian, **September 5, 1863**

Died in a field hospital, near Gettysburg, Pa., **William H. Herring**, of Sampson County, N.C., Company F, 20th Reg't N.C.T. He left the comforts of home, for the hardships of a camp life, choosing rather to undergo the sufferings of a soldier than to live under a Government of fanaticism and tyranny. He discharged the duties of a soldier with heroism and fortitude. He received a wound in the right breast at the battle of Gettysburg, after which he was captured and carried to the hospital, and lived about two weeks, dying July 20th.

—A friend, *Wilmington Daily Journal,* November 11, 1863

Fell at the battle of Gettysburg, **Lieut. Francis C. Wilson**, of Co. F, 20th Reg't N.C.T., in the 20th year of his age. He volunteered as a private in the ranks of the 2nd Company (Holmes Riflemen) from Sampson, his native county, feeling it the duty of young and unmarried men to enlist. In the battles around Richmond at Gaines' Mill, he received a wound in the foot that disqualified him for service for a considerable time. Having returned to his command soon after the battle of Fredericksburg, he was unanimously elected to the 2nd Lieutenancy of his company, and being exposed to very severe weather and privations, he was prostrated by Chronic Rheumatism with Pneumonia, the attack being so powerful as to prevent his walking. At the time of the enemy's advance at Chancellorsville, he was carried to a private house. Here the most affecting and trying circumstances were brought to bear upon him in this feeble state of health. Imagine his condition at this time, the Yankees crossing the Rappahannock, his division ordered to march, him sent to a private house, and on the 3d day of the fight at Chancellorsville information being carried to him that his brother, *Lieut. John J. Wilson*, (56) was instantly killed, that the 3rd Lieutenant while trying to secure the valuables of his brother, was severely wounded and his Captain at home sick. Lieut. Wilson soon recovered from this attack so as to take command of his company, and until his Captain returned, the duties devolving upon him as the only commissioned officer were very laborious, yet he never faltered but marched with his company to Pennsylvania. In the bloody battle at Gettysburg on the first day his Captain was wounded and the command falling on him, soon exposed him to the deadly aim of the enemy and the fate of his brother. Francis was a member of Mingo Lodge, No. 206. We cannot refrain from mourning the loss of those gallant and heroic young officers, whose loyalty as privates and skill in command were tried on the bloody field and found to be of the highest order. Each fell while leading the same command, though at different times and places. Severely indeed has the blow fallen on his doting relatives and friends.

—*Wilmington Daily Journal,* January 22, 1864

Lines in memory of **James Thomas Watson**, Company C, who was killed in the memorable battles around Richmond, at Gaines' Mill, on the 27th June 1862, and **Lt. Giles H. Watson**, Company C, later Captain of Company E, who was killed in the late battle (near Locust Grove, Va.), 6th May 1864, both belonging to the 20th N.C. Reg't:

> My bothers are dead—their sparkling eyes
>   Have lost their lustre now;—
> Death, cold and dreadful, passed them by
>   And smote their blooming brows.
>
> My brothers, my brothers! how can it be,
>   That I must give thee up?
> To think that I, so far from thee,
>   Must drink that bitter cup.
>
> My brothers in blooming youth are dead!
>   No sister by their side
> To watch or ease their aching head—
>   Thus all alone, they died.

> My brothers are dead, their loss I mourn:
> And sorrow fills my breast—
> Their bodies fill an earthly tomb;
> I trust their soul's at rest.

—Sister Bettie, Fair Bluff, N.C., *Fayetteville Observer,*
June 27, 1864

In recording the death of a friend and brother in arms with whom we have been associated from childhood by the strongest ties of friendship, our hearts and hands tremble with sorrowful emotion. We are reminded by every word we pen, that we are paying the last tribute of respect to one whose hand we shall never grasp again, whose voice shall never be heard, and whom we shall meet no more on earth. Such are our feelings when we record the death of our friend **Serg't. James H. Davis**, who volunteered in Company H, 20th N.C. Infantry, on the 10th of May 1861, and took an active part in the battles around Richmond, South Mountain, Sharpsburg, 1st Fredericksburg, Chancellorsville and Gettysburg, where he was instantly killed on the 1st day of July 1863. He was a good soldier and a sincere friend to his country's cause; was at his post at all times, and always did his duty without a murmur. He was beloved by all who knew him, especially his comrades in the army.

May the ashes of this noble young man repose in peace.

—Helenus, *Fayetteville Observer,* July 25, 1864

Ransom G. Hawley, son of John Hawley of Sampson County, N.C. volunteered May 2d, 1861, in Co H, 20th Reg't N.C.T. He was captured by the enemy in the Wilderness on May 12th 1864, and carried to Point Lookout, where sickness and death took him, on July 14th 1864, from all hardships, trials, privations, dangers and suffering. He was a very consistent member of the Baptist church and was much beloved as a member of the church and neighbor. He was an affectionate son and kind brother.

—*Fayetteville Observer,* October 27, 1864

Died suddenly of disease, 21st Oct, 1864, near Unionville, Robeson County, **John P. Ashley**, only son of W. H. Ashley, aged 19 years 3 months and 4 days. He leaves a kind mother, and two affectionate sisters to mourn their loss. He was one of the first to bid adieu to home and loved ones in defense of his country. He was a member of Co. C, 20th Reg't N.C.T. He fought bravely with his regiment through the campaign of Va. until he was wounded and taken prisoner at Gettysburg. He remained in a Yankee prison (Fort Delaware and Point Lookout) fifteen months before exchange—was at home but two short weeks when God called his spirit to a better land.

—Cousin, *Fayetteville Observer,* October 27, 1864

It is not often our duty to record the fact, that a mother, who, with Spartan devotion, gave up every son, has been bereaved of all. Bur in the present notice we behold three of the same family successively falling in the service of their country, **Messrs. Warren, Hope**, and **Harris Newell**, sons of Mrs. Elizabeth Newell, all of Mecklenburg County, N.C. **Warren Newell** was a member of Co. A, 20th Reg. N.C.T., and is spoken of in letters from his officers in the highest terms of commendation. He performed his duty without a murmur. He was at his post on all occasions, and a braver soldier cannot be found. On the first day's fight at Mechanicsville, the company was much exposed to the fire of artillery, through which he proceeded in so cool and decided a manner as to satisfy all to his courage. On the second day the enemy were repulsed, and retreated to Cold Harbor. Our young friend, sick and previously excused by the surgeon, rallied his strength and joined his comrades as they went into battle. A charge being made by our men, he was struck in the forehead by a rifle-ball, fell with his face to the enemy and died without a struggle on the 27th of June 1862, in the 23rd year of his age. He is now at rest. The Captain eulogizes his noble and gallant conduct, and assures his friends that had he lived he should have been promoted.

Hopie Newell was destined to die in the field hospital, on the morning that he was 17 years old. Every one acquainted with him pronounces him to have been a very pleasant and amiable young man. So far as known he had not an enemy in the camp. He was greatly esteemed and beloved by all.

The third and last, **Mr. Harris Newell**, was a member of Co. A, 11th Reg. N.C.T., and died in Winder Hospital, on the 27th of August 1864, in the 23rd year of his age. What has been remarked of the first, is equally true of this one, with respect to his noble and gallant conduct as a soldier. He participated in the battles of White Hall, Gettysburg, Bristow Station, Wilderness, Hanover Junction, and Cold Harbor; and in all these engagements, he acted in the most patriotic and courageous manner.

—*North Carolina Presbyterian,* **January 25, 1865**

Mr. James Cedric Killett died at his home at Haw River about 2 o'clock Tuesday morning, aged about 73 years. He was a Confederate veteran and was a member of Co. E, 20th Reg., N.C. State Troops. He was wounded at Gaines' Mill, June 27, 1862, and again at Chancellorsville in May 1863. This latter wound caused his discharge in July 1863, as he lost his middle finger and the use of his hand. His remains were laid to rest in Linwood Cemetery at this place yesterday afternoon with Masonic honors.

—*Alamance Gleaner,* **February 24, 1910**

Last Thursday afternoon about two o'clock **Capt. James W. Wright** died in his room at the Clinton Hotel. His health had been failing for only a short time. A few weeks ago he went to Seven Springs hoping to recuperate and after his return continued to decline very rapidly, but he was on the streets most every day until just a few days before he died and very few people in town knew that he was dangerously ill. Deceased was 75 years of age and a member of the Holiness Church. He was a son of Isaac Wright and a grandson of John Wright, a patriot of the Revolutionary War, who on his return from the war beat his sword into ploughshares and began to clear and cultivate his farm in McDaniels Township. Deceased had only one brother, the late John C. Wright of Coharie, and three sisters, Mrs. Haywood Boykin, of Lisbon, Mrs. John Murphy, of Pender county, and Mrs. Dr. Videl, of Florida, all of whom preceded him to the grave many years ago.

Deceased was a brave fearless Confederate soldier, and in 1861 at the beginning of the Civil War he volunteered in Company F. 20th North Carolina Regiment and after one year of service as a private he was elected Captain of his company, which position he held until he was captured. He was wounded in the seven days fight around Richmond at Gaines' Mill and also in that famous charge at Gettysburg. He was captured at Rappahannock Station, Virginia at the end of October 1863. First confined in Washington D.C., he was then transferred to Johnson's Island, Ohio and held there until his release in June 1865. After the surrender he returned home and soon married Miss Mary A. Boykin, daughter of the late Loftin Boykin, to this union was born two children, Mrs. J. D. Johnson, of Garland, and Mr. Thos. L. Wright, a rising young attorney of Ardmore, Okla. His married life was short, his wife died many years ago when he was a young man, yet he never married again. About

10 years ago he quit farming and came to Clinton, Sampson County, and was appointed carrier on R.F.D. No. 1. He was the first R.F.D. carrier appointed in Sampson County and rendered efficient service for about ten years. Deceased was a devout Christian and is gone to be with Him whom he served.

The funeral was conducted from the hotel by the Rev. T. M. Lee and the remains were laid to rest in the Clinton Cemetery by the side of his wife. The pallbearers were: Messrs. C. C. Corbett, A. F. Johnson, Walter Draughon, V. J. McArthur, John A. Beaman and J. A. Ferrell. The floral offering was very profuse and beautiful. THE NEWS DISPATCH sympathizes with the bereaved ones.

—*The News Dispatch,* **October 5, 1911**

Vann J. McArthur, born Feb 19, 1846, departed March 12, 1914, married Miss Catherine Boney, daughter of Mr. Wright and Linda Boney, June 9, 1864. To them were born seven children: Mrs. A. D. Williamson, of Beulah, Mrs. Whitfield Tart of Clinton, Mrs. Aubine Lewis of Faison, Mrs. O. C. Williams of Newton Grove, Messrs. W. O. of Rocky Mount, J. A. of Clinton, and O. P. of Raleigh. All of whom survive him. Of the seventeen grandchildren that have blessed the homes of his children all save one, Ruth Williamson, a sweet little girl of nine years old, who died Jan. 20, 1908, survive him. At the age of 14 he joined the Baptist Church at Mt. Gilead and was an earnest member until about thirty years ago when he united with the Universalist Church at Red Springs. Making his home in Clinton a few years ago, he became a leading factor in the establishment of his church home in Clinton and was a charter member of the Clinton Church. In his own church he held many positions of honor and trust, and was for two terms President of the Universalist State Convention. His very last public act, feeling that death was at hand, he made a deed to his church conveying valuable property as site for parsonage. For several terms he was Chairman of the Board of County Commissioners, and for a number of years he had been Post Master at Clinton, which position he held at the time of his departure.

In the Civil War he joined Company F, 20th N.C. Regiment and served two years. Here he received two painful wounds, one in each arm. He received the first one at the battle of Gaines' Mill in 1862. He was wounded again at Fox's Gap, Maryland in September 1862, resulting in the amputation of his left hand. He was discharged from duty in February 1863. Thus handicapped he fought the battles of life and, assisted by his faithful companion, reared a family whose lives will do honor to his.

—**A friend,** *The News Dispatch,* **March 26, 1914**

The passing of **Capt. David J. Broadhurst**, whose death occurred at his home in Goldsboro, N.C., on August 20, removes a beloved character from the daily activities of that community, with which he had been intimately associated for more than a generation. He was a native of Wayne County, of an old-line family running back to colonial days, and was seventy-two years of age on the first day of last March, his beloved wife having the same birth month and year. Their golden wedding anniversary was celebrated last January, the happy occasion being a family reunion with "open house" to their friends in old-time Southern hospitality.

At the outbreak of the War Between the States, David Broadhurst, at the age of seventeen, volunteered in Company K, 20th North Carolina, of Duplin County, of which he subsequently became captain, serving with such bravery that he was especially mentioned for his gallantry by President Davis. Captain was with Jackson at Chancellorsville and left his good right arm on that memorable field. Going home after his crucial hospital experience, he faced the future fearlessly and determinedly as he had faced the foe in battle, and he was a powerful force in the work of rehabilitating that section and leading his people out from the ordeal of Reconstruction, and they accorded him at all times their confidence, their gratitude, and their loyalty.

On January 5, 1866, he married Miss Martha J. Baker, daughter of the late Col. Jesse J. Baker, and to this union ten children were born, eight of whom, with their revered mother, survive him. These are: Mrs. John Farrior, of Portland, Oregon; R. S. Broadhurst, of Americus, Ga.; J. J. and F. K. Broadhurst, of Smithfield; Mrs. Lila B. Winkleman, of Goldsboro; Edgar Broadhurst, of Greensboro; Capt. Hugh H. Broadhurst, of the 8th Cavalry, Fort Bliss, Tex.; and Charles S. Broadhurst, of Goldsboro.

—*Confederate Veteran*, Volume 24, Number 11, November 1916

21st Regiment North Carolina Troops

We learn by a letter received by a friend in this City, that there is much sickness in the 11th, *Col. William Kirkland*'s (57) Regiment, [later 21st Regiment North Carolina Troops]. The regiment is encamped eight miles west of Manassas Railroad. The diseases were for the most part contracted on Bull Run. *Lt. Col. James M. Leach,* (58) the Surgeons, and the Chaplain have been sent off for treatment, all of them being sick. **Capt. John H. Boyd**, Company L, is dead. He bravely filled his position during the memorable day of the 21st July, on the Manassas Plains.

—*North Carolina Standard,* September 4, 1861

Died of typhoid fever on the 6th of September, at Camp Hardee, near Manassas, **Robert D. Herring**, of Surry County, N.C. When there was a call for Volunteers, he willingly stepped forward in defense of his country, and joined *Capt. Bazillia Graves*' (59) Company C, 11th Regiment N.C. Volunteers. He has left an aged father and mother, brothers and sisters to mourn. His remains were brought home and buried at his father's.

—*North Carolina Standard,* October 5, 1861

Died in Winchester, Va., Hospital, 9th June, **Carlos W. Miller**, of Forsyth County, of Co. D, 21st Reg't. He was about 19 years of age, and participated in the fight at Manassas Junction, and afterwards was attached to Jackson's Division and was in all the fights in the Valley of Va., up to the great contest at Winchester.

—*Fayetteville Observer,* September 1, 1862

Died in hospital at Charlottesville, 13th July, from the effects of a wound received in battle at Cross Keys, Virginia, **John A. Hester**, Company D, aged about 23 years, of Forsyth County.

—*Fayetteville Observer,* September 22, 1862

Killed at 2nd Manassas, 28th August, **George C. Hartman**, of Co. F, 21st Reg't, about 28 years of age. He was in the first fight at Manassas and then in Jackson's Division, was in all the fights in the Valley of Virginia and on the Peninsula up to the great contest at Second Manassas, where he was stricken down by a ball through his head. He was of Stokes County.

—*Fayetteville Observer,* October 6, 1862

Through the politeness of a friend, we are permitted to lay before our readers the following interesting letter from Brig. Gen. Trimble, to the father of the lamented **Lt. Col. Saunders F. Fulton**, of this State, who fell recently gallantly bearing the flag of his regiment. Such a tribute from the pen of his commander will be gratifying to his friends:—

Samuel Fulton, Stokes County, N.C.:   Front Royal, Va., Oct. 1, 1862

DEAR SIR:—The names of those who nobly die for their country have ever lived in a people's grateful memory. He who falls in battle, inscribes his name upon the records of his country's glory in characters which can never perish while freedom lives. Such a man was Lieut. Col. Fulton, of North Carolina. At an early period he entered the army, and joined the 21st North Carolina Regiment, in which, by promotion, he had obtained the rank of Lt. Col. His regiment was attached to the brigade commanded by me, and brought into every action which took place in Northern Virginia, from the battle of Winchester on the 28th of May, to that of Manassas on the 28th of August—including all the actions near Richmond—that is to say in all Jackson's battles. I, therefore, who knew him well, can speak from personal knowledge of his merits.

He mingled in a remarkable degree, kindness and civility with discipline and military duties. He was the favorite of every soldier. His merits were exhibited without pretension; and his courage, the chief element of his character, shown without bravado, and always surpassed the expectations of his friends. In many charges against the enemy, the battle flag was seen in his hands leading the regiment to victory. His death wounds were received while thus bearing the colors in the charge at Manassas, on the 28th of August. He expired the next day with the same flag waving over him, which he had borne in triumph against the foe.

I have felt constrained my dear sir, to offer this faint tribute of respect to the virtues and gallantry of your son, who I considered one of the most valuable officers of my brigade, and whose honorable and gentlemanly deportment gained my warmest esteem. Accept, sir, my sincere and deepest sympathy in the distress you and your family must feel for the loss of such a son. May this testimony to the merits and manner of his death assuage, in some degree, the pangs of those who knew him and loved him well. His State should be proud of his name, and ever cherish his memory, and her sons should now and hereafter emulate his virtues and patriotism. I write this from a sick bed, where I am suffering from a wound, or I should write more at length.

I am, sir, respectfully your obedient servant,
    J. R. TRIMBLE,
    Brig. Gen'l. 7th Brigade.
—*Greensborough Patriot,* **October 23, 1862**

Died.—At Ferguson Hospital, Lynchburg, Va., December the 5th, **Samuel M. Williams**, of Company L, 21st Regiment North Carolina from Stokes County. He was taken sick at Gordonsville, and sent to Richmond to the Hospital where he was sick for several weeks and recovered as he thought, and went to his Regiment where he was but a short time and when he was taken sick with pneumonia sent to the above named place and died in his 21st year. He was a citizen of Stokes County, N.C.

—*Greensborough Patriot,* **March 19, 1863**

Private Philemon J. Leinback of Forsyth County, of the 21st N.C. Regiment, Company D, fell at the battle of Williamsport, Md., on the 6th or 7th of July, while defending the wagon trains during the retreat from Gettysburg. He was the first who volunteered in the Pfafftown District, and left home at the beginning of the war; he stood the balls and shelling in ten severely contested battles, and came out unhurt, and about 12 months ago he was detailed as Brigade harness maker; and when coming back from Pennsylvania, the enemy attacked the wagon trains, where he sacrificed his life. The writer of this was told by a soldier from the army, that a few minutes before he fell, he told his companions that he would die before he would surrender anything in his care.

He left home on the 11th day of June 1861, and was not permitted to see home any more. A recent letter from a soldier in the army states, that he was a noble soldier, and ever at his post where his duty called him. His age was 23 years and nine months.

—*People's Press,* November 6, 1863

Died at Guinea Station of smallpox, on the 27th May 1863, **Daniel W. Reynolds**, of Co. M, 21st N.C.T., in the 27th year of his age. He has left an affectionate wife and one child to mourn their irreparable loss.

—*Greensborough Patriot,* February 11, 1864

Slowly, from amidst the hoarse roar of the battle and the sulphurous canopy which shrouds the ensanguined field in Virginia, come tidings which fill many a Southern home with deep and unutterable grief. Though the shouts of victory which electrify the country can never reach the dull cold ear of the brave dead who are sleeping their last sleep upon the field which their valor helped to win, yet the paeans of triumph may serve to pour a balm into the stricken hearts, grieving for the friends who return no more.

Among those whom our community may justly mourn, is the lamented **Capt. Samuel C. James**, Company L, who fell pierced by a stray bullet, after the repulse of the enemy at Drury's Bluff, on the morning of the 16th inst., while ministering to the wants of a fallen comrade.

—A friend, *People's Press,* May 26, 1864

Killed in battle, on the 18th of April 1864, while charging the enemy in the town of Plymouth, N.C., **Corp. James G. Wilkinson**, of Charlotte, a member of company L. 21st N.C. Regiment, aged 39 years. He was for many years a consistent member of the Presbyterian Church. For three long years he has fought against those who have waged a relentless war against an unoffending people. Thus a mother's last offering on the altar of her country, and a widowed wife's all of earth has been swept away by one fell stroke. His brother **Neill**, Company B, 53rd Regiment sleeps on the bloody field of Gettysburg, where he fell July 3, and James on the now classic banks of the Roanoke where the hands of veteran comrades have kindly laid him.

—Pastor, *North Carolina Presbyterian,* July 6, 1864

The Richmond Enquirer makes the following interesting extract from a letter written by a gentleman at Gordonsville to the editor:—

Private Wm. Sprinkle, (60) of Co. D, 21st N.C.T. (my old regiment), reached here yesterday from the Valley, with a severe wound in the left shoulder, received in the battle of Cedar Creek on the 19th inst. He informs me that Gordon was the moving spirit of the occasion, and had he been left unmolested by Gen. Early to carry out his plans to the end, no disgrace would have befallen our arms. He also gives me the sad intelligence of the death upon the battle field of **Major William J. Pfohl**, commanding 21st N.C. Troops. This gallant young soldier was shot through the thighs, while leading his regiment into the thickest of the fight, and, before the ambulance corps could carry him out of further danger, a shell struck his head, scattering it to pieces, and, of course, killing him instantly. Maj. Pfohl was a native of Salem, N.C., and joined the army on the same day as myself, April 16th, 1861. Upon the organization of our company, the Forsyth Rifles, he was elected its orderly sergeant, and, by his gallant conduct, equable temperament, and urbanity of manner, gained the esteem of all in the regiment, until, rising step by step, he became its Major. For two long years he followed the immortal Stonewall Jackson; during that period participating in the famous Valley and Richmond campaigns; the campaign against Pope, embracing the battles of Cedar Run and second Manassas; the first invasion of Maryland, with the siege and capture of Harper's Ferry and the sanguinary engagement of Sharpsburg; the bloody battles of Fredericksburg and Chancellorsville, and no harm befell him until at the bloody battle of Gettysburg, Pa., he received a wound which temporarily disabled him. Very speedily, however, he rejoined his command, and again shared with the dangers at Plymouth, N.C., Drury's Bluff and Cold Harbor, Va.; participating with Gen. Early in every engagement from Richmond to Lynchburg, Va., to the very gates of Washington. More recently he was engaged at Winchester at Fisher's Hill, and finally at Cedar Creek, where he fell a martyr to the cause of Liberty.

His death removes another of the little band that survives of the original 87 members that composed the Forsyth Rifles. Death has been busy with them in every form, and now there are but six left of those who formed the company when it first left North Carolina. Eighty-one fill soldier's graves.

He was interred in the Presbyterian church-yard at Strasburg, Va.

—Fayetteville Observer, **November 3, 1864 and** *People's Press,*
November 24, 1864

Vincent W. Haizlip, whose death occurred on May 19, 1914, was born in Pittsylvania County, Va., January 7, 1836. At the outbreak of the War Between the States he was in the prime of young manhood, with a wife and two children. In May 1861, he enlisted in Company G, 21st North Carolina Troops, and served in all the principal campaigns and engagements in which the Army of Northern Virginia took part up to the second battle of Manassas, where he was twice wounded. From a private he rose to a first lieutenant and was commanding his company when he fell severely wounded in the left leg. At the same time fell also his Major, Saunders Fulton. He was off duty for about a year on account of his wounds, but again entered the service in 1863 as a member of Company H, 2d North Carolina Cavalry, commanded by William Henry Lee, son of Gen. R. E. Lee, and served as an officer in this command until the surrender. At the close of the war he returned to his desolated home. Like many another, broken in fortune, he turned his footsteps to the undeveloped West. With his wife and children he began life anew in Illinois. Success crowned his honest efforts, but there were few veterans of the Stars and Bars in that State. After a residence of seven years, he moved to Texas in 1873 and located in Grayson County, where he had resided continuously since. He was married four times. The twelve children of the first three wives survive him, with the last wife, who was faithful and devoted in his long illness.

—Confederate Veteran **Volume 22, Number 7, July 1914**

22nd Regiment North Carolina Troops

Died in Richmond, on the 19th June, of typhoid fever, **Alpheus Adolphus Ross**, aged about 21 years, a member of Capt. C. C. Cole's Guilford County Company E.

—Fayetteville Observer, **July 7, 1862**

Died at Camp Winder Hospital, Richmond, 15th June, of typhoid fever, **Alpheus F. Sapp**, in the 20th year of his age, member of *Capt. Harper Evans Charles'* (61) Company E, 22d Regiment.

—*Fayetteville Observer,* **July 14, 1862**

Died in the hospital at Richmond, July 15th, **John Watson Yates**, from a wound received in the battle at Mechanicsville, June 26; a native of Guilford, in Capt. C. C. Cole's Co. E.

—*Fayetteville Observer,* **August 4, 1862**

In memory of my oldest son, **Lieut. Eli H. Winningham**, of Company I, 22d Reg't N.C. State Troops. At his country's call he left school and volunteered in the first company from Randolph County; he discharged his duties faithfully for twelve months, went through the battle of Seven Pines unharmed, but through fatigue he was attacked with bilious fever and putrid sore throat, and died at Richmond, Va., July 17th, aged 22 years and 18 days. He was a dutiful son, a professor of religion. He said to the Doctor you must not think I am afraid to die, for I left home a Christian, and have tried to remain one in the camp. His death is a great loss to Ma, sister and brother, but we hope our loss is his eternal gain.

> But now my son is gone,
> To him there is no morrow,
> Though time with us rolls on,
> He's free from pain and sorrow.
> Beloved by those he left behind,
> No foe he had at home,
> He was ever gentle, good and kind,
> But the Lord bid him come.
> Then fare thee well, loved one,
> Ofttimes we'll think of thee,
> And when we're called from time to come,
> Oh may we follow thee.

—Ma, *Fayetteville Observer,* **September 8, 1862**

Died of Typhoid fever, Sept. 30th, 1862, at the residence of Mr. Tom Flemming, in Loudoun County, Va., **Lieut. James Logan Greenlee**, Company K, in the 22d year of his age. At the close of the first session of Davidson College, after the call made by Lincoln, he came home, and although in bad health, resolved to volunteer in defense of his country. A company then being raised by his father, he was elected First Lieutenant; but the company afterwards disbanding he went as a private to Capt. Charles H. Burgin's company, and was in the battles of Mechanicsville, Gaines' Mill, the Monday evening fight below Richmond, Cedar Run, and two days at Second Manassas, in all of which he was found a soldier bravely standing to his Forty First, being made Orderly Sergeant, and then promoted to a Lieutenancy for gallant conduct on the battle field.

At the battle of Manassas, being in command of his Company, he was, in making a charge, struck with a shell on the side of his head. Rising from the fall, he called to his men, "I am not killed; on to the charge," and he gallantly led on. This was his second wound. I conversed with his captain and many others who were acquainted with him on the battlefield, all testify to the fact that none was more loved by the officers or privates. Improving, but still weak and ill, he bid fair to join his company but the Yankees coming on him, he got out of bed and walked three miles and soon died. His servant Stephen by intrigues made his escape out of the hands of the Yankees and followed him. God in his mercy led him to the house of kind ones to minister to his dying wants.

—S. W. M., *North Carolina Presbyterian,* September 8, 1862

Died—At St. Charles Hospital, Richmond, on the 1st of December, of chronic diarrhea **Levi P. Hardister**, a member of Company L, 22nd Regiment, N.C.T., aged 25 years. He went through the great battles around Richmond unhurt; but soon after, disease seized upon his system, from which he never recovered. He was among the brave and noble boys that left "Oak Grove" settlement, in Randolph County, 18 months ago, to go in defense of his country's noble cause. He was one of three brothers who enlisted for the rights of the South; and while his remains lie in Oakwood Cemetery, one other brother lies numbered with the dead at Petersburg, and the other brother in arms is left alone, with no kind brother near,

> Should he fall in battle,
> To bear him from the field.

He has left a kind father, a loving and heart-stricken mother, brothers and a sister to mourn their loss.

—*Greensborough Patriot,* December 18, 1862

Died recently of disease in camp near Richmond, **Leander C. Nichols**, of the 22d Reg't., Company B, from McDowell County, aged 23. **John P. Goforth**, aged 21, Company K, also from McDowell County, was killed at Shepherdstown, Va., September 20, a few days after the battle at Sharpsburg.

—*Fayetteville Observer,* January 12, 1863

Killed on the battle field near Fredericksburg on the 13th of December 1862, **Sergeant Whit J. Luther**. He was a native of Randolph County, N.C., aged 26 years and 5 months, and a son of Martin & Sarah Luther. He was a member of Co L, 22d Regiment N.C. Troops. He participated in twelve regular fought battles, and at the battle of Cedar Run, the other officers being absent, he was in command of Co. L and led his brother soldiers nobly through, acting the part of a brave and noble soldier. It was hard for him to be killed after performing so many kind duties, and had made his escape through so many battles, and had done so much for the cause of the South, and then being hit by a random shell which killed him instantly. His remains were taken up after having been interred a month near Fredericksburg and brought to his native home in N.C., and reinterred side by side with his little niece in the church yard at Oak Grove. He has left a father and mother, a brother in Co L, *Private Josiah Luther,* (62) one brother at Wilmington, three sisters and many friends to lament his early death.

—Parthena L., *Greensborough Patriot,* February 5, 1863

F. Marion Hooper, of *Capt. J. A. Hooper's* (63) Company, E, 22nd N.C.T., was killed at Chancellorsville, Va., while bearing dispatches for Gen. Pender. The ball piercing his cheek and passing directly through his head killed him instantly. He was at the battle of Frayser's Farm, June 30, 1862, and had been wounded in both legs.

—*Greensborough Patriot,* May 28, 1863

Killed—At Chancellorsville, in the battle of the 3d of May, **Sergeant Josiah Presnell** of Co. I, 22d Regt. N.C.T., aged 26 years. He fell pierced with six minie balls, within a short distance of the enemy's line, having passed unharmed through 14 previous battles. He leaves

a young and interesting wife to mourn his loss, while all who knew him feel bereft of a generous friend. He was buried on the field of victory. He was a farmer in Randolph County.
—*Greensborough Patriot,* **June 11, 1863**

It is with heartfelt sorrow that I announce to his numerous friends and relatives the death of my esteemed brother-in-law, **Robert L. Phillips**, of my company. I offer the following lines as a feeble Tribute to his memory, and if possible offer some consolation to his distressed relatives.

He fell while bravely charging the enemy in his breastworks at "Wilderness Swamp," near Fredericksburg, Va., on Sunday, May 3d, 1863. He faltered not, but fought bravely till he fell, having his left leg broken by a minnie ball. He said he called to me when he fell, but I was knocked down by a shell probably about the same, and failed to hear him. Shortly after he fell, he was struck I suppose by a shell, shattering both thighs.—I stayed with him, and had every attention paid him that I could employ, until he was removed to Richmond on the Wednesday following, at which place he died on Saturday the 9th of May.

Robert entered the service last March as a "volunteer conscript." He remained at home with his loving wife, as long as he could consistently with honor. In his short stay with us he endeared himself to all his comrades by his kind deportment. But he is gone, forever gone, from this world of trouble and trials, turmoil and strife, we humbly hope to a land where peace and happiness eternal reigns.
—Lieut. M. T. Mitchell, (64), Co. "H," 22d,
Daily Bulletin, **June 19, 1863**

John R. Frazier fell in the late battle at Fredericksburg on May 3. This noble youth, having arrived at the age of 18 a few months before the battle, and when called, though afflicted with rheumatism to lameness, responded and went to his country's service. He joined Co. E, 22d Regiment, N.C. Troops. From his short stay with his comrades in the army, there can be but little said of his military capacities, but having been acquainted with him ever since his early school boy days, I can add, that he was one among the first of his classmates.
—*Greensborough Patriot,* **July 16, 1863**

Killed in the battle of Gettysburg, July 1st, 1863, **Lieut. John H. Palmer**, of the 22d Reg't N.C.T., Company I, in the 24th year of his age. He was a native of Randolph County, and among the first to volunteer in defense of his beloved country. He had been wounded at the battle of Chancellorsville. Thus has fallen one so young, and promising, in the opening bud of manhood. He died a true patriot and soldier, fighting the enemies of his country and home.
—*Fayetteville Observer,* **September 14, 1863**

Lt. Col. Christopher Columbus Cole, 22d N.C. Regiment, perished May 3d, 1863, at the hard earned and glorious victory of Chancellorsville. He was formerly Captain of Company E of this Regiment. He was struck in the breast by a ball, and killed instantly. Col. Cole was a native of Greensborough, and was favorably known for several years as Editor of the *Times.*
—*Greensborough Patriot,* **September 17, 1863**

Corporal Wesley C. Siler of Randolph County, left his home and dear friends at an early period of this unholy war, and went to the tented field to give his time and labor to defend the rights of his country. He was a member Company E, 22d N.C. Regiment.

His health generally was very feeble, but he was ever ready to do what was his duty;

and often went on the march when his very countenance told plainly that nothing but the purest of motives kept him with his company; he would often, ere the day's march ended, be forced to fall beside the road and remain there for hours to have his strength renewed; this done he would close up with his company again.

He most bravely followed his commanders in charging the enemy from their many strongholds, from the battle at Seven Pines to that terrible contest at Gettysburg, where he was mortally wounded, and expired in a few hours.

—*Greensborough Patriot,* September 17, 1863

Killed at Gettysburg, **Corp'l. Hezekiah D. Perry**, Co. L, 22d Reg't N.C.T., of Randolph County. He had been wounded in the eye at the battle of Fredericksburg and furloughed for several months. On July 3, 1863, he received the fatal blow far from his father, mother, brothers and sisters, who ofttimes think of him while he is moldering in the grave in the State of Pennsylvania, with no kind father or mother to place the tomb-stone at his head and inscribe thereupon the epitaph of their departed son.

—*Fayetteville Observer,* September 21, 1863

Lt. Isaiah S. Robbins, aged 25, Company I, 22d Regiment, fell in the bloody battle of Gettysburg, in a distant land, far from home and kindred in Randolph County, while faithfully discharging his duties in defense of his native country, on July 1, 1863. He had also been wounded in the fighting at Chancellorsville, in May. He was a member of New Salem Lodge, No. 209.

—*Greensborough Patriot,* September 24, 1863

Corp. Harrison H. Rollins, Company I, 22d Regiment, fell May 3d, gallantly fighting where the contest was the greatest and the battle raged the fiercest; his "sun went down while it was yet day," on the blood-stained field of Chancellorsville, far away from his native home, with nothing to mark his resting place but the little mound of earth that covers his immortal remains.

—*Greensborough Patriot,* September 24, 1863

William A. Rich who had been unable to do any work for a number of years died Tuesday evening about 7 o'clock at his home here. He was 68 years of age. During the Civil War he served in Company E, 22nd Regiment N.C.T. He was wounded in the chest at Gettysburg. Mr. Rich was captured July 6 and held a prisoner of war at Fort Delaware until he was exchanged in October 1864. He was twice married and is survived by a widow and several sons and daughters, nearly all of whom live here. The funeral was held yesterday afternoon and the remains were buried at New Providence.

—*Alamance Gleaner,* November 28, 1912

23rd Regiment North Carolina Troops

Died at Garysburg, Northampton County, on the 20th inst., of pneumonia, **John C. Teal**, aged 23 years. He was from Montgomery County and leaves a wife and four helpless children.

—*Fayetteville Observer,* July 29, 1861

Died on May 2, in Richmond, Va., of an accidental wounding at Yorktown on the 23d ult., **Serg't. John W. Fleming,** of the Granville Targeteers, Co. E, 23d Reg't. He was a Granville native and was aged 22.

—*Fayetteville Observer,* June 2, 1862

We have received word of the deaths of three members of Company D, 23d Reg. N.C. Troops: **Malcolm C. Nicholson, Robert D. Thomas,** and **Willis Watkins.** Malcolm joined the 23d in May 1861, and died of a disease in May 15, 1862. He was buried the next day in an old graveyard about seventeen miles from Richmond. Robert, a resident of Richmond County, enlisted in May 1861, aged 18, and died at Petersburg the following April. Willis, also from Richmond County, enlisted in May 1861, aged 19, and died of pneumonia in Richmond the following May.

—*Fayetteville Observer,* June 2, 1862

Killed on the battle-field at Seven Pines, May 31st, in the 19th year of his age, **Alfred E. Hoyle,** of Lincoln County, a member of Co. K, 23d Reg't N.C.T.

—*Fayetteville Observer,* June 30, 1862

Edmund J. Christian, 26, of Montgomery County was killed in the late battle before Richmond, on 31st May, at Seven Pines whilst nobly and gallantly discharging the duties of his position (Major of the 23d Reg't, N.C. Troops). Having been severely wounded in three different places, he refused to leave the field, when urgently begged to do so, and while still going on, urging his men forward, he received the fourth and fatal wound. He leaves a bereaved mother and sisters. He was a member of Blackmer Lodge, A.Y.M., No. 127.

—*Fayetteville Observer,* July 7, 1862

Died on the 11th June, from the effects of a head wound received in a battle near Richmond at Seven Pines, **2nd Lieut. Albert M. Luria,** of the "Granville Stars," Company I, 23d Reg't N.C.T. He had previously served with the 2nd Battalion Georgia Volunteer Infantry.

—[July 7, 1862] *Fayetteville Observer*

Messrs. Editors.—

Permit the pen of friendship to record a feeble tribute to the memory of **Franklin Wall Dumas,** who was killed at the battle of Seven Pines, near Richmond, on the 31st ultimo. He volunteered in the 1st Montgomery Company, the "Montgomery Volunteers," Company C, at the early age of 16, and remained in connexion therewith until his death. Under the provisions of the Conscription Act he expected soon to be temporarily released from the arduous duties pertinent to camp life, and his numerous friends and relations were anticipating much real enjoyment from the pleasure of his company again, but he was cut down on the battle field amid the roar of cannon, and the clash of arms. He fell there *because it was his duty,* and as such, regardless of consequences, must be done.

—O. H. D., *Fayetteville Observer,* July 14, 1862

Killed in the battle at Malvern Hill, on Tuesday evening, July 1st, 1862, **Serg't. William J. Phillips**, a member of Company D, 23d Regiment, N.C. Troops. He was killed instantly by a cannon ball, on entering the battle field. He was from Richmond County, aged 22 years.

—*Fayetteville Observer,* July 28, 1862

John F. Garrett, of the Pee Dee Guards, Company D, 23d Reg't. N.C. Troops was mortally wounded at the battle of Malvern Hill, July 1, 1862, aged 25 years. He was the son of Capt. Thos. Garrett of Richmond County. In every engagement he was found with his musket on his shoulder doing his duty. While his regiment was charging a battery at Malvern Hill, he was shot in the thigh in two places—the bone shivered. He was carried to Howard Grove Hospital in Richmond, where he lingered until the 25th of September, when death put an end to his sufferings. To his attentive younger brother who remained with him during his sickness, he remarked that he "was going home to die no more."
—*Fayetteville Observer,* **November 20, 1862**

Died of congestion of the lungs in Richmond, Nov. 21, **Serg't. Solon S. Hicks**, Company G, 23d Regiment. He was wounded at Mechanicsville, in June 1862, but had returned to duty by September. He was from Granville County and was 21.
—*Fayetteville Observer,* **January 12, 1863**

Died at Sharpsburg, Md., 25th Sept., of wounds received during the battle of the 17th, **Serg't. William J. Amis**, of Company I. of Granville County, in his 21st year.
—*Fayetteville Observer,* **February 9, 1863**

Died, at the residence of his parents, near Rockingham, Richmond County, on the 3d ult. after a prolonged illness, **Hiram H. Hailey**, in 30th year of his age. He entered service in June 1861. Through a period of about 18 months he experienced many privations and endured many hardships. A member of Co. D, 23d Reg't N.C.T., his first campaign was in the army of the Potomac, which, through rain, sleet and snow, through a long and dreary winter, in the face of the enemy and within sight of his Capital, stood a wall of defense to the South. Subsequently this army falling back he was with it on the Peninsula, and though not actually engaged was exposed to fire at the battle of Williamsburg. Still later he was with the troops who made that long and toilsome march into Maryland, where he participated in several bloody engagements. Shortly after this his health failed and in Jan'y 1863 he reached home. For several long months his family and friends watched by his bedside with alternate hopes and fears, and all that love and friendship could accomplish was done, but all was in vain. His work was done.
—*Fayetteville Observer,* **February 9, 1863**

Died, from a wound received on the battle-field at Chancellorsville, May 3d, **James S. Knight, 1st Lieut.** Co. D, 23d Reg't N.C.T., in the 25th year of his age. Lieut. Knight completed his collegiate course at Chapel Hill in May 1861. At the organization of the "Pee Dee Guards" of Richmond County, he was elected to the position of 1st Lieut. After a few months' service, and at the withdrawal of the former Captain, he became Captain, by the entire vote of the company, who later served under him during the arduous campaigns of Manassas and Yorktown,—the majority of whom were still side by side with him on the memorable field on which he lost his life. However, at the re-organization of the regiment, in accordance with the privilege extended to all the regiments last Spring, Capt. Knight and his subordinates, commissioned and non-commissioned, were ousted, and new officers elected. That this seemingly ungrateful proceeding on the part of the company emanated more from a mere desire for novelty and change than from any real prejudicial feeling (in the case of Capt. Knight at any rate), is manifest from the fact that, after he had returned home and volunteered as private in the cavalry service, Company C, 59th Regiment (4th N.C. Cavalry), he was re-elected to fill a vacancy in the 1st Lieutenancy of the company, and with the same degree of unanimity that had before marked a high appreciation of his manly virtues. It was thus under happy circumstances that he fell. Having gallantly conducted through the fiery ordeal of Saturday that band of fearless boys, in the very moment of victory, the fatal bullet was sped that laid him low. Comrades were near to soothe his dying moments and perform the last sad duties to his mortal remains.

—*Fayetteville Observer,* **February 9, 1863**

To the long catalogue of martyrs who have died upholding the banner of freedom in the face of the enemies of liberty, we this morning add the names of **William Pines Dunlap**, killed on the 3d of May at Chancellorsville, and **James Richard Knight**, both of Company A, wounded unto death in the same fight. They both volunteered in May 1861, and joined the Ellis Anson Rifles, of this county. They were each 21 years of age. They were wounded at the battle of Seven Pines, returned home on furlough, and as soon as their wounds were healed, returned to their regiment. W. P. Dunlap was killed instantly. J. R. Knight was desperately wounded, and died in a few weeks after the amputation of his leg, at Globe Hospital, Richmond, Va.

—*North Carolina Argus,* **August 28, 1863**

Killed, in the battle of Chancellorsville, May 3, **Kenneth McKenzie**, son of Bethune B. McKenzie, of Richmond County, a member of the Pee Dee Guards, Company D, the first company from his native county. He enlisted in May 1861 at age 18 and was in the fight at Malvern Hill where he had been wounded.

—*Fayetteville Observer,* **September 14, 1863**

Killed in the battle of Chancellorsville, Va., May 3d 1863, **Private Wiley P. Davis**, only son of Ann and E. Davis, of Montgomery County, N.C. Wiley belonged to Co. C, 23d Reg't N.C.T. He volunteered the 4th of March 1863 and joined the company at Fredericksburg, Va. the 22d of March, at the age of 18 years and 1 month. Wiley was in camp just six weeks. While he was fighting bravely he was pierced by a musket ball through the head and died instantly, on that beautiful Sabbath morning. He sleeps under the soil of Virginia far from his home and friends.

—Sister Mollie, *Fayetteville Observer,* **January 4, 1864**

Killed, instantly, on the battle field of Chancellorsville, the 3d May 1863, **Serg't Brantley Harris**, a member of Co. C, 23d N.C. Reg't, son of Parsons and Abigail Harris of Montgomery County, N.C. He was one of the first to respond to his country's call, and volunteered in the above company on the 27th day of May 1861, with two of his brothers. Before he was 20 years of age he had shared all the danger and hardship in which his company had been exposed, had been frequently complimented by his commanding officer for his courage and good conduct on the battle field. He was appointed 1st Serg't for gallantry on the battle field, which post he filled to the complete satisfaction of his company. He was nominated for the Badge of Distinction for his gallantry at Chancellorsville.

—*Fayetteville Observer,* **January 21, 1864**

Died, in the hands of the cruel foe, **Joseph B. Norwood**, a member of the "Granville Stars," Company I, 23d Regiment, N.C.T., aged 29 years, leaving to weep for him a loving wife, one sweet little cherub, and many friends. He was taken prisoner at Gettysburg and sent to Fort Delaware, then Point Lookout, Maryland, where he died of chronic diarrhea this past January.

—*Raleigh Register,* **June 8, 1864**

Died at Bell Plains, Va., **Thomas F. Powell**, son of the late P. M. Powell, Esq., of Powellton. He joined the army early in the war as a private in Company C and was appointed Sergeant Major in May 1862. He was captured at the battle of South Mountain, September 14, and held prisoner at Fort Delaware until his exchange in October. He was appointed Adjutant of the 23d N.C. Troops in July 1863. He was wounded in the leg and captured on the 8th of May during the battle of Spotsylvania Court House, and died on the 17th. It is a source of pleasure to his numerous friends to know that he found a friend and brother in the Chaplain, the Rev. Jos. Jones, of the 20th Michigan. He was in his 21st year. He made a profession of religion and joined the Baptist Church in the fall of 1859.

—*Fayetteville Observer,* August 4, 1864

Died on 21st Sept. 1864, in the hands of the enemy, **John S. Shipp**, eldest son of Mr. Wm. T. and Mrs. H. M. Shipp of Gaston county, N.C., age 18 years, 2 mo's and 14 days, and a member of Co. K, 23d Reg't, N.C.T. He was mortally wounded at Winchester, Virginia on the 19th.

—*Fayetteville Observer,* December 12, 1864

[The following is one of a number of memorial addresses or reports that were given from time to time about Confederate soldiers. While it is not a true obituary, it gives interesting information about Colonel Daniel Harvey Christie and is slightly edited.]

Daniel Harvey Christie was born in Frederick County, Va., in March 1833. His father was Robert W. Christie, who with his family, when his son was quite young, settled in Louden County, Va. At the age of sixteen Daniel Harvey found employment as a teacher at Heathville, Northampton County, Va., and there met the Rev. Robert B. Thompson, a minister of the Methodist Protestant church, who afterwards induced him to settle in Nansemond County. He met Miss Lizzie A. Norfleet, of Suffolk, Va., and won her hand and heart; they were married on the 22nd day of November 1855. During the first two years succeeding his marriage his residence was in Norfolk, Va., where he was engaged in the tobacco and commission business. From Norfolk he went with his family in 1858, to reside in Henderson, N.C., and there conducted a military school until 1860, when he returned to Suffolk for a brief period. When the tocsin of war was sounded in 1861 he was called by his North Carolina friends to the position of major of the Thirteenth North Carolina Infantry, which was organized at Weldon, N.C., and subsequently became the Twenty-third, with Major Christie as its colonel, a gallant regiment, with a gallant, brave, and handsome colonel.

He was in the battle of Seven Pines, where his horse was shot out from under him and he was injured in the fall. At Gaines' Mill he was wounded in the leg and returned to duty in September 1862. Having previously made for itself, under its intrepid leader, an enviable record for daring and bravery, the regiment won for itself fresh laurels at Gettysburg. In the battle at the latter place Colonel Christie was in the front in command of Iverson's Brigade, when he was shot through the lungs. Though the ball was extracted, the wound proved fatal shortly afterwards at Winchester, where he died at the residence of a Mrs. Smith, who nursed him tenderly until the end came.

Mrs. Christie, with her three children, was a refugee at Henderson, N.C., when she received a telegram from her husband saying he had been wounded and was slowly on his way home. A day or two later the lieutenant-colonel of the regiment telegraphed her to come at once to Winchester to see her husband who had grown worse. She started immediately on the sad journey, but made slow progress, owing to the imperfect facilities for travel, and the difficulties growing out of Gen. Lee's retreat. A week had elapsed when she reached her destination. It was during this weary week that Colonel Christie, longing to see his young wife, continued to sink slowly, and as the days passed by and she came not, to ask, "Is she coming?"

Upon arrival at Winchester Mrs. Christie was met by two officers of her husband's regiment—Dr. Vines E. Turner, formerly the adjutant, but at that time quartermaster, now living at Raleigh, and Captain James Johnson, of Charlotte, N.C.—who had remained to meet her. Their countenances indicated unmistakably sad news for her, and she implored them at once to tell it all, her suspense being extremely painful. The first to speak was Dr. Turner, her husband's dearest friend, who, with tears in his eyes and tremulous voice, could only say, "He is no more." He had died on Friday morning, July 17, 1863, just two days before her arrival. He is buried in the Stonewall Cemetery, at Winchester, where lie the bodies of so many of the South's most gallant and noble men.

[His death inspired the writing of the poem "The Dying Soldier," and the *Gold Leaf* also published it and the following information about its composition. Wilbur P. Kilby wrote the story as well as the information on Christie's career and death.—Ed.]

The following article, which, in addition to its historical value, is of such local character as to prove interesting to our readers, has been taken from the Richmond *Dispatch* of February 23, 1896:

SUFFOLK, Va., Feb. 14th, 1896.

Having noticed the call for the republication of the poem entitled "The Dying Soldier," it gives me great pleasure to furnish for your columns an exact copy of the pathetic composition, as it was originally written by "Matilda" and sent by her to "Lizzie." I may add that I have obtained this copy from "Lizzie" herself, who is still living, and a resident of this place. Before I proceed to give an account of its origin, let us all read the poem once more. Here it is:

The Dying Soldier.
BY MATILDA.
[Affectionately inscribed to Lizzie A. Christie.]

I am dying; Is she coming? Throw the window open wide,
Is she coming? Oh, I love her more than all the world beside;
In her young and tender beauty, must, oh! must she feel this loss?
Savior, hear my poor petition; teach her how to bear this cross.
Help her to be calm and patient when I moulder in the dust;
Let her say and feel, my Father, that Thy ways are true and just.
Is she coming? Go and listen; I would see her face once more;
I would hear her speaking to me, ere life's fevered dream is o'er;
I would fold her to my bosom; look into her soft, bright eye;
I would tell her how I love her, kiss her once before I die.
Is she coming? Oh! 'tis evening, and my darling comes not still,
Lift the curtain; it grows darker; it is sunset on the hill;
All the evening dews are falling; I am cold—the light is gone,
Is she coming? Softly, softly comes death's silent footsteps on,
I am going; come, kiss me; kiss me for my darling wife;
Take for her my parting blessing; take the last warm kiss of life,
Tell her I will wait to greet her where the good and lovely are,
In that home, untouched by sorrow; tell she must meet me there.
Is she coming? Lift the curtain; let me see the failing light;
Oh! I want to love to see her; surely she will come to-night!

Surely ere the daylight dieth I shall fold her to my breast;
With her head upon my bosom, calmly I could sink to rest.
It is hard to die without her. Look! I think she's coming now;
I can almost feel her kisses on my faded cheek and brow;
I can almost hear her whisper, feel her breath upon my cheek.
Hark! I hear the front door open. Is she coming? Did she speak?
No! well drop the curtain softly, I shall see her face no more
Till I see it smiling on me on the bright and better shore.
Tell her she must come and meet me in that Eden, land of light;
Tell her I'll be waiting for her where there is no death—no night;
Tell her that I called her darling, blessed her with my dying breath,
Come and kiss me for my Lizzie; tell her love outliveth death.

It so happened that while Mrs. Christie was a young girl, and a pupil at Buckingham Female Collegiate Institute, in Buckingham County, Va., she met and became the warm friend of Matilda C. Smiley, one of her schoolmates. Of Miss Smiley it could be truthfully said, "*Poeta mascitur non fit.*" She was a born poet. She had been sent to the institute to be educated by her friend or guardian, the late Rev. George W. Nolley, a minister of the Virginia Conference of the Methodist Episcopal Church, South. She wrote poetry with a great deal of ease, and soon became noted for her compositions. She had left school and married Mr. Alpheus Edwards, of Washington D.C. Soon after Mrs. Christie's return to Suffolk she told the story of her sorrow in a letter addressed to Mrs. Edwards, who at once sat down and, with the information imparted by the letter, wrote "The Dying Soldier," which embodies the thoughts suggested by Colonel Christie's last words for "Lizzie." The poem was first published in the Richmond *Christian Advocate* of March 23, 1864, and has since appeared in a volume of southern poems, and frequently in newspapers. This, however, is the first time the full story of its origin has been published. Mrs. Edwards wrote and published her first volume of poems while she was a pupil at the Buckingham Institute and afterwards became quite famous as a poet.

—*Gold Leaf,* **March 19, 1896**

Superintendent R. H. Brooks, of the North Carolina Soldiers' Home, writes the GOLD LEAF to chronicle the death of another Confederate veteran. **Mr. Joseph N. Orrell**, an inmate of that institution from Vance County, died on Sunday, aged 61 years. He was a member of Company G, 23rd North Carolina State Troops, and enlisted in June 1861, serving under that splendid commander, Col. Charles C. Blacknall, of Kittrell. He was captured at the battle of Gettysburg and imprisoned at Fort Delaware and Point Lookout. He was released in February 1865.

The deceased was well known to many of our readers. He had his weakness, but he was a good natured, inoffensive man and his own worst enemy. During the latter part of his life he was greatly afflicted and suffered much bodily pain. He was a good soldier and served his State and country well. Mr. Orrell had been in the Soldiers' Home since December 1899. Thus another one of the "Old Guard," the immortal heroes who followed Lee and Jackson and their compatriots of 1861–1865 has crossed over the river to rest under the shade of the trees.

—*Gold Leaf,* **August 2, 1903**

Another one of our most highly esteemed citizens has passed to the great beyond when **Mr. Zack E. Lyon**, who lived just north of town, answered the sudden summons of the Master early Monday morning.

Mr. Lyon was apparently in good health, although he had complained for some time with a trouble of the heart. He was on the streets here Saturday afternoon and remarked to a friend that he was feeling very well, except the heart affection. He had just gotten out of bed and dressed himself when the summons came.

He was a member of the Methodist Church. He was a Confederate Veteran, having served his country through the entire struggle between the states from 1861 to '65. He was wounded in the leg and captured at Gettysburg and exchanged in October 1863. He returned to duty in Company E and remained with the 23rd until he was paroled at Appomattox Court House.

Mr. Lyon is survived by one daughter, Mrs. R. H. Whitfield and Hugh Lyon Whitfield, the son of a daughter who died a number of years ago who made his home with his grandfather, and numerous other relatives throughout this and adjoining counties. The funeral was conducted from the home Tuesday afternoon and the remains were laid to rest beside those of his wife, who preceded him some years ago, in the Mitchell grave yard north of town.

—*Creedmoor Times-News,* **May 1, 1918**

24th Regiment North Carolina Troops

Died near Meadow Bluff, Western Virginia, on Friday, the 11th of October, **James A. Currie**, son of Archibald B. and Jannette Currie, of Robeson County, aged twenty-one years, four months and eight days. About the last of May, he joined the "Highland Boys," Company G, under command of Capt. T. D. Love, (65) and on the 5th of July, bid adieu to his family to enter upon the duties, undergo the hardships and endure the privations incident to a soldier's life. Having spent some time at Garysburg and Weldon, his Regiment (14th Volunteers) was ordered to join Floyd's Brigade in Western Virginia, and there, after suffering the severest hardships, he fell victim to that most fatal of diseases, Pneumonia, and died.

—*North Carolina Presbyterian,* **November 9, 1861**

Died of Typhoid fever, at Blue Sulphur Springs, Greenbrier County, Va., October 21st, in the 28th year of his age, **Neil A. Clark**, of Robeson County, N.C. He was in the Highland Boys, Company G, 24th Reg., North Carolina Volunteers and leaves a widow and two small children to mourn the loss of a patriotic husband and father.

—*North Carolina Presbyterian,* **November 23, 1861**

Died of disease at Meadow Bluff, Western Virginia, on the 10th of October, **Daniel A. Conoley**, of Robeson County, N.C., a member of the "Highland Boys," Company G, aged 24 years. Also, on the 12th of October, at Meadow Bluff, Western Virginia, **William C. Conoley**, brother of Daniel, and member of the "Highland Boys," aged 22 years, of pneumonia.

—*North Carolina Presbyterian,* **November 23, 1861**

Died on the 19th of November, of typhoid fever, at Blue Sulphur Springs, Va., **William H. Drumwright**, in the 24th year of his age, of Capt. John L. Harris' (66) Company H, Col.

Clark's (67) 14th Reg. N.C. Vols. He was a young man of fine education and feeble health, yet he went as a private, and served in that capacity until his death.

—*North Carolina Standard,* December 21, 1861

James G. Cobb (son of the Rev. J. H. Cobb), of this county, lately a volunteer in the Cumberland Plough Boys, Company F, 24th Regiment, N.C. Regiment, has died in Western Virginia while, as a soldier and Patriot, he was engaged in defense of Southern rights and constitutional liberty; marching over Mountain and valleys, and suffering privations and hardships, which none but patriots could endure. He breathed his last at Meadow Bluff, on Nov. 7, 1861, and his body lies buried in a strange land.

—*North Carolina Presbyterian,* January 4, 1862

Died at the Blue Sulphur Springs, Va., on the 9th of Dec., **Neil McLellan**, in the 22nd year of his age.

He was a Soldier of the 24th N.C. Regiment, Company F, and like many of his comrades has fallen a victim to disease. He suffered long and severely, first from camp fever, then from jaundice, and lastly from pneumonia, but "not a murmur or complaint was ever heard to escape his lips."

—*North Carolina Presbyterian,* January 11, 1862

Died, at his father's residence in Cumberland County, on Friday the 17th inst., **James L. Culbreth**, aged about 18 years. He volunteered with *Capt. Charles H. Blocker,* (68) in the Cumberland Plough Boys, Company F, 24th Regiment; his company was immediately ordered to Western Virginia, and where, no doubt, from the many privations and hardship of the army, he contracted the disease which terminated his life. His company having come back to Petersburg, he was granted a furlough to visit his home again and loved ones there. He came home, was taken sick and died in a very short time. He joined the Methodist E. Church when very young. His remains lie silently in the grave by the side of a pious and devoted mother.

—*Fayetteville Observer,* February 3, 1862

Departed this life at Staunton, Va., on the 3rd ult., in the 25th year of his age, **James H. Malloy**, son of Mr. Duncan and Isabella Malloy, of Robeson Co. N.C. He was a member of the Presbyterian Church, at Lumber Bridge. He entered the Freshman Class at Davidson College, on the first of October 1859, where he continued two years. He joined the army last July, under the command of Captain Blocker, of the Cumberland Plow Boys, 14th Regiment N.C. Volunteers, Company F.

—*North Carolina Presbyterian,* February 8, 1862

Private John Calvin Smith of the Highland Boys, Co. G, 24th N.C.T., was among the first to respond to his country's call and manfully endured all the hardships and privations of winter campaign in Western Virginia. He died of typhoid fever at Murfreesborough, N.C., April 15, 1862. He has left a widowed mother, a sister, and four brothers.

—*Fayetteville Observer,* April 28, 1862

Captain William Bryant Gulley, of the Clayton (Johnston County) Yellow Jackets, Company C, fell on Tuesday, the 1st instant, while gallantly fighting at the head of his Company, in the desperate charge of Ransom's Brigade against the Yankees at Malvern Hill. Capt. Gulley fell immediately on receiving the fatal wound, and lived only long enough to breathe out an invocation to his gallant men to "fight on." Capt. G. was by trade a printer, a member of the Raleigh Typographical Society, was for some years employed in this office, and left it to join the army, going in as First Lieutenant of the Clayton Yellow Jackets, and being promoted to the Captaincy of the Company upon its re-organization at the end of the twelve months for which it had first enlisted. The printers of the South have done their full duty in this war, and have shown that their "shooting-sticks" are not the only shooting implements which they can handle.

Capt. Gulley's remains were brought home on Friday by his brother, **Sergeant John D. Gulley**, (69) and were interred on Saturday with military honors.

—*Raleigh Register,* July 9, 1862

Died in the Howard Hospital at Richmond, Va., June 28th, from a wound received in battle near Richmond, **Joseph A. Campbell**, son of John C. Campbell of Robeson Co., a private in Co. G, Highland Boys, 24th N.C. Reg't. He was among the first to volunteer when his company was gotten up at Floral College May 1, 1861. He died in the 20th year of his age.

—*Fayetteville Observer,* August 4, 1862

Died in Crow Hospital, Richmond, Aug. 8, 1862, from the effects of a wound received in the battles before Richmond, **Corp'l. Hugh. W. W. McDougald**, Co. G, 24th Reg't, N.C.T. He was from Robeson County and leaves a widowed mother and a devoted sister.

—*Fayetteville Observer,* September 8, 1862

Killed near Sharpsburg, Md., Sept. 17th, **John G. McNair**, aged 33 years. He was a citizen of Robeson Co., N.C., and a member of the 24th Regt., N.C.T., Company G. In 1852 he united with the Presbyterian Church at St. Pauls, where he remained an honored member till the day of his death.

—*North Carolina Presbyterian,* October 25, 1862

Died of disease at Winchester, Va., Oct., 16th, **John Paisley Fairlee**, youngest son of Neill and Jennet Fairlee of Robeson County, in the 21st year of his age—a member of the "Highland Boys," 24th Regt., N.C.T., Company G.

Paisley was the last of four noble sons who have been laid in the grave in early manhood. The hearts of his parents were drawn to him as their only surviving son, who would cheer and support them in their declining years. He passed through the battles below Richmond unhurt, and his elder brother, Capt. Fairlee, was killed. His death is the more grievous in that he was the last of the sons, who have passed within less than two years. Two elder sons and their wives both died shortly before him.

—*North Carolina Presbyterian,* November 29, 1862

Died on the 19th of Sept., in the 25th year of his age, **John McIntyre McNeill**, son of Lauchlin and Mary P. McNeill, of Robeson County, N.C. He was named after the late the Rev. John McIntyre. He was a member of the "Highland Boys," Company G, and shared in all the privations, exposures and forced marches last fall and winter under Gen. Floyd in N. W. Va. He bore his part in the bloody strife before the City of Richmond. He was in the charge at Malvern Hill, when its summit was mantled with sheets of fiery flame, and when the earth beneath was crimsoned with the rain of human gore, but he escaped unharmed. He aided in the capture of Harper's Ferry. He was at Sharpsburg on the memorable 17th Sept., and when the fury of the battle on that dreadful day was nearly spent and the victory about to perch upon the folds of our banners, he received from a random shot of the enemy, a ball which penetrated the vital parts of his body, which he survived only two days, and after having crossed the Potomac the fourth and last time, he sank in death, where he now fills a solitary but an honored grave.

—*North Carolina Presbyterian,* December 13, 1862

Among the many gallant dead who fell amid the terrible carnage at Fredericksburg, Va., in the battle of Dec'r. 13th, 1862, was **Corp'l. James D. McAlister**, Co. G (Highland Boys), 24th Reg't N.C.T., in the 21st year of his age, and son of Mr. and Mrs. James D. and Mary McAlister, of Robeson County, N.C. He enlisted in June 1861. From the balmy atmosphere of Carolina his Reg't was transferred to the command of General Floyd in Western Virginia. It is needless to recount the many trials and hardships to which our brave troops were subjected in that bleak country. The dreadful hand of disease soon laid hold upon many of them—among them James. For weeks he lay upon a bed of straw with naught but the rough hands of his comrades to soothe his heated brow as he slowly recovered. In the battles before Richmond, at Malvern Hill, at Sharpsburg and at Fredericksburg, he was conspicuous for his gallant bearing. At the latter battle, when his musket had become hot from its deadly fire, when the first shouts of victory ran along the line, his brain was pierced by a rifle ball; and thus he fell and died with the flag he had loved so ardently floating triumphantly beside him.

—*Fayetteville Observer,* February 23, 1863

Died, on the 19th of Sept. last, from the effects of a wound received in the battle of Sharpsburg, **John J. McNeill**, Co. G, 24th Reg. N.C.T. This blow has fallen doubly heavy on his bereaved parents, followed so soon by the death of another son, the noble and generous Angus. On the banks of a little stream that winds its way into the Potomac, we made grave, and with bursting hearts and unutterable anguish we saw the earth close over him, who but a few hours before was in all the strength of manhood.

—*Fayetteville Observer,* February 23, 1863

First Serg't. Archibald P. McKinnon, of Robeson County, was mortally wounded in the battle of Fredericksburg, Dec'r 13th, 1862. He lingered but a few days and died in an infirmary near the battle field on the 17th Dec'r. He was a member of the "Highland Boys," Co. G, 24th N.C. Reg't, and at the time of his death was 24 years old. During the period of his illness he was sensible of no pain, his body being paralyzed from the effect of his fatal wound. His last resting place is near the blood-stained field upon which he fell, where many of his brave associates are filling the honored soldier's grave beside him.

—*Fayetteville Observer,* April 6, 1863

Died at Atkins' Landing, August 5th, of typhoid fever, **Obediah W, Pearce**, of Person County, Co. A, 24th Reg't N.C.T. He was captured at Malvern Hill in July last year and held at Fort Columbus, New York, then transferred to Fort Delaware. He was being transported for exchange to Atkins' Landing in Virginia when he died.

—*Fayetteville Observer,* July 15, 1863

Killed, near Drury's Bluff, at Bermuda Hundred, on the 26th of May 1864, **Merrell Rimmer**, of Co. H., 24th Regiment N.C. Troops, in the forty-first year of his age. He leaves a wife, one child, and many friends to mourn his loss. He volunteered and joined a company in 1862. While charging the enemy's breast-works, he received a minie ball in his head, and fell dead. His body lies resting in his camp blanket under the silent clods of the great James River; his spirit is gone to rest with his little babes who were just before him

—*Hillsboro Recorder,* June 15, 1863

Died, in the Field Hospital, near Chester, Va., June 2d, 1864, from a mortal wound received that morning in a charge on the enemy's rifle-pits, at Bermuda Hundred, **John H. M. McLean**, eldest son of Daniel H. McLean, Esq., of Robeson County, and 1st Lieutenant in Co. G ("Highland Boys"), 24th Reg't N.C.T., in the 27th year of his age. Nature had endowed Dr. McLean, in a high degree, with the elements of the good and successful physician. The war broke out about the time he was completing his medical course, and like many other brave and generous youths, he laid aside his books and sacrificed the labor, time and money he had expended in acquiring knowledge of his profession, together with a bright and hopeful prospect of success, and volunteered a private in the ranks.
—*Fayetteville Observer,* **June 16, 1864**

Died at his residence in Cumberland County, on the 24th inst., in the 36th year of his age, **John Henry Smith**, of a wound received in the battle near Petersburg. He was a member of Co G, 24th Reg't. He leaves a wife and four small children. He was a member of the Presbyterian Church
—*Fayetteville Observer,* **June 30, 1864**

Killed, on the 18th of July, in the Trenches near Petersburg, Va., by a mortar shell, **Owen D. Jones**, a member of Co. F, 24th N.C.T., aged 18 years. He joined the army about the last of April 1864. He was the eldest son of Mr. Hardy and Mrs. Martha A. Jones. He was a good boy and equally as good as a soldier.
—*Fayetteville Observer,* **October 20, 1864**

25th Regiment North Carolina Troops

Died of disease at Grahamville, S.C., on the 23d ult., **Benjamin F. Curtis**, from Buncombe County, of the Pisgah Guards, Co. I, 25th N.C. Vols.
—*Fayetteville Observer,* **April 7, 1862**

Died at Kinston, on the 14th April, of brain fever, **Daniel M. Davis**, aged 18, and on the 18th May, **Benjamin F. Warren**, aged, 25, both members of the Pisgah Guards, Co. I, 25th Reg't., and both from Buncombe County.
—*Fayetteville Observer,* **June 2, 1862**

Captain Ephraim Young, of Company E, 25th Regiment N.C. Troops, died of fever at Kinston on the 22d of June, at the residence of the Post Master at Kinston, from whose family he received every attention and kindness. He was from Transylvania County, and was about 26 years of age. He left home as third Lieutenant of *Capt. Francis Johnstone's* (70) Company and on the reorganization of the Regiment, he was elected Captain without opposition.
—*Asheville News,* **July 3, 1862**

DIED,—At the Hospital in the city of Richmond, on the 22d day of July, **Henry C. Merrill**, aged 19 years, 11 months and 7 days.—He left his father's residence early last March, and attached himself to Co. H, 25th Reg. N.C. Troops, then at Grahamsville, S.C. He died from a wound which he received, while his regiment was storming the enemy's battery at

Malvern Hill on the 1st of July, when so many of our brave countrymen fell. He, with many others, lay on the battle field all that night. Next day when the wounded were collected and carried to the various hospitals, he and an elder brother (B. W. Merrill, of Co. F, 14th N.C. Troops), were laid side by side on the same cot. They were both wounded the same evening, and when the blood was washed from off the face of the latter Henry recognized his brother. Thus met the youthful warriors after a separation of fifteen months.—They both died in the same hospital, Henry surviving his brother 12 days.

—*Asheville News,* **August 14, 1862**

Roland C. Osborne, son of E. Osborne, of Haywood County, died of typhoid at the Hospital at Petersburg, on the 5th of August 1862, in the 26th year of his age. He was a member of Co. F, 25th Reg't N.C.T., and although unable for duty he kept at his post in that gallant Reg't during the bloody contest before Richmond until the last days when he was sent back sick. Convinced that he could never get well he greatly desired to go home to die.—But the privilege was denied him, and he died among strangers.

—*Asheville News,* **October 2, 1862**

Written by Mollie Glenn upon the death of her brother, **Napoleon L. Glenn**, who died at Wilson Hospital, N.C. He was born in Buncombe County, January 1st, 1843, and died July 1st, 1862, of Typhoid Fever. He entered the service about the first of July 1861, in Company F, *Capt. Thomas Lenoir,* (71) 25th Regiment N.C.T. The Regiment went from Asheville to Raleigh, then to Wilmington, Grahamsville, S.C., and finally to Kinston, N.C. He was complaining for several days at Kinston, and the day the Regiment received orders to go to Richmond he went to the Doctor to take his name to go to the Hospital with some six more of that Company. When the Regiment started he was sent to Goldsboro' and remained there some three days, then was taken to Wilson Hospital, 24 miles from Goldsborough, lingered on till the first July, and died. He had for some time been a member of the M. E. Church and a professor of religion.—How glad I was to hear that my dear brother died shouting and praising God. I hope to meet him in a better land—in the sun-bright clime.
French Broad, N.C.

—*Asheville News,* **October 9, 1862**

Died at Richmond, **James P. Lance**, a member of *Capt. Thomas Young's* (72) Company H. He was one of the wounded at Sharpsburg.

—*Fayetteville Observer,* **February 9, 1863**

Major William S. Grady, of the 25th N.C. Regiment and formerly Captain of Company G, died a few days since, from the effects of a wound received in front of Petersburg on the 30th of July last. In the fight at the Crater he was wounded in the right side of his chest and in both arms. He remained in a Petersburg hospital until October, when he received a furlough, and later died at Greenville, South Carolina on October 20. He was 40 years old and was a most gallant and accomplished officer.

—**Originally published in the** *Asheville news,* **and reprinted in the**
Fayetteville Observer, **December 1, 1864**

On February 16, 1913, **Serg't. George M. Clayton** answered the last roll call. Early in 1861, when a boy of sixteen he had donned the grey, enlisting in the Cane Creek Riflemen, a company made up in Cane Creek Valley and commanded by *Capt. Fred Blake* (73) and which afterwards became Company H, 25th North Carolina Regiment. He became orderly sergeant of the company and participated in nearly all the engagements of his regiment from the beginning of the Seven Days' Battle about Richmond until he was captured at Five Forks, Virginia, April 1, 1865. He was held prisoner at Hart's Island in New York Harbor, and paroled in June 1865.

He was an active Mason, loyal and charitable. He was a member of the Zeb Vance Camp, No. 681, U.C.V., and was laid to rest by the Masons and members of his lodge. He leaves a wife and three children—two sons and one daughter—also two brothers and one sister.

—*Confederate Veteran* **Volume 21, Number 6, June 1913**

26th Regiment North Carolina Troops

Died at the hospital in Carolina City, on the 14th instant, of Typhoid Fever, **William H. Broughton**, a member of the Wake Guards, Company D, 26th Regiment N.C.T., in his 21st year. He leaves a widowed mother, sisters and a brother to mourn for him.

—*Raleigh Register,* **October 23, 1861**

Died at Carolina City, on the 23d of Oct'r, **Robert W. Goldstone, Esq.**, Postmaster at Prosperity, Moore County, in the 36th year of his age. He was a volunteer in *Capt. William P. Martin's* (74) Company H—a Lieutenant—of the 26th Regiment of N.C. Volunteers. He was attacked with fever, and being of a frail and delicate constitution, fell a victim to its ravages. He has left a devoted wife, an aged father, two brothers and four sisters. He was a consistent member of the Methodist Church. His remains were sent home to the family burial ground, accompanied by *Lt. Clement Dowd,* (75) *Private Enoch S. Cagle* (76) and A. B. March.

—*Fayetteville Observer,* **November 11, 1861**

John E. Matthews, 1st Lieutenant of Company G, the Chatham Boys, died at Carolina City, November 13th, 1861, of fever and measles. A heavy blow has fallen on the family as he was the only son of exceedingly kind parents, and brother of two lovely sisters.

—*North Carolina Standard,* **November 23, 1861**

Dr. Daniel M. Shaw enlisted in the "Moore County Independents," Company H, 26th N.C. Regiment, in June 1861. In October he was promoted to Assistant Surgeon and transferred to the Field and Staff. He contracted measles or fever and died at the hospital in Carolina City, on the 29th day of November 1861. He was aged 25 and leaves an aged mother and a brother and sister.

—*North Carolina Standard,* **December 7, 1861**

Died in the hospital at Carolina City, on the 23d December 1861, of Pneumonia, **John F. Turner**, son of Wm. D. Turner, Esq., a member of the Wake Guards, Company D, 26th N.C. Regiment in the 23rd year of his age. He was a member of the Methodist Episcopal Church.

—*North Carolina Standard,* **January 25, 1862**

Died at the Hospital, Kinston, on the 14th inst., of typhoid fever, **Orderly Sergeant Benjamin McLauchlin**, son of Duncan McLauchlin of Cumberland County, in the 18th year of his age. He was a member of *Capt. James C. Caraway's* (77) Anson County Company, K, 26th Regiment; and his remains were brought to this county for interment in the family burial place.

—*Fayetteville Observer,* **April 21, 1862**

Company K, "Pee Dee Wildcats," 26th Regiment N.C.T.

On March 31st 1862, **Private Luke Turnage** died in Anson County of brain fever. He was aged 21.

On April 1st, **Serg't. John Q. Neal** died in Anson County of typhoid fever. He was aged 28.

On April 1st, **Private Edmund P. Huntley** died at Goldsboro of typhoid fever. He was a farmer and was 18 years old.

On April 2d, **Corp. Thomas C. Knotts** died in Anson County of typhoid fever. He was 28.

On April 9th, **Private William H. Teal** died at Kinston of typhoid fever. He was aged 20 and a farmer.

On April 9th, **Private Samuel T. Sanders** died at Goldsboro of typhoid fever. He was 23.

On April 9th, **Private Alexander Rickets** died at Goldsboro of typhoid fever. He was 22.

On April 14th, **Serg't Alexander P. Short** died at Goldsboro of typhoid fever. He was 24.

All these soldiers enlisted July 1, 1861, and were from Anson County. Their deaths are supposed to have been caused by the exposure and fatigue from that awful retreat from Newbern.

—*North Carolina Argus,* **April 24, 1862**

Departed this life with disease at Kinston, N.C., on the 27th ult., **Jesse C. Womble**, in the 20th year of his age. He was a member of *Capt. William Webster's* (78) Company E from Chatham County, and fought in the battle below Newbern. He died far away from home, though he was consoled by the presence of his father during the last days of his sickness. Jesse was a member of the Baptist Church, for more than three years.

—*North Carolina Standard,* **May 4, 1862**

Messrs. E. J. Hale & Sons: Please announce in the Observer the death of **Hugh Keith** and **Troy Everett** both privates of my company. Keith died at the Hospital at Wilson, on the 26th of April, of Consumption and rheumatism, in the 33d year of his age. He was a pious man and in all respects a good soldier. Everett died of disease at the Hospital, Kinston, on the 29th of April, aged about 18 years. He was a noble little fellow. Though small and quite young he bore himself manfully in the fight at Newbern. He was of an amiable disposition and faithful in the performance of every duty.

Yours, very respectfully,
Clement Dowd, Capt. Company H, 26th Regiment,
Camp Magruder, near Kinston, May 19, 1862.

—*Fayetteville Observer,* **May 26, 1862**

Died at his father's, near New Hill, in Wake County, on Sunday 11th of May 1862, **Paschal Segroves**, aged about 28 years, a private in *Capt. O. R. Rand's* (79) Company D, 26th

N.C. Regiment. He was in the battle below Newbern and fought to the last. He was taken prisoner and kept on a vessel about three weeks, and was then sent to the hospital, where he stayed some four weeks—was then paroled and returned home. His disease was a low type of fever, which baffled the skill of his physicians.

—*North Carolina Standard,* May 31, 1862

The following letter from Col. Vance, speaks for itself. It is, indeed, extraordinary that Gen. Branch should have praised in his report, by name, a number of persons who took part in the battle of Newbern, and should have made no allusion to these officers, who fell while bravely fighting for their country. The friends of these officers, the army, and the people generally will thank Colonel Vance for his timely and eloquent allusion to these brave men, who sealed their devotion to the cause with their blood:—

HEADQUARTERS 26th REG'T., N.C.T.
KINSTON, May 28, 1862.
Editor Standard:—
Sir:—With the many lies whether official or simply officious, that have appeared in the papers in regard to my share in the battle of Newbern, I have not seen proper to interfere, being content to rest my case in the hands of my companions in arms, *who were in the fight.* But, Sir, in the case of a gallant officer and chivalrous gentleman who yielded up his life on that unfortunate field, I feel it due the noble dead that I should speak. I allude to **Maj. Abner Bynum Carmichael**, 26th Reg't N.C. Troops. In the official report of Gen. Branch, his name *is not mentioned.* Surely, surely, when so much fulsome adulation is lavished upon those who fought and escaped, the aged parents and numerous friends of a brave and intrepid soldier might have expected at least to hear from his commander a mention of his fate, if not his heroism. I wish them to know at least that his immediate commander was not indifferent to his merits, either as a man or as a soldier, and that his memory is cherished, fresh and green, in the hearts of the entire regiment.

The same remarks are applicable to the brave **Capt. William Pinckney Martin**, Co. H., these two officers being the highest in rank who fell that day.

Very respectfully,
Z. B. VANCE,
Col. 26th Reg., N.C.T.

—*North Carolina Standard,* June 4, 1862

Died in the hospital at Richmond, on the 9th inst., after a brief illness of typhoid fever, **William A. McLauchlin**, son of Duncan McLauchlin of this county, aged about 20, of Co. K, 26th N.C. Vols. This is the second son of Mr. McLauchlin who has perished by fever in the army, whilst another, *Capt. J. C. McLauchlin,* (80) to whose company they belonged, had a narrow escape in the late battle at Richmond, being slightly wounded in the head by a fragment of a shell at Malvern Hill.

—*Fayetteville Observer,* July 21, 1862

Messrs. Editors: Drury's Bluff, July 12, 1862.
Please announce the death of **Private Duncan Kelly**, a member of Co. H, 26th Regiment N.C. Troops, who died in the North Carolina Hospital, at Petersburg, 20th of June 1862, in the 21st year of his age. He left College, gave up home and all its sacred endearments, to participate in the great contest for liberty and independence. During the twelve months he served, no one discharged the difficult duties of a soldier's life more faithfully than he did; always at his post, he did whatever duty was before him faithfully. He acted the part of a brave man during the battle of Newbern. He came to Virginia to aid in driving back

the invading foe, but he fell a victim to disease and died a few days after he left his native State. Thus ended the brief career of this patriotic young man—he fell in the path of duty.
—A friend, *Fayetteville Observer,* **July 28, 1862**

Samuel W. C. Siler, aged 22, of the "Chatham Boys," Company G, 26 Reg't. N.C. Troops, died in the Winder Hospital at Richmond, July 12, 1862, of disease. He was born in Chatham County, N.C.; was the son of Samuel Siler, a worthy citizen of the same county. He volunteered in this company in June 1861—has been in two or three battles, in which he behaved with courage such as only a true soldier can possess. Besides his parents he leaves brothers and sisters.
—*North Carolina Standard,* **June 30, 1862**

Died in Petersburg, Va., on the 30th ult., of fever, **Serg't. William Henry Harrison Davis**, Co. H, 26th Reg't N.C.T., in the 22d year of his age. He volunteered in Capt. Wm. P. Martin's Company, the "Moore County Independents," on the 3d June 1861. In the battle of Newbern he conducted himself nobly, as well as in the more recent battles around Richmond. Soon after the battle of July 1st he was taken sick and sent to Petersburg, where he died. In recording the death of Serg't Davis, we deeply sympathize with his relatives and friends.
—A comrade in arms, *Fayetteville Observer,* **August 4, 1862**

The officers who prepare lists of casualties in battle are so careless in writing names that innumerable errors occur in the printing. Proper names should always be written plainly. In Virginia papers the name of Hiram Evans is given as among the killed on the night of 25th June, the first day of the late battles near Richmond. Subsequently the name was printed O. H. Jones. Both were wrong. The name intended was **Orpheus Hiram Evans**, only son of Oren S. Evans, of Chatham County, who fell while on picket duty near King's School House, Virginia, in Co. E, 26th Reg't (Col. Vance's). He had been more than a year in service, had gone through the battle of Newbern unharmed, and had escaped the physical and moral evils of camp life, to perish almost the first day of his arrival in Virginia. When the war broke out he was not 18, and was engaged in the study of medicine. The blow is a crushing one to father, mother, and sisters—the only son and youngest child in the family.
—*Fayetteville Observer,* **August 4, 1862**

Martin A. McKinnon died in Petersburg, August the 9th, aged about twenty-five years. He was a member of the "Moore County Independents," Company H, 26th North Carolina. He participated in the fights at Newbern and Richmond, and escaped untouched by the ball of an enemy, only to be seized by that fell destroyer of man, "Typhoid Fever." He leaves his aged parents and a large circle of friends. He was a consistent member of the Presbyterian Church. This is the second time since the commencement of the war, that these aged parents have been bowed in sorrow over the loss of a son.
—*North Carolina Presbyterian,* **September 20, 1862**

Died in Petersburg, Va., on the 2d October 1862, of Typhoid Fever, **Sergeant Daniel G. Beckwith**, son of Green Beckwith, Esq., of Wake County, in his 22d year. He was a member of the Baptist Church at Holly Spring, Wake County. He volunteered in the company raised at Holly Spring (Capt. Oscar R. Rand's, Company D, 26th Reg. N.C.T.) and was made O. S. [Orderly Sergeant] of that company, the duties of which he performed with ability and fidelity. He was in the battle of Newbern and bore an active part in that bloody struggle, being one of the last to quit the field, was consequently taken prisoner and carried to Fort Columbus, N.Y., and subsequently to Fort Delaware, being kept in close confinement and on bad fare until he was exchanged and returned to his regiment in August. His constitution, naturally delicate, was so worn down that he gradually sunk to the tomb.

—*North Carolina Standard,* **November 7, 1862**

Died at the 1st N.C. Hospital, Petersburg, 10th inst., **Isaac N. Johnson**, of Chatham County, and a private in Company E, 26th Reg't, N.C.T. He had just attained his 18th year, and without waiting to be enrolled he went at once to camp to join with his friends and associates in beating back the invaders of our soil. After a very fatiguing march in Eastern N.C., he was taken with measles. The exposure to which he was subjected brought on typhoid fever, which proved fatal.

—*Fayetteville Observer,* **January 19, 1863**

Killed at Rawls Mill, Martin County, N.C., 2d November 1862, **John P. Winfield** of Anson County, aged 32 years 2 months and 20 days. He was a private in Capt. J. C. McLauchlin's Co. K, 26th Regiment of N.C. Troops. In May last he bid adieu to friends and relatives. After spending a few weeks in peace and quietude on the tented field, the company had an engagement with the enemy at King's School House, Virginia, on June 25, where he received a flesh wound in the right arm. He then returned home. His arm having convalesced, he again returned to camp. Not long after his arrival, the company was again engaged with the enemy in which engagement he was instantly killed by a shell. He left a wife and four children.

—*North Carolina Argus,* **February 3, 1863**

Capt. A. Carmichael desires to acknowledge in this public manner his obligations to those whose kindness has been shown in matters growing out of the death of his son, **Major A. B. Carmichael**, who fell nobly at his post at Newbern on the 14th of March 1862. He remembers with gratitude the first attempts to recover the body of his son, made by the late Gen. Branch. These advances were rejected by Gen. Burnside, the commander of the U.S. forces occupying Newbern. The request was renewed by Gen. Ransom while commanding the advance brigade of Gen. Holmes' army; and seconded by the earnest solicitations of the late gallant Col. Campbell of the 7th N.C.T., a former friend of Gen. Burnside. To these Capt. Carmichael acknowledges his indebtedness; and also to Col. Leaventhorp of the 11th (Bethel) Regiment, and to Lieut. Col. Gordon of the 1st N.C. Cavalry, a fellow-townsman of Major Carmichael, for their kind efforts to interest others in securing the body. But the aged father is especially indebted to the untiring exertions of His Excellency Gov. Vance, both while Colonel of the 26th regiment N.C.T., to which Major Carmichael was attached, and also after he had acceded to the Chief Magistracy of the State. Also he returns his thanks to Mr. Alex. Justice of Newbern, through whom Gov. Vance finally secured the remains of his friend and fellow-soldier. Capt. C. also thanks Col. Barnes, Aid to the Governor, for his promptness, in the absence of Gov. Vance, in forwarding the body from the city of Raleigh.

—**Wilkesboro, N.C., April 1st, 1863,** *North Carolina Standard,* **April 10, 1863**

SIR:—The object of this letter is to recommend Cadet H. K. Burgwyn, of North Carolina, for a commission in the Artillery of the Southern Confederacy. Mr. B. is not only a high-toned Southern gentleman, but in consequence of a highly practical as well as scientific character of his mind, he possesses qualities well calculated to make him an ornament not only to the Artillery but to any branch of the military service.

T. J. JACKSON,
Prof. Nat. Phil. And Inst'r Va. M. I.
LEXINGTON, VA., April 16th, 1861.

To L. P. WALKER, Sec'y. War.

The discriminating and sagacious character of the Professor has been fully attested by the career of the pupil, **Henry King Burgwyn,** from the moment he entered the services to the day on which he met a soldier's fate on the bloodiest field of the war, and while, colors in hand, he was leading his men on to victory, for on that day the enemy were signally repulsed. When Newbern fell, he was the last man of his Regiment to cross the Creek on the retreat, having refused to enter the boat until all were safely passed over. On this occasion young Burgwyn was Lieut. Colonel of the 26th Regiment, the Colonel being the present Gov. Vance.

From this State we follow the subject of our narrative to the bloody fields around Richmond, winding up with the terrific fight at Malvern Hill, in which his Regiment, the 26th, was unsurpassed for heroism by any troops on the field. On the resignation of Col. Vance, when he became Governor elect of this State, young Burgwyn was elected Colonel, and soon thereafter we find him again in service in his native State. In the critical campaign in Martin County, when the enemy was threatening disastrous consequences to the region of the Roanoke River, we find Col. Burgwyn performing signal services, especially in the engagement of "Rawl's Mills, "where he displayed a cool judgment and indomitable courage of which a veteran of many years" standing might have been proud. In all the course of his career, so well calculated "to turn the head" of one so young, Col. B. displayed modesty so commendable that he silenced the tongue of envy, and won the confidence of his brothers in arms. When, on Gov. Vance's resignation, it was suggested that he was too young for the Colonelcy, Gen. D. H. Hill thus wrote of him: "Lieut. Co. Burgwyn has showed the highest qualities of a soldier and officer, in the camp and on the battle field, and ought, by all means, to be promoted." As we have seen, Col. B. did receive the promotion, and subsequently was strongly recommended for the office of Brigadier General.

We have thus given a brief sketch of the career of one whose death in the very outset of manhood prompts the question: "If he was such in the gristle, what would he not have been in the bone?" His last words, after sending a farewell to his parents and family, were, "Tell Gen. Hill I can lead my Regiment no farther. My men have behaved well, and will behave well."

We conclude this imperfect tribute to Colonel Burgwyn with the following letter received by his father from the officers in his Regiment:

H. K. Burgwyn, Esq., Raleigh, N.C.

DEAR SIR:—Captain Young has undertaken to give you the sad news of your son's death, but I cannot let the opportunity pass without expressing my deep sympathy with his bereaved parents and family, as well as testifying to the gallant and soldierly manner in which he met his death. He was one of 11 shot bearing the colors of his regiment, and fell with his sword in his hand, cheering his men on to victory. The ball passed through the lower part of both lungs and he lived about two hours. Among his last words, he asked how his men fought, and said they would never disgrace him. He died in the arms of Lieutenant Young, bidding all farewell, and sending love to his mother, father, sister and brothers.

It was my painful privilege to assist Captain Young to inter his body under a walnut tree about one mile west of the town on the North side of the turn-pike road, 75 yards N. E. of a medium sized stone farm house, which has a yellow barn on the opposite side of the road leading from Gettysburg to Chambersburg. There are several graves under the tree, but his is directly east of the tree, with the head straight towards it. I have given this description that in case none of us should ever return, and this reaches you, you might still recover his remains. I cannot attempt to offer consolation to friends so bereaved, but can only mourn with them the loss of one of my most cherished friends. His death, however, was so noble and so glorious that it was all a soldier could desire.

Allow me, sir, to subscribe myself with great respect.
    S. P. Collins, Gettysburg, PA.
    July 3, 1863
            —*Raleigh Register,* July 22, 1863

  Killed, in the battle of Gettysburg, **Harmon H. Wilcox**, of Moore County, a Private in Co. H, 26th Reg't. Scarcely 17 years had passed over his youthful head when he, being inspired by noble patriotism, seized his musket and went forth to share the fate of his fellow soldiers. Although he sleeps upon the far distant plains of Gettysburg, far away from his home and friends, he is not forgotten but will ever live fresh and bright in our memory.
    —A friend, *Fayetteville Observer,* July 27, 1863

  Died, the 2d of July, from a wound received the 1st July, in the battle of Gettysburg, Pa., **Ashly F. Muse**, of Moore County, N.C., a private in Co. H, 26th Reg't N.C.T. son of Jesse Muse, Esq., aged 21 years 6 months and 4 days. He was a member of the Baptist Church at Bethlehem. He was a student in the Academy at Jackson Springs. He was in feeble health, but notwithstanding, he returned home and laid aside his books and volunteered April 1862, in defense of his country. He fought through the battles around Richmond and in Eastern N.C.; he endured many fatiguing marches; he would often be seen after a battle on his knees praying for the wounded; he would always remark in his letters to his parents that if he fell in the midst of the enemy not to grieve for him for he put his hope and trust in God. In the first of the charges at Gettysburg, he received his death wound on the second day in the evening he died. He called a friend to sit down by him; he said I am going to die and I want you to promise me to write to my father and tell him I was wounded mortally in the battle at Gettysburg while fighting for the independence of my home and country, and I die near the battlefield; tell him I am not afraid to die, for all is well with me. He fills a soldier's grave upon the far distant plains of Gettysburg.
    —Sister M. J. M., *Fayetteville Observer,* August 31, 1863

  On the night of the 2d July 1863, of wounds received on the 1st, at the battle of Gettysburg, Pa., **Serg't William Preston Kirkman**, son of Dr. George Kirkman of Chatham County, N.C., a member of Co. G, 26th Reg't N.C.T., aged 26 years, 10 months and 16 days. He volunteered in June 1861, and cast his lot among the "Chatham Boys." He was in the battle of Newbern in March 1862, and none fought more bravely or contended more earnestly than he, and unfortunately he was taken prisoner with a few more of his company. He was paroled and exchanged some time during the following summer, at which time he rejoined his Reg't. He participated in several fights and long marches. He had been acting Orderly Sergeant for sometime before his death, which post he filled to the complete satisfaction of his Company; always ready at any hour of the night, after a long and wearying march, to draw provisions for his comrades, which they knew was always done true and faithful by Preston. He was wounded in the evening of the 1st. He was heard to say he was mortally wounded—that he must die. He lived till the night of the 2d. He lies near Gettysburg, Pa., with two of his companions-in-arms in the same grave.

  We cannot close without bestowing a passing eulogy upon his father, Dr. George Kirkman, for his active patriotism and manifest kindness to the soldiers, and especially to the

"Chatham Boys," by whom he is designated the *soldiers' friend*. He has given 4 sons to the service—does all he can for the comfort of the soldiers and advancement of the cause.

[His brothers, all of Company G, George E. Badger Kirkman and Henry Clay Bascom Kirkman, died of wounds received at Gettysburg, and Wiley Prentiss Kirkman was captured at Gettysburg and died at Point Lookout, Maryland, March 10, 1865.—Ed.]

—A friend, *Fayetteville Observer,* September 21, 1863

William M. Persons, of Moore County, a member of Co H, 26th N.C.T., was wounded the first day of the battle at Gettysburg. He was captured by the enemy on July 30 died in the hospital at Winchester, Va., the 3d of August. Surrounded at home by everything necessary to make a man happy in this life; his constitution weak, it was natural to suppose that he would shrink from the hardships and dangers of a soldier's life, but as soon as his country called upon him, he left home, wife and children, and all that was dear to him, and nobly took his stand with his country's defenders. He did his duty like a true man and patriot. Long and nobly did he battle for his country on the bloody field of Gettysburg. After the hottest of the fighting was over, he turned round to me, with blood streaming from his breast and said, "I am killed; tell my wife and children good bye for me." I saw him next day and had hopes that he would recover, but the fatal bullet had done its work too well.

John B. Martin, of Moore County, age 28, a member of the same company and Reg't, died at the same place, the 1st day of August, of wounds received at Gettysburg. He had been captured and died in the hands of the enemy. He was an honor to his Co. and Reg't, an honor to his country, a model soldier and a most worthy man.

James A. N. McLeod, also of Moore County, member of the same company and Reg't, died near Gettysburg the 3d of July, of wounds received on the 1st. To those who knew him well nothing need be said. Father, mother, sister, friend, yours was a great sacrifice upon the altar of your country. The brave, gentle and unassuming soldier is gone. I loved him almost as much as my own gentle, youthful brother who fell and sleeps near him. The thunder of 300 cannon was their lullaby. They sleep in a strange land. But they will sleep as sweetly there as if at home in their own land and church yard.

—Friend, *Fayetteville Observer,* September 21, 1863

On David's Island, N.Y., on the 7th of September 1863, **Lieut. Marion J. Woodall**, of Wake County, N.C., Co. D, 26th N.C. Troops. He entered the army as a private and for meritorious conduct was promoted by his comrades in arms to a Lieutenancy. He received a slight wound in the battle at Newbern, N.C., and has been with the gallant 26th in all its hard-fought battles, perils and sufferings around Richmond, at Fredericksburg, Chancellorsville, in Maryland and Pennsylvania. He was wounded in the battle of Gettysburg, in the left knee and was taken prisoner and carried to David's Island, N.Y. The ball lodged near the bone and had to be cut out. Afterwards mortification ensued, and the leg was amputated; but his system had been so weakened that he could not survive, and he expired after upwards of two months of intense suffering. He leaves a sorrowing widow and his suffering little ones.

—*Fayetteville Observer,* October 12, 1863

Messrs Editors:
Permit me to announce the death of **Corp'l. Neill McDonald**, of Co H, 26th N.C.T., he having fallen in the battle of Bristow Station, Va., on the 14th Oct'r. 1863. He was a native

of Moore County, and enlisted at Carthage on the 3d June 1861 for twelve months. About the first of March 1862 he re-enlisted for two years or during the war. He fell while charging the enemy's lines behind the railroad. We feel that we have lost one of our best comrades, and I hope is at rest where the sound of cannon and the rattle of musketry will be heard no more.

—A friend, *Fayetteville Observer,* November 2, 1863

Corp'l, John A. J. Moran, a member of Co. G, 26th Reg't N.C.T., and son of William and Elizabeth Moran of Chatham County, was wounded in the head at Gettysburg, July 1st, 1863, captured by the enemy and sent to David's Island, New York Harbor, where he died about the 28th of August. He enlisted in June 1861, and was one of the first to compose the "Chatham Boys." He leaves a loving wife, kind parents, and brothers and sisters.

—*Fayetteville Observer,* November 9, 1863

I am much pained to announce the death of my brother, **Neill T. Smith**, who died of wounds received at Bristoe Station on the 15th ult. He was born in Moore County, July 25th, 1836. He survived only one day after the battle. He was a member of Co. H, 26th Reg't, N.C.T. He volunteered when first his country called, and has ever been found at his post. He leaves an aged father, doting mother, loving wife, fond sisters, and one sweet little daughter to mourn their loss. We were looking for him home when the news came that he was no more. Oh! How happily we would have welcomed him to the home he left in '61, to which he never again returned.

> Things we prize are first to vanish,
> Hearts we love to pass away,
> But a brother slain in battle
> Grieves the heart from day to day.

His name must be added to that catalogue of heroes who have laid down their lives for their country. He was deeply afflicted by the calamities and sufferings of the present war (as he wrote home a few weeks previous to his death that the only pleasure he saw was when he was reading his Bible).

—Sister, *Fayetteville Observer,* December 21, 1863

William H. Gee, of Co. E, 26th Reg't N.C., was wounded in the knee in that terrific engagement at Bristow Station, Va., Oct 14th 1863, and died Nov. 7th, aged 31 years. He participated in several battles, doing his whole duty, escaping injury up to the bloody battle of Gettysburg, Pa., where he received a slight wound from which he soon recovered and returned to his company. He bore his sufferings with much fortitude. While in the Hospital a kind lady presented him a Bible, which he read as long as he was able, and then gave it to his nephew who was present, requested him to carry it home to his mother and tell her to read it. He was the only son of his parents, who deeply mourn their irreparable loss.

—*Fayetteville Observer,* December 28, 1863

Killed instantly, at Gettysburg, Penn., July 1st, 1863, **William A.** and **Henry B. Garrett**, Co. G, 26th Regiment, N.C.T., and sons of the Rev. Jacob and Anna Garrett, of Chatham County, N.C.

At the first sound of the war cry William forsook his home and attached himself to the "Chatham Boys" Company, then being organized. For two long and trying years he had undergone the hardships of the camp, the fatigues of the march, and the exposure and danger of battle. At Gettysburg, while charging the enemy, he fell to rise no more. Henry,

though not among the first to volunteer (owing to his age) did so before he became 18 and connected himself with the same Co. and Reg't. They both fill an honored soldier's grave in the grove fronting Gettysburg.
—*Fayetteville Observer,* **February 11, 1864**

With profound regret we announce the deaths of **Sgt. James N. Ellis,** of Chatham County, aged 26, **James W. McDaniel,** also of Chatham County, aged 29, and **William H. Crutchfield,** from the same county, aged 29, Co E, 26th N.C.T. Serg't Ellis was wounded and captured at Gettysburg. He was confined at Fort Delaware, and then was taken to Point Lookout, Md., where he died January 23, 1864. James McDaniel was also wounded and captured at Gettysburg, sent to Fort Delaware, then to Point Lookout, where he died November 13, 1863. William Crutchfield was captured in Maryland July 4, 1863, sent to Fort Delaware, and died of smallpox at Point Lookout, Md., in December.
—*Fayetteville Observer,* **March 17, 1864**

Died in the General Hospital, Richmond, Nov. 26th **George Washington Hood,** from Caldwell County, in the 24th year of his age. He was a member of Co. F, 26th Reg't. and died from wounds received in the fight at Bristoe Station, October 14, 1863. He was first wounded at Malvern Hill, July 1, 1862, and again at the battle of Gettysburg.
—*Fayetteville Observer,* **May 12, 1864**

The reported death of **Lt. Col. John Thomas Jones,** of 26th Reg't N.C.T. has been confirmed. He was well known to the writer as a young man of more than ordinary promise and among the first of those spirits who left the University of N.C. and entered the ranks as privates in a Company from Chapel Hill in April '61; was in the 1st N.C. Reg't at the battle of Bethel; after serving out the period for which they had volunteered, young Jones immediately entered the army again. He served as Captain of Company I and was promoted to Major just before the battle of Gettysburg where he was wounded by a shell fragment. On May 5, 1864, he was killed at the battle of the Wilderness.

We are also sorry to learn that **Edward S. Jones,** Sergeant Major of the Regiment, son of Dr. J. B. Jones of Chapel Hill (who was wounded in the knees at the Wilderness and captured on the 6th), has lost a leg above the knee. His father has gone for him. He died May 19th. It is not known if his father arrived before his death.
—*Fayetteville Observer,* **May 30, 1864**

G. H. Sudderth, Company I, 26th Regiment, fell at Gettysburg on that memorable first of July. He was the youngest son, aged 23, of devotedly pious parents, residing in Caldwell County, and though young, he early in the war followed the example of three of his elder brothers (one of whom fell since at Bristow), and forsook a happy home to serve his country. Having fought through several bloody battles, he fell at Gettysburg, pierced through the body by a minie ball, and died next day. As soldiers we regret, as friends we mourn his loss.

In charging the enemy at Bristow Station, on the 14th of Oct. 1863, fell **Lieut. Joseph G. Sudderth** of Co. I, 26th N.C. Troops. He was a member of a highly respected family residing in Caldwell County. He served as a private in the ranks till the Fall of 1862, when he was chosen by his comrades to serve them as Lieutenant. As a soldier he did his duty; being seriously wounded in the forehead at Malvern Hill, and slightly in the foot at Gettysburg. He was shot through the body at Bristow, and died in an ambulance a few miles

from the field on the night of the next day (15th), and was buried by a weeping brother. He was a young man of excellent qualities; moral and intelligent, amiable and affectionate.
—*Fayetteville Observer,* July 7, 1864

Killed, at the battle of the Wilderness, on the 5th of May, **Charles Chalmers Roberts**, of Moore County, Co H, 26th Reg't N.C. Troops, in the 24th year of his age. He entered the army in the Spring of 1861, for twelve months. At the expiration of that time he promptly volunteered for the war before conscription was even talked of. He was one of the color-bearers of the Reg't, and stood bravely by them on many a hard fought field, among them the ever memorable one of Gettysburg, in which he received a slight wound, but soon recovered and promptly reported himself for duty, and again took his stand by the colors of the 26th Reg't., there proudly to stand until his country was freed from the ruthless hand of the invader; and there he was firmly standing on the 5th of May when a minie ball entered his head, killing him instantly.
—*Fayetteville Observer,* July 14, 1864

Killed on the battle field in the Wilderness, on the 6th of May, **Sergt. Lauchlin A. Currie**, Co. H, 26th N.C. Troops, aged 24 years and 1 month. He was among the first to respond to his country's call, having volunteered in the first company that left his native county (Moore) in 1861. For three long years of war and bloodshed he was found at his post battling against our common enemy (being wounded at Gettysburg), till at last he was pierced by the fatal ball which ended his short life on earth.
—*North Carolina Presbyterian,* July 27, 1864

Serg't Nathaniel Foster, Co E 26th N.C. Reg't, died at Chimborazo Hospital, Richmond, Va., on the 7th June 1864, of typhoid fever. It is seldom that we are called upon to mourn the loss of a more obliging friend, generous comrade, and sincere patriot and devoted Christian, then was Serg't Foster. Enlisting in May 1861, at age 18, he has ever since been found at his post none doing their duty more cheerfully than he. He had participated in some of the most severe battles of the war, was wounded at Gettysburg, taken prisoner and held at David's Island. He was exchanged in August and returned to his command in January 1864. He passed through the battles of the Wilderness and Spotsylvania unhurt, when he was seized with the disease which terminated fatally. He has left a wife, father, mother, brother, sisters and a large circle of friends and relatives to mourn their loss. Sgt Foster was a member of the Baptist Church.
—**A comrade in arms,** *Fayetteville Observer,* August 11, 1864

Fell mortally wounded in the bloody battle of the Wilderness, Va., on the 5th of May 1864, and died on the 13th, **Private William P. Blue** of Co H, 26th N.C. Troops, in the 23d year of his age. He was a native of Moore County, N. C; volunteered into the Confederate service on the 13th of May 1862; and since that time has ever responded to the call of duty, until he received the fatal blow. He had passed through many hard fought struggles, receiving a slight wound in left hand on the bloody field of Gettysburg, Pa. He was a young man of quiet, unassuming manners. He was an obedient son, and most kind and affectionate brother.
—*Fayetteville Observer,* August 29, 1864

Killed, in a charge on the enemy's works at Reams' Station on the 25th August, **Joseph G. Ellis**, Co E, 26th N.C. Reg't. As soon as he arrived at the age of 18, he left his happy home in Chatham County, N.C., and cast his lot with the defenders of his oppressed country. For more than two years he was in the field ready to meet the enemy whenever he might come. On the 25th ult., in a charge ordered on the Railhead near Reams' Station, a minnie ball pierced his forehead, causing instant death. The deceased was aged about 20 years; and is the third son of James Ellis, who has died in the service of their country. They were members of this company. The first, **William B. Ellis**, aged 22, died of typhoid fever in the hospital at Richmond, in June 1863. **Serg't. James N. Ellis** was left at Gettysburg, Pa. when Gen Lee fell back from that place, to care for our wounded; fell into the hands of the enemy; contracted a disease in northern prisons which proved fatal, Jan'y 1864, and he died at Point Lookout, Maryland. The afflicted parents of these three noble youths who have so freely offered up their lives for our independence, and have been cut down in the very bloom of life, have our warmest sympathy.

—A comrade in arms, *Fayetteville Observer,* September 12, 1864

Corpl. John J. Record, a member of Co G, 26th N.C.T., was killed on the morning of the 21st of August, while charging the enemy's skirmishers near Globe Tavern, Virginia, when a ball passed through his head, which caused his death in a few hours.

In June 1861 this young man volunteered, and was one of the first to compose the "Chatham Boys." He participated in many hard fights and long marches. He was captured at Bristoe Station October 14, 1863, and held prisoner at Point Lookout, Maryland. He was exchanged in1864, and returned to his command. He was a member of Rocky River Lodge, No. 159.

—*Fayetteville Observer,* October 27, 1864

The remains of the late **Henry K. Burgwyn, Jr.**, Colonel of the 26th regiment N.C. Troops, who fell on the bloody field of Gettysburg, while gallantly leading his men, the colors of his regiment in his hand, will reach this city on Saturday afternoon.—They will at once be taken to the Episcopal Church, where at 5 o'clock, the funeral services of the Church will be read, and thence they will be carried to the Memorial Cemetery for interment. It is most fit that he should sleep in the dear sod of his nativity and his affections.

—*Wilmington Journal,* June 14, 1867

Mr. Nathan Brewer, of this county, met with a horrible death last Friday. He was threshing wheat on that day at Mr. Josiah T. Dart's in Matthews Township, and, in attempting to step over the rod that connected the horse-power with the thresher, the end of his pants was caught and the rapidly revolving rod threw him down, and, before the machinery could be stopped, he was fatally injured. One leg was broken in two or three places and the other was pulled off, besides severe injuries to his body. He lingered in great agony for three or four hours before death relieved his sufferings. The deceased was a son of the late Amos Brewer and during the late war was a gallant Confederate soldier (being a member of Co. E, 26th N.C. Regt.) and was wounded at Gettysburg. He was captured March 25, 1865, near Petersburg, held prisoner at Point Lookout, Maryland, and released in June after taking the Oath of Allegiance.

—**Originally published in the *Pittsboro Record*, and reprinted in the *Alamance Gleaner,* August 4, 1887**

WASHINGTON, April 15—**Senator Zebulon B. Vance**, of North Carolina, died at his home, 1726 Massachusetts avenue, in this city, at 10:45 o'clock last night. He had a stroke of apoplexy at 10 o'clock in the morning. He had been suffering for some time from paralysis and a complication of diseases, but the end was so sudden and unexpected as he was regaining his health, and it was thought was on the road to recovery.

ZEBULON B. VANCE.
BY HON. KEMP P. BATTLE.

Zebulon Baird Vance was born in Buncombe County, North Carolina, May 13th, 1830. His father was a merchant of that section. His mother's father, Zebulon Baird, was one of the trusted citizens of Buncombe, for many years chosen as representative in the General Assembly. His father died when he was quite young. His mother devoted herself to his training. Her means were slender, however, and his education was confined to Pike's arithmetic and Webster's spelling book. But young Zeb had an inquiring mind. He read every book that was within reach and being gifted with great quickness and a strong memory early in his boyhood he began the accumulation of the stores of illustrations and stories which afterwards made him famous as a speaker. A gentleman from the senior class of the University, traveling in Buncombe, met young Zeb Vance and was amazed to find this half grown country boy so conversant with the Bible, Shakespeare and Scott's novels. He then predicted his subsequent success.

ENTERS THE POLITICAL ARENA.

In 1852 Vance went to the University of North Carolina, where he spent a year. He stood first in his class. He then began the study of law and soon was admitted to the bar. He made Asheville his home, and was at once influential with the jury, his humor and ready eloquence never failing of an effect on the mind of the average mountaineer. Vance went early into politics. He was elected to the Legislature in 1854. He was one of the most prominent men in that body.

His peculiar powers were not fully developed, however, until 1858, when he took the stump in opposition to the late W. W. Avery as a candidate for the National House of Representatives in the mountain district. When Vance announced his intention to oppose Avery he was applauded for his gallantry, but laughed at for his supposed folly. In this campaign Vance, then only 28 years of age, displayed those qualities of a stump orator and leader of men for which he afterward became conspicuous and unequalled in the State. By his power of presenting arguments and facts and by his winning ways he stole away the hearts of the people. He was elected by as large a majority as the year before had been given to his Democratic predecessor. In Congress he was an active and watchful member. He took sides strongly and labored earnestly against secession, at the same time warning the country against coercion of the Southern States by force of arms. His appeals for the Union in Congress were earnest and powerful, but when Sumter was fired on he cast his lot with his native State and took up arms against the Union.

TOOK UP ARMS FOR HIS COUNTRY.

Whatever Vance did he did with all his might. He was one of the earliest volunteers marching to the seat of war in Virginia as a captain in May 1861. His promotion soon came. He was elected colonel of the 26th Regiment North Carolina troops, in August 1861. He was among the brave fighters who drove McClellan to his ships on the James, and brought his regiment off safely when Branch's little army was overwhelmed by Burnside at Newbern. He was a faithful and gallant officer, and civilians and soldiers united in the demand that he should be the next Governor of North Carolina. He was chosen by an overwhelming majority in 1862; two years later over the late Governor W. W. Holden. As Governor of North Carolina Vance displayed talents for which even his most ardent admirers had not given him credit. He exhibited administrative and executive powers of the highest order. It was his province to execute largely the functions of a war minister, and when the full history of the war shall be written it will be found that Zeb Vance excelled all Southern Governors in vigor and ability in these regards. In the midst of the very death struggle of the war, he insisted that the military should be subordinate to the civil powers. It should be known and remembered throughout the civilized world that all during the time when the Confederacy was vainly fighting for life, and when one-fourth of the State was over-run by contending armies, the great privilege of the writ of habeas corpus was never suspended. North Carolina had a Governor brave enough to enforce its mandates in the midst of conscript camps.

ELECTED SENATOR.

In 1870 he was elected to the Senate of the United States, but on account of the disabilities imposed by the fourteenth amendment to the constitution, was not allowed to take his seat. In 1872 he was defeated for the same high office by a coalition between Judge Merrimon and the Republicans. He was nominated for Governor of North Carolina by the Democrats in 1876, and elected by a large majority over Settle. He received the degree of LL. D., from Davidson College in 1867.

In 1878 he was again the nominee of the Democrats for United States Senator, and was this time elected. This position, to the credit of North Carolina, he held to the day of his death. His fame as a statesman was widespread. He was known all over the Union as leader of the Democratic wing of the Senate. He was ever fearless in his efforts for that which would benefit his constituents.

HE WAS TWICE MARRIED.

Senator Vance was twice married. His first wife was Miss Harriet Espy. To them were born four sons, all of whom survive. His second wife was Mrs. Florence Martin, of Kentucky. Their home on Massachusetts Avenue, in Washington, was the resort of all North Carolinians who visited Washington. Their mountain home, Gombroom, was a beautiful retreat for the mountain-loving Senator. He was aptly styled "The Sage of Gombroom."

—*Gold Leaf,* May 3, 1894

This community is saddened by the death of **William G. Murchison**, which occurred the 13th inst., from an attack of pneumonia. I have known Mr. Murchison all of my life and know the high regard and the esteem his neighbors had for him. He stood high in church and Sunday school work for the last forty years. Mr. Murchison was an ex–Confederate soldier, a member of Company G, 26th N.C. Regiment, and since the great battle of Gettysburg he had not seen many days that he was not suffering from the wound by a Yankee minnie-ball. He was captured after the battle and held prisoner at David's Island in New York Harbor and was later exchanged in September and returned to duty. He was a member of the Christian Church at Pleasant Hill, and he lived on his comfortable little farm in South Alamance to a ripe old age.

—*Alamance Gleaner,* February 20, 1902

Mr. **Andrew H. Courtney**, a prominent citizen of Caldwell County, died Wednesday at his home near Hartland, in the county, on pneumonia, aged 72. He was a Confederate veteran, Company F, 26th Regiment, and lost a badly wounded leg at Gettysburg after he was captured. He was exchanged in September 1863 and retired to the Invalid Corps. He was treasurer of Caldwell County for 10 or 12 years. A wife and nine children survive.

—*Alamance Gleaner,* May 25, 1909

27th Regiment North Carolina Troops

William D. Cook died in Greensborough, June 14th. The deceased, on the appearance of Lincoln's Proclamation, though at the time in delicate health, at once promptly volunteered his service in defense of the South, and joined the Guilford Grays, Company B, 27th

N.C. Regiment. He was stationed at Fort Macon, where he remained until he became too feeble for military duty and returned to Greensborough, where he lingered with the typhoid fever for several days, then died. He was about 25 years of age.
—*Greensborough Patriot*, June 11, 1861

At Fort Macon, on the 30th of July, of typhoid fever, **George J. Sloan**, Company B, 27th N.C. Regiment, son of James Sloan, Esq., of Greensborough. He was in the 26th year of his age. He marched with his company, the Guilford Grays, to the defense of Fort Macon, where he served, without intermission, to the time of his death. His remains were attended home by a detachment of his comrades.
—**Originally published in the** *Greensboro Patriot* **and reprinted in the** *Fayetteville Observer,* **August 12, 1861**

Samuel A. Hunter, Company B, 27th N.C. Regiment, fell in the battle near Newbern, Friday 14th inst., when he was struck by a shell fragment. He was from Guilford County and enlisted in June 1861.
—*Way of the World*, April 5, 1862

Corporal John D. Collins, "Guilford Grays" Co. B, 27th Regiment N.C.T., enlisted in April 1861 at age 20 and died at Camp Jackson near Drury's Bluff, Va., June 17, 1862, of typhoid fever. He was from Guilford County.
—*Greensborough Patriot*, August 7, 1862

During the last month, the following members of Company C died: **James F. Barrow**, at Camp Jackson, aged 19, typhoid fever; **John W. Sutton**, hospital at Petersburg, Va., aged 19, bilious fever; **John W. Jump**, hospital in Petersburg, Va., aged 29, of chronic diarrhea; **William H. Waters**, at Petersburg, aged 32, of typhoid fever; and **Leonidas Herring**, hospital at Petersburg, aged 32, of meningitis, all of Lenoir County, N.C.
—*Fayetteville Observer,* August 18, 1862

Died, at Sharpsburg, Maryland, September 19th, of wounds received in the battle of the 17th Sept., **Sergeant Thomas Clay Carmichael,** aged 20 years. Sergeant Carmichael was wounded in the thigh, the wound was severe (the bone being shattered to the hip), and he had laid without attention so long (two days and one night) that the Federal surgeon declined to operate, saying it would only add to his suffering and give him no relief.

A few days before the battle, he wrote to his father speaking of and foreshadowing his fate; begging his father to take no thought of him, and not to tell his mother of the letter, it would make her unhappy.

Charles Parker, a young friend and neighbor, buried him, placing a board over his head and his name and regiment upon it.

> Slowly and sadly he laid him down,
> From the field of his fame fresh and gory;
> He carved not a line; he raised not a stone,
> But he left him alone in his glory.

—**A friend,** *Hillsboro Recorder,* October 2, 1862

Died, on the 19th of September 1862, near Sharpsburg, in Maryland, **Capt. Jason P. Joyner,** Company E, 27th Regiment N.C.T., in the 20th year of his age. This young and gallant officer was mortally wounded in the battle of Sharpsburg on the 17th of September. From the ranks he rose rapidly to the head of his company, having occupied almost every subaltern position in the short space of six months. He was twice unanimously elected Captain of his company. His military knowledge combined with his genial disposition and kindness of heart, gained for him the confidence and love not only of his command, but of the whole regiment, both officers and men. The number of the enemy's bullets through his clothes, attest his fearless courage and heroic firmness in times of danger. Pierced with four balls, he remained calm and undaunted at his post until mortally wounded by the fifth, the fatal one. His brother ran to him and asked him if he was hurt much? His reply was: "I am killed, brother." These were his last words upon the field. He was borne to his camp by four of his men, where he was tenderly nursed by a kind friend, and where he calmly breathed his last. His remains were taken to Charlestown [VA, now WVA] and neatly buried.

Dear friends, our beloved Captain is gone! We will cherish his memory as long as our hearts continue to throb. He sleeps quietly in a soldier's grave, near the spot where the first armed ruffian and invader of our homes received a just reward, upon the scaffold of his hellish and diabolical purpose. He leaves a devoted mother, an affectionate sister, two loving brothers, and a host of warm and sincere friends to mourn his loss.

—R. W. J., *North Carolina Standard,* October 14, 1862

When the conflict was raging on the battlefield of Sharpsburg, and the issue was doubtful, an order was given to charge the lines and batteries of the enemy. Promptly and nobly was the order executed. **Captain William Adams** and his Guilford Grays, Company B, 27th North Carolina, were in that terrific charge, when he received his death wound. When he fell, some of his gallant comrades wished to bear him from the field. The last utterance of his noble spirit was, *"Leave me and fight on!"* A nation's fame and a people's gratitude should not allow the names, the words and the deeds of our heroes to die.

Capt. William Adams was the son of Peter and Sarah Adams, and was born in Greensborough, N.C., on the 18th of February 1836. The affectionate liberality of his worthy father gave him the advantages of a good education, and he never forgot the moral teachings of his patriotic and Christian mother. Captain Adams graduated at our University in June 1858. He chose the profession of law, and was admitted to the bar in February 1860. Lincoln's proclamation, the cause of war and all our woes, was issued on the 15th of April 1861; and on the 23rd, the Guilford Grays were on their way to Fort Macon. A nobler band of boys never entered their country's service, and William Adams was their first–Lieutenant. For more than sixteen months he endured the toils and privations of army life. His affectionate heart was every day longing for home, but duty kept him in the camp. He soon became Captain of his company, and his comrades say he was a brave and accomplished officer. He promptly obeyed the orders of his superiors in command; and while he was firm in discipline, he was kind and generous to his men.

He commanded his company at the battle of Newbern, and did all that courage could do, to prevent that disaster. He was with his company, in a reserved corps during the seven days battle before Richmond, and he went with the army with the expedition into Maryland. He fought his last battle at Sharpsburg, and there at the post of duty and of danger, he died. At Shepherdstown his sad and weary comrades laid him in a quiet grave. He sleeps now on the confines of his country, by the banks of the beautiful Potomac. He was a member of Greensborough Lodge, No. 76, A.Y.M., and a member of the Zeta Psi Fraternity, at our University.

—*Greensborough Patriot,* November 6, 1862

Died, in Charlestown, Va., on the 19th ultimo, **Elbert Thomas Riddick, First Lieutenant** of Company F, 27th Regiment of N.C. Troops, of wounds received on the 17th of September, in the memorable battle of Sharpsburg. Lieut. Riddick was a native of Gates County, N.C., son of Joseph Riddick, Esq. deceased, and was in the twenty-third year of his age at the time of his death. He volunteered as a private in the first company that organized in Perquimans, the county in which he then resided. He conducted himself with great coolness and courage in every engagement in which he participated, and finally fell a victim to his own generosity, endeavoring to save from the hands of the enemy, the body of a dying comrade.

—*North Carolina Standard,* December 2, 1862

A number of Company B, 27th Regt. N.C. Infantry, have passed since leaving Rapidan Station, on our march to join the army of the Potomac.

R. D. Brown, Guilford County, died of typhoid in the hospital at Richmond, Sept. 21, 1862, aged 22; **Hugh A. Hall**, at Richmond, Sept. 19th, of typhoid; he was a farmer and was 20; **Robert S. Coble**, 22, Frederick, Md., Sept. 12th, of fever; **Alfred F. Coble**, aged 20, **James M. Edwards, R. Leyton Smith**, a farmer aged 22, and **Samuel Young**, also a farmer aged 19, were killed at Sharpsburg, Sept. 17th; **William W. Underwood**, farmer, aged 28, and **Robert L. Donnell**, 24, both of whom were wounded at Sharpsburg, the former having died in the enemy's Hospital, Sept. 29th, and the latter, after his capture and leg amputation, at the house of a friend in Chester, Pennsylvania,, Nov. 30th; and **William H. McLean**, a farmer, aged 22, of disease in the hospital at Winchester, Oct. 24th. Our Company B has sustained a loss not to be repaired, and our country and State, some of its best citizens.

—*Greensborough Patriot,* December 18, 1862

Died, near Pink Hill, Lenoir County, N.C., on the 3d day of December 1862, **Benjamin Franklin Nunn, 1st Lieutenant** of Company D, 27th Regiment, N.C. Troops, of wounds received on the 17th of September, in the memorable battle of Sharpsburg. Lieut. Nunn was a native of Lenoir County, N.C., son of James Nunn, Sr., dec'd, and was in the twenty-fourth year of his age at the time of his death. He volunteered as a private in the first company that organized in Lenoir County

Died of pneumonia in the hospital at Staunton, Va., the 30th day of October 1862, **Jesse Isler Nunn, 1st Sergeant** of Company D, 27th Regiment N.C. Troops, in the twentieth year of his age. Serg't. Nunn was a native of Lenoir County, son of James Nunn, Sr., dec'd. He fought bravely at the battle of Newbern. The deceased left a widowed mother and several brothers and sisters and many friends to lament their loss.

—*North Carolina Standard,* January 2, 1863

Died, on the 14th of December 1862, **Milton B. Robson**, Company G, 27th N.C., in the 23d year of his age. He joined the army in June 1861, and went to Fort Macon, where he stayed several months; then he was ordered to Virginia. He fought in the battle of Sharpsburg with undaunted bravery. The many trials and hardships he underwent he bore with great patience and resignation. He was a true and gallant soldier, but now he has fallen. While forming the line of battle at Fredericksburg on Friday he was mortally wounded, and died on Sunday morning. May God comfort his bereaved and aged father and distressed friends, and may they all met in heaven, where they will part no more, and be happy forever

—Laura, *Hillsboro Recorder,* January 28, 1863

On 3d March, in Greensboro, N.C., of typhoid fever, in the 27th year of his age, **William P. Wilson, Adjutant 27th Reg't.** Previously he had been 3rd Lieutenant of Company B. He had safely passed through the battles of Newbern, round Richmond, Harper's Ferry, Sharpsburg (where he was slightly wounded) and at Fredericksburg, Va. He was a good soldier and a young man of promise, in the prime of life. He will be remembered by the young of Fayetteville, where he once lived.

—*Fayetteville Observer,* **April 6, 1863**

Died in Richmond, Va., on Saturday October 24th, of wounds received in the battle of Bristoe Station, October 14th, **Joseph W. Rankin**, a Private in the Guilford Grays, Company B, 27th North Carolina. The deceased was one of the very first volunteers from Guilford County. Soon after Gov. Ellis ordered the Guilford Grays to Fort Macon, Mr. Rankin, then at Mr. Lindsey's Classical School, volunteered; he was but little over 18 years old. He was wounded at the battle of Sharpsburg and later returned to duty. He endured for years the chosen hardships of a private soldier, and fell, pierced through the lungs, in the most bloody and daring encounter at Bristoe. He was a member of the Presbyterian Church of Alamance.

—*Greensborough Patriot,* **November 13, 1863**

Died in Richmond on the 24th of Oct., from a hip wound received at Bristow Station on the 14th ult., **Robert D. Weatherly, Serg't. Major** of the Guilford Grays, 27th Regiment, N.C.T., aged about 23 years. At that disastrous fight, many of Cooke's and Kirkland's brigades were killed, wounded and captured. Robert was taken to Richmond and in a day or two after, his father and mother arrived and were with him until his death—some four or five days afterwards. His remains reached this place on Monday morning and were interred in the Presbyterian burying-ground the following day.

—*Greensborough Patriot,* **November 20, 1863**

The Guilford Grays lost a number of men at Bristoe Station.

Lieut. John H. McKnight fell mortally wounded there, on the 14th of October 1863. He was left on the field and died during the night. In the morning his comrades found his remains and buried him there. He was from Guilford County and was 18 when he enlisted.

William F. Hunter was 22 when he enlisted at Fort Macon in June 1861. He was wounded in the battle of Sharpsburg but soon returned to duty. He was wounded in the leg and arm at Bristoe Station. His arm was amputated and he died at Richmond November 9th.

Henry Crider was 27 when he enlisted in April 1862. He was wounded at Sharpsburg and returned to duty in November. He was killed at Bristoe Station.

John Canady was also 27 when he enlisted in February 1862. He was killed at Bristoe Station.

John T. Sockwell enlisted at Fort Macon in August 1861, aged 18. He was killed at Bristoe Station.

—*Greensborough Patriot,* **December 3, 1863**

Capt. Joseph A. Williams, from Pitt County, Co. H, 27th N.C. Troops, has died of wounds received at the battle of Bristow Station, Oct. 14th, 1863. He entered the Army in April 1861 and was elected Captain in March 1862. He was in the Fredericksburg battle in December and was wounded in the hip and returned to duty sometime in 1863. He was 24.

—*Wilmington Daily Journal,* **December 17, 1863**

Died in Hospital No. 9 at Richmond, on the 8th of November last, **John A. Quinn** of Albertson's Precinct, Duplin County, N.C., about 30 years of age. He volunteered in April 1861, and joined *Captain William T. Wooten's* (81) Company D, in which he faithfully served his country to the time of his death, having been in every battle in which the 27th regiment was engaged, down to the battle of Bristow Station, when he was mortally wounded with a severe thigh wound. After his death his remains were brought home, and on the 6th instant, interred in the family burying ground. Poor John was a brave, patriotic, and faithful soldier, an honest man, and a good citizen, and has left behind him a wife and three children, also, 3 brothers who have faithfully served their country,—to which I will add, his precinct has furnished 98 volunteers, and no conscripts nor has any man hired a substitute, and out of the 98 volunteers, 14, just 1-7th part of the whole number, have offered up their lives upon the altar of liberty. Honor to poor John's name; for if it is true that "Cowards die many times, whilst men of true courage never suffer death but once," he never died but once. Peace to his ashes.

—Chocolate, *Wilmington Daily Journal,* **December 30, 1863**

Died, at General Hospital, Richmond, Va., on the 30th day of October 1863, of wounds received in the battle of Bristow Station, **Captain James Devereux Bryan**, Company A, while gallantly leading his men in that deadly but unequal conflict with a superior force of the enemy.

When it was first discovered that this unholy war was inevitable, and when all the good and brave of the South rushed to arms at their country's call, he grasped his gun and chose for himself the true post of honor—a private's station—in the ranks. On the final organization of the company of his choice—the Goldsboro' Rifles—under *Capt. Marshall Craton*, (82) he was appointed Orderly Sergeant and elected Captain in April 1862. He was born on the 25th day of September 1838, and was therefore a little over 25 years old at his death. He was a son of Gen. Henry Bryan of Sampson County, and leaves two brothers surviving him in the army. At the battle of Bristoe Station, wounded three times, at short intervals, he still continued to cheer on his men; but a fourth bullet felled him to the ground and he had to be carried off the field. It was while being carried off by his brother and one or two members of his company, that he received the fatal wound which terminated his life. He was carried subsequently to Richmond, where he suffered intensely for two weeks during which he had all the care and attention which medical skill and kind friends could bestow. It is a consolation to his immediate relatives to know that, during most of the time and up to the moment of his death, he had all the benefit of the eminent skill and tender nursing of Dr. Jno. W. Davis of Goldsboro, who, when he could do no more for the living hero, performed the last sad office to the dead patriot by bringing home his corpse for interment. He was a communicant of the Methodist Episcopal Church; he was buried in Sampson County.

—Amicus, *Fayetteville Observer,* **January 4, 1864**

Killed, in the battle of Bristoe Station, Oct. 14th, 1863, **Private James H. Parker**, a member of the Goldsboro' Rifles, Co. A, 27th Reg't N.C. Infantry. He was the son of James R. Parker of Wayne County, N.C., and enlisted in the above company, with two of his brothers, on the 15th day of April 1861, then under the command of Capt. Marshall D. Craton.

He served with his company in all its subsequent campaigns, was in the battles of Sharpsburg, Md. (where he was severely wounded), Fredericksburg, Va., and several other engagements of less note, in each of which he greatly distinguished himself for his unflinching bravery. He gave up his life on the ill-fated field of Bristoe, where with his comrades he had breasted a perfect storm of shot and shell unhurt, until the order was given to fall back; in doing so he lingered to assist in conveying from the field the body of his Captain, who was mortally wounded, and while thus engaged, the fatal bullet pierced his head and he yielded up his life to God who gave it.

He is gone, and a braver man has not fallen during this wicked and relentless war which is now being waged against us by our vandal foes of the North.

—Julian, *Fayetteville Observer,* **January 21, 1864**

Died, at General Hospital No 1, in Richmond, Va. on the 17th day of January 1864, **Edward Ballard Sasser**, of Co A, 27th N.C. Reg't. In April 1861 he joined the Goldsboro Rifles at Fort Macon, N.C., which company afterwards was placed in 27th Reg't, and participated in every battle in which the regiment was ever engaged, but luckily escaped until the unfortunate affair at Bristoe Station on Oct. 14, 1863, where he received a wound in the left knee which finally caused his death. Deceased was a native of Wayne County, and was in the 31st year of his age. He told his brother, who attended him in his last moments, that he did not fear to die, that his soul would soon be at rest, and asked him to meet him in Heaven.

—A True Friend, *Fayetteville Observer,* **February 29, 1864**

Died a prisoner at Point Lookout, Maryland, of chronic diarrhea, **Serg't E. M. Crowson**, of Co. B 27th Reg't N.C.T. He enlisted in April 1861 at age 21. He was captured during the fight at Bristoe Station, held prisoner for a while in Washington D.C., then sent to Point Lookout.

—*Fayetteville Observer,* **March 17, 1864**

Roderick Cotton Davis of Chapel Hill, N.C., aged 25, enlisted at Fort Macon in June 1861. He was the eldest son of Dr. J. Z. Davis of that place, and grandson of General R. C. Cotton of Pittsboro, N.C. He remained in the ranks for the greater part of three years, nobly discharging his duty, till on the bloody field of the 5th at the Wilderness he was killed. A few moments before his death, he entrusted to a friend and comrade his last earthly message for the far distant loved ones. "Tell them I die resigned: may they all meet me in heaven."

—*Raleigh Register,* **June 7, 1864**

Killed, in the battle of the Wilderness, May the 5th, 1864, **Samuel McLean**, in the 33rd year of his age. He was a member of Co. B, 27th N.C. Regiment, and entered the army in the spring of 1863, where he remained, faithfully discharging all his duties as a soldier, never being absent except 18 days last winter, when home on furlough until he fell in the desperate battle of the Wilderness. His head was pierced by a ball causing immediate death, and he quietly sleeps, buried by his own brothers, beneath the pleasant shade of two large oak trees by the roadside about a half a mile from the field on which he fell.

—*Greensborough Patriot,* **July 7, 1864**

Died on the 13th July 1864, in Camp Winder Hospital, Richmond, **William M. Paisley, Orderly Sergeant** of Co. B, 27th N.C.T., and eldest son of James Paisley, was born on the 3d March 1842, and received his death wound through the lungs on the 15th June 1864, in Virginia. He joined the church at Alamance in the fall of 1858. Soon after President Lincoln's "proclamation," William Paisley, with his father's consent, left school, and volunteered in the "Guilford Greys." He remained in this company till his death. Though he passed through many bloody engagements he never received a scratch before the 15 July 1864. He died with his father at his side.

—*North Carolina Presbyterian,* **August 10, 1864**

Captain Benjamin S. Skinner fell a victim to his country's cause in the battle of Reams' Station, Virginia, on the 25th of August 1864. The fatal bullet penetrated his head just above his left eye killing him instantly. He was born in Perquimans County, N.C., in 1839, of wealthy and influential parentage. He graduated with distinction at the University of Massachusetts in the Summer of 1860. Possessing an innate love of agricultural pursuits, he returned to his home and devoted himself to the cultivation and improvement of the rich land which had fallen to his lot from the domains of his father.

But when the war drums beat, he enlisted in May 1861, as a private in the ranks. At Sharpsburg, Maryland, on the 17th day of September 1862, when so many brave hearts were crushed by the deadly missiles of our foes, Captain Skinner received a severe wound in his arm which fractured the bone. While at home convalescing, he was betrayed and captured and carried to Newbern, North Carolina, where he was kept in prison for several months. Released, he rejoined his command. The bloody conflict in which he lost his life, was, indeed, a time that tried men's souls; but Cooke's brave brigade was equal to the emergency. It was in a charge upon the enemy's lines of entrenchment that Captain Skinner fell, with the shout of victory upon his lips. His body reposes quietly in his rude grave far from the home of his childhood. A little mound of earth, an unpolished head board with the inscription: "Capt. B. S. Skinner, Co. F, 27th North Carolina Troops, killed Aug. 25th 1864," is all that marks the spot where his comrades with sorrowful hearts laid him away.

—R. W. J., *Daily Confederate,* **September 13, 1864**

Died, in the city of Richmond, on the 7th instant, of a wound received at Reams's Station on the 25th of August, **Lieut. Thomas J. Strayhorn**, of Company G, 27th Regiment, North Carolina Troops. He was 34. He had served the county of Orange for a number of years as Public Register, and afterwards as County Trustee, to the satisfaction of all his friends. Although not subject to military duty, when Gov. Ellis ordered the Orange Guards to Fort Macon he volunteered his services, and left Hillsborough with the company on the 20th day of April 1861. While in service he was detailed for various duties, and while absent from the Company, he was elected Lieutenant, which he accepted and remained with the Company until the memorable day on which he fell. He was at the head of his command, leading his men on to victory, and just as he ascended the enemy's works he received a shot which eventually terminated his earthly existence. He died peacefully and calmly.

—*Hillsboro Recorder,* **September 21, 1864**

The sad intelligence reached us on Monday, that **Serg't Daniel W. McConnell**, of Co. B 27th Regiment, N.C. Troops, expired on that morning from injuries received by the explosion of a shell. Death in the army need not surprise us at any time; yet he was so youthful, so full of life and buoyancy, that we confess that we were not prepared to realize this fearful news.—He was only a little over nineteen years of age. He was in command of his company at the time he was stung, to borrow a soldier expression, by the explosion of the shell, *Capt. John A. Sloan* (83) being in command of the regiment and his commissioned officers being all absent or dead.

—*Greensborough Patriot,* **September 22, 1864**

Died at Point Lookout, Sept. 18th, 1864, **Private George H. Woolen**, aged 26 years. He volunteered in April 1861, and he was a member of the Guilford Grays, Company B, at the time of his death. He was wounded at Sharpsburg, September 17, 1862, and later returned to duty. He was captured during the fighting at Bristoe Station, October 14, 1864, and held at the Old Capitol Prison in Washington D.C., before he was sent to Point Lookout. Far from home and friends he languished on a bed of sickness, no fond parent, nor much loved sister to smooth his dying pillow. No wreath of fame encircled his brow. Neither was his spirit cheered by the glory of his country's freedom. But still, he died for his country and his name will never be forgotten by the devoted hearts of his parent at home and long, long will his memory be cherished in the heart of his cousin.

—M., *Greensborough Patriot,* **December 1, 1864**

The Hillsborough community was shocked by the sudden and sad intelligence of the death of **Roscoe Richards**, son of Capt. Henry and Eliza Richards, of this place, who died at Trenton, in Jones County, on the 21st instant, in the 24th year of his age, after a short but painful illness.

At the breaking out of the war he went with his company, the Orange Guards (Co. G, 27th Regt. N.C.T.), and was with the famous Regiment in all its engagements during the war. He was wounded in the hand at the Battle of Sharpsburg in 1862 and again in the hand at the Wilderness, May 5, 1864. Returning to duty, he was wounded in the arm a few days later at Spotsylvania Court House. He surrendered at Appomattox Court House, April 9, 1865. He leaves kind and loving parents, brothers and sisters. He was a member of Eagle Lodge, No. 71, F. and A. M.

—*Hillsboro Recorder,* **August 28, 1867**

On Sunday morning **Mr. John E. Randolph**, who lived with his sons at House Station, 3 miles from Greenville, was found dead in bed. Mr. Randolph was quite old and had been feeble for some time. He was a life-long Democrat, a gallant Confederate soldier and a good citizen. He leaves several children, all of whom are grown. He enlisted in Pitt County in April 1861, at age 29. He served in Company H, 27th North Carolina. He was wounded in the ankle during the fight at Sharpsburg, September 17, 1862, and later returned to duty. He was again wounded in the wrist and hand at Reams' Station in August 1864, was with General Lee at the Appomattox surrender, April 9, 1865.

—*Daily Reflector,* **December 13, 1909**

Mr. Joseph T. Westbrook, one of Newton Grove's oldest citizens, passed away at his home here on Monday, June 28, 1910, in the eighty seventh year of his age. He was active and strong for one of his years and was sick only a short time before his death, dying almost suddenly. He was born and reared in Westbrook's township, Sampson County. In early manhood he married Miss Phoebe Elderidge, of Johnston County, who preceded him to the grave a few years ago. To this union were born nine children six of whom still survive him, viz: Messrs. J. F. and J. L. Westbrook, of Newton Grove, and Mr. A. T. Westbrook, of Johnston County, Mrs. Joe Royal, of Clinton, Mrs. Line Herring, of Dunn, and Mrs. J. W. Weeks, of Newton Grove, and a host of grandchildren and great grandchildren to mourn their loss.

He was an Old Confederate Veteran and served in Company A, 27th North Carolina. He was captured in the fight at Bristoe Station October 14, 1863. He was held prisoner at Point Lookout and exchanged in February 1865. He was a member of the Methodist Epis-

copal Church South at Newton Grove. After the close of the war he moved into Newton Grove Township to the place we know as the Cox Place. Mr. Westbrook was a very successful farmer and made considerable property during his life.
—*The News Dispatch,* July 14, 1910

28th Regiment North Carolina Troops

Died from the measles at Wilmington, on the 8th Dec., **Lewis A. Williams**, from Yadkin County, in the 18th year of his age, a private in *Capt. William H. A. Speer's* (84) Yadkin Stars, Company I.
—*Fayetteville Observer,* January 20, 1862

Died, at the encampment of the 28th North Carolina Regiment, Company E, Wilmington, N.C., on the 31st day of Dec. 1861, **Hugh W. McAulay** of Montgomery County, about 26 years. Though for several years in feeble health, he left father, brothers and sisters, all the comforts and pleasures of home, and went forth to help drive off the invaders from our soil.
—**One of His Brethren,** *Fayetteville Observer,* January 20, 1862

Died at the General Hospital at Goldsboro,' on the 24th of March, of typhoid fever, **Private George R. Earnhardt**, of Stanly County, of *Capt. John A. Moody's* Co. (85) (K), 28th Reg't.
—*Fayetteville Observer,* April 14, 1862

Died a prisoner in the Hospital at Fortress Monroe, Virginia, on June 30th, **Baxter B. Morris**, Co. G, 28th N.C.T. He had been wounded in the knee and captured during the fight at Hanover Court House, Virginia, May 27, 1862.
—*Fayetteville Observer,* June 21, 1862

Died in Hospital at Charlottesville, on the 6th inst., after he was shot through the lungs in the battle of Cedar Run, **Edwin P. Wade**, of Montgomery County, of Co. E, 28th Reg't, in the 24th year of his age.
—*Fayetteville Observer,* September 29, 1862

Near Fredericksburg, Va., on the 14th Dec., of a wound received on the 13th, **R. Alexander Morrow**, of Orange County, in his 21st year; he was a private in Co. G, 28th Reg., N.C.T. He joined the Presbyterian Church at Chapel Hill when he was 17 years old. He had been captured at Hanover Court House, May 27, and later released.
—*North Carolina Presbyterian,* January 10, 1863

Died, of typhoid pneumonia, at Emory Henry College, Virginia, in the 22d year of his age, **R. C. P. Faucette**, son of Thomas D. and Ann Faucette, of Orange County, N.C. The deceased was a member of the 28th N.C. Regiment, Company G, formerly under Capt. George Johnston, and since under *Capt. George McCauley.* (86) His Captain said he was a good man, and as good a soldier as ever was. He belonged to the Baptist Church. He fought in eight battles, waded the Potomac four times, and came out of all unhurt, which he attributed to the kind hand of Providence, for he said he believed in prayer.
—*Hillsboro Recorder,* February 4, 1863

Died at Howard Grove Hospital, near Richmond, March 18, of wounds received in the battle of Fredericksburg in December last, **John W. Roper**, Co. E, 28th Reg't, aged 22 years. He was a member of the Montgomery Grays and had been in the service since August 1861.
—*Fayetteville Observer,* June 22, 1863

Died, on the 19th of July, near Gettysburg, Pa., of wounds received on the 3d, **Elijah Graham Morrow**, of Orange County, Captain Co. G, 28th Regiment N.C.T. He was captured during the battle of Fredericksburg, December 13, 1862, and released a few days later. He was wounded at Chancellorsville but returned to duty just before the battle at Gettysburg. There he was wounded in the leg and captured by the enemy. His leg was amputated and he died in the hospital.
—*Fayetteville Observer,* August 14, 1863

Died at the residence of his father, in Yadkin County, on the 17th inst., **James Dallas Conrad**, Company F, son of Joseph and Elizabeth Conrad, aged 19 years. He volunteered as soon as he became 18 years of age, and being taken sick came home, returning to his company, however, as soon as he recovered, and was wounded and captured at the sanguinary battle of Gettysburg. With great difficulty, his father brought him home, where he lingered some time, suffering considerably. He bore his sufferings patiently.
—*People's Press,* September 24, 1863

It is with sorrow that we record the death of **Private Lucian Lloyd**, who was captured and died from a wound he received in the battle of Gettysburg the 3d of July. He volunteered on the 27th of August 1861, in Company G and did his part well as a soldier. Mr. Lloyd was loved by all the boys of the 28th Regiment. He was my tent mate and mess mate, and I loved him as I did a brother, and deeply deplore his death. The last words that I ever heard him say were that he wanted peace. He was captured at Fredericksburg and released soon afterwards. He leaves his father, mother, brothers and sisters, and many friends and comrades who mourn his early death.
—James F. Craige, (87) Co. G, 28th N.C.T., *Hillsboro Recorder,* September 30, 1863

Serg't John E. White, from Gaston County, enlisted in Company B, 28th N.C. Regiment, in July 1861, at age 29. He was wounded at Gaines' Mill, Virginia, in June 1862, but returned to duty later. He was captured at Gettysburg and died of chronic diarrhea, 3d Nov., 1863, at Point Lookout, Maryland, prison camp.
—*Fayetteville Observer,* February 25, 1864

Edmund Moose, of Stanly County, 1st Lieut. Company D, 28th Regiment, was wounded and captured at Gettysburg. He was sent first to a hospital in Baltimore, then to Chester Hospital, Pa., where he died September 27 of his wounds and exhaustion.
—*Fayetteville Observer,* February 29, 1864

Died at Chapel Hill, on the 9th inst., **Capt. George Burgwyn Johnston**. He was born in Hillsboro, August 17, 1849, the son of the Rev. Samuel I. Johnston, well known for many years as the Rector of St. Paul's, Edenton, and graduated at the University of North Carolina, bearing away the highest honors of his class. In June 1860 he was married to Miss Nannie Taylor, daughter of Dr. Charles E. Johnson of Raleigh, and in the same month selected to be one of the Tutors in the University. When the war broke out, he forthwith volunteered and served with the Orange Light Infantry of the "Bethel Regiment," 1st Regiment N.C.

Infantry, six months. He was subsequently promoted to a Lieutenancy, in the 28th N.C. Troops, Company G, and then Captain. He was captured at Hanover Court House, Virginia, May 27. Though he had escaped by swimming the river, he returned to the enemy and gave himself up, that he might share and perhaps alleviate the captivity of his men. He was held in several forts, the last being Johnson's Island, Ohio in June 1862. The severities of his imprisonment there laid the foundation of the disease which would eventually take his life. He was officially exchanged in November 1862. In January 1863, he was appointed Assistant Adjutant General of General James Lane's Brigade in the Army of Northern Virginia, which he held till the progress of his disease, consumption, obliged him to resign it in the summer of 1863. He returned to Chapel Hill, and after months of declining health sunk into the grave. He was a noble character, a Christian gentleman, a member of the Episcopal Church, and warmly beloved by family and friends.

—*Fayetteville Observer,* **April 18 & 21, 1864**

Killed on the 12th day of May, at Spotsylvania, C. H., **Nevin Clark**, Captain of Co. E, 28th Reg., N.C.T., Lane's Brigade. He was the son of John Clark, of Montgomery County, N.C., and was in the 30th year of his age. Capt. Clark volunteered early in the war, was elected 3rd Lieut., and at the re-organization of the Regiment was elected 1st Lieutenant. He was first in active service near Newbern, where his Regiment covered the retreat of our army; then at Hanover Court House, and the seven day's fight around Richmond, in which he was wounded in the arm, but still remained in command until sent to the rear by order of the surgeon. Time and again did he go with the gallant Lee, Lane, and others, to the enemy's land; was at Harper's Ferry, Sharpsburg, Shepherdstown, Fredericksburg, Chancellorsville, Gettysburg, the Wilderness, and the bloody field near Spotsylvania. Gallantly did he lead his men and cheer them on to meet the foe. He was a member of the church of Mt. Carmel. Thus the father has lost two noble sons, and with his family and friends mourn their loss. **Maj. George Clark** was killed at Gettysburg, and Capt. Nevin Clark at Spotsylvania—both well educated Christian gentlemen, of more than ordinary promise.

—*North Carolina Presbyterian,* **February 1, 1865**

Daniel Foust Morrow, Esq., of Burlington, died at Rex Hospital, Raleigh, Tuesday afternoon. Mr. Morrow had not been in good health for several months, and a few weeks ago he went to Raleigh for an operation from which he had almost recovered when he was taken ill from another trouble and death followed soon afterward. He was born in Orange County about 68 years ago, but for 20 years or more has made his residence at Burlington. He was mayor of the city for several years and has been a Justice of the Peace for a long time. He served his country honorably as a Confederate soldier in his young manhood days. He enlisted in Company G, 28th N.C.T., in September 1861, at age 19. He was captured at Hanover Court House, May 27, 1862, and held prisoner on a New York Harbor Island, before he was exchanged in the summer. He was wounded at Chancellorsville, and was promoted to a Lieutenancy when he returned to duty. He was surrendered at Appomattox Court House, Virginia, April 9, 1865. He is survived by his widow and five children, 3 sons and 2 daughters, four brothers, and a large and influential family connection. His remains were interred at the cemetery at Burlington yesterday afternoon with Masonic honors, he being a bright Mason and having been a W. M. at one time. He was a member of Camp Ruffin, United Confederate Veterans, in Burlington.

—*Alamance Gleaner,* **February 17, 1910**

On the 9th inst., at the Soldiers' Home in Raleigh, where he had been for a few months, **Mr. William Stewart Dixon** passed away, aged about 70 years. His nearest living relatives are some nephews and nieces. He was never married. His remains were brought up and buried at Hawfields. He was a member of Company F, 28th N.C.T. Mr. Dixon was wounded at Gettysburg and later reported back for duty.

—*Alamance Gleaner,* November 28, 1912

29th Regiment North Carolina Troops

DIED.—At Cumberland Gap, on the 26th of April, after an illness of four weeks with typhoid fever, **Private William Malcombe Hensley**, of *Capt. Bacchus Proffitt's* (88) Company K, 29th Regiment N.C. Troops, aged 17 years. He was a good soldier—brave and true—having the confidence of all who knew him, at home and in the army. He was born and raised amid the green hills of Yancey County; and though poor, speaking after the manner of man, yet in the language of the Scripture he was rich. He heard the cannon roar around the stormy Cumberland on the 22d March, but now he sleeps at its rugged base.

—**Samuel J. Westall,** (89) **Co. B, 29th Reg., N.C. Troops,**
Asheville News, May 8, 1862

DIED,—In the hospital, near Cumberland Gap, on the 27th ult., of pneumonia, **Silas M. Ray**, of Buncombe County, a member of *Captain Wiley Parker's* (90) Company H, 29th Regiment N.C. Troops, and son of the late Archibald Ray, of Buncombe County. He received during his illness every attention and kindness, and was assiduously nursed and cared for by one of the kindest of men. His remains were brought home for interment, and now rest by the side of those of his father. Peace to the ashes of the gallant dead.

—*Asheville News,* May 29, 1862

James W. Patterson, son of J. R. and Nancy Patterson, 2d Lieut. in Company G, 29th Regt. N.C. Troops, died at Parrotsville, Tenn., Dec. 17, 1861. He was born in Yancey County, June 4, 1838—was raised by religious parents, and at the age of 15 joined the M. E. Church at a Camp Meeting held at Burnsville Camp Ground. His body was brought home at the command of *Lt. Col. William Walker,* (91) and deposited in the place selected by himself before he left home. He was one among that valiant band who was instrumental in crushing the rebellion in East Tennessee and taking and trying those Bridge burners. He was at the time just recovering from sickness, and though not able, took an active part in these proceedings. After which he was taken with a relapse of measles, of which he died after ten days suffering.

—**A friend,** *Asheville News,* September 4, 1862

DIED,—In Knoxville, Tenn., on the 15th of July 1862, **Hugh L. Gudger**, Private in Co. C, 29th Reg. N.C.T. He was the son of Mr. Robert L. and Mary Gudger, of Turkey Creek, N.C. He was born in April 1843, in Buncombe County. In April last he joined the army at Cumberland Gap, and in June, while camped at Bean's Station, he was attacked with measles. He did not suffer a great deal, nor was he thought to be dangerous. In fact, he was thought to be recovering. But being sent forward to Knoxville for the purpose of getting a furlough, he is supposed to have taken cold, which, with the fatigue of the journey, produced a relapse, ending in death after two weeks of confinement in the hospital.

He suffered and died among strangers, far from the home of his youth and the friends that he loved! He wrote to his father, but that letter was not received in time for his father to visit him. He also wished to see his brother, *Capt. John W. Gudger* (92) of Company C; but when he found that this could not be, he murmured not, but was patiently resigned to the will of God.

—E. C. Wexler, His Chaplain, *Asheville News,* September 25, 1862

We announce with sincere regret the death of **Lieut. Col. Thomas F. Gardner**, late of the 29th N.C. Regiment. He had served as 2nd Lieutenant of Company B before he was promoted to Major in September 1861. In the fall of 1862 he was captured by the enemy and exchanged near Vicksburg in December. He had resigned his commission in March 1863 in consequence of bad health—chronic diarrhea and a bout with pneumonia while in Kentucky—and returned to his home in Yancey County, where he died on the 31st of May. He was a good man and a gallant and faithful officer.

—Originally published in the *Asheville News* and reprinted in *Way of the World,* July 9, 1863

Marcus D. L. Garmon, Company C, 29th N.C. Troops, a native of Buncombe County, died in the stage on his way home from the army at Cumberland Gap, without a relative or friend to minister to his wants, or hear his dying words.

—*Asheville News,* October 30, 1862

30th Regiment North Carolina Troops

Josiah Johnson of New Hanover County was 27 when he joined the Duplin Turpentine Boys, Company E, 30th Regiment. He caught the typhoid fever and died at Smithville [now called Southport] November 13.

—*Wilmington Daily Journal,* November 20, 1861

Obed Carr was aged 44 when he enlisted in the Duplin Turpentine Boys, Company E, 30th Regiment. He died from typhoid pneumonia at Camp Wyatt on November 16.

—*Wilmington Daily Journal,* December 2, 1861

Died in Wilmington at Camp Wyatt, from typhoid fever, on the 1st December 1861, **Samuel W. Thomas Dunn**, son of the late Col. J. A. Dunn of Union County, N.C., in the 17th year of his age. He was a volunteer in *Capt. James Kell's* (93) Company K.

—*Fayetteville Observer,* January 20, 1862

Died of typhoid fever in a Wilmington hospital, **Elisha Moseley**, of Pitt County, around the first of June. He was 19. On June 15th, **Thomas Edwards** of Edgecombe County also died in a Wilmington hospital from typhoid fever. He was 35. Both were members of the Sparta Band, Company F, 30th Regiment.

—*Fayetteville Observer,* July 7, 1862

Capt. John G. Witherspoon's Company K, 30th Reg. N.C. Troops, has lost the following men on the Virginia battlefields of the 27th June and 1st of July.

Serg't. Andrew F. Steel from Mecklenburg County was 28 when he enlisted in September 1861. He was wounded at Gaines' Mill, May 27, and died in early July.

Serg't. Sidney Tedder resided in Mecklenburg County and was 31 when he enlisted. He was killed at Gaines' Mill.

Private George W. Davis of Mecklenburg County enlisted at age 17. He was killed at Gaines' Mill.

Private James R. Robinson of Union County was 16 when he enlisted September 1861. He was killed at Malvern Hill July 1.

CAMP NEAR RICHMOND, July 17th, 1862.
To the friends of those of Co. K, 30th Regiment, N.C.T., that fell in the late battles:
It is with much regret that we have been unable to send home the remains of those that were most dear to you. Although lifeless, it would have been a gratification for you to receive their remains, but the necessity of the case was such that we could not even pay them the respect that was due them. Two of them fell almost touching me, and notwithstanding that you and we have to mourn their loss, we can say they were among the most pious and better prepared to meet their fate than some of us would have been. Though they sleep far away from you we wish peace to their ashes and happiness to their immortal souls. All but one, Sergeant Steele, was killed instantly, and from the manner in which he had a note written to me concerning his private affairs shows he was remarkably cool. Apart from business his note was farewell, tell my wife good bye, also for her to pray to meet me in heaven, where the roaring of cannon and the sound of musketry is not heard, to walk the golden streets.

Very Respectfully,

JOHN G. WITHERSPOON, Captain Company K.

—*Daily Bulletin,* **July 22, 1862**

Captain William T. Arrington, Company I, 30th Regiment N.C. Troops, enlisted at age 40 in Nash County in September 1861. He was killed at Malvern Hill July 1, 1862.

—*Wilmington Daily Journal,* **July 22, 1862**

Died at the Winder Hospital, Richmond, Va., on the 22nd Sept., 1862, of Typhoid Fever, **Murdock A. McIver**, in his 21st year. He was a member of *Capt. Jesse Wicker*'s (94) Co. H, Moore Co. Rifles, 30th Regt. N.C. Troops, with which he had for the past 12 months performed all the duties appertaining to a soldier's life. He was born in Moore Co., where he resided until the commencement of this war, then enlisted in August 1861.

—*North Carolina Presbyterian,* **October 11, 1862**

Killed on the 17th day of September 1862, on the heights of Sharpsburg, Maryland, **Andrew Jackson Dunn**, of the 30th Regt. N.C.T., Company K. He was a citizen of Providence, Mecklenburg County and early joined the ranks of the defenders of his country, leaving behind him, among the endearments of the home, a devoted young wife. He had bravely passed through many a hard fought contest of this war, and gloriously fell with his face toward his foe. True, but a few days before, I saw him; he bade me adieu with his usual warm and heart-some smile. He fell amid the raging of that terrible conflict; as the mountain tops were wrapped, and the valleys beneath were shrouded in the battle-smoke—lighted up by the glaring flash of artillery. It was in this grand and terrible scene that his noble spirit, with many gallant ones went up to God who gave it.

—*North Carolina Presbyterian,* **November 15, 1862**

Died in the Hospital at Staunton, Va., 12th Dec., **James R. Stephenson**, aged 31 years, a private in Company K, 30 Reg't. He was a native of Mecklenburg County and enlisted there in September 1861. He was badly wounded at Sharpsburg, September 17 and died as stated.

—*Fayetteville Observer,* **November 15, 1862**

Died in Clinton, Sampson County, N.C., on the 26th Dec. 1862, **George H. Draughon**, only son of G. W. Draughon, in the 20th year of his age, a member of Co. A, 30th Reg't N.C.T. Having encountered the dangers and toils of the battles of Mechanicsville, Cold Harbor and Malvern Hill, around Richmond, the toilsome march from Richmond to Maryland, and there undergoing the labor and hardships of a soldier's life in the battles of South Mountain and Sharpsburg, without a single blemish to his person or character, he was at last fallen a victim to disease so usually contracted in Camp, and now sleeps in his quiet grave.

—*Fayetteville Observer,* **January 26, 1863**

Edward McIver, a private in Co. H (Moore County Rifles), 30th Reg't N.C. Troops, departed this life from pneumonia at Port Royal, Va., on the 18th of Dec. last, aged 24 years and 22 days. He enlisted last April and in a few short weeks he was engaged with the enemy in the hard fought battles around Richmond, and in quick succession the battles of Second Manassas and Sharpsburg, in all of which he made himself useful in driving back the foe. He was not found faltering or wanting at his post. His illness was short. He was ministered to by a skillful (N.C.) physician, and had the attentions of a particular friend and near neighbor, who stayed by him till his days were numbered and followed him to a cedar tree in Academy Square, that marks his last resting place. He was the only stay and support of an aged and widowed mother and three sisters.

Buffalo, Moore Co., N.C.

—*Fayetteville Observer,* **January 26, 1863**

Died, near Fredericksburg, about the 20th of December last, **Duncan McDougald**, son of William McDougald of Moore County, aged 26 years and 10 months. He was a member of Company H (Moore County Rifles), 30th N.C.T., and died of a wound received in the battle of Fredericksburg, on the 13th of December. He lived seven days after having undergone the painful operation of amputation of the left leg. He was in the battles below Richmond and also in the battle of Sharpsburg, where he was taken prisoner—was sent to Ft. Delaware and kept there for three weeks, then paroled, sent to Richmond and immediately exchanged, and soon after rejoining his Company received the fatal wound at Fredericksburg. He was born in Scotland, Island of Jura, and was three years of age when his father and family emigrated to N.C. in 1839. He was of the eighth generation of McDougalds in Jura, the first of whom belonged to the House of Lorn. His name and baptism are recorded on the Session Book of the Church of Scotland in Jura, where for three or four generations his ancestors served as the Ruling Elders in that Church. He now lies in the land of his adoption, for which he thought proper to fight and die in order to protect it, four thousand miles away from the land of his sires and the place of his birth. He was a member of Crain's Creek Lodge, No. 213.

Farewell, dear brother, your warfare's o'er; you will never answer to roll call any more upon the earth, and another name is added to the roll of martyrs for the cause of the Confederacy.

—D., *Fayetteville Observer,* **March 30, 1863**

Died, in Richmond, at the Chimborazo Hospital, on the 29th of March inst., **Sergeant Thomas D. Wolf**, of Co. K, 30th Regiment N.C.T., in the 22d year of his age. He was from Mecklenburg County and had braved many a hard fought field, from the earliest period of the war up to the present, and suddenly fell a victim to disease in the cheerless hospital.
—*Daily Bulletin,* April 15, 1863

David B. Stedman, a Private of Company H, 30th Reg't N.C.T., died of typhoid pneumonia the 13th of April 1863, in his 22d year. He was a brave and gallant soldier who had distinguished himself in the series of battles around Richmond, and the severe battle of Sharpsburg and the first battle of Fredericksburg. He was from Chatham County and was a member of Buffalo Lodge, No. 172, of Free and Accepted Masons.
—*Fayetteville Observer,* June 8, 1863

Died, at Camp near Fredericksburg, Va., of pneumonia, on 13th May, **Private Doctor Hughes**, of Co. H, 30 Reg't. The deceased had been in eight hard-fought battles, and always conducted himself bravely. He was buried to-day (14th) in a beautiful cedar hedge, about half a mile from the railroad, with religious services by the Rev. A. D. Betts.
—*Fayetteville Observer,* June 8, 1863

Died of pneumonia, in Hospital at Richmond, Va., **Privates Andrew Cole** on the 2d April, and **Kenneth H. McIver** 6th June 1863, at Chimborazo Hospital, of wounds received at Fredericksburg; he was the son of D. D. McIver of Moore County. This is the second son this honored father has given as a sacrifice to his country. Two others remain in the service. Killed at the battle of Gettysburg, Pa., 1st July 1863, **Private Louis M. Wicker**. He was a member of Buffalo Lodge, No. 172, of Free and Accepted Masons.

All belonged to Co. H, 30th Reg't N.C.T. They have been faithful soldiers in the army of the Confederate States for nearly two years. At their country's call they went forth to assist in driving the invading enemy from our soil. Being always at their post, they were never known to falter from performing their whole duty. They were among the many who sacrificed their lives upon the altar of liberty.
—J. J. Wicker, Capt. Comd'g Co., Camp near Orange C. H., Va.,
Aug. 7, 1863, *Fayetteville Observer,* August 17, 1863

Died, at Gordonsville, Va., Nov. 9th, 1863, **Lt. Col. William W. Sillers**, 30th Reg't N.C.T., of wounds received in the late battle near Kelly's Ford on November 7. Col. Sillers was in the 25th year of his age. He volunteered in Company A and was elected 1st Lieut. At the re-organization of the Reg't. he was elected Major. Since that time he has been with them wherever the thunders of battle shook the hills of the "Old Dominion." His blood mingled with the stream which crimsoned the heights of Malvern Hill, where he was wounded in the arm. He had just been promoted to Lt. Col, when at the head of his Reg't he was killed.
—*Fayetteville Observer,* November 23, 1863

Died of disease Nov. 29th, 1863, in hospital at Gordonsville, Va., **Private Anderson Cook**, of Alamance County. He was 43 years old. Also, on the 9th February 1864, at camp near Orange C. H., Va., **Private Thomas Pool** of Orange county. He was 18 years old. Both of Co. H, 30th N.C.T.
—*Fayetteville Observer,* February 24, 1864

Capt. John G. Witherspoon of Co K, 30th Reg't, was shot through the breast at Kelly's Ford, on the 7th of Nov, and died a prisoner on the spot a few hours afterwards, aged 26. He was from Cabarrus County and enlisted in September 1861. He was a brave and gallant soldier.

—*Fayetteville Observer,* March 17, 1864

Rufus Weeks was killed on the 19th ult. near Spotsylvania C. H., Va. He was a member of Co. K, 30th Reg. N.C.T. This heroic young man, aged 19, volunteered at the beginning of the war, and has participated in the service of the Army of Va., from Sharpsburg to the battle of the Wilderness. He was wounded in the shoulder at Sharpsburg but returned to duty in October. He was at home but once from the day he entered the army till he fell, and that was on a furlough of eleven days, last winter. It was during this furlough that the writer first knew him and found him to be a warm hearted and heroic man. His only brother was wounded about the same time that he was killed. These were the only sons of their mother, and she a widow. She has struggled hard in their absence, and now her heart is broken, while she weeps for her children.

—Pastor, *North Carolina Presbyterian,* June 15, 1864

Charles Center, Company H, 30th N.C., from Harnett County, enlisted at age 40. He was wounded in the head and captured at Spotsylvania Court House, May 12, 1864, and died in a Washington D.C. hospital on May 31st.

—*North Carolina Argus,* June 16, 1864

Last Wednesday morning about 8 o'clock **Mr. Judson Hobbs** died at the home of his daughter, Mrs. Julia Smith's in McDaniel's Township. Mr. Hobbs was about 67 years of age. At the outbreak of the war he volunteered his services in Company A, 30th N.C.T., and went through the entire four years of the war and was a brave Confederate Soldier. He was captured at Winchester, Virginia, October 19, 1864, and held prisoner at Point Lookout, Maryland, until his release on June 27, 1865. Deceased was a member of the Methodist Church and is said to have lived a consecrated Christian life. The funeral services were conducted by the Rev. T. M. Lee, and the remains were laid to rest in the family burying ground in the presence of a large concourse of people who had gathered to pay their last respects to their neighbor and friend. He leaves a devoted wife and seven children to mourn their loss.

—*The News Dispatch,* April 14, 1910

31st Regiment North Carolina Troops

Died of disease in the "Post Hospital," Washington, N.C., on the 19th Dec. 1861, **Private Benjamin F. Pitman,** of Robeson County, in the 19th year of his age. He was a member of *Captain Condray Godwin*'s (95) Company A, 31st Regiment North Carolina Troops.

Fort Hill, N.C., Dec. 19, 1861.

—*Fayetteville Observer,* January 6, 1862

William Thomas Parker and **Calvin Cox**, both of Anson County and members of the "O. K. Boys," Company B, 31st N.C. Regiment died in the Hospital at Washington. William was 18 and Calvin was 19. Both died in mid-December.
—*North Carolina Argus,* January 30, 1862

Died of disease on Roanoke Island, on Dec. 26th, 1861, **James S. Carlisle**, private in Capt. C. Godwin's Company A, 31st Regiment, N.C. Troops, in the 26th year of his age. He was from Robeson County and leaves a widow and child to mourn their loss.
—*Fayetteville Observer,* February 3, 1862

Died at home of disease in Harnett County, **Joseph F. Cutts**, son of William and Martha Cutts, of Harnett County. He was upon Roanoke Island at the time of its fall, belonging to Company C, 31st Regiment N.C. Troops. He was taken prisoner and paroled, then fell sick. He spent near five long weeks in the hospital at Raleigh, and was then conveyed to his mother's, in a supposed improving condition; but soon after reaching there he breathed his last. His soldier brethren attended the burying of his body on the 6th.
—*North Carolina Standard,* April 14, 1862

Captain Andrew W. Betts departed this life the 16th ult. He had been a member of the Baptist Church some ten or twelve years, and was at his death an ordained, active and zealous minister of the Gospel. When the war commenced he felt it his duty to exert himself for the defense of his home and the rights of the South. He, as a Christian, consulted his pastor as to the propriety of a minister of the Gospel engaging in military operations, after which he raised a company, headed it, and led in defense of the rights of the Confederacy. He, with his Company C, 31st Regiment, was taken prisoner in the defense of Roanoke Island and paroled, in order to an exchange. He returned home diseased about the 26th of February, from which he lingered until the 15th ult., when he was attacked with purpura hemoragic, which terminated his life on the 15th. He was interred on the evening of the 17th, by those of his company who heard of the sad event in the presence of a large concourse of people. He left an affectionate wife and seven children to lament his loss.
—*North Carolina Standard,* May 17, 1862

Died on the 28th ult, very suddenly, at Camp Whiting near Wilmington, N.C., **David W. Johnson**, son of T. O. Johnson and a member of Co. I, 31st N.C. Reg't., from Harnett County. From the time of his enlistment (Oct. 1861) to the day of his death, he was never upon the "sick list" and never known to murmur on account of any duty assigned him; on the evening previous to his death his brother asked him why he went on dress parade while suffering with such pain; he replied he wanted to be at his post and do his duty as long as he lived. The next morning at the sound of the reveille, he arose from his hard bed with an aching head and fevered pulse, went into line, answered to his name, returned back and laid down and died in a short time. He had been captured on Roanoke Island and later released.
—*Fayetteville Observer,* February 9, 1863

Lt. William O. Tutor, Co. I, 31st N.C. Reg't., of Harnett County, enlisted in October 1861. He was captured on Roanoke Island February 8, 1862, and released later in the month at Elizabeth City. He died of typhoid pneumonia at the hospital in Wilmington January 29, 1863.
—*Fayetteville Observer,* February 16, 1863

James C. Bird, of Anson County, a member of the "O. K. Boys," Company B, 31st N.C.T., enlisted in October 1861 and was later captured at Roanoke Island in February. He was released later in the month and returned to duty. Receiving a wound at White Hall in December, he came home and taking the Typhoid Fever, he died on the 11th inst.

—*North Carolina Argus,* **February 19, 1863**

Serg't. George W. Barber, and **Private Willis J. J. Wilson**, of Company D, 31st Reg't. N.C.T., have died. Both were from Wake County, N.C. George was 22 when he enlisted in September 1861. He was taken prisoner at Roanoke Island February 8th and released later in the month. He died of disease on March 7th, 1863. Willis was 18 when he enlisted in September 1862. He died the 7th of March 1863, after a severe attack of typhoid fever, at Charleston, S.C.

—*North Carolina Standard,* **March 17, 1863**

Privates Adolomus Massey and **James P. Ferrell**, Company H, 31st Reg't. N.C.T., of Wake County, N.C., have died. Private Massey was 18 when he enlisted in 1862, and he died in the Hospital at Wilmington, N.C., on the 19th day of February 1863, of typhoid fever. Private Ferrell enlisted at age 20 in October 1861. He was captured on Roanoke Island and later paroled. He died in the hospital at Charleston, S.C., on the 19th day of March 1863, after a brief illness of typhoid fever.

—*North Carolina Standard,* **March 31, 1863**

Died at the Marine Hospital, March 27th, **Doctor Peter Barton Custis**, aged 39 years.

The deceased was a native of Newbern, in which place he devoted himself to the practice of his profession, until the commencement of the war. Taken prisoner at New Bern, exposed to the hardships and fatigue of camp life, his constitution always delicate, began to sink; yet it was only in response to the most urgent solicitations of his friends that he consented to leave active service and accept the position of Surgeon in charge of the Marine Hospital at Wilmington. During the autumn of last year while the fire of yellow fever was raging fiercely around, Dr. Custis remained faithful at his post, earning for himself the esteem and respect of those to whom moral courage is a virtue. He lost a large amount of property when New Bern was captured, but no expression of regret ever fell from his lips.

—*Wilmington Daily Journal,* **April 1, 1863**

The following members of Company D, 31st Regiment N.C.T., have died. **Serg't. Richard A. Smith**, enlisted in Wake County in September 1861, at age 20. He was captured at Roanoke Island in February and released a few weeks later. He contracted typhoid fever and died March 23d, at Savannah, Ga. He was a member of the Baptist Church and a brother of the late **Samuel A. Smith**, Company G, 3rd Regiment N.C.T., who died in 1862. Private Samuel A. Smith, of Wake County, was 21 when he enlisted in September 1861. He was also captured and released at Roanoke Island and died of disease at home on March 24. **Private David Roberts**, from Johnston County, enlisted in September 1861, aged 18. Captured and released at Roanoke Island, he later died of disease at Charleston, South Carolina, March 18. **John B. Whitley** enlisted in Wake County at age 18, in September 1862 and died of disease on the 18th inst., at Charleston, S.C.

—*North Carolina Standard,* **April 14, 1863**

Died of pneumonia in the hospital at Wilmington, 22d February, **James K. Smith**, in the 19th year of his age, private of Co. B, O. K. Boys, 31st Reg't, son of W. E. and Mary

Smith, formerly of Richmond County. As soon as he arrived at the age of 18 years he volunteered in *Capt. Charles B. Lindsay*'s (96) company. Of him, his Captain says, "Jimmy was a noble boy, loved by officers and men. Never was an order given that he refused to obey; always at his post. In fact, if he had any faults, I was unable to discover them."

He was in the battle below Kinston, and soon after that fell a victim to camp fever. He was sick but a short time, and for the last few days was attended by his father and mother. His Bible, given to him by his sorrow-stricken mother, was found under his head after his death.

—*Fayetteville Observer,* **April 20, 1863**

Privates Benjamin Parnell and **Edmund M. Phillips**, both of Robeson County, N.C., and both members of Company A, 31st N.C. Regiment, have died. Private Parnell passed away in the Hospital at Wilmington, N.C., on the 26th of March 1863, of typhoid fever. He was 31. Private Phillips died in the Hospital at Charleston, S.C., on the 11th of March 1863, after a brief illness of typhoid fever. He was 24.

—*Fayetteville Observer,* **May 4, 1863**

The following members of Company E, 31st Reg. N.C. Troops, have died.

Serg't. Abner C. Pope, of Orange County, enlisted in October 1861. He was captured at Roanoke Island in February 1862 and later released. He died of disease at Charleston, South Carolina, April 3, 1863. He was about 27.

Private Joseph A. Tinnen, from Orange County, died of disease this March at Charleston, South Carolina.

George M. Ray, of Orange County, enlisted at age 30. He was captured and released at Roanoke Island. He also died in Charleston of disease on April 3.

John W. Porterfield, and **James H. Porterfield**, who died of disease at the Citadel Hospital, in Charleston, S.C., were both from Orange County. Both were captured and released at Roanoke Island.

John H. Douglas, who died in April of typhoid fever at the General Hospital, in Macon, Ga. was from Alamance County and 18 years old.

Private John W. Jordan, who died of diphtheria in December at the General Hospital, in Goldsborough, N.C. was from Orange County and was aged 21 years.

Private David W. Rhew, who died of disease February 11 at the General Hospital, in Wilmington, N.C., was from Orange County.

Though they fell by the hand of disease, they are as much martyrs to the cause of Southern Independence as those who have fallen in battle, being ever ready to discharge their duties.

—*Hillsboro Recorder,* **May 6, 1863**

Died of disease in the hospital at Charleston, May 28th, **William H. Blalock**, aged 20, and in Wilmington, June 28th, his elder brother, **Jesse Blalock**, died of typhoid. Both were from Orange County and both were in Company E, 31st N.C. Regiment.

—*Fayetteville Observer,* **July 13, 1863**

Died, on the 22d of July last, from the effects of a wound received in the battle of Morris Island, Charleston, South Carolina, **Captain Allen B. Parker**, of Co. I, 31 Reg't N.C. Troops. He was from Harnett County and was 25 when he enlisted in October 1861. He was captured at Roanoke Island and later released.

—*Fayetteville Observer,* **September 28, 1863**

Andrew Lawrence, Co G, 31st Reg't., was 19 when he enlisted in Hertford County, September 1861. He was one of the many captured at Roanoke Island and later freed. He fell mortally wounded at Battery Wagner, Charleston, South Carolina, 18th July and died on the 28th.

—*Fayetteville Observer*, October 12, 1863

Died, near Cedar Grove, on the morning of the 13th ult. of chronic Diarrhea, in the 29th year of his age, **John Faulkner**, Co. E, 31st, N.C.T. He was a poor man, but with that unselfish patriotism and love of country volunteered early in the war in Company E raised by *Capt. Jesse Miller*, (97) now commanded by *Capt. Julius Allison*. (98) Thus have fallen, in defense of their country, three of five brothers—a sorrow to the aged mother. His wife preceded him, followed by the babe that he never saw.

—*Hillsboro Recorder*, April 13, 1864

Died, in Chimborazo Hospital, Richmond, on the 24th of May, of a chest wound received in the battle near Drury's Bluff, **Lieut. Junius A. Liles**, Co. B, 31st Reg't, son of James A. Liles, Esq. of Anson County, aged 37 years. With the exception of the time he was on parole as a prisoner after his capture on Roanoke Island and release, he remained in active service to the time of receiving his fatal wound. I have known Lieut. L. since the days of childhood and seen him *tried* under various circumstances. In the camp, on the weary march, on the battle-field, where death rode on every breeze and the ground grew red with blood, his cheerfulness, vivacity, coolness and bravery never left him. He died as he had lived, a patriot and Christian gentleman, his last thoughts being of his home and his country, and his last words "tell my mother I am willing to die, and have done my duty."

—*Fayetteville Observer*, June 13, 1864

The following members of Co. K, 31st Regt, N.C.T., have died: **Serg't. Caleb Dixon** and **Alexander Willis.**

Serg't. Dixon was a very pious young man, ever at his post, responding to every duty with cheerfulness unparalleled; doing credit to himself and pleasure to his commander, until 31st of May, when he fell while on a most gallant charge under a most galling fire. So composed was his feeling, that a smile even lingered on his lips while death held him motionless. He was from Chowan County and was 20 years old.

Private Alexander Willis was also a brave and noble soldier, who always held the confidence of his officers and comrades up to the ever memorable 31st of May, when he was wounded and almost instantly killed, and though he could not speak, he seemed reigned and calm. He was from Chowan County and was captured during the fighting on Roanoke Island.

—*Daily Confederate*, June 20, 1864

Killed, and buried on the battle field near Drury's Bluff, on the 16th of May 1864, **Capt. Samuel P. Collins**, Co. A, 31st Regiment N.C.T., of Orange County, in the 32d year of his age. He fell while gallantly leading his company in a charge on the enemy's works, nobly battling for the independence of his bleeding country. He had been 2nd Lieutenant of Company E prior to his promotion. He has left an affectionate wife and four little daughters, a father, mother, two sisters and many friends, to mourn.

—*Hillsboro Recorder*, July 20, 1864

Died of wounds, in the enemy's hands, on the 9th of June 1864, **Stephen L. Clark**, a member of Co. E, 31st N.C.T., aged 17 years and two months. He enlisted in September

1863 and had passed through the first battle on the south side of Richmond, and on the 31st of May he went with his regiment to Cold Harbor, where he, with many of his comrades, were killed or wounded. Having received a severe wound, he fell into the enemy's hands, and only lived nine days. He had been a member of the Presbyterian Church two years.

—*Hillsboro Recorder,* **August 3, 1864**

Sgt. John P. Dewar, Co I, 31st N.C.T., and youngest son of A. H. Dewar of Harnett County, was shot through the head by a sharpshooter near Petersburg, Virginia and instantly killed on the 30th June 1864. He enlisted in October 1861 and was taken prisoner on Roanoke Island and later released. He was a faithful member of the Methodist Church, and leaves his aged parents and brothers and sisters.

—*Fayetteville Observer,* **August 22, 1864**

Died, at Camp Winder Hospital, Richmond, Va., on the 5th day of July last, **Joseph W. Porterfield**, of Orange County, in the 22d year of his age. He received a mortal wound near Petersburg, on the 1st day of June. His sufferings were great until the day of his death. He was a member of Company E, 31st N.C. Troops and had volunteered and joined the company in 1861. He leaves a mother, a brother and sister.

—*Hillsboro Recorder,* **August 24, 1864**

One by one we are called upon to mourn departed friends: one by one the choicest and noblest of our youths are sacrificing their precious lives on the altar of liberty. Old Anson mourns many of her best and bravest, but for none that have fallen has more sincere sorrow been felt than for **Capt. John F. Forte**, Co. A and **Serg'ts. J. N. Hancock** and **James N. DeBerry**, Co. B, 31st Regt, who fell at Fort Harrison.

Capt. F. was originally a private in Co. B, but escaping from Roanoke Island, he was elected to a Lieutenancy in a company formed at Wilmington, composed of such men of the 31st as were not taken on that ill-fated island. The company retained its organization, and he was afterwards promoted to the Captaincy.

Serg't. Hancock, a native of Randolph County was engaged in teaching in Anson at the beginning of hostilities, and volunteered early in '61 at age 29. He was captured and released at Roanoke Island.

Serg't. DeBerry—poor Jimmy! He enlisted at 18 in October 1861. What could be too good to say of him? Light-hearted, generous, brave, amiable, truthful and honorable, and his sorrowing friend who pens these lines, his intimate and trusted companion for many weary months of war's hardships, who loved him as a brother, offers his humble tribute to his worth as a soldier and to his claims to the praise and remembrance of all who prize *true goodness* and *true greatness*.

—*North Carolina Argus,* **October 27, 1864**

Died on the 2d of Oct. 1864, near the battle-field, **Daniel McLean Jones**, son of Nat. G. and Mary M. Jones, 1st Lieut. Co. I, 31st N.C.T. He was from Harnett County and enlisted at age 18 in October 1861. He was among the many captured on Roanoke Island and then released. He died from wounds received in the advance of Clingman's Brigade upon "Fort Harrison," below Richmond. He fell with his face to the foe, with his country's flag in hand, while twenty yards in advance of his Company, which he then commanded.

—*Fayetteville Observer,* **November 10, 1864**

John A. Martin, son of G. W. and Susan Martin, of Merven, Anson County, N.C., died in the Howard's Grove Hospital, Richmond, Va., on the 11th of August 1864. At the breaking out of the war he volunteered in the Company called O. K. Boys, now attached to the 31st Regiment, N.C.T., as Co. B. He was taken prisoner on Roanoke Island, and after he was exchanged rejoined his Regiment. He was wounded in the fight at White Hall in Lenoir County, December 16, 1862. He was in the memorable defense of Charleston, S.C. His Brigade (Clingman's), being ordered to Petersburg, he was wounded very severely at Drury's Bluff in May 1864, and was sent to Richmond, and after lingering several months in severe suffering, he closed his career in resignation and peace. He was a useful and consistent member of the M. E. Church South.

—*North Carolina Argus,* December 22, 1864

32nd Regiment North Carolina Troops

We are grieved to record the death of this gallant and noble-hearted young man, who fell in the battle below Richmond on Tuesday last. **Lieut. Leonidas J. Merritt** was second in command of the Chatham Rifles, 2nd Company I, 32nd Regiment North Carolina troops; and we learn from his Captain (Capt. William London, (99) who passed through this place on Sunday), that he was struck with a Minnie ball, which entered his side through his arm, and came out under his shoulder blade. He died almost instantly. His last expressive was, "come on, my brave boys!"

Lieut. Merritt was wounded in the battle of Wynn's Mill, and was relieved for some weeks from duty on this account, during which time he occupied his seat as a member of the Convention. He returned voluntarily to his company; as under the conscription law he was exempt, being a Clerk of one of the Courts in Chatham. We conversed with him the day before he returned, and we know, as his conduct shows, that he was actuated by the loftiest sense of duty. His fellow-citizens of Chatham were urging him to be a candidate for the Legislature, and his election would have been certain if he had consented to run, and this also would have exempted him from the conscription; but he told us he was in for the war, and he could not think of leaving the brave boys who composed his company, and who had stood by him in battle. We knew him intimately, and we mingle our regrets with those of his numerous friends.

—*North Carolina Standard,* July 9, 1862

In Franklin County, 14th August, **Rufus E. Egerton**, in the 19th year of his age, the third son who departed this life within the space of a month. Deceased was a member of the "Franklin Rifles," 5th (now 15th) Reg't. He transferred to 2nd Company K of the 32nd on July 4, 1862.

—*Fayetteville Observer,* September 1, 1862

Died on the 3d July, from wounds received on the first day of the battle near Gettysburg, **Archibald J. Davis**, of Franklin County, in the 25th year of his age, of 2nd Company K, 32d N.C. Regiment. Before transferring to this company, he was a private in Company L, 15th N.C. Regiment (5th Regiment N.C. Volunteers).

—*Fayetteville Observer,* July 27, 1863

Killed, on the 3d of July, in a charge at Gettysburg, Pa., **Corporal Thomas D. Clegg**, of 2nd Company I, 32d N.C.T. He volunteered May 1861; his absence from home was but brief; he soon returned with a furlough on account of bad health; recovering from which, he hurried back to camp, endured many fatiguing marches, was wounded at Malvern Hill, again came home, and returned to come no more. He bid all adieu with tears streaming down his cheeks, at the same time saying, "I will see home and friends no more." His mother, sisters and brothers are left to mourn for their loved one. He professed religion in the 12th year of his age, joined the Methodist Church. His life in camp can be no better described than by an extract from a letter to his mother, written by a comrade, in which he said: "Cousin Tom was a brave and good boy; all the company speak of him as a Christian; none doubt but that he is now peaceful and happy." Although he fills a soldier's grave upon the far and distant plains of Gettysburg, his friends will never cease to remember with affection his many virtues and have no doubt but that he is gone to his reward in Heaven, where he will meet with his brother, who, also, gave his life for his country.

—Sister, *Fayetteville Observer,* August 17, 1863

We have learned with profound regret that **Robert D. Brooke**, of 2nd Company I, 32d N.C.T., fell on the battle-field of Gettysburg, mortally wounded, July 1st in his 22d year. His remains could not be recovered. Robert was among the first to volunteer in the defense of his country, serving first in Company M, 15th Regiment N.C.T. (5th Regiment N.C. Volunteers).

—*Fayetteville Observer,* January 21, 1864

At the residence of this brother, Henry G. Williams, Esq., in Nash County, on the 9th March, **Lt. Col. William T. Williams**, aged 23 years, died.

Col. Williams volunteered in April 1861, and was elected Captain of the first Volunteer Company from Nash County. He served as Captain, Company H in the 12th Regiment N.C.T. (2nd Regiment N.C. Volunteers) until the Fall of 1861, when he was elected Lieut. Colonel of the 1st Battalion N.C. Infantry. He commanded the Battalion until it was organized into the 32nd Regiment N.C.T., and was elected to the same position in this Regiment, which position he filled with much credit.

A short time before his death he resigned the office of Lieut. Col. of the 32nd Regiment and soon received the appointment of Assistant Surgeon in the C. S. Navy.

Col. Williams made a popular commander and was greatly beloved by those who knew him both in the army and at home. Few men have been gifted with a higher order of talent, and none gave better promise of future usefulness and distinction.

—*Daily Confederate,* April 18, 1864

John Turner, Co. E, 32d Reg't N.C. Troops, was mortally wounded through bowels, in the great and bloody battle near Spotsylvania, C. H., on the 12th May, a.m., and died the following evening. He was born in Catawba County, aged 20 years, 5 months and 11 days. He was regarded by his company and regiment as a true friend, a gallant and obedient soldier. He was among the first to volunteer his services, and served about 12 months in 2d Reg't N.C. Vols. (12th Regiment N.C.T.), but was subsequently transferred to the 32d Reg't. N.C.T., where he remained until he received his fatal blow. He had been blessed with excellent health, and shared the hardships, toils and privations addicted to cruel and fratricidal wars with fellow soldiers without a murmur for three long weary years. He fell in a great cause, and at the post of duty—planting the colors of the 3d Army Corps that was shot away, the flag which the 32d has the honor of carrying, and which floated over Carlisle Barracks, farther North than any other Confederate flag has yet been unfurled in that territory.

And a further consolation is that he died calm, and in hope of a high and lasting immortality.

—*Carolina Watchman,* **July 18, 1864**

Killed, at the battle of Spotsylvania Court House, Va., on the 10th of May 1864, **Edmund Carey Brabble, Colonel** of the 32d Regiment of North Carolina Troops, aged 26 years, 4 months and 5 days.

Born in Currituck County, N.C., he early entertained a strong desire for a complete education and devoted his youth to the acquisition of knowledge. He entered Dartmouth College, New Hampshire, and in 1857 he graduated with high honors. Upon his return to his native State, he studied Law, and was admitted to the bar in 1860. He was appointed Solicitor for the county of Tyrrell in October 1860, to which place he had removed in his youth. The records of the Courts in that county attest the estimation in which he was held. Early in the year of 1861, Mr. Brabble raised a volunteer company in his adopted county, to repel the foot of the invader. He succeeded, and was soon at the head of as brave and efficient a company as any who have periled their lives and fortunes in this long and bloody war. At the head of his company (A), Captain Brabble passed through the different fortunes of war until his skill, his bravery and his high character attracted the attention of his Generals, and he was promoted to the rank of Colonel of the 32d Regiment N.C. Troops. Wherever duty called him, he was seen, calmly and bravely battling for Southern Independence. Upon the bloody heights of Gettysburg, at Mine Run, upon the Rapidan where the gallant 32d fought for five days, and at various places, upon the blood-drenched soil of Virginia, he gained a name never to be erased from the records of fame. Upon the evening of the 10th of May 1864, two days before "the bloody 12th," at Spotsylvania Court-House, Va., amid the smoke and roar of battle, he fell at the head of the brave Regiment, which he had commanded so long and so successfully. He fell, shot through the breast, and died without a perceptible struggle. It would seem as if he had a presentiment of his untimely fate, for before the battle, he had administered to him the Sacrament of the Last Supper of our Lord and Savior. In his lone grave, near the battle-field, where he fought so bravely, he sleeps his last sleep. The thunders of the cannon, of friend and foe, fall alike unheeded upon his dull ear.

When heroism is no longer praised—when patriotism is but a name, and loyalty is no virtue; when friends cease to praise, and brothers and sisters fail to weep over their departed dead; when nations cease to be grateful, and virtue to have its reward, *then,* and not till then will the name of Edmund C. Brabble be forgotten.

—*Daily Confederate,* **September 17, 1864**

Major D. Gregory, one of the oldest and best known citizens of Elizabeth City died at his home on North Road Street Monday morning, following an illness of several weeks. Mr. Gregory was 78 years old. He had an attack of Influenza last year which left him hopelessly weak and ailing.

He was a veteran of the Civil War, 1st Company H, 32nd Regiment N.C.T., and a native of Camden County. He had been a resident of this city about 30 years. He is survived by two daughters and four sons. The daughters are: Miss Bessie Gregory and Mrs. M. G. Wright, both of this city. The sons are, Richard, Howard and Frank Gregory of Norfolk, and Eddie Gregory of this city.

—*Elizabeth City Independent,* **January 27, 1920**

Col. G. B. Alford, President of the Oscar R. Rand Memorial Association, reports the following deaths in the membership of that camp during the past year:

On the 8th day of November 1921, there passed into the great beyond the soul of **1st Lieutenant Calvin Pritchard**, who died as he had lived, a true soldier of Christ. He was in his ninety-first year. Mr. Pritchard was born in Bertie County, N.C., February 25, 1831. He followed Lee and Johnston through the War Between the States, giving four years of his life to the service of his country as a soldier of the Confederacy. He was in Company G, 32nd Regiment of N.C. Troops. He was captured during the Battle of Gettysburg and held prisoner at Johnson's Island, Ohio, from July 1863 until he was transferred to Point Lookout, Maryland on March 14, 1865, and exchanged on the 22nd. After the war he returned home and assumed the heroic task of rebuilding a ruined and desolate country. In all relations of life he was to be relied on, giving his time and strength in any good work. In 1871 he was married to Miss Maria Ward, of Franklinton, N.C., a woman noted for her beauty and intellect. To them five children were born, and of them two sons and a daughter survive him; his wife died some years ago. In late years he made his home with his daughter, Mrs. W. A. Seagraves, at Holly Springs, N.C., where he was tenderly cared for. He joined the Baptist Church about seventy-five years ago and had served as deacon for over fifty years. He was a member of the Oscar R. Rand Camp No. 1278 U.C.V., of Holly Springs, and his death has taken from that membership a comrade tried and true.

—*Confederate Veteran* "Comrades at Holly Springs, N.C."
Volume 30, Number 2, February 1922

33rd Regiment North Carolina Troops

Died of pneumonia at Camp Mangum, near Raleigh, on the 9th inst., **Goodman Arnett**, of Robeson County, aged 41, a soldier in *Capt. Robert Wooten*'s (100) Company G, 33rd N.C. Regiment.

—*Fayetteville Observer,* January 20, 1862

Died near Gordonsville, Va., on the 2nd inst., of typhoid fever, **Lewis W. Kimbrough**, aged 19. He was from Huntsville, N.C., where his parents still live to mourn the loss of a son. Before he was eighteen he volunteered in *Capt. George C. Stowe*'s (101) Company I against the advice of his friends, who believed his constitution too feeble to bear the exposure and hardships of camp life, but he could not be prevailed on. He was later promoted to Company A and then to the Regimental Band.

—*People's Press,* June 27, 1862

Killed in the battle at Cedar Mountain, Va., on the 9th August, **John McNatt**, from Robeson County, a private in Capt. Robert Wooten's Company G, from this place, aged 28 years. He leaves a wife and three children. He was in the battles of Newbern, N.C., Hanover C. H., Va., and other engagements during this war.

—*Fayetteville Observer,* September 1, 1862

Died:—In Winchester, Va., of a wound received in the Sharpsburg battle, **Lieut. Hugh Alex Hill**, of Co. A, 33rd N.C. Regiment. He was a native of Iredell County, aged 30, and was a doctor there before his enlistment.

—*Greensborough Patriot,* October 25, 1862

Died near Fredericksburg, Va., on the 17th of December 1862, **John P. Martin**, of Co. D, 33rd Regiment, N.C.T. He was 30 years old and was from Richmond County. He was a consistent member of the Presbyterian Church of Smyrna for five years. The sad tidings fall truly heavy upon an aged and doting mother and two fond sisters who alone constitute the remaining family.

—*North Carolina Presbyterian,* **March 21, 1863**

Died, in the Hospital at Guinea Station, near Fredericksburg, Va., of Typhoid Fever, on the 19th of January, **William G. Carr**, aged 28 years and 22 days. He was a member of Co. F, 33d Reg. N.C.T. He left home on the 15th of July last, at his country's call, and leaves to mourn his loss a father, mother, two brothers, and four sisters.

—*Hillsboro Recorder,* **April 8, 1863**

A letter from William J. Callais, (102) of Co. G, 33d Reg't, to a friend in this town, states that his brother, **1st Lieut. John Dudley Callais**, was killed in a charge by Lane's Brigade on the enemy on Monday the 4th, in the battles near Fredericksburg [Chancellorsville]. He was an excellent officer, and we learn that his Colonel (C. M. Avery), speaks of him with high respect. Circumstances have placed him for most of his service in command of his company, and his conduct at Newbern, in Jackson's battles with Pope and Banks in the Valley, at Harper's Ferry, at Sharpsburg, at Fredericksburg, and on the Rappahannock, was ever consistent with his character for cool and determined bravery. He had a family and many friends here who deplore his loss.

His brother was wounded in the right hip, but hoped soon to be able to rejoin his Company. He gives the following list of casualties in the Company up to the time when his wound obliged him to leave it, viz: Killed: Lieut. John D. Callais, Corpl. Jas. Gardner, Privates R. C. Lineback (103), John Brock (104) and H. Slater (105).

—*Fayetteville Observer,* **May 18, 1863**

Serg't James Gardner of this place, aged 19 years, 33d Reg't of N.C.T., Co. G, fell with the ever lamented Callais, in the thickest of the fight at Chancellorsville, being of his devoted band who rushed forward numbering forty and came out of the awful struggle numbering six. One of the earliest volunteers, he enlisted at the age of seventeen, and though so young has breasted the storm of war in fourteen battles, and won the highest esteem and confidence of men and officers. After two years duty in camp and field, he applied for a furlough, and returned home for the first time a few weeks ago on a short visit to his widowed—now desolate mother—and hurrying back to war and duty *before* his furlough expired, has met a soldier's death. Let him receive a hero's reward and live in the hearts of his countrymen along with others who sicken and die at their post of duty. All honor to their *sacred* memory.

—*Fayetteville Observer,* **May 18, 1863**

Died May 10 at Camp Gregg, Caroline County, Va., on the 3d of June, **Private D. D. Webb**, of Co. K, 33d Reg't N.C.T., in the 22d year of his age. He was born and raised in Richmond County and served 12 months as a soldier. Early in life he joined the Methodist E. Church. He died very suddenly of congestive fever. He has left his parents, brothers and sisters to mourn.

—*Fayetteville Observer,* **July 20, 1863**

Serg't William F. Guthrie of Hyde County enlisted in Company B, 17th Regiment in May 1861. When the company disbanded, he joined Company H, 33rd Regiment. He died in the General hospital in Wilson, 9th inst., from a wound received in his leg at the battle of Chancellorsville, aged 22 years.

—*Fayetteville Observer,* July 27, 1863

Died at Gordonsville, Va. Sept 1, 1862, of chronic diarrhea, **James T. S. Gibson**, in the 20th year of his age, and **William H. Gibson**, at the same place, on Sept. 5, 1862, in the 22d year of his age. At Lynchburg Hospital, Nov. 19th 1862, with chronic diarrhea, **Virgil A. Gibson**, in his 28th year. All were members of Co. K, 33d N.C.T., and sons of Dempsey Gibson, of Richmond County, N.C. Thus passed away all of his sons. They had been in service but a short time before death seized them.

—*Fayetteville Observer,* July 25, 1864

Died, at Orange Court House, Va., on the 18th June, of wounds received at the battle of the Wilderness, May 6th, 1864, **Colonel Clark Moulton Avery**, 33d Reg't N.C. Troops.

Col. C. M. Avery was a citizen of Burke County, North Carolina, a graduate of the University of the State, and a member of a family occupying a prominent position in the State since the beginning of the Mecklenburg Declaration of Independence—distinguished alike in the first as in the second Revolution—pouring out their blood freely upon the altar of their country's freedom in both. Already in this war have three of the brothers, each occupying marked positions in the State, fallen; while a fourth is now a sufferer from the third severe wound received in battle.

Col Avery began the war as a Captain of the 1st North Carolina Volunteers, and as such participated in the battle of Bethel. At the disbanding of that regiment in November 1861, he received at the hands of Gov. Clarke, the appointment of Lieutenant Colonel of the 33d N.C.T., of which Brig. Gen. Branch was then Colonel, and Maj. Gen Hoke, Major. Upon the promotion of Colonel Branch, before the complete organization of the regiment, Lieut. Col. Avery was called upon to finish that labor. How well he accomplished this, as he did the other duties devolving upon him, the brilliant record this veteran regiment has written in the bloody history of this war, bears true and most honorable testimony. In January 1862, he was commissioned Colonel.

Col. Avery, while holding the centre of the line at the battle of Newbern, in March following, long after it was carried by the enemy on the right and left, was finally overpowered, and his gallantry, while saving a large portion of Gen. Branch's small command from capture, cost him, with others of his regiment, seven months close confinement in Northern prisons He was thus deprived of the privilege of leading his men in the glorious campaigns of the summer of 1862, but returned in time to participate in the battle of Fredericksburg in December of that year.

Shortly after this battle, his long and severe confinement in foreign prisons had so shattered his health, he found the hardships of the campaign, the exposures of camp, the rigors of the winter climate of the Rappahannock, so severe as to confine him in his bed. Under the advice of his Surgeon and the recommendations of the Medical Board of the division, he applied for a leave of absence, which was readily granted by the commanding General.

He returned to camp, however, in ample time to prepare his regiment for the campaign of 1863, and those who witnessed the thorough police and inspections of arms, accoutrements and camp, the drills and dress parades of his command at "Moss Neck," will long remember the neatness of his camp and the soldierly bearing and appearance of his regiment. On one of those occasions the distinguished and now lamented Maj. Gen. Pender, struck with the accuracy of drill and thorough discipline of the regiment, remarked to the writer, "if all our Colonels were Averys, our army would indeed be invincible."

At the battle of Chancellorsville, Colonel Avery was severely wounded, but returned to take part in the Pennsylvania Campaign, and was slightly wounded in the memorable charge upon the heights of Gettysburg, July the 3d, but remained with his regiment.

From this time until the opening of the present campaign, he devoted himself to the organization of his regiment and its discipline, interrupted only by the duties incident to the campaign to Bristoe and Mine Run during the fall; and the fruit of his labors have been seen by all who are familiar with the performance of its duties by the regiment in the arduous marchings and bloody battles of the last two months. Its history in this as in other campaigns of the war, not only reflect credit upon its gallant and lamented commander, but will fill a proud page in the "Record of Honor" which the sons of the old State are making for North Carolina.

Having passed safely though the memorable battle of the 5th instant, which will ever be remembered by the gallant men of Heth's and Wilcox's commands, and as long as the events of this war are cherished by a grateful people, will illustrate with renown the history of those two divisions, repulsing as they did the onset of two corps and a half of General Grant's army. Col Avery was badly wounded in the right thigh about daylight on the morning of the 6th, while leading his men against the renewed attack of the enemy. An attempt was made to remove him from the field, but two of his officers, bearing the litter, *Lieuts. John G. Rencher* (106) Company K of Chatham, and *John D. Fain* (107) Company C of Warren, were severely wounded in the attempt. While lying in this helpless situation, he was wounded in the neck and body, and his left arm was badly shattered. In this condition he was subsequently borne to the field hospital of the division, and had every attention that skillful surgeons and devoted friends could render. His arm was amputated and his leg would have been, had it been thought safe, but it was the opinion of his medical advisers that the shock his system had already undergone was too great to permit the second amputation.

Col. Avery so long survived his terrible wounds, that the hope of his valuable life being spared, faint at first, grew into form and expression; and though from the character of his injuries his friends in the army thought they were prepared for the news of his death, its announcement shed the deepest gloom upon his devoted regiment and the brigade to which he belonged, and his many friends and admirers. He had so warmly attached his immediate regiment and brigade to him by his urbane manners and dignified deportment as a man, and his untiring industry and gallant bearing as an officer, that his loss to them was freely acknowledged, and found expression in universal gloom and outspoken sorrow. But his loss to the army was manifested by the earnest interest his corps and division commanders took in his welfare and their sincere regret at his death.

Col. Avery died far from home; but among strangers his services and merits found him friends; and the warm patriotic ladies of Orange C. H., attended to his wants and administered to his sufferings as only woman can. His friends would gladly have attended at his bedside had circumstances permitted; and the writer of these lines envies those whose place was near him, but is consoled by the belief that the recollections of a most intimate association, in all the dangers of the field, and the social recreations of the camp for nearly three years, which had united them with "hooks of steel," was unbroken and untarnished, as was evident from his last conversations and the fevered mutterings of his wandering faculties in the hour of death.

—*Fayetteville Observer,* July 28, 1864

The remains of the late **Lieut. William H. Massey**, Company G, 33rd N.C.T., who was killed and buried at or near Newbern, at the taking of that town in 1862, were brought to this place last Saturday, and re-interred on Sunday, at the family burial place in this vicinity. Notwithstanding that the weather was gloomy and inclement, the attendance was large; for it is the only sad privilege now left us to honor those who surrendered their lives in behalf of a cause in which our best interests, our dearest hopes, and our most holy affections were enlisted—a cause now, alas! crushed and broken, oppressed and insulted, but honorable to us still.

—*Wilmington Journal,* **March 22, 1867**

34th Regiment North Carolina Troops

Died of disease at High Point, on the 14th ult., **William P. Oliver Davis**, a member of the "Oakland Guards," Company D, from Rowan County. He was aged 20. Died at the same place, on the 28th ultimo, from measles, **Joel J. Overcash**, a member of the same company.

—*Carolina Watchman,* **December 2, 1861**

Died of disease at High Point, on the 18th December, **Nathaniel S. Suggs,** of Montgomery County, in the 19th year of his age, of *Capt. Jesse Spencer*'s (108) Montgomery County Company K.

—*Fayetteville Observer,* **February 3, 1862**

Died in Goldsboro on the 14th inst., of typhoid fever, **George W. Means**, eldest son of Wm. Means, Esq., of Mecklenburg County, aged 23 years. He was a volunteer in *Capt. William R. Myers'* (109) Company G, 34th Reg. N.C.T.

—*Western Democrat,* **March 25, 1862**

Died, on Wednesday the 16th inst., in Richmond, from a gunshot wound in the leg, in Monday's fight near that place, **Orderly Sergeant John W. Davenport**, a member of *Capt. McGee*'s (110) Company G. from Mecklenburg County. The deceased leaves a wife and three little helpless children to mourn their irreparable loss. He had been a consistent member of the Methodist Church for many years.

—*Daily Bulletin,* **July 30, 1862**

Died at St. Charles Hospital, Richmond, Va., on July the 28th, from a wound received in the battle near Richmond, **John F. Sechler**, in his 41st year, from Rowan County. He was a member of *Capt. William Lowrance*'s (111) Co. D, 34th Reg. N.C.S.T. For a number of years he was a member of the A. R. Church and later transferred his membership to the Presbyterian Church, of which he was a member when he died, and to which he was devoted in his love. Before he left home for the field of strife, he made such arrangements that in the event he never returned home, his entire estate with the exception of a few hundred dollars, should go to the church of which he had long been a consistent member.

—*North Carolina Presbyterian,* **August 23, 1862**

In defense of Southern Rights and Independence, we have lost, in immediate action, and from the effects of camp life, our comrades in Company D, **Lieuts. John P. Parks** (112) and **Robert T. Cowan**, (113) who were killed, gallantly leading us on in the battle field at Frayser's Farm; and **Lieut. Samuel H. Douglas**, who died of disease contracted in camp—who was not killed by our enemy's balls—but whose life was as honorably sacrificed as those of the battled, and as willingly laid down. Lt. Cowan leaves a young wife and two little ones.

—Monroe M. Gillon, (114) *2d Lieut., Company D, Carolina Watchman,* **September 22, 1862**

Col. Richard H. Riddick, 34th N.C.T., died a few days ago near Fairfax C. H., Va., of wounds received in battle at Manassas, Virginia, September 1. He was 37. Col. Riddick was a native of Gates County. When the North Carolina regiment was raised for the Mexican war, young Riddick volunteered and served out his term to the entire satisfaction of his officers. In 1855, he was appointed a Lieutenant in the 1st Regiment of U.S. Cavalry, in which he remained until the difficulties broke out between the North and South, when he immediately resigned.

At an early period he tendered his services to Gov. Ellis, who appointed him Assistant Adjutant General, and he immediately proceeded to the organization of the State Troops. After the appointment of Adjutant General Martin, he became a member of Gen. Gatlin's staff and his Assistant Adjutant General. During this period, being at Manassas pending the first battle, he was volunteer aide to Gen. Longstreet and behaved with great gallantry.

In the re-organization of the army, he was elected Colonel of the 34th N.C. Regiment. In the battles around Richmond he displayed great tact and courage until his wound at Gaines' Mill obliged him to leave the field. In the battles around 2nd Manassas he bore himself at the head of his command with great coolness and gallantry until he fell mortally wounded. His men rushed to his assistance, but he said to them, "Go on! I am shot, but not conquered." He lingered until the third day, when he calmly expired.

—Fayetteville Observer, **September 29, 1862**

Died at Scottsville, Virginia, July 18th 1862, **Corporal William R. Macon**, Co. K, 34th N.C.T., of a wound received June 26th, in the fight at Mechanicsville near Richmond. He was a native of Montgomery Co., aged 23 years, 6 mos. and 4 days. He had been in service nearly one year when he died. I have known him since childhood; he was loved by all who knew him at home and by all his fellow soldiers in camp. He did all a brave soldier could; he left home and friends so dear to go and help drive the vandal foe from our land. Although his body lies moldering far from his native home, where no friend can go, his memory will be green, for his name will never die. He has left behind him a kind mother and father, three sisters and two brothers.

—Fayetteville Observer, **January 5, 1863**

Died of fever in Cleveland County, 10th Nov., while home on a sick furlough, **Hugh Williams**, in the 29th year of his age, of *Capt. S. A. Hoey's* (115) Company H. He was appointed Musician in the spring of 1862 and had been captured and released at Warrenton, Virginia in September.

—Fayetteville Observer, **January 26, 1863**

Died of consumption in the hospital at Richmond, June 13th, 1862, **Joseph Junius Sloan**, Co. D, 34th Regiment N.C. Troops, aged 26 years and nine months. He served previously as Sergeant Major of the Regiment. The deceased, though of feeble constitution,

volunteered against the advice of his physician and friends, and sealed his devotion to his country by his death. He was a good soldier, a pleasant companion, and a fast friend.
—*Friend, Carolina Watchman,* **May 11, 1863**

Died in Seabrook's Hospital, in Richmond, Va., 17th May 1863, **Noah R. Freeman**, Company K, 34th, aged 27 years, 3 mos. and 7 days. Owing to bad health he was never in any battle until the last battle at Chancellorsville, Va., when he fell mortally wounded, and died in a few weeks from his wounds and typhoid pneumonia. He was a member of the Christian Church. He leaves a wife and three small children.
—**R. W. Freeman,** *Fayetteville Observer,* **August 17, 1863**

Died at home, on the 3d inst., from the effects of a wound received at Chancellorsville, **William H. Hall,** a member of Co. K, 34th Reg't N.C.T. He was from Montgomery County and was 37.

Captured on the 3d July, on the bloody hills of Gettysburg, **Serg't George W. Coggin**, a member of Co. K, 34th Reg't N.C.T. He was held at Fort Delaware and died there September 29, 1863.
—*Fayetteville Observer,* **August 24, 1863**

Killed, near Gettysburg, July 1st, **Major George M. Clark**, about 23 years of age, of the county of Montgomery. He was a student at the University when the war began. He hastened home, and made up a company in his native county, of which he was Lieutenant and later Captain of Company K. For two years did he faithfully serve his country, having been in all the battles through which that Regiment (the 34th) passed. After the battle of Chancellorsville, he was made Major of the Regiment, and was killed on the first day of the Gettysburg fight.
—*Fayetteville Observer,* **September 14, 1863**

A brother of John M. McInnis was killed near Gettysburg, Penn., July 1st 1863, **Allen M. McInnis** in the 22d year of his age, a member of Co. K, 34th N.C.T. He was wounded in the battle of Gaines' Mill in June 1862, and only returned to his company a short time before he received the fatal ball. He did his duty well and faithfully, "undergoing in behalf of his company the most severe dangers, privations and toils, until at last, while in the heroic discharge of his duty, he fell within a few feet of the enemy's guns. Although the remains of one rest among the mountains of Virginia and the other near Gettysburg, Penn., we feel assured they together enjoy a happy immortality."
—*North Carolina Presbyterian,* **October 24, 1863**

Killed in the battle of Gettysburg, 1st July, **Orderly Serg't Norman J. McLeod**, Co. K, 34th Reg't N.C.T., aged 25 years, 2 months and 3 days, a native of Montgomery County, where he resided till he joined the army in the Spring of 1861. He was in a number of hard fought battles and was a cousin of the late Major George M. Clark. He fell with his face to the foe like a soldier falls.
—**Brother,** *Fayetteville Observer,* **October 26, 1863**

At Point Look Out, Md., of chronic diarrhea, on the 29th of Feb, 1864, **William A. Kilpatrick**, of Co. D, 34th Reg., N.C.T. aged 28 years, 3 months and 8 days. The deceased was not a man of vigorous constitution, yet he responded early to the call of his country, and volunteered in the 34th Regiment. He was wounded at Chancellorsville in May but returned to duty before the fight at Gettysburg. On the retreat from there, he was taken

prisoner on July 14th and carried to Washington City, and from thence to Point Look Out where he died, leaving fond parents to mourn his untimely death.
—*North Carolina Presbyterian,* May 11, 1864

Among those who have fallen in defense of Southern Independence, should be mentioned the name of, **Color Sergeant Theo J. H. Kistler**. In September 1861, he joined the "Oakland Guard." (Co. D, 34th N.C.T.) from Rowan County, and served with unwavering devotion, in the ranks, for the period of two years. In the campaigns of 1862–63, in Virginia and Maryland he was ever found vigilant at his post until he was wounded, unfortunately, in each campaign—first at the 2d Manassas and second at Culpeper C. H., Aug. 1st, 1863. After the campaign of '63 had ended, he was appointed Color Sergeant of his Regiment, and served in that capacity until the 23rd of May 1864, when he was mortally wounded at Jericho Mills, Virginia, and died the subsequent day.
—**A comrade,** *North Carolina Presbyterian,* August 10, 1864

Killed instantly, carrying the colors in front of his regiment, in the battle near North Anna River, 23d May 1864, **Capt. Nevin C. McLeod**, Co K, 34th N.C.T., aged 28 years, 9 months and 26 days. He was born in Montgomery County. He volunteered 9th Sept 1861 and served as a non-commissioned officer until the battle of Richmond. He was then elected 2d Lieut. He served truly and faithfully as an officer and soldier, except while wounded, until the fatal ball took his life. He was wounded in the battle of 2nd Manassas, 25th Aug 1862, and again at Gettysburg on the 2d day in the leg. About the 1st of May he was promoted to Captain of his Company which he had bravely commanded ever since May 1863.
—*Fayetteville Observer,* August 22, 1864

35th Regiment North Carolina Troops

Capt. Joseph P. Jordan, of Henderson County, commanding Company G, of the 35th Regiment, was taken ill with typhoid fever before the battle of Newbern, and was removed to Raleigh, and had been confined ever since under medical treatment, at the Yarborough House. A few days ago we learned that he was better and likely to recover, but on Tuesday morning last he grew worse and died suddenly. His remains were carried home for interment. Capt. J. was a good citizen and soldier, and a useful member of the House of Commons.

—*North Carolina Standard,* April 26, 1862

Lieut. James Amzi White of Company H, the "Mecklenburg Farmers," 35th Regiment, died on the 8th inst., of Typhoid fever, after an illness of four weeks, at his residence in Mecklenburg County, N.C. At the organization of his company, he was elected Orderly Sergeant. During eight months service he was never known to miss a roll-call or a drill, and discharging the duties of the office so faithfully, he was styled by his commanding officer, "the best Orderly in the Regiment." At the late battle in Newbern, in which he participated, he was highly complimented, both by his field and company officers, as a man of undaunted courage; and in the retreat, his Col., calling for volunteers to form a rear guard, although wearied and exhausted he was the first man to offer his service. As a proof of the high estimation in which he was held by his company, at the late reorganization, was unanimously elected 2nd Lieutenant.

—**Leander Query,** (116) **1st Sergeant Company H,** *North Carolina Presbyterian,* **June 28, 1862**

Died at the St. Charles Hospital, Richmond, on the 22d, from wounds received in the battle of Malvern Hill, on the 1st July, **Private James L. Cameron**, of Co. C, 35th Reg't, of Moore County, aged 24 years.

—*Fayetteville Observer,* **July 28, 1862**

Died in the hospital near Drury's Bluff near Richmond, 3d Aug., of typhoid fever, **Charles Cox, Jr.**, Company A, 35th, aged 28 years. The deceased fought gallantly in nearly all the battles near Richmond. He was born in Onslow County.

—*Fayetteville Observer,* **September 8, 1862**

Died at home Onslow County, 5th Aug., of a wound received on the head in the Battle of Richmond, at Malvern Hill, July 1st, **John L. R. Langley**, of Co. A, 35th Reg't, in his 27th year.

—*Fayetteville Observer,* **September 29, 1862**

Died at the General Hospital in Petersburg, Va., of typhoid, on the 22d of July, **Kenneth A. Campbell**, in the 19th year of his age. He was a member of Capt. Kelley's Company C, 35th Regt., N.C. Troops. Although no missile from the enemy did the fatal work, he is nevertheless among the many martyrs who have yielded up their lives. He was a consistent member of the Presbyterian Church at Euphronia.

—*North Carolina Presbyterian,* **November 1, 1862**

Killed, in the battle of Fredericksburg, on the 13th Dec., **Major John McDonald Kelley**, in the 26th year of his age. Maj. Kelly was a student at the University of N.C. When the war broke out he came home to his native county, Moore, and raised a company. Just before his company was ordered away, Union Church was enjoying a precious season of grace, when the Captain and many of his men came out on the Lord's side, and became soldiers of the cross as well as soldiers of their country. His company was accepted on the 12th of September 1861, and was put into the 35th Regiment as Company C. He was in the battle at Newbern, in two pitched fights before Richmond, and at Malvern Hill, when he was promoted to the office of Major. He was at the reduction of Harper's Ferry, and engaged in the bloody scenes at Sharpsburg, and finally closed his career in the battle at Fredericksburg. All testify that Maj. Kelly was a brave officer and a Christian gentleman. He was a member of Carthage Lodge, No. 181, A.Y.M.

—*North Carolina Presbyterian,* **January 10, 1863**

Died of cold and exposure in an ambulance near Gordonsville, Va., 18th November, **Allen E. McDonald,** in the 26th year of his age, of Capt. Kelly's Company C, 35th Reg't. He was in the battle at Newbern, below Richmond, Malvern Hill, Reduction of Harper's Ferry and Sharpsburg.

—*Fayetteville Observer,* **February 16, 1863**

Private Marshall Hodge of Co. C, 35th Reg't N.C.T., died at the General Hospital in Wilmington, March 25th, 1863, aged 24 years. He was in the fight at Newbern, in the several battles below Richmond, at Sharpsburg and Fredericksburg and various other skirmishes. He leaves an aged father and mother, two brothers and a sister.

—*Fayetteville Observer,* **April 20, 1863**

Died, in the General Hospital at Raleigh, on the 11th day of August 1862, **John Monroe**, of Moore County, N.C., aged 22 years 2 months and 28 days. He belonged to the Presbyterian Church at Cypress. He volunteered in Capt. Kelley's Co. C, 35th N.C.T. He was in several engagements with the enemy and came through unhurt, but was at last seized with a violent sickness and only survived ten days, when he died. He died away from home and among strangers; but he said nothing disturbed him in death only he wished to be brought to his home when he died. He leaves a father, mother, two brothers and three sisters. His remains will be brought to his native home and interred in the burying ground where he spent many a happy day.

—Sister M. J. M., *Fayetteville Observer,* **September 21, 1863**

Died, at General Military Hospital, Wilson, N.C., on September 22d, **Private Asa J Gunter**, of Co D, 35th Reg't, of Chatham County. He met with his death in the following manner: While attempting at Nahunta Depot, on W & W R R, to step on the morning train of cars which was conveying his Reg't to Weldon, he was thrown between the cars, his right leg dreadfully mangled and left foot crushed. He was carried to the hospital at Wilson, where all human aid was rendered him but proved unavailing, and in a few hours he expired. He was 22. For more than two years he had served as a soldier. He was severely wounded in a desperate charge with his regiment at Malvern Hill on the 1st July 1862, and fought bravely in other engagements with the enemy. He leaves a kind father, mother, brothers and sisters, at home, and two younger brothers in service.

—*Fayetteville Observer,* **November 2, 1863**

The following men of Company C (Moore County Scotch Riflemen), 35th Reg't N.C.T., have been killed in the late battles around Drury's Bluff.

1st Lt. Neill R. Kelly, a Moore County native was hospitalized May 14 in Richmond with arm and chest wounds. He died June 2.

2d Lt. Malcom Ray, Jr., also a Moore County native, was wounded at Malvern Hill, July 1, 1862. He was again wounded at the battle of Fredericksburg, December 13th. He was hospitalized in Richmond May 14th with arms and chest wounds and died May 28th.

Sgt. John A. Patterson, a Cumberland County native, died at Jackson Springs; he was 23.

Private John A. G. Johnson, a Moore County native, had been captured in the fall of 1862 and released in late September.

Private Nathaniel Morris fell in the prime of his manhood. He was 18.

—*Fayetteville Observer,* **June 16, 1864**

Died in the Seabrook Hospital, Richmond, Virginia, 27th May 1864, of wounds in the right arm and right lung received in the battle near Bermuda Hundred, Virginia, on the 20th May, **Private Archibald Johnson**, a member of Co. C, 35th Reg't, N.C.T., aged 26 years. He was born in Moore County.

—*Fayetteville Observer,* **June 27, 1864**

We regret to learn that **Col. John G. Jones** of the 35th Regiment is among the number of those who fell in one of the earlier battles in front of Petersburg. He was gallantly leading his regiment in a charge on the enemy's works when he was struck. He rose and was shot down again, rose once more and was still going forward when shot a third time. He was carried to a hospital in Petersburg; but soon afterwards died from the effects of his wounds.

He was born in Person County. His parents were poor and unable to afford him such educational advantages as he desired; but his own thirst for knowledge, his energy, industry and self-reliance enabled him to overcome the difficulties of his situation. Having pursued the usual preparatory course of study, he entered as a student at Wake Forest College, and graduated with credit, just before the commencement of the war. He was a member of the Baptist Church, and his thoughts had been directed to the Gospel ministry. Indeed he had decided to enter on this sacred work when, the war breaking out, he felt that the country needed the services of all her sons, enlisted as a soldier, and was made Captain Company E. From this position he rose successively to the office of Major, Lieutenant Colonel and Colonel of the 35th Regiment, to which his company was assigned. Attached to Ransom's Brigade, he bore a meritorious part in all the arduous services of that command, ever deporting himself in a manner worthy of the Christian patriot and officer. In the battle of Plymouth, a few months ago, he distinguished himself by his coolness, daring and skill; and a strong and important fortification which he succeeded in capturing was named in honor of him. He was killed in a charge on the enemy's works near Petersburg, June 17.

He had fallen from a wound, rose and was shot again, rose once more and was stumbling forward when shot a third time

—Originally published in the *Biblical Recorder* and reprinted in the
Daily Confederate, July 1, 1864

Died, at Richmond, Va., on the 25th of May, **John Crausbey Stone**, of Chatham County, N.C. He was the son of Mr. Carney P. Stone. He died of Pneumonia, in the 23rd year of his age. He joined in February 1862, Capt. Hardy Lasater's Company (now Capt. Robert Petty's) of the 35th Regiment, Co. D. Captain Lasater was killed at Malvern Hill.

He was in the fights at Newbern, Harper's Ferry, Sharpsburg and the late battles at Drury's Bluff, and was with Gen. Ransom in East Tennessee. He has left disconsolate parents, a brother and a sister.

—*Daily Confederate*, July 23, 1864

Solomon N. Cole, Malcom A. McNeill and **Neill A. Patterson**, all of the 35th Regiment N.C.T. and all of Company C, 35th Regiment, recently departed this life in the army defending our country.

Private Cole was a native of Moore County and was 37 when he enlisted in September 1861. He entered the hospital at Petersburg on June 17, 1864, with wounds in his left arm, hand, and chest and died on August 13, 1864.

Private McNeill, also a Moore County native, entered the army in September 1861, aged 30. He was wounded in the leg near Petersburg, June 17, 1864, and sent to a hospital where he died July 12.

Private Patterson was a native of Cumberland County and was 18 when he enlisted in September 1861. He was wounded at the battle of Sharpsburg but returned to duty the following month. He was killed in the fighting around Petersburg, June 17, 1864.

All three were members of Crain Creek Lodge No. 213.

—*Fayetteville Observer*, December 22, 1864

36th Regiment North Carolina Troops
(2nd Regiment North Carolina Artillery)

At Fort Fisher, N.C., on Thursday, 12th of June, **William John McLauchlin**, 2nd Company B, of Robeson County, son of Duncan McLauchlin, dec'd., aged 23 years, 4 months. He was (his Captain writes us) a correct and upright man. The deceased was a private in "Starr's Light Battery."

—Fayetteville Observer, June 30, 1862

In Harnett County, at the residence of his brother-in law, Hector McLean, on Friday the 28th ultimo, **Mr. Alexander Ochiltree**, 2nd Company B, aged 38 years. Mr. Ochiltree volunteered as a soldier in Starr's Artillery Co., was taken sick whilst on duty with his company at Fort Fisher, and allowed to come home on furlough, hoping soon to return; but he continued to decline until relieved by death. He leaves a widowed mother, sisters and one brother in Texas. He was generous and kind and died with manifestations of peace with his God.

—Fayetteville Observer, December 8, 1862

At Dixons, on Tar River, of Pneumonia, November 24th, 1862, **Dixon Burton**, a private in the Cape Fear Light Artillery, 1st Company C. Mr. Burton was a good soldier, ever ready to do his duty. He was buried on the banks of the River.

—Wilmington Daily Journal, December 11, 1862

At Fort Fisher, Dec'r 30, **Corpl. William T. Jones**, 2nd Company C, of Cumberland County, aged about 21. He died of lockjaw, consequent on cold being taken in a wound received by the bursting of a gun more than a week previous to his death. He entered the service at the beginning of the war as a member of the Fayetteville Independent Company and was at the time of his death a member of *Capt. K. J. Braddy's* (117) Artillery Company, 2nd Company C. His remains have been brought home for interment.

—Fayetteville Observer, January 19, 1863

Killed, in the battle near Kinston, on the 14th ult. **George W. Gee**, a Private in "Starr's Light Artillery," 2nd Company B. The deceased was formerly a member of the "Independent" Company of this place, and served with that company on the Peninsula. At Kinston, he fell nobly at his post. In the language of one of his companions, on that occasion, "his bravery was not reckless, but cool and determined, being the last man to leave the gun." His kindness to the sick among his associates marked him as one always to be sought for when affliction came. True he leaves no father, no mother, no wife nor child to mourn for him, but he has left *one* whose grief time itself can never assuage, that one is an *only* sister. May God comfort her.

—Fayetteville Observer, February 2, 1863

Andrew Weir, a native of Scotland, was killed at Neuse Bridge in December last. He served in the British Army during the Crimean War and took part in the siege of Sevastopol. He was a member of Co. F, 1st N.C. Reg't, during the Peninsula Campaign, under Magruder, was taken prisoner at Roanoke Island, and when exchanged obtained a transfer from Capt. Murchison's Company to Starr's Light Battery. At Bethel, Roanoke Island, Kinston and

Goldsboro,' he exhibited that heroism which is ever characteristic of the Scotch soldier. In that terrific fight at Neuse Bridge, while in the act of firing one of the guns, he was struck in the head by a canister shot and killed instantly. The Confederacy has lost no braver soldier that this generous stranger who died fighting for Southern liberty.

—*Fayetteville Observer,* **March 9, 1863**

At Camp Lee, near Richmond, 21st April, of Bronchitis, **Corporal Zephaniah W. Burgess**, 1st Company, Latham's N.C. Battery, 36th North Carolina Regiment, in the 21st year of his age.

—*Fayetteville Observer,* **April 27, 1863**

At the residence of his mother in this county, **Mr. Joseph G. Thaggard**, Company K, in his 29th year. The deceased had been a member of the Baptist Church for ten years. He volunteered about two years ago in October 1861 as a Private and was promoted to Corporal the following year. In December 1862 he was transferred as a Private to Company E, 44th Regiment N.C.T. He performed his duty as such until about two months ago, when he was attacked with chronic diarrhea and placed in a hospital at Lynchburg where he obtained a furlough, and got home on the 7th of this month, where he lingered, often conversing with friends on the subject of death, telling them that he was prepared and willing to die at any time, and on the 18th he died in the full triumph of a christian faith.

—*Fayetteville Observer,* **November 30, 1863**

Died at his father's residence in Johnston County, of chronic diarrhea, **Julius Westbrook**, son of Uriah and Saby Westbrook, aged 20 years. He entered the service of his country when he arrived at the proper age; was with his company nearly two years, when he was seized with the fatal illness that ended his life. He was a member of Co K, 36th N.C.T. He leaves a father, mother, sisters and brothers.

—E. Price, *Fayetteville Observer,* **August 25, 1864**

Killed, at Fort Fisher, January 15th, 1865, in the 22d year of his age, **Sergeant Michael H. Turrentine**, 2nd Company D, of this place. In the beginning of the war, responding to the call of patriotism, he became a volunteer defender of his native land. Captured at the fall of Roanoke Island, when exchanged, he again joined the army, and was assigned to duty at one of the garrisons, first at Fort Caswell, and then to Fort Fisher. Here he remained, except when the garrison was ordered to Charleston, till his death, sustained by a sense of duty. In the last fatal assault he fell, heroically rallying his comrades and urging them to meet and repel the foe. Pierced by two balls, his body instantly released his brave spirit, which, spared the humiliation of surrender, passed at once from the conflicts of earth, to the peaceful presence of that God whom he served. For several years he was a member of the Presbyterian Church.

—*Hillsboro Recorder,* **February 2, 1865**

In the Hospital at Fort Fisher, January 11th, 1865, **Hugh McGoogan**, aged 34 years. He was a member of Co. B, 36th Reg. N.C.T., and faithfully discharged his duty as a soldier until about two weeks before his death, he was taken with typhoid pneumonia, which soon ended his existence. He was for several years a member in the Presbyterian Church, and died in the full triumph of a christian faith. He leaves a mother, sister, wife and one little son.

—A friend, *North Carolina Presbyterian,* **February 8, 1865**

In the early morning of November 22, 1922, at Rocky Mount, N.C., the spirit of comrade **Frank J. Weathersbee**, passed into that land where now rest Lee and Jackson. In 1862 he enlisted in the army of the Southern Confederacy, was assigned to the 36th North Carolina Regiment, and stationed at Fort Fisher, N.C., where he served in the Signal Corps until the capture of the fort in early 1865. He was wounded in the battle of Bentonville, receiving a Minie ball in his thigh. In the absence of surgical attention, the ball was not removed, and he carried it for sixteen years, when it became so troublesome that he had an operation to remove it. The wound was a stubborn one and never healed entirely. He was seventy-seven years of age when death called him. Thus went the life of a gallant son of the Confederacy and a faithful member of Newbern Camp U.C.V. May his rest be sweet!
—*Confederate Veteran* **Volume 31, Number 3, March 1923**

37th Regiment North Carolina Troops

Died at the hospital in Newbern, on the morning of the battle there, **John L. Varner**, a member of *Capt. James M. Pott's* (118) Company C, from Mecklenburg County. He was 25.
—*Fayetteville Observer,* **April 14, 1862**

Killed on the 7th inst., by accident on the railroad between Richmond and Gordonsville, Va., at Louisa Court House, **Hugh Franklin Icehower**, of Mecklenburg County, aged 24 years 1 month, a member of Company I, 37th Regiment.
—*Fayetteville Observer,* **May 26, 1862**

Died in Richmond, on the 31st May, from the effects of a wound received in the head, during the engagement with the enemy at Hanover Court House, **Lieut. George R. Gilbreath**, of the 37th Reg't N.C.T. Company F.
—*Fayetteville Observer,* **June 23, 1862**

The remains of **Colonel Charles Cochrane Lee**, commander of the 37th Regiment North Carolina State Troops, arrived at this city yesterday morning in charge of *Capt. Wm. Fetter,* (119) one of the Aids of Col. Lee. He fell and expired instantly, in front of the enemy, having been pierced by a Grape shot from the enemy's Battery during the fight at Frayser's Farm, Virginia, June 30. He previously had been Colonel of the 1st N.C. Infantry (6 months 1861), the "Bethel" Regiment. As a token of respect to the remains of Col. Lee, on their arrival, all places of business were closed and deep gloom pervaded the entire community.—*Charlotte Bulletin, 4th.*

The above announcement will sadden many hearts. Col. Charles C. Lee was the son of our highly esteemed fellow citizen. He was an accomplished and gallant officer, and many hard fought fields attest his devotion to the land of his birth. He was greatly esteemed in this community as one of the most amiable and chivalrous of men, and his untimely death is deeply lamented.

Col. Lee was a native of Charleston, S.C., but at early age removed to Asheville, N.C. At the age of eighteen he received a cadet appointment to West Point, where he graduated in the class of 1856 with distinguished honor, and was attached to the army as a Lieut. in the Ordnance Department. Having served three years in a manner highly creditable to himself, he resigned from the army to assume the position of Commandant of Cadets, in the N.C. Military Institute, then just entering on its existence.

In the fight at Hanover Court House, in the carnage around our beleaguered capital, he exhibited marked daring and gallantry. He leaves behind him a devoted wife, and aged father, late Col. of the 16th Regt. which suffered so terribly in the wilds of Western Va., who served his country until the infirmities of age compelled him to resign,

Col. Stephen Lee has lost three sons since this war commenced, all noble and promising young men. Truly he has laid a costly sacrifice upon the altar of his country.

—*Asheville News,* **July 10, 1862,** and *North Carolina Presbyterian,* **August 16, 1862**

Died on June 28th at Fortress Monroe, Virginia, after he was wounded in the leg and captured at Hanover Court House, **Sterling H. Russell**, Co. I, 37th Regiment. He was 23 and was from Mecklenburg County.

—*Fayetteville Observer,* **July 21, 1862**

Lieut. Col. William M. Barbour, (120) now commanding the 37th N.C. Troops, in his report of its casualties in the late Battles near Richmond, thus mentions the circumstances attending the death of the gallant Col. Lee:—

Col. Lee was killed by a ball from a cannon on the 30th of June, late in the evening. His regiment, with the rest of Gen. Branch's brigade, was charging a battery and had driven the enemy before them for a considerable distance. When about 100 or 120 yards from the battery as he shouted "On my brave boys!" he fell. Adj. Wm. T. Nicholson (121) was a few feet from him; he at once raised him up and asked him if he was hurt—"Yes" was his reply. Colonel, are you hurt much? was then asked. He was unable to answer this question, and almost instantly died in the arms of his adjutant, who brought his body from the field, with such of his personal effects as were not blown away.

A better man or braver officer never fell at his post of duty. When his death was announced to the regiment, his men wept as if they had lost a father.

—*Fayetteville Observer,* **July 28, 1862**

The following soldiers in Capt. Owen N. Brown's Company C, 37th Reg't. from Mecklenburg, have died since April 27:

Private Joseph A. Kerns died at Kinston April 27. He was 25.

Private Hugh E. McAulay died of typhoid fever May 23 in Lynchburg, Virginia. He was 21.

Private Clement R. Nantz died of typhoid fever in the hospital at Lynchburg, Virginia. He was 32.

Private T. S. Luckey died of disease at Richmond, Virginia, June 12. He was 18.

Private Franklin C. Williams, aged 24, died in the hospital at Richmond June 23.

Private Charles S. Wallace., aged 18, died in the hospital in Richmond, June 25.

Private Thomas C. Wilson, aged 18, died at Richmond of typhoid June 30. He had been discharged June 23 due to general debility.

Private C. R. Williams, aged 21, died in the hospital at Petersburg of diarrhea, July 1st.

Private John B. Blakeley, aged 27, died at Brook Church, Virginia, June 30, 1862.

Corporal David H. Fidler, aged 38, died in a Richmond hospital July 17.

Private Alexander Warsham was wounded in the lungs in the Richmond battle of June 27. He died July 8.

Corporal John A. Bell, aged 24, died at Brook Church near Richmond, July 8.
W. F. M. Blakeley, aged 20, died July 12th..
James J. Gibson, aged 24, died near Richmond, July 3.
—*Fayetteville Observer,* **August 25, 1862**

Died, in the County of Wilkes, N.C., on the 9th of September 1862, **1st Lieut. John Kerr Smith**, son of the Rev. P. and A. M. Smith, aged 34 years, 6 months and 19 days. In August 1861, Lieut. Smith was licensed to practice law, and entered the profession of his choice. In January 1862, the war having assumed so serious a type, he relinquished his fond anticipations of success at the bar, and entered his country's service as a private under *Capt. C. N. Hickerson*, (122) Company B, 37th Regiment N.C. Troops. Early in April following, he was promoted to a Lieutenancy, and as such remained in service till wounded in one of the series of battles below Richmond, when he resigned his commission and returned home to die from the effects of wounds received while defending the soil of the "Sunny South" upon the banks of the Chickahominy. It is said, that at one time during the battle, the command of the company devolving upon him, he pressed his command onward, nothing daunted by the falling of his comrades on either hand, eagerly intent upon victory and the independence of the land of his birth, until he himself fell, insensible to the surrounding scenes.
—*North Carolina Standard,* **October 3, 1862**

Killed on the first day of September 1862, at Ox Hill, Virginia, **William Leroy Sample**, Company C, 37th, in the 20th year of his age. He was the second of three sons whom a widowed mother surrendered to the Confederate service. Having safely passed through nine successive battles, he fell a victim to the rage and violence of the enemy, receiving a mortal wound in the morning, and dying on the same night. He leaves his desolate mother and orphan brothers and sisters.
—*North Carolina Presbyterian,* **November 15, 1862**

Died at Charlottesville, Va., October 15th, from a hip wound received in the Battle of 2nd Manassas, August 29th, **William F. Henderson**, of Capt. Brown's Company C, from Mecklenburg, 37th Reg't. He was 24.
—*Fayetteville Observer,* **December 8, 1862**

Died:—Of typhoid fever, five miles of Richmond, Va., July 24th, 1862, **Pickens Lewis Triplett**, son of Dorcia and Thomas Triplett, of the 37th Reg. Co. F, N.C. Troops, aged 26 years 3 days. He participated bravely in the battle at Newbern, from thence he had a long wearisome and much exposed march, ere he reached the place of his final dissolution near Richmond.

Died:—Of Typhoid fever in Weldon, N.C., Sept. 21st, 1862, **William T. Triplett**, son of Dorcia and Thomas Triplett, of the 37th Regt. Co. F, N.C. Troops, aged 25 years 5 months and 10 days. William T. was brother of the above said Lewis Triplett. These two young men left home at the same time. William participated with great courage and bravery in the battles of Hanover and Richmond. He was a bible reading christian—never failed to read the bible and offer up his prayers before retiring to rest at night.
—*Greensborough Patriot,* **April 23, 1863**

Died of wounds at Richmond, Va., in the 1st Ga. Hospital, on the 19th of May, **William Augustus Henderson** of Company C, 37th, in the 19th year of his age. He was a son of Mr.

Robert Henderson, who died a few months since. During his soldier's life of seven months, his letters were always hopeful, but contained a presentiment that he would never return. He enlisted in November 1862, and at the battle at Fredericksburg, December 13, 1862, was wounded in the head. He recovered and rejoined his company in time for the fight at Chancellorsville in May where he was again wounded and this time died.

—*North Carolina Presbyterian,* August 1, 1863

Died, in Chimborazo Hospital, Richmond, Va., July 23d, 1863, of typhoid fever, **Robert F. Ragan**, aged 18 years and ten months. He was a member of Company H, 37th Regiment N.C.T. He was wounded during the fight at Hanover Court House, May 27, 1862, and later discharged because of disability. He reenlisted sometimes later and was promoted to Corporal. He was wounded at Chancellorsville, taken to the hospital where he contracted fever and died.

—*Daily Bulletin,* August 10, 1863

The sister of this gallant officer of the 37th N.C. Reg't, who lost a leg and was captured at Gettysburg, has received the sad intelligence of his death. A letter from an officer in General Lee's army informs her that his own nurse, *Private Wm. Goss*, (123) of his Reg't, who remained to nurse him, writes that after an illness of four days with a severe attack of fever, he died on the 24th of July, at Chambersburg, Pa.

If a conscientious discharge of duty without display can endear the memory of the dead to the living, **Major Owen N .Brown** will long be remembered with a sad pleasure by all who knew him. Shortly after the beginning of the war he volunteered as a private in Captain Potts' Company C from Mecklenburg, was soon elected Lieutenant and afterwards to the Captaincy of that company; and shared with it, all the hardships of the Western Virginia campaign; and then returning immediately to engage in the battles of Hanover C. H., in front of Richmond, Fredericksburg, and other sanguinary conflicts of his country. His relation to his men as an officer did not make him forgetful of his duty to them as fellow-citizens. Towards them he was ever courteous and kind; he loved his men as a brother, and they were devoted to him. He was for several years a member of the Presbyterian Church. His life was short, but long enough to make his friends hold his name in everlasting remembrance.

—*Fayetteville Observer,* August 24, 1863, and *North Carolina Presbyterian,* September 26, 1863

Wesley Lewis Battle, youngest child of Hon. Wm. H. Battle, 2d Lieut. in the 37th Reg't N.C. Troops, Company D, was wounded in the arm at the battle of Gettysburg, July 3d, and died in the hospital there Aug. 22d following amputation of his shattered limb, aged 19 years and 10 months. His brother Junius fell at the battle of South Mountain in Maryland. They both were taken prisoners mortally wounded, both lingered in hospitals and were kindly cared for by strangers; both died in peace and are laid in what is now to us foreign land.

In the letter received by Mrs. Battle from the Reverend W. Burton Owen, Chaplain of the 17th Miss. Reg't, prisoner at Gettysburg, he writes—"I have conversed frequently and freely with your son in regard to the future. He delighted in religious services. He received the Communion Aug. 19th at the hands of the Rev. Mr. Willing of the Episcopal Church. Just before he died he said, 'Jesus has taken all the fear of death away.'" Precious words to the faithful mother who had trained his early feet in the way they should go!

—*Fayetteville Observer,* September 21, 1863

Died in Bailey's Factory Hospital, Richmond, August 5th, **Rufus James Hartin**, from a wound received in the battle of Gaines' Mill, near Richmond, June 26th 1862, of Co. F, 37th Regiment, aged 23. He was a native of Wilkes County.
—*Fayetteville Observer,* **November 23, 1863**

Died of fever on the 10th of September 1863, a prisoner of war at Point Lookout, Md. **Hugh L. Torrence**, a member of Company C, 37th N.C.T. Thus in the prime and buoyancy of life has fallen another brave man, a victim to the hardships of a Northern dungeon. He was 25. He faithfully served through many hard fought battles and was wounded at Gaines' Mill. He returned to duty in early winter. He fought on and fought well till the 3d day of July 1863, when in a charge at Gettysburg, Pa., he was overpowered and compelled to surrender himself to the enemy. Thence he was conveyed to Point Lookout, Md. He died away from home, and had no friends to soothe his head in his last hour. He leaves fond parents and relations.
—*North Carolina Presbyterian,* **April 20, 1864**

Died, in Petersburg, May 26th, of wounds, **Sergeant Major Thomas Charles Wright**, 37th N.C. Troops, aged 18 years and son of the late Dr. Thomas M. Wright of Wilmington, N.C. Thomas Wright fired with patriotic fervor, some months since left the Virginia Military Institute where he was a cadet and received the appointment of Sergeant Major of the 37th N.C. Troops. In the capacity of he was fearlessly and gallantly discharging his duty in the thickest of the fight at the Wilderness, May 5th, when he received the wound from which he died. He is survived by his mother, sisters, and a brother.
—*Fayetteville Observer,* **June 2, 1864**

A letter from a Surgeon in Lane's Brigade says in reference to the death of this gallant young officer, who but a few months ago left the Lexington Military Institute for active service in the field:

Lieut. Charles T. Haigh fell on the evening of the 12th ult. at Spotsylvania Court House while gallantly leading his company (Co. B, 37th N.C.T.) in charging a yankee battery. A member of his company reports that he was shot through the head, the ball entering above the right eye and coming out on the left and back part of his head. Our men were unable to hold the ground on which he fell, and consequently I was unable to secure his remains.

Col. Barbour had no officer whom he esteemed more highly than Charlie, and although he had been with us but a short while, he had won the esteem of every officer and man in the regiment. His conduct was such in the battle of the 12th as not only to elicit the commendation of officers and men of his own regiment, but his gallantry was such as to attract the attention of Gen. Lane, who complimented him highly for his bravery and efficiency.
—*Fayetteville Observer,* **June 9, 1864**

Private Junius C. Battle, 12th Regiment N.C.T., Companies B and D, and **Lieut. Wesley Lewis Battle**, 37th Regiment N.C.T., Company D, youngest sons of Judge Battle, volunteers in the late Confederate army, were buried in Chapel Hill, on the 16th inst.

Junius Battle, 12th Regiment, Companies D & B, died at Middletown, Md., on the 2nd October 1862, from the effects of a shattered ankle at the battle of South Mountain. Lewis Battle, 37th Regiment, Company D, died at Gettysburg, Penn., August 22nd, 1863, having been mortally wounded in the disastrous charge on Cemetery Hill, July 3rd.

We learn that their brother R. H. Battle, Jr., who went on for their remains, on his mission of love met with the same sympathy from the kind strangers who had soothed with tender nursing the dying soldiers.

Their remains were met at Chapel Hill by many of their surviving comrades. The companions of their happy college days, with weeping eyes sang a requiem to their memory, in the Village Church, where they so long worshipped; and spread flowers over the mound, under which they who in life loved one another so well now peacefully repose, to be parted nevermore.

—*Wilmington Journal,* **April 26, 1866**

Charlotte, N.C., June 24.—**Dr. John Brevard Alexander**, 1834–1911, one of the best known citizens of this county, died tonight after a long illness. Fourteen years ago Dr. Alexander was stricken with paralysis and for several weeks past he has been at the point of death. Dr. Alexander was the author of "Reminiscences of the Past Sixty years," and other works dealing with the life of the days before the war. The funeral service will be held tomorrow and will be conducted by the Masonic Lodge of which he was an honored member. The service at the home will be in charge of the Rev. J. L. Caldwell.

At the very beginning of the conflict he offered his services to his State and the Confederacy, and served as a sergeant in Company C, Thirty-Seventh North Carolina Regiment of Infantry. He was in Branch's Brigade, known as Lane's after the death of the former in battle. He had participated in the Newbern, the Hanover, Va., and the Mechanicsville fights and was in the Gaines' Mill engagement of June 1862 while serving in the ranks. Just after the battle last mentioned he was commissioned as surgeon in the army of the Confederate States of America. He had already passed his examination previously, but some time was required for the issuance of the papers. This occurred just before the Frazier's Farm fight, which was a part of the Seven-Days' battle. Dr. Alexander served the army faithfully in the capacity of surgeon in those days, when surgeons were badly needed, until about a year later when his health failed, necessitating his retirement from the service and his return to his home. He was then given an appointment as examiner for the home guard and for such as the soldiery as were at home on furloughs. He continued in this position until the close of the war.

It was three years prior to the war, in 1858, that Dr. Alexander was happily married to Miss Annie Lowry, daughter of Samuel Lowry and Mary Johnston of this county. The marriage occurred at Davidson College. Mrs. Alexander's death occurred February 17, 1893, after the family had removed to this city. Dr. Alexander had returned to his country practice after the war, remaining there until 1888 when he moved his family to Charlotte and opened a drug store on South College Street. Later it was located on North Tryon street between Fifth and Sixth streets on the site at present occupied by The Presbyterian Standard building. The family resided at the North Tryon street place where Dr. Alexander's last days were spent. In 1896 Dr. Alexander retired from the drug business and from his practice in connection therewith. In the same year he was elected on the ticket of the People's party a member of the Senate of North Carolina General Assembly, where he served conspicuously. Retirement in his latter years gave him opportunity for the writing of three books, "The Early Settlers of the Hopewell Section and the Hopewell Church"; "The History of Mecklenburg County" and "Reminiscences of the Past Sixty Years." The last named was the last of these, having been issued in 1908. As throwing sidelights on memorable times whose story can scarcely be now told by word of mouth by those who lived in the midst of them, these are of high value.

—*News and Observer,* **June 25, 1911, and** *Charlotte Observer,* **July 25, 1911**

Andrew J. Reed, a member Gainesville Camp, No. 12, U.C.V. has died. He was born in Caldwell County, N.C., and enlisted in December 1861, at age 19. He was wounded in the right leg at the Battle of Cedar Mountain, August 9, 1862, and discharged the following October. He belonged to Company G, 37th N.C. Regiment.
—*Confederate Veteran* **Volume 24, Number 9, November 1916**

38th Regiment North Carolina Troops

The following members of the Richmond Boys, Company E, 38th Regiment N.C.T., have died.

George Kelly died before we left home.

John Crouch, a Richmond County native, joined our company in last October, aged 24. He died of the fever in Raleigh, January 1.

Eben N. Kelly was a Richmond County native and joined the company in October last, aged 26. He died in Raleigh January 3.
—**Oliver H. Dockery, (124) Captain, Company E.,** *North Carolina Standard,* **January 25, 1862**

A report has been received that **Alexander McKay, Thomas Garrett, Henry C. Morgan**, of the "Richmond Boys," Company E, 38th, have died.

Private McKay was born in Richmond County and enlisted in October 1861, aged 20. He died in Raleigh of pneumonia, January 19, 1862. Private Garrett from Montgomery County was 17 when he enlisted in October 1861. He also died in Raleigh of pneumonia, January 3, 1862. Private Morgan, also a Richmond County native, was 16 when he enlisted in October 1861. He died in Raleigh of pneumonia, February 7.
—*Fayetteville Observer,* **February 10, 1861**

Colon R. C. McKenzie and **Daniel B. Graham**, members of Captain Murdock McLaughlin's Carolina Boys, Company K, 38th Reg't., have died. Both were from Cumberland County. Corporal Graham, aged 24, died April 3, of disease, at Petersburg. Private McKenzie, aged 27, also died of disease at Petersburg, March 13th.
—*Fayetteville Observer,* **April 14, 1862**

Messrs. Editors:

Please allow space in your columns for a tribute to the memory of **Lieut. Angus Shaw**, late of Capt. McLauchlin's Company K, 38th Regiment N.C.T., who died of wounds July 18th. I have known Lieut. Shaw intimately for the past ten years, and can speak advisedly of his great worth and integrity of character. I served with him, in the ranks, in the 1st (Bethel) Regiment for six months, and when he was by my side, as was usually the case, I always felt there was near me, at least, one true man—one who would do his duty let the consequences be what they might. Many times, when it was thought an engagement was imminent, I have heard him declare that in this revolution, he was ready to die upon the battlefield, and would rather bequeath to his children that heritage of glory than any other he could bestow. The exhibition of this courage upon the battlefield of Mechanicsville, June 26, and to him, the fatal field near the Chickahominy, caused his Colonel to say, "Lieut.

Shaw is one of the bravest men I ever saw." He died of wounds received in battle, having fought a good fight.

—*Fayetteville Observer,* July 28, 1862

Lieutenant Lewis F. Haynes, of Yadkin County, was 18 years old at the time he entered the army, and had been for four years a member of the Baptist Church. He was attached to the 38th Regiment N.C.T., and was First Lieutenant of Company B. He fought conspicuously brave through the late battles before Richmond for five days. He was injured internally by the bursting of one of the enemy's bombs, at Malvern Hill, and was also struck by a minnie ball.—These injuries resulted in an attack of typhoid fever of which he finally died on the 29th day of July. His remains were brought home by his bereaved father, and he now sleeps near his family with others of our sons and brothers who have sacrificed their lives in the same glorious cause.

—*North Carolina Standard,* August 27, 1862

It is painful to record the death of our much esteemed, very dear and loved brother, **James T. Bostick**, who was killed in one of the battles before Richmond, at Ellison's Mills, on the 26th of June, in the 22d year of his age. He was in Company E ("Richmond Boys"), 38th Reg't N.C.T. He volunteered in November, and went into camp at Raleigh the 20th of December. After some time he was detailed to go to the Hospital to nurse the sick. So kind and warm-hearted was he that he gave up his bed and blankets to the sick, to render them comfortable. When he could have a few spare hours during the night, he would lie on the hard benches, without any covering. In a few weeks, after so much exposure, he was taken with severe Pneumonia, from which he suffered intensely—came home on a sick furlough, and for three weeks was very unwell, and before he was at all able to perform military duty, he longed to be again in the army. Contrary to the remonstrance of his Physician, and the entreaties of his friends, he bade adieu to all who were near and dear to him.

His wishes were: "If I die in camp, bury me there: if I am killed in battle, bury me on the battle-field."

After receiving the fatal wound, he lived but a few hours. Would that we could have been by his side, to alleviate his intense sufferings. But no father, mother, sisters or brothers were there. Dearest "Jimmie," thou art gone; thy grave is in a strange land, in old Virginia; but our true hearts will often linger around thy tomb. He was a consistent member of the Cartledge Creek Baptist Church, Richmond County, N.C.

—Sallie L. & Annie J. Bostick, *Fayetteville Observer,* October 27, 1862

Died at Upperville, Va., on the 17th of last September, **Lieut. Duncan A. Black**, Co. K, 38th N.C. Troops, of a wound received in the battle of Second Manassas, on the 30th of August, aged 24 years, 2 months and 16 days. Lieut. Black was born in the Island of Jura, Argyleshire, Scotland, and was 3 years old when his parents immigrated to this country. Four years ago, he joined the Presbyterian Church of Galatia. When his company was organized, he was elected a non-commissioned officer, and upon his election he wrote to his Pastor for advice, saying, "There are so many office seekers, I am content to fight for my country a private in the ranks. I have no desire for office, what shall I do?" Before the war broke out, he was engaged in teaching. He labored and toiled for months with others of like sentiments to fill up the ranks of the Carolina Boys, now Co. K, 38th Regt. N.C. Troops. During his painful sufferings from the wound, the ladies of Upperville attended upon him as a brother. When he died, they procured a coffin for him, and buried him in the Episcopal graveyard of Upperville; the ladies strewed his grave with flowers as a token of their feelings towards this patriot. Many daughters have done virtuously, but the daughters of Upperville excel them all. Lieut. Black has left parents, brothers and sisters, to mourn their loss.

—North Carolina Presbyterian, **November 8, 1862**

We are permitted to publish the following letter from his Colonel in reference to the death of this gallant soldier and estimable gentleman, **Lieut. Angus Shaw**, Company D.

Mrs. Angus Shaw:—My Dear Madam:—Permit me at this late hour, to express my deep sympathy at the loss you sustained when the late much lamented, and greatly missed, Lt. Shaw fell. My dear madam, he was an ornament to his regiment and was considered as one of our noblest and bravest officers. When any perilous adventure was to be undertaken and a cautious, brave and prudent officer was wanted to lead it, he was selected, and when a volunteer was wanted for any secret, confidential and unknown peril, he was always among the first to offer his services to lead it. On the bloody field of Mechanicsville, where our Regiment was so badly cut up in charging a battery, Lt. Shaw was among the foremost, leading his men where honor called him, and in as gallant a charge as was ever made, he was wounded. At the same time I had the misfortune of receiving a serious wound, and only rejoined my Reg't one month ago. I knew your gallant husband while a member of the Bethel Reg't, and had formed an attachment for him that will never be erased, and none fell on that fatal day whose loss I deplore more.

May God, who watches over all, soon send peace to our unhappy country and protect you, is the prayer of the friend of your husband.

Wm. J. Hoke, Col. 38th N.C.T.
January 28, 1863, Camp Gregg, Near Fredericksburg, Va.
—Fayetteville Observer, **February 16, 1863**

The following members of the "Carolina Boys," Co. K, 38th Reg't., have died. **James A Snead** died near the first of July 1862, from wounds received in the battle of Mechanicsville, near Richmond, June 26; he was 18. **John L Campbell,** a Cumberland County teacher, died in Richmond September 9th. He was 46; **H. McL. Campbell**, aged 18, was captured at Frederick, Maryland, September 12 and held at Fort Delaware until exchanged in October. He died in Richmond Nov. 12th; **Lauchlin Ray**, a Cumberland County farmer, aged 30, died at Mount Jackson, Virginia, Nov. 18th; **Daniel A. McPhaul**, aged 18, died at Lynchburg, Virginia, Dec 19th, 1862.

—Fayetteville Observer, **March 9, 1863**

Messrs. Hale & Sons:

For gratification of the parents and friends of the deceased soldiers of my company, would you please allow space in your columns for the publication of the following list of deaths in Co. H, 38th Reg't N.C.T.:

Serg't W. L. Hill, died of typhoid pneumonia at Camp Mangum, near Raleigh, Feb'y 4, 1862, aged 26. **Private John Clodfelter** died in Weldon, Feb'y. 2, of typhoid pneumonia, aged 21. **Private S. M. Bingham**, at home in Randolph County, Febr'y. 24, of typhoid fever, aged 23. **Private Charles L. Hatcher,** died in Petersburg, Va., Feb'y 26, of typhoid pneumonia, aged 16. **C. L. Crisco**, age 20, died in Richmond, Va., June 8. **Whitson O. Kearns**, died of disease in Goldsboro,' June 13, aged 22. **E J. Henley**, died of disease near Richmond, June 25, aged 18. **N. H. Cranford,** aged 22, **A. M. Dorsett**, age 21, and **D. N. Miller**, age 23, were killed in action at Mechanicsville, Va., June 26. All three were farmers.; **Claton S.**

Lewis, aged 20, was killed at Frayser's Farm, June 30. He was farming in Randolph.; **A. C. Steed**, aged 21. died in Richmond, July 2, of wounds received at Mechanicsville. **T. W. Bell**, ditto, July 10. He was 26 and a farmer in Randolph County; **Milton Stevens**, aged 24, died of disease in Petersburg, July 10. He was also a farmer in Randolph County; **P. W. Carter**, aged 20, died of disease near Richmond, August 13. He farmed in Randolph County; **N. H. Carter**, aged 18, a farmer in Randolph County, was killed at Second Manassas, August 30. **N. E. Russell**, aged 20, also a farmer in the above county, was killed at Shepherdstown, Va. Sept. 20. **J. M. Scarlott,** also a farmer in Randolph, aged 18, died of chronic diarrhea in a Richmond hospital, Oct'r 19.

I would say to the parents and friends of the above-named deceased soldiers, that they were always good and obedient, always at their posts and never refusing duty. Those who have been stricken down by disease doubtless contracted the same while undergoing the many hardships of the camp and hard marches. Though regardless of the hardships and privations, they hesitated not, but did everything that was enjoined upon them with alacrity, knowing that the good of their country demanded it. Those who have been killed in action are now sleeping beneath the sod of the gory fields of battle upon which they fell. Let their parents and friends be consoled with the thought that they fell while engaged in a noble cause, that of defending their rights, their homes, and the loved ones who made their homes precious to them.

The vacancies that have thus been made by the above-named deaths will be hard to fill. Those of the company who have survived, and were strongly bound to them by love and affection, deeply mourn their loss and sympathize greatly with their relations and friends.

—W. L. Thornburg, Capt. (125), Comd'g Co. H, 38th Reg't N.C.T.,
Camp Gregg, Near Fredericksburg, March 23, 1863,
Fayetteville Observer, March 30, 1863

Died August 9th, 1862, at his father's residence in Sampson County, N.C., of a wound received at the battle before Richmond at Frayser's Farm, **Ezekiel M. Boyett**, aged 21 years. He was a member of the Church of Christ, at Six Runs, Sampson County, N.C. Early in the war he enlisted in Company D, 38th Regiment, and proved to be a brave soldier, but having been wounded near Richmond in the memorable 7 days' fight he was sent home, where he lingered only a few weeks when he died.

—*Fayetteville Observer,* May 25, 1863

Killed, at Gettysburg, in the battle of the 1st July 1863, **Daniel McDuffie**, a member of Co. K, 38th regiment, N.C.T., aged 28 years. As a soldier he served his country faithfully and gallantly, undergoing the most severe dangers, privations and toils, until at last, in the heroic discharge of his duty, he fell within a few feet of the enemy's guns. He had his membership in the Presbyterian Church at Sandy Grove. He leaves aged parents, a sister, and brothers.

—*North Carolina Presbyterian,* September 12, 1863

Corporal William Thomas Tyson, of Richmond County, of Co. E, 38th Reg't, was wounded and captured at Gettysburg on the 1st July. He died a prisoner on David's Island, New York Harbor, on the 26th. He was 22 and leaves a wife and one child.

—*Fayetteville Observer,* September 28, 1863

Died at the residence of his brother-in-law, J. A. McLauchlin, in this town, on Thursday morning the 24th ult., **Captain Daniel A. Monroe**, Co. K, Carolina Boys, 38th Reg't, aged

34 years and 6 months. Capt. Monroe volunteered in the Lafayette Light Infantry Co., 1st Reg't. After serving the term for which that Reg't volunteered, 6 months, he again volunteered as a private in the Carolina Boys. He was elected Lieutenant; afterwards he became Captain of the Co. He was in all the arduous service through which his company passed and was recently detailed on special duty. He died of disease of the liver.

—*Fayetteville Observer,* **October 5, 1863**

Died a prisoner on the 13th of January, on David's Island, New York Harbor, of wounds received at the battle of Gettysburg, **Sergt. Leonidas Pearsall**, a member of Co. A, 38th N.C. Regt. He was engaged in fourteen battles, previous to the one in which he was wounded and captured, and displayed courage and coolness.

—*North Carolina Presbyterian,* **February 17, 1864**

Died, at Point Lookout, Md., on the 13th of March last, **Serg't. Daniel McMillan**, Co. K, 38th N.C.T., 23 years of age, a native of Robeson County, and son of Col. A. McMillan. He volunteered in 1861, and was in the battles of Chancellorsville in May 1863, where his chief commander, Stonewall Jackson, fell. He was in the Pennsylvania campaign, and on the return of the Army he was taken prisoner on the Potomac, at Falling Waters, on the 14th July, near where Gen. Pettigrew was slain; was sent to Frederick City, where, after four days fasting and marching, he was kindly entertained by the citizens. After spending one month in Baltimore jail he was sent to Point Lookout, and there on the inhospitable shore of the Chesapeake he lingered and suffered of chronic diarrhea and affection of the lungs till his death. Thus ended the short career of a youth who was dearly beloved by his friends and esteemed by all who knew him.

—*Fayetteville Observer,* **April 18, 1864**

Killed, at the battle of Spotsylvania, May 12th, Private **William B. Sedberry**, in the 20th year of his age. He had enlisted in Company E, 38th one month earlier on April 5th. He was a member of the M. E. Church. He leaves a father and mother, brothers and sisters.

—*Fayetteville Observer,* **June 16, 1864**

Died at Hill's Corps hospital, on the 25th May 1864, from wounds received in battle near Spotsylvania C. H., May 12th, 1864, **Corporal William McP. Geddie**, of Co. K, 38th Reg. N.C.T., son of William and Agnes Geddie, of Cumberland County. He was captured near Sharpsburg and paroled in late September. He was 27.

—**Brother,** *North Carolina Presbyterian,* **August 10, 1864**

Died at his Father's residence near Boonville, Richmond Co., June 15th 1964. **Terrell Chance**, a Private in Co. E, 38th N.C.T., of chronic disease, in the 30th year of his age. He leaves a father and mother, sister and brother. He was ever at his post of duty; even when he was not able to perform duty he would go with his company. He was in many battles; he fought through the memorable Chancellorsville, Spotsylvania C. H., Wilderness and other battles. He was finally obliged to give up. He was sent to a Hospital, where he was furloughed. Went home. But his journey in this life was out. In two days after he arrived at home, death seized him and he calmly expired in the arms of his Father.

—**A soldier friend,** *Fayetteville Observer,* **August 29, 1864**

Died in Alexander County, on the 27th August, **Thomas J. Flowers** Company G, 38th. He had been in the army for some time, enlisting in November 1861, and had returned home. He was 47 and was discharged under the age provision of the Conscription Act. Scarce two weeks had passed, when he was called by death.

—*Carolina Watchman,* **September 19, 1864**

Died October 19th, of disease contracted in a Northern prison at Elmira, New York, **Jacob H. Lewis**, Private in Co H, 38th N.C.T. He was captured at Falling Waters, Maryland, July 14, on the retreat from Gettysburg

—*Fayetteville Observer,* **December 15, 1864**

Died, on the 18th of June 1864, at Richmond, Va., from wounds received at Noles' Station, Va., May 23d, 1864, **Sgt. Maj. Agrippa S. Hardister**, 38th Reg't N.C. Troops, and son of Asberry and Cynthia Hardister, of Randolph County, N.C. He first served as 1st Sergeant of Company H of the 38th. For nearly three years he patiently endured the privations and hardships of camp, weary marches, and all the many bloody battles in which the Army of Northern Virginia has been engaged, and while gallantly charging the enemy at Noles' Station, received a wound which proved mortal. He was a member of the M. E. Church for several years.

—*Fayetteville Observer,* **December 15, 1864**

Randol R. Jackson, of Sampson County, a member of Company C, 38th Regt., N.C. Troops, was born October the 9th, 1834, volunteered in October 1861, fought through the campaigns of 1862 and 1863 and 1864, receiving three wounds and finally was fatally wounded near Petersburg, June 22d, 1864, and died at Weldon July 29th, 1864, aged 29 years 9 months and 20 days. He leaves a wife and two children. He was a member of Mingo Lodge, No. 206, of Sampson County.

—*Fayetteville Observer,* **December 22, 1864**

Mr. Ephraim S. Shipp, of Clinton, died last Friday at his home on Stetson Street after a long period of sickness with Dropsy. He was a good man about 67 years of age, an old Confederate soldier and stood well in his community and county. He was 17 when he enlisted as a substitute in Company D, 38th Regiment N.C.T., in February 1862. He was wounded in the leg at the Battle of Chancellorsville and served until he surrendered at Appomattox. He leaves three sons and two daughters to mourn their loss. The funeral services were conducted Saturday morning from the residence of the deceased by the Rev. B. F. DeLoatch and the remains laid to rest in the town cemetery in the presence of a large circle of relatives and friends.

—*The News Dispatch,* **June 27, 1912**

Maj. Murdock McRae McLaughlin was born in Cumberland County, N.C., May 7, 1833, and died in Cheraw, S.C., on December 15, 1913. At the beginning on the war he enlisted in and was made Captain of Company K, 38th Regiment, which was assigned to Pender's Brigade, Jackson's Corps. He participated in the Seven Days' fight, and particularly the first day, when his regiment lost heavily as it, with the 44th Georgia, charged down the hill to the edge of Ellison's Mill pond, across which the enemy was entrenched. He was afterwards promoted to Major, and served with Jackson at Cedar Mountain, Second Manassas, and in the Maryland campaign, being with Jackson at the capture of Harper's Ferry. While Jackson marched from Harper's Ferry to Sharpsburg, Major McLaughlin was left with A. P. Hill's Division (to which his brigade belonged), to take charge of the captured stores; but the next day he was marched to Sharpsburg, where the division arrived just in time to hold the Confederate right against Burnside, who had succeeded in crossing the bridge over Antietam Creek.

At Chancellorsville he was with Jackson on the famous flank march, and was within a hundred yards of the General when he fell. Major McLaughlin picked up Jackson's cap the next morning. In the fight the day after Jackson fell, Major McLaughlin was severely wounded, being shot through the face with a Minie ball, and was not able for further duty. General Pender in his official reports spoke highly of him.

After the war Major McLaughlin moved to Cheraw, S.C., where he established a high school that had a far-reaching reputation. He became one of the leading educators of the Carolinas. In 1874 he married Miss Cornelia McKay, who, with two sons and one daughter, survives him. In recent years he had devoted himself to Sunday school work in the Presbyterian Church, of which he had been a lifelong member. No one stood higher in the hearts of his acquaintances. He truly loved his neighbor as himself.

—*Confederate Veteran* **Volume 22, Number 2, February 1914**

Commander W. L. Glenn, of De Soto Camp, No. 220, U.C.V., at Hernando, Miss., sends a list of losses in membership during 1916 and says: "We are rapidly passing away, and in a few more years the last Confederate will have gone to his reward." One was formerly from North Carolina.

—**Alfred W. Dockery, 1st Lieutenant (126) Company E, 38th North Carolina Infantry,** *Confederate Veteran* **Volume 25, Number 2, February 1917**

39th Regiment North Carolina Troops

Died the same day, March 27, near Clinton, Tenn., **John Humphrey**, aged 18, and **Samuel Rose**, aged 20. Both were members of Company C, 39th Regiment and were from Cherokee County.

—*Fayetteville Observer,* **April 28, 1862**

DIED,—At the Hospital on Reems' Creek on the 19th of February, **Calvin Burgess**, a member of *Capt. Hugh Harvey Davidson's* (127) Company C, 39th Regiment from Cherokee County aged about 26 years. He was afflicted with phthisic pulmanolis, and died of hemorrhage of the bowels following five weeks sickness, leaving a family of three small children. He was a quiet, peaceable man, and as far as his health would permit, a good soldier. He fell in a good cause, and was the first to die of disease in the Battalion, which speaks well of the care of the officers and judicious treatment of the Surgeons. Peace to his ashes.

—*Asheville News,* **March 3, 1862**

Died recently, **Columbus C. Matlock,** aged 21, and **John D. Dalton**, aged 23, of Capt. Alfred Bell's (128) Cherokee County Company B, 39th Regiment. Both were from Macon County, and both died April 24th at Clinton, Tenn., of disease.

—*Fayetteville Observer,* **May 19, 1862**

Died of disease near Lenoir's Station, Roane County, E. Tenn., on the 16th Nov., 1862, of typhoid fever, **James O. Case, 1st Lt.** Co. D, 39th N.C. Regiment, in his 31st year. He was a man of the strictest moral character and most undoubted integrity, of strong feeling and determined courage. He had been a member of the Baptist Church 7 or 8 years. He leaves a wife and three small children.

—*Asheville News,* November 27, 1862

Died of disease near Clinton, Tenn., **Thos. H. Ammons**, April 28, Madison County, aged 28, and **George W. J. Moore**, April 30, Macon County, aged 43, Members of *Capt. Bell's* (128) Company B, 39th Reg't.

—*Fayetteville Observer,* June 2, 1863

North Carolina is bereaved in the death of so able and true a man as **Col. David Coleman**, of Buncombe County. He was a superior lawyer and a logical thinker, and was a man of sterling worth. His age is stated to have been 60 years. He was unquestionably one of the ablest of the Western men. He was graduated at the University in 1842. He was in the U.S. Navy for eight years. He was Solicitor in his district at one time and served in the Legislature several times. He was a very gallant soldier, and was Colonel of the Thirty-ninth N.C. Troops. He was wounded in the leg at Murfreesboro, Tennessee, December 31, 1862. He was in the battle of Chickamauga, and at the end of the war was paroled in June 1865 at Shreveport, Louisiana.

—*Fayetteville Observer,* March 15, 1873

40th Regiment North Carolina Troops (3rd Regiment North Carolina Artillery)

Lieut. James W. Kincey, of Lenoir, of the "Lenoir Braves," Company A, died of disease at Fort Warren, Boston, on the 19th of Dec. 1861. He had been captured at Fort Hatteras in August 1861.

—*North Carolina Standard,* January 1, 1862

In Fort Caswell Hospital, of typhoid fever, in Smithville, N.C., on the 24th Oct., **Wm. B. B. Thompson,** Company F, son of Samuel and Nancy Ann Thompson, of Robeson county, in the 29th year of his age. He was a farmer before his enlistment.

—*Fayetteville Observer,* November 3, 1862

Died, in the hospital at Smithville, of typhoid fever, on the 15th November, **Mr. W. J. Bracy,** aged 21 years. The deceased was a volunteer from Robeson County, in *Capt. M. H. McBryde's* (129) unattached Company E, N.C.T. He left his father and mother eight months since to enlist in his country's service but alas! he has been called to meet his God.

—*Fayetteville Observer,* December 8, 1862

At Fort Fisher, very suddenly, of congestive chills on the 1st inst., **Philip R. Herrington, Jr.,** 27, of Capt. Tait's Bladen Artillery Guards, 2nd Company K. The deceased was a citizen of Bladen Co. and a farmer there. He was an exemplary member of the Presbyterian Church, and was a member of the Masonic Fraternity. He was a noble soldier, a good citizen, a

loving husband, a pious and devoted christian. He leaves a wife and many relatives to mourn after him.
—*Fayetteville Observer,* March 2, 1863

Died at Camp Lee, near Richmond, 21st April, of Bronchitis, **Corporal Zepheniah W. Burgess**, 1st Company, Latham's N.C. Battery, in the 21st year of his age.
—*Fayetteville Observer,* April 27, 1863

Died, February 22d, 1864, of typhoid pneumonia, in hospital at Smithville, N.C., **Malcom Culbreth**, Company E, 40th N.C. Regiment, in the 43d year of his age. The deceased was born in Robeson County. For more than fifteen years he was a consistent member of the M.E. Church. As his end drew near his confidence in God remained unshaken, and he calmly sank to rest. He leaves a mother, sister and brother.
—*Fayetteville Observer,* May 12, 1864

Intelligence has just reached us, that **Robert Walker Anderson**, Company G, 40th N.C. Regiment, Captain of Ordnance in Cook's Brigade, fell in the battle of Wilderness Creek, near the dividing line between Spotsylvania and Orange counties, Va., on Thursday the 5th inst. Of the particular incidents connected with his death, we are without information.

Captain Anderson was born on the 23d January 1838; entered the Sophomore class at the University of North Carolina in the summer of 1855. His class consisted of 94 members, and there were few, it is believed, of the whole numbers that were not prompt to enter the army, at the earliest call for their service. Two of the seven who shared the first distinction with him, one subsequently, Tutor in the University, W. C. Dowd, the other Capt. W. C. Lord, are in their graves. The five survivors are all promising officers in the Confederate service.

Immediately after receiving his degree, Capt. Anderson was, on the recommendation of the Faculty, appointed Tutor of the Greek Language in the University, and discharged the duties of his chair with universal acceptance during the two following years. At the beginning of the war, he was a candidate for orders in the Protestant Episcopal Church, but under the conscientious convictions of duty, suspended his preparation for the sacred calling, to which his life was to have been devoted, that he might contribute his share to the vindication of the rights of his injured country. He accepted a position on the staff of his gallant brother, the late Gen. George B. Anderson, and was seriously injured, when the former was fatally wounded at the battle of Sharpsburg. Shortly after his brother's death, he passed the requisite examination to secure an appointment in that branch of the service in which he was engaged, with increasing reputation at the time of his death.

He was married on the 28th April 1863, to Rebecca, eldest daughter of P. C. Cameron, Esq., of Hillsboro,' N.C. How sad the reflections, that one brief year has sundered forever, two congenial spirits united by the tenderest of human ties.
—*Raleigh Register,* May 14, 1864

Henry T. C. Chance, a private in Co. E, 40th Reg't, N.C.T., son of Richard Chance and wife, died at Fort Holmes on the 6th inst, of Typhoid fever, aged 20 years 4 months and 9 days. He was the only son of his parents, much loved and esteemed by them, and upon whom they depended for assistance and protection in their declining life. About one month before his death he addressed a letter to the writer informing him that God for Christ's sake had pardoned his sins and that he desired his name enrolled on the Church book. And one of his comrades in arms informs us that he maintained the christian faith to the last—and was able to say to his last word, that he was not afraid to die.

—**Thomas Gibson**, *Fayetteville Observer,* **October 27, 1864**

Died of typhoid fever, in hospital at Fort Holmes, N.C., 15th ult, **Private Samuel Martin**, son of Amos Martin of Bladen County, aged 24 years and two months, a member of Co K, 40th N.C.T. Though cut down in the prime of manhood the writer has great reason to believe that he has retired from this world of strife to share the reward of the righteous. He had been a member of the Missionary Baptist Church for 7 years. His remains now rest in the burying ground at Smithville, while his memory lives in the bosom of his comrades.

—*Fayetteville Observer,* **November 3, 1864**

Dr. W. H. Green, a prominent druggist of Wilmington, N.C., died suddenly in the month of January 1914. He was born in Newbern, N.C., December 21, 1843, and lived there until the beginning of the war when he entered the war as a private in 1st Company H, 40th Regiment North Carolina Troops, at the time being only eighteen years old. He was a member of the famous Latham Battery, a North Carolina artillery organization which demonstrated its efficiency and bravery on many noted fields during the four years of strife. In 1863 he was detached as sergeant major of the battalion of Maj. J. C. Haskell, to which Latham's Battery was attached, and served as such during the remainder of the war. At the close of the war he was acting adjutant of his regiment.

He had an active career as an artilleryman, participating in the famous battles of Cedar Run, Second Manassas, Chantilly, Warrenton Springs, Fredericksburg, Gettysburg (where the battery was in action three days), Spotsylvania, Second Cold Harbor, and throughout the siege of Petersburg and the retreat to Appomattox, where he was paroled.

Returning to North Carolina, he made a beginning as a pharmacist at Newbern and continued his studies and practice in New York City, where he was graduated in 1869. He went to Wilmington, N.C. in 1870 and entered the drug business, in which he continued for forty-four years.

In July 1875, Dr. Green was married to Miss Frances Iredell Meares, who, with three daughters and two sons, survives him. He was a member of the Episcopal Church and for many years a vestryman. He was also a member of the Royal Arcanum.

Dr. Green was a genial, whole-souled man, never too busy to lend assistance to any one in trouble or to speak a kind word in greeting. His long and useful life was one of service and benefit to his generation.

—*Confederate Veteran* **Volume 22, Number 6, June 1914**

Mr. Amos Neil Johnson died at his home near Ingold last Saturday night about 10 o'clock, at the ripe old age of 94 years, seven months and 27 days. He was a son of Samuel and Ann Johnson, and was born July 29th 1820, in the two story log house now standing in the back yard of his late residence, where he spent the greater part of his long and useful life of nearly 95 years. He was a devoted member of the Methodist Church. He professed religion under the ministry of the Rev. Henry Gray, on August the 7th, 1842 at "Parker's Meeting House"—now Andrews Chapel and now on the Sampson Circuit. He connected himself with the church at Johnson's Chapel which was first built by Samuel Johnson in 1856 about one mile from Ingold, its present location. He served in the Confederate army in Company "K" 40th Regiment stationed at Fort Fisher. He was taken prisoner at the fall of Fort Fisher on the 15th of January 1865 and held prisoner at Point Lookout, Va., until

July the 3rd of the same year, when he was discharged. Mr. Johnson was a successful farmer and business man. He married Miss Ellen Herring, of Bladen County, and to this union was born six children, one girl, Mrs. B. L. Culbreth, who died nearly a year ago, and five boys, Mr. A. F. Johnson, of Ingold; Messrs. J. D., J. S. and E. N. Johnson, of Garland, and Mr. Geo. M. Johnson, of Barto, Fla. His devoted wife preceded him to the grave several years ago.
—*The News Dispatch,* April 1, 1915

Duncan Alexander Buie, one of the oldest Confederate twins, died at his home in Buies, N.C., on October 3, 1918. He would have been eighty-five years old on November 3, 1918. His twin brother, David Calvin Buie, survives him.

The *VETERAN* for August 1915, page 378, gave a short account of these twin brothers in the Confederate army. They were in their year at Davidson College when the war began, went home, enlisted in August 1861, in Capt. Malcolm McNair's company, and shortly were put on detached service. Duncan was ordered to Wilmington and appointed quartermaster sergeant of the 40th North Carolina Regiment of Heavy Artillery. He remained at Baldhead Island until the fall of Fort Fisher, marched through Wilmington the day it was evacuated to Kinston, N.C., and was in the battle there on March 9. He went from there to Bentonville and surrendered with General Johnston April 27, 1865. He then walked home, reaching it sometime in May.

He is survived by his wife, who was Miss Kate McGeachy, and two daughters, Miss Kate Buie, who lives at the old home, and Mrs. J. T. Kenyon, of Washington D.C.; also three sisters and two brothers besides the twin survives him. He was the son of Archibald and Flora McInnis Buie and was born at Philadelphia, N.C., November 12, 1833.
—*Confederate Veteran* **Volume 26, Number 11, November 1918**

41st Regiment North Carolina Troops (3rd Regiment North Carolina Cavalry)

Killed on the 17th inst., in a skirmish near Smithfield, Isle of Wight, Va., **Neill A. Kelly**, of "Highland Rangers," *Capt. Murchison*, (130) Co. D, 3d Reg't, N.C. Cavalry, and only child of Wm. John Kelly of Cumberland County. Mr. Kelly was killed instantly while charging the enemy—a ball piercing his heart. He was much beloved and respected by his entire company for his good moral character in Camp and his gallantry in time of action. The officers and men of his company deeply sympathize with his bereaved parents. His remains were brought through this place on Saturday in charge of two of his late comrades on its way to his home.
—A comrade, *Fayetteville Observer,* May 25, 1863

Privates **John B. Stevens** of Onslow County and **Isaac James**, also from Onslow County, Co. B, 3d N.C. Cavalry, died while on the recent scout in Eastern N.C. The former at Gatesville, N.C., May 6th, 1863, and the latter at Woodville, N.C., May 4th, 1863.
—*Wilmington Daily Journal,* June 1, 1863

Died, on the 9th of July, at the residence of his father in Harnett County, N.C., after a protracted illness, **John H. Hodges**, 5th Sergeant of Highland Rangers, Company D, 41st Regiment North Carolina Troops.

He was with us but a short time, and while in the company, he portrayed the qualities of a good soldier and useful member of our company. Those who were with him in his last hours, are left with the comfortable hope that he died in the triumph of faith; that for him death had no sting, and the grave robbed of its victory.

—*North Carolina Standard,* **August 23, 1862**

Private Francis B. Ferrell, Company G (Scotland Neck Cavalry), 3rd N.C. Cavalry, was killed in the late skirmish with the enemy near Greenville, N.C., on the night of 30th December.

—*Wilmington Daily Journal,* **January 12, 1864**

David Clark Camp, Brv't. 2d Lieut. Co. G, fell in a fight with the enemy near Greenville, N.C., on the night of the 30th of Dec. 1863. In the memory of his comrades live the immortal words of the expiring hero—"boys they have killed me, but fight them."

—*Fayetteville Observer,* **February 11, 1864**

Marshall and **Hiram Williams,** Onslow County, of Co. B, 3d N.C. Cavalry were killed in recent fights with the enemy. D. C. Marshall fell at Hanover Court House, May 31st, and Hiram S. Williams fell the day following near Ashland, Virginia.

—*Wilmington Daily Journal,* **July 16, 1864**

In the Confederate Hospital at Petersburg, on June the 25th, 1864, of wounds received in battle near the city on the 21st of the same month, **Lieut. David W. Simmons**, of Co. B, 3d Regiment of N.C. Cavalry, in the 24th year of his age. He volunteered and joined the army as a private in the early part of 1862 soon after graduating with collegiate distinction at Chapel Hill. For his known ability, true merit and soldierly bearing, he was soon promoted by his comrades to a Lieutenancy. When in the bloody contests around Richmond, the command fell upon him, by the killing and wounding of his ranking officers, they saw that their confidence had not been misplaced. His last words were, "tell my relatives that I have tried to bear it like a man and to die like a soldier."

—A friend, *Wilmington Daily Journal,* **July 21, 1864**

Died, in the Hospital in Richmond, Va., on the 29th of July, **Private Archibald McRay**, 25, Co. D, 3d Reg't N.C. Cavalry, eldest son of John and Catharine A. McRae of Harnett County, N.C., of a wound received in the head in battle near Petersburg on the 21st of June in the vicinity of Richmond. He was 28 years of age, and had been a faithful soldier for nearly three years. He leaves a father and mother, four sisters, seven brothers, a large number of relatives and many friends to mourn his loss. He has been a member of the Presbyterian Church for about three years,

—A brother, *Fayetteville Observer,* **August 22, 1864**

In the General Hospital No. 24, Richmond, Va., on the 30th July 1864, of a wound received near Atlas Station on the 27th May 1864, **Private James Corbett**, of Co. A, 3d N.C. Cavalry, in the 27th year of his age. He entered the service in the Spring of 1862, leaving his home and friends to embark on this great ocean of war. His conduct as an obedient and dutiful soldier, and his unflinching firmness in the hour of trial, when the swift messengers of death fell thick and fast around, amid the din of battle's wild rage, and the sharp

crack of the rifle, whose notes seemed to stifle with the moans of the slain, need no comment from the pen of those who are left to mourn their loss.
—A Brother Soldier, *Wilmington Daily Journal,* August 29, 1864

Died on the 13th inst., at Pettigrew Hospital, Raleigh, N.C., of Typhoid Pneumonia, **Noah H. Sutton** of Lenoir County. The deceased was a member of Co. E, 3rd N.C. Cavalry, was a good soldier, a true patriot, and a faithful christian. He leaves a wife and three children,
—*Daily Confederate,* February 16, 1865

Col. G. B. Alford, President of the Oscar R. Rand Memorial Association, reports the following death in the membership of that camp during the past year:

James M. Utley died at his home in Holly Springs on January 13, 1921, in his seventy-seventh year. He was born and reared in this county, and in 1861, at the age of nineteen, he volunteered in Oscar R. Rand's company, but was transferred to Company I, 3rd N.C. Cavalry, and served four years for the Confederacy, taking part in some big raids. In the passing of this good man the Holly Springs Baptist Church lost a faithful member and the Oscar R. Rand Camp of Veterans a true comrade, his family a devoted father. Surviving him are his wife and seven children.
—*Confederate Veteran* Volume 30, Number 2, February 1922

43rd Regiment North Carolina Troops

John Morton died of pneumonia in a Raleigh hospital April 9, two months after he had enlisted. He was 20. **Eli P. Winfree** also died of brain fever in a Raleigh hospital April 14. He enlisted in February and was 27. Both were from Anson County and were members of the Fisher Light Infantry, Company H, 43rd Regiment.
—*North Carolina Argus,* April 24, 1862

Died in Wadesboro, Anson County the 25th instant, of typhoid fever, **Sergeant Arthur L. Singer,** aged 26 years. Mr. Singer came to this place nearly two years ago from Philadelphia, at the solicitation of Jno. Ruscoe, who about that time commenced, in connection with Capt. J. C. Caraway, the coach making and blacksmithing business in Wadesboro. For the space of two years, lacking two months, he lived among us, laboring diligently at his business, and conducting himself in all things, soberly, orderly, gentlemanly. His deportment was unexceptionable. He was a Sabbath School teacher, punctual and attentive—regular in attendance at church. Such was his mode of life up to the time *Capt. John H. Coppedge's* (131) Company H, in which he volunteered, left for Raleigh. He was taken sick in camp, and, though sick, marched with his company from Camp Davis to Fort Johnson, though advised by a physician to remain at the camp. When his regiment left for Petersburg, being too unwell to accompany it, he returned home, sick of the fever. He arrived on Sunday. On Monday morning I visited him, found him in bed, and though very sick, thought he would recover. So thought many others; but on Tuesday a great change took place. It was evident that he was fast sinking into the arms of death, and on Wednesday morning he died—a martyr to the cause of Liberty and Southern Independence. Every attention was paid to him. He was faithfully attended by a skillful physician, and kindly nursed and ministered unto. All that human means could do was done.

—*North Carolina Argus,* June 26, 1862

Died of disease in camp, near Petersburg, Va., on the 13th inst., **Richard T. Talent**, of *Capt. C. H. Sturdivant*'s Company K, 43rd Regt. N.C. Troops. A farmer in Anson County, h e volunteered last February at age 26, and went with his company into camp of instruction at Raleigh, N.C., where he performed his duty as well as any, and since he has taken the rounds with the Regiment.

—*North Carolina Argus,* August 7, 1862

1st Lieutenant Thomas W. Baker lost an arm and was captured by the enemy at Gettysburg, July 1st. He died of the wounds and amputation on July 26th. He was the youngest of five brothers who have been in the army, and the only one who has suffered any material hurt in the various engagements in which some of them have participated. He first went as a private in the Lafayette Company of this town (Fayetteville), which was Co. F in the Bethel Reg't, and at the end of that term of service obtained a commission in Company D, the 43d Reg't. The community sympathizes with his aged mother and a large family connection in this sad affliction.

—*Fayetteville Observer,* August 17, 1863

July 2d, 1863, at the field infirmary of Rodes' Division, near Gettysburg, Pa., of wounds received in the battle of the preceding day, **Lieut. William W. Boggan**, Company H, 43d Regt. N.C. Troops, aged 21 years, 7 months and 17 days. At an early period of the present struggle, he joined one of the "volunteer" companies from the county, and departed to the "field of duty." Soon after the reorganization of his Regiment, under the act of Congress of April, '62, he attached himself to Co. H, of the 43d N.C. Regt., and in this, as in the Company to which he had formerly belonged, Company K, 26th Regiment N.C.T., his merit and proficiency soon won for him the honorable promotion of Lieutenant, which he held up to the time of his death. He entered the fight on the evening of the 1st of July, was mortally wounded in the left leg and died at 7½ o'clock the next morning. Borne, fatally wounded, from the field, at the close of a contest in which he had done his whole duty, the last sounds that reached his dying ear, as he was being carried to the rear, were shouts of victory from those with whom he had shared the dangers and the glory of that terrible day. He endured fatigue, cold heat, hunger and indeed all the hardships and privations incident to a soldier's life with a patience and resignation that were really astonishing. He scarcely ever complained. Even while he lay at the camp-fire with his leg all broken and shattered, not a murmur escaped his lips. In his last hours his mind was much engaged about his brother who was then on the field.

—**Chaplain (132), 43rd,** *North Carolina Argus,*
August 20, 1863 & September 3, 1863

Killed instantly, at the battle of Gettysburg, July 3d, 1863, **Serg't. S. Thomas Sikes**, of Wadesboro, Anson County aged 17, of Co. H, 43d N.C. Regt. He was the son of B. F. and J. B. Sikes. It is a sad duty to record the death of our gallant youth. Ever faithful in the discharge in the arduous and perilous duties of a soldier, he won the respect of his comrades and the confidence of the officers of his company. When there was an important and dangerous post to be guarded, his Captain thought he hazarded nothing in entrusting it to the care of Serg't. Sikes and his squad of men. But he was struck by a minie ball through his temple and fell bravely fighting the foe. He lies like many others in a soldier's grave in the enemy's land. No rude stone will be erected to mark his resting place—no flower will be planted by the hand of affection to adorn his grave. The place where he lies will soon be lost to sight of, but let his gallant bearing in the field never be forgotten by his sorrowing comrades. And while his bereaved friends may deplore his untimely death, let them be proud to be informed that he lived like a soldier and died like a hero.

—**Chaplain 43D N.C. REGT.**, *North Carolina Argus,* **August 27, 1863**

Killed at Gettysburg, Pa., July 1st, 1863, **James Briley**, of Anson County, aged about thirty-two years. He was a Corporal in *Captain R. T. Hall*'s (133) Company I, 43d Regiment of N.C. Troops. He enlisted in March 1862, and arriving at the city of Raleigh, he was attacked by measles. He then returned home on furlough. Having convalesced, he again returned to camp. After experiencing many long, tedious, and toilsome marches, and undergoing many privations incident to camp-life, he was again taken ill with fever, when he again returned home on furlough. Having regained his strength, he again reported for duty. After enduring many other hardships and laborious marches, the Company at last came in contact with the enemy. Whilst the balls were flying thickly and rapidly around him, and his comrades were falling on his right and on his left, he bravely stood at his post in discharge of his duties until forced to the ground by the piercing of a ball through his head. He left a wife and two children.

—*North Carolina Argus,* **September 3, 1863**

Died October 15, 1863, at Camp Winder Hospital, Richmond, Va., of dysentery, **James A. Treadaway**, Co. H, 43d N.C. Troops, in the 21st year of his age. He was from Anson County and was badly wounded in his left leg on the first day of the Gettysburg battle. His leg was amputated a few days after the fight. He was captured by the enemy and sent to a hospital in Baltimore. He was exchanged in late September and sent to the Richmond hospital where he died.

—*North Carolina Argus,* **November 5, 1863**

Died in a Hospital near Gettysburg, Pa., July 6, of wounds received in the battle of 1st July, **George G. Gay**, Company F, 43rd N.C.T., of Halifax County, aged 24. He died a prisoner of the enemy at age 26.

—*Fayetteville Observer,* **November 23, 1863**

Died of pneumonia in the Hospital, Richmond, 17th Dec., **Corporal M. C. Britt**, Co. F, 43d Reg't, in the 20th year of his age. He was from Halifax County.

—*Fayetteville Observer,* **March 31, 1864**

Killed, in battle, **Daniel Turner Hundley**, Co. G, 43d Regt N.C. Troops, by a grape shot, on Monday the 30th of May, near Mechanicsville, Virginia. His brigade had handsomely repulsed the enemy when they were ordered back. The enemy fired upon them as they turned back, when he received his death wound. He had a younger brother standing nearby when he was shot down. Sad indeed was the task that devolved upon this young brother to communicate this sad intelligence to his widowed parent. Mr. Hundley was 23 years old last April and leaves a mother, seven brothers and two sisters to mourn his loss. I hope he is at rest, where the wicked cease from troubling and the weary are at rest.

—**A friend**, *Daily Confederate,* **June 16, 1864**

Private George W. Tice, Company K, 43d N.C. Infantry, died at Howard's Grove Hospital, in the 18th year of his age, on the 24th of May, from the effects of a wound received on the 16th inst., at the battle of Drury's Bluff. He came from Lenoir County and joined in March this year. The family of the deceased has the sympathies of every acquaintance, yet no one more deeply grieves than the author of this notice. My loss is common with theirs; my regrets alike enduring. Rest in peace!

—A friend, *North Carolina Argus,* July 28, 1864

Died at Chimborazo Hospital, Richmond, July 14th, 1864, **Ashley S. Kornegay**, of the 43d Reg't N.C.T., Company A, Grimes' Brigade. He was 18 and one of the braves of Duplin County that responded to the call of his country in her great struggle for liberty. He returned home after the battle of Plymouth, where he was permitted only to remain a few weeks, before returning to his Regiment in Virginia, He received a severe wound in the hip at Cold Harbor, June 3. He then took the fever, which proved fatal. Providence has seen fit to call him in the spring time of youth at 18 from deadly strife, and he will be deeply mourned by his devoted relatives and friends.

—**By his schoolmate,** *Wilmington Daily Journal,* **August 3, 1864**

Killed, instantly in battle, near Bethesda Church, Va., on the 30th day of May 1864, **Corporal George Barber**, of Co. K, 43d N.C. Reg't. He joined in Anson County where he was a farmer. He was 19. I surmise that a poor tribute from one who well knew the subject of this brief notice, will not pass unappreciated by his parents, relatives and friends. Although a longer time having elapsed since his death and this date, than habit has made a custom, I hope that I will not again enkindle the deep grief that naturally existed on the first reception of the sad intelligence—the delay being caused by active and fatiguing duties, beyond our control. The qualities of a good soldier were, certainly, always visible in the demeanor of Corporal Barber. While in camp he was faithful and obedient in the discharge of all duties incumbent upon him; and on the march, when the energies of all men are tested, he was firm and untiring in his efforts to discharge his duties, however fatiguing and laborious, and oftentimes at great sacrifices to himself. In the repeated conflicts with the enemy, in which he participated before his death, he was particularly distinguished for his bravery and heroism. On the evening of his death, not long before the monstrous deadly missile struck its fatal blow; when the regiment was subject to a terrific enfilading and effective fire, from the concentrated guns of the enemy, he, amid some confusion, exclaimed, "Brave comrades, form on me."

—B. A. J., *North Carolina Argus,* August 11, 1864

Killed, instantly, on the 21st of August, in the 19th year of his age, in an engagement with the enemy near Charlestown, Va., [now Charles Town, WVA] **Sergeant Joseph M. Hammond**, of Anson County, son of H. B. Hammond, and a member of Co. H, 43d N.C. Troops.

—*North Carolina Argus,* September 1, 1864

Killed on the field of battle at Fisher's Hill, Valley of Virginia, near Winchester, on the 22d of September 1864, **Julius C. Pinkston**, aged 27 years, a member of Co. H, 43d N.C.T. He leaves a kind wife and two little boys and an affectionate mother to mourn his loss. He was one of the first to bid adieu to home and loved ones in defense of his country.

—*North Carolina Argus,* November 15, 1864

Died of disease at Harrisonburg, Va., Nov. 29th, 1864, **Thomas. L. Gales**, Co. I, 43d Reg't. N.C.T. He enlisted in Anson County, at age 37, February 1863. After the battle of

Gettysburg, he was left behind to nurse the wounded and was captured by the enemy. He was moved to Baltimore in October and paroled in November. He returned to duty in early 1864, was taken sick and died. He leaves a wife and nine children and many relatives and friends to mourn his loss.

—*North Carolina Argus,* December 8, 1864

Near New Market, Va., Nov. 25th, 1864.
Mr. Editor: Please publish the following list of our brother officers of the 43rd N.C.T. who died during our late and current campaigns:

Capt. William Clark Ousby, Company F, was killed July 1, at Gettysburg, minutes after the battle opened. He was buried there as well as conditions would allow.

Capt. Henry Allston Macon, Company H, aged 23, was slightly wounded at Gettysburg, July 1. He was killed at the battle of Plymouth, N.C. in April 1864.

Capt. Levi Parkinson Coleman, Company G, age 27, was wounded in the fighting at Drewry's Bluff, May 16, 1864, and died near there June 8th.

Lieut. Julius J. Alexander, Company B, was wounded at Gettysburg July 3, and captured during the retreat two days later. He died at Gettysburg, July 15th.

Lieut. Thomas Wilson Baker, Company D, was wounded in the arm and captured at Gettysburg. His arm was amputated and he died July 26th.

Lieut. William Willington Boggan, Company H, was wounded at Gettysburg July 1, and died the next day.

—*North Carolina Argus,* December 12, 1864

Died, at the residence of his father in this county, on the 4th instant, **Allen Rhew**, of Co. E, 43d N.C.T., aged 18 years, 3 months and 9 days. He enlisted in Hillsborough in May last, and was at Raleigh, Weldon and Goldsborough. On arriving at the age of 18 he was transferred to the 43d N.C. Regiment, and went through all the fighting in the Valley, at Fisher's Hill and at Winchester, at which latter place he was severely wounded. He was taken to Staunton, where he remained sometime laboring under the effects of his wound and a consuming fever. He then obtained a furlough for sixty days absence, and arrived at Hillsborough on the 16th of November. On reaching home his disease had made such progress that all the attention and kindness of his friends were unavailing, and he fell a victim to the great conqueror. He leaves a father, mother, three brothers and three sisters to mourn their loss. He sleeps calmly in that honored home, the soldier's grave.

—*Hillsboro Recorder,* December 14, 1864

Lieut. Stephen W. Ellerbee, Co I, 43d N.C., died at Hospital in Winchester, Va. on the 31st of July 1864, from a wound received in battle at Snicker's Ferry on the 13th of the same month. He was born in the county of Richmond, N.C., where his entire boyhood was spent. Becoming early wedded to an amiable and accomplished lady, he moved to Anson County. At the breaking out of the war, he left home and all those comforts and endearments—a lovely wife, two prattling children to enliven his household with their innocent mirth, and a prospering farm. He enlisted as a private in the company in which he met his death. His comrades, however, soon evinced their appreciation of his excellent qualities as a man and soldier, by promoting him to a Lieutenancy.

—**His friend**, *Fayetteville Observer,* December 22, 1864

Captain Caswell Sturdivant, of Co. K, 43d N.C.T., died in hospital at Winchester, Va., on the 30th of September 1864, of wounds received in the battle near Winchester, Va., on the 19th day of the same month. Early on the morning of the 19th day of September, the bombing of the distant cannon was heard in the quiet camp of Rodes' Division, and as the sun rose, the warlike sounds began to usher in from all around, demonstrating, to many of us that day would be an eventful one, and that the households of many brave, heroic and virtuous men would be wrapped in mourning. Orders to march speedily came, and as the troops, in their martial robes, moved noiselessly and steadily on, could be seen the stately and manly form of the Captain, determined to do his duty at whatever cost. Arriving on the field of carnage amid the roar and clash of arms, the Brigade was hurled against the advancing columns of the enemy, and having driven them in utter route and confusion was ordered to fall back and establish a permanent "line." The command of the Regiment, at that time, devolved upon Capt. Sturdivant, and while he was exposing himself, endeavoring to place a portion of his command in places more secure, some of the companies being much exposed, the enemy firing upon them with both artillery and musketry, and their ranks being thinned every moment, he was struck by a solid shot from one of the enemy's batteries. He was quickly removed from the scene of action to the hospital at Winchester. His wound was pronounced painful but not serious. In the misfortunes of war, he fell a prisoner in the hands of the enemy. We had fondly indulged in the hope of hearing of his early recovery and speedy return to his own land loved. But alas! We hope in vain! The sad news of his death is borne to us; the grief more unutterable because he died in the hands of a cruel enemy, in a hostile land, where no kindred, nor his wife, could stand around his couch and speak soothing words of consolation in his dying moments.

—*North Carolina Argus,* December 22, 1864

The remains of **Capt. Hampton Beverly**, Co. H, 43d N.C. Troops, were brought to the residence of his widowed mother, near this town, last week, and interred on Saturday in the family burial ground near the family residence. He fell near Petersburg, in the fighting on the afternoon of the 2d of April 1865, on the east side of the town, and on the retreat of the army, during the night of that day, his body was carried off by the sorrowing members of his company, and buried in a gentleman's garden one mile and a half west of Petersburg, from whence they have been removed to their last resting place in this county.—

—**Originally published in the** *N.C. Argus* **October 18, and reprinted in the** *Wilmington Journal,* **April 26, 1866**

Thomas Stephen Kenan was born April 12, 1838. He obtained his first education at the old Grove Academy at Kenansville, under the venerated the Rev. James Sprunt, an institution that educated many of the brightest young men of the Cape Fear section; he then spent a year at the Central Military Institute at Selma, Ala., and entered Wake Forest College, completing the freshman course in June 1854. That fall he entered the sophomore class at the University of North Carolina, where he graduated in 1857 with the degree of A. B., and the next year the University conferred on him the degree of A. M. Having determined to become a lawyer he spent two years studying law with Chief Justice Pearson at Richmond Hill and entered upon the practice of law at Kenansville in 1860. In 1859 the "Duplin Rifles," a military company, was organized in Kenansville, and in 1861 this company volunteered in a body under Thomas Stephen Kenan as its captain, and was assigned to the First or Bethel Regiment and afterwards to the Second Regiment. At the end of the year it was reorganized and assigned to the 43d Regiment and Colonel Kenan was made Lieutenant-Colonel. He was elected Colonel of the 38th Regiment upon its reorganization. He declined that office, preferring to remain with the 43d Regiment, and on April 24, 1862, he was elected Colonel of that regiment. He was assigned to Daniel's Brigade and engaged in the operations before Richmond. He had previously served a year in Virginia, and after joining the Daniel Brigade he served again in North Carolina until he joined General Lee, who was then preparing for the Gettysburg campaign. Then he was assigned to the Rode's division, and it carried the flag to Carlisle, Pa. Returning to Gettysburg on the first of July, Colonel Kenan was in the hard fight on Seminary Ridge that day and was under fire all the next day, his regiment supporting a battery of artillery on Seminary Ridge, and on the third day he participated in the desperate assault on Culp's Hill. While leading a charge he fell severely wounded, and while being borne to the rear in an ambulance train the next day he was captured and confined on Johnson's Island, a prisoner of war until March 1865. He was paroled, together with a number of other prisoners, but was never exchanged.

After the war he continued to serve the state as a lawyer, attorney-general and clerk of the North Carolina Supreme Court for twenty-five years. He died December 23, 1911, and is buried in the historic Oakwood Cemetery in Raleigh.

—*News & Observer,* December 24, 1911

44th Regiment North Carolina Troops

Died in the Hospital at Raleigh, on Monday the 19th of May 1862, **Eli P. Freeman**, aged 27 years, 7 months and 12 days. He was a carpenter in Montgomery County. He was a respected member of the Christian Church. The deceased was a volunteer from Montgomery County, in *Capt. William Moffitt's* (134) Company H, 44th Regiment.

—*Fayetteville Observer,* May 26, 1862

The remains of this gallant and lamented officer, **Colonel George Badger Singeltary**, reached this city at an early hour on Sunday morning, and at 10 o'clock, were escorted by the 54th Regiment, Col. John Wimbish, and a procession of citizens to the Cemetery, where after the reading of the burial service by the Rev. Dr. Mason, they were interred. A braver and more noble man than George Badger Singeltary never lived or died.

Of the skirmish in which Col. Singeltary fell, we have been enabled to gather the following particulars. The fight took place at Latham's Mill, on Tranter's Creek, nine miles from the town of Washington. Our men were stationed behind a temporary breastwork, and Col. Singeltary, without either pistol or sword, was sitting on a log with his head exposed over the breastwork. While in this position he saw a Yankee soldier skulking in the bushes and acting as if he wished to get a shot at him, whereupon the Colonel ordered one of his men to shoot the Yankee, and had no sooner done so than he received a ball in the head and breathed but for an hour afterwards. Besides Col. Singeltary, we lost two men—**Corporal Louis J. B. Edwards** (135) Company I and **William H. Heathcock** (136) Company F and had three men—we did not learn their names—wounded.—The Yankee loss was about 20 killed, and 50 more or less severely wounded. Our men made good their retreat in an orderly manner after Artillery was brought to bear on them.

—*Raleigh Register,* June 11, 1862

Daniel L. McMillan died at his father's residence in Montgomery County, 7th July 1862, of Typhoid fever, while at home on sick furlough. At the time of his death he was 2d

Lieutenant in the Montgomery Guards, Co. H, 44th Reg't N.C.T. He was a farmer there and was 24. He was a member of Mt. Olivet Lodge, No. 164.

—*Fayetteville Observer,* **August 8, 1862**

Died near Petersburg of typhoid fever on the 18th inst., **Capt. Baker W. Mabrey**, of Company B, 44th Regt. He had been but a short time in camp, and acquitted himself gallantly at the recent fight at Tranter's Creek, near Washington. He was 30 years old from Edgecombe County.

—*Fayetteville Observer,* **September 29, 1862**

Died on the 19th March in Hospital at Goldsboro,' of small-pox, **Sergeant Claiborne Harris**, of Co. F, 44th Reg't, aged about 20 years and 11 days. He was a good soldier and well beloved by all who knew him. He was a native of Montgomery County, and leaves a father, mother, brothers and sisters to mourn his loss.

—Sister, *Fayetteville Observer,* **April 20, 1863**

Died on the 23d of May, of Typhoid Fever, in the Chimborazo Hospital, Richmond, **Preston H. Wooley**, son of Calvin W. Wooley, Esq., of Montgomery Co., N.C. The deceased was born the 7th day of August 1844. He had a frail constitution, but was too spirited and manly to claim an exemption from service. He volunteered in the 44th N.C. Reg't, Company F, reached camp on the Saturday previous to the advance of our troops on Newbern. Though wholly unaccustomed to military life and to hardships of any kind, he discharged all the duty devolved upon him promptly and faithfully, throughout the campaign from Newbern till after the falling back of our forces from Washington, and from the representations of many soldiers, they saw very hard times. When the brigade to which he belonged reached Richmond, he was taken sick and sent to the hospital. In a very few days his father reached him and had everything done for him that was in the power of man to do, but all to no avail. Thus has perished another noble youth in defense of his country.

—A friend, *Fayetteville Observer,* **June 15, 1863**

Killed in the battle near Bristow Station, on the Orange and Alexandria Railroad, in Prince William County, Va., on the 14th Oct., **Lieut. John C. Montgomery**, son of Dr. J. H. Montgomery, of Montgomery County, of Co. F, 44th Reg't N.C.T., Kirkland's (formerly Pettigrew's) Brigade, whilst gallantly leading his company in a charge against the enemy, and heroically encouraging them by pointing to their colors flying in their front; by a minnie ball penetrating his forehead just above his left eye, killing him instantly; in the 27th year of his age. A Surgeon of his Brigade (Dr. W. H. L.), in communicating the sad intelligence of his death to his parents says: "We all hear testimony of his worth and mourn his loss; his Regiment had no officer more efficient or gallant than he, and I am sure no one was more beloved by his men." His remains were grossly outraged by his murderers on the battle field, by robbing him of his arms and other property, stealing from his finger a ring which he had playfully taken from a friend when he was last home.

He sleeps in the cold embraces of death under the soil of Virginia, far from his home and friends and the scenes of his youth; but he will ever live in the hearts of his relatives and friends, who will fondly cherish his memory.

—*Fayetteville Observer,* **November 16, 1863**

Died of chronic diarrhea, at the residence of his father, near Pittsboro,' 7th of Nov., after a protracted illness of three months **Sergt. Henry A. Dismukes**, aged 22 years and 7 months, of Co. E, 44th Reg't, N.C.T. For near two years he had been battling in his country's defense—After much suffering in camp, he was prevailed on to be placed in a hospital, where he remained several weeks, after which he obtained leave of absence, and returned home; hoping there by the many attentions and kindness of fond parents, brothers and sisters, and with the aid of medical skill to be perfectly restored; but after lingering two weeks he peacefully died. He leaves parents, seven brothers (five in the Confederate service) and six sisters.

—Sister, *Fayetteville Observer*, December 21, 1863

Died of chronic diarrhea at Staunton, Va., Oct. 15th, 1863, **Matthew A. Coggins**, of Montgomery County, of Co. H, 44th N.C.T., aged 31 years 4 months and 20 days. He had been in service 1 year and 7 days when he died, and had been in several skirmishes but passed them all unhurt. Thus has fallen the last of three soldier brothers, a crushing blow on their aged father. He was esteemed by all who knew him at home and loved by his fellow soldiers. He leaves an affectionate wife, lovely little daughter, aged father, sisters and brothers, to mourn his early loss.

—*Fayetteville Observer,* March 4, 1864

Died, of meningitis at Raleigh General Hospital, No. 7, on the 9th of March, **Richard A. Sykes,** son of Henry and Eliza Sykes, of Orange County, in his 25th year. He was a Private in Company G, 44th Reg., N.C.T. He is the third son that has died in the army. He was captured at the South Anna Bridge in Virginia in June 1863 and was paroled at Fortress Monroe later in the month. He returned to his command in January 1864. He leaves a kind Mother and many friends to mourn his loss. He was a consistent member of the Baptist Church.

—*Hillsboro Recorder,* March 30, 1864

Died, of pneumonia at his residence in Chatham County, N.C., 27th Nov'r, 1863, **Sg't. Elijah O'Bryan,** Company E, 44th Reg't N.C.T., in the 31st year of his age. He leaves a wife and one child and many friends to mourn their loss. He left home and volunteered his services to the Confederate army, 11th March 1862. He was in 4 battles, Newbern and other places. He was taken sick in July with the bilious fever and remained in camp seven weeks; was then sent to Lynchburg Hospital and there remained three weeks; was furloughed, returning to his home where he lived 2 months with much suffering which he bore with patience.

—*Fayetteville Observer,* April 25, 1864

Killed instantly, in battle, at the Wilderness, on the 5th of May 1864, **Capt. John C. Gaines**, Co. F, 44th Reg't, N.C. Troops, Kirkland's Brigade, and son of the late Col. James L. Gaines, of Montgomery County, N.C., in the 27th year of his age.

His Regiment had been relieved after having charged and carried the enemy's works in gallant style, and on retiring Capt. Gaines was killed by a minnie ball piercing his head. He entered the service in March 1862, as 1st Lieutenant of the company, which he had assisted to raise by volunteering, and upon the death of *Capt. D. D. DeBerry*, (137) which happened shortly after the Company was organized, he was promoted to the Captaincy, which position he held and served gallantly up to the time of his death.

—**A friend**, *Fayetteville Observer,* July 14, 1864

Died on the 4th June 1864, from wounds received on the 2d June at Cold Harbor, Va., **Sgt. Murdoch D. McLeod,** Co H, 44th N.C.T., aged 23 years, 5 months and 14 days. He was the third brother that has fallen in the last twelve months. His first brother, Sgt K. J. McLeod, fell at Gettysburg, 1st July 1863, and his next, Captain N.C. McLeod, fell on the 23d of May, and then he fell on the 2d June—three of the noblest brothers that were ever in Confederate service have fallen in the short space of twelve months. Murdoch volunteered 16th of March 1862, and served through all the fights and marches which that noble regiment passed through without ever being wounded until the fatal ball struck him. He leaves an affectionate father, two sisters and two brothers.

—*Fayetteville Observer,* **August 22, 1864**

Another of Pitt County's Confederate soldiers and good citizens answered the final roll call this morning about 4 o'clock, when **Mr. Edward P. Fleming**, Company B, 44th Regiment N.C.T., passed away at his home five miles from Greenville. He was farming in the county when he enlisted at age 22 in January 1862. He held the rank of Corporal at the end. He was among those who surrendered at Appomattox Court House April 9, 1865. He was 72 years of age and is survived by three sons, Messrs. J. E., C. E., and Bithel Fleming. His wife died only two weeks ago and he soon follows to join her "Beyond the River."

—*Daily Reflector,* **October 31, 1912**

45th Regiment North Carolina Troops

Died of disease at Camp Mangum, near Raleigh, 12th inst., **Private Thomas Vincent**, from Rockingham County, a member of "Guilford Light Infantry," Co. C, 45th Reg't N.C. Troops, in the 20th year of his age.

—*Fayetteville Observer,* **April 8, 1862**

Died July 17th, in camp near Petersburg, Va., of typhoid fever, **William H. Kellam**, from Guilford County, a member of Co. B, 45th Reg't N.C. Troops, aged about 21 years.

—*Fayetteville Observer,* **July 28, 1862**

Died of disease, near Petersburg, 20th July, **Private Samuel Taylor**, of Co. C, 45th Reg't, aged 37, of Guilford County. Also, on the 26th, **Private Julius Story** of the same Co. and county where he farmed, aged 17. He entered service as a substitute. Died of fever in camp, near Petersburg, of fever, 21st ult., **Simeon Casper**, a carpenter in Rowan County, a member of Co. B, 45th Reg't N.C. Troops. He was 23.

—*Fayetteville Observer,* **August 4, 1862**

Died of typhoid fever in the Second N.C. Hospital at Petersburg, Va., August 3rd, 1862, **Private Absalom Aldred**, a farmer in Guilford County, and member of Co. C, 45th Regiment N.C. Troops. He was 24, a faithful soldier, and greatly beloved by all who knew him. Died of typhoid fever in Petersburg, at South Carolina Hospital, July 25th, 1862, **Private William Cummins White**, member of Company C, 45th Regt. N.C.T., aged 36 years. He resided in Guilford County, N.C., where he farmed, and was the son of Benjamin and Margaret White. Mr. White was a well-trained, able and willing soldier, and respected by all his comrades in arms.

—*Greensborough Patriot,* **August 14, 1862**

Died in First N.C. Hospital, Petersburg, July 6th, of typhoid fever, **Private Munroe Ingold**, of Company C, 45th N.C.T., aged 17 years, and a native of Guilford County, N.C. He was a farmer there and had enlisted as a substitute.

—*Fayetteville Observer*, **September 15, 1862**

Lieut. T. A. Price, aged 23, **Sergeant David Kallam**, a tobacconist in Rockingham County, aged 26, both of Company A, and **Sergeant John S. Dalton**, a merchant in Rockingham County, Company D, aged 25, died of typhoid fever, near Petersburg, all of the 45th Reg. N.C. Troops and all members of Cherokee Lodge, No. 197, A.Y.M. They were from Rockingham County, and they died between August 2–6, 1862.

—*Greensborough Patriot*, **December 11, 1862**

Died at his residence in Halifax County, near Weldon, on the 26th of January, of typhoid fever, **Dr. William L. Johnston**. Last summer he became Assistant Quarter Master with the rank of Captain to the 45th N.C. State Troops. He was 39 and leaves a devoted wife and six children to mourn his loss. He was a consistent member of the Methodist Protestant Church.

—*North Carolina Presbyterian*, **February 7, 1863**

1st Lieutenant Wilson D. Moore died in camp near Goldsboro,' N.C. on the 5th inst., from the effect of vaccination for smallpox after a confinement of 19 days. The best medical skill was brought to bear on his case, but his sufferings were so great and the symptoms of the disease so unchangeable that the administering of medicine was of no effect. His remains accompanied by his wife and brother were carried to his home for interment. He was a native of Rockingham County, N.C., a farmer there, and was in the 29th year of his age. He leaves a wife and two little children.

—*Greensborough Patriot*, **February 9, 1863**

Died in the Peace Institute Hospital at Raleigh N.C., on the 20th February 1863, **Andrew M. Irvin**, Company G, 45th Regt. N.C. Troops, in the 33d year of his age, of Erysipelas caused from vaccination. He was an ardent, enthusiastic and obedient soldier. His remains were brought to his native county (Rockingham) for interment. He was a farmer there, and he leaves a brother.

—A friend, *Greensborough Patriot*, **March 26, 1863**

Col. John Henry Morehead, of the 45th Regiment, died at Martinsburg, Va. [now West Virginia] a few days ago of typhoid fever. Col. Morehead was a gallant officer—a noble and generous hearted man.

—*Greensborough Patriot*, **July 9, 1863**

Died February 16, in Danville, Va., on the 15th inst., of brain fever, **Serg't. William C. Irvin**, Co. G, 45th Regt., N.C. Troops. He was from Rockingham County and a consistent member of the M. E. Church for five years. He was 23.

—Fannie B., *Greensborough Patriot*, **February 24, 1864**

Died at Camp Terrell, near Orange Court House, a., 6th February, **Joseph J. Willett**, of Company C, 45th Reg't, aged 38 years. He resided near Jamestown, N.C., and leaves a wife and several children to mourn his loss. He was wounded and captured at Gettysburg, hospitalized and held prisoner at David's Island, New York Harbor, and exchanged in August.

Died in the hospital at Salisbury, N.C. February 16th, 1864, **William R. May**, of Company C, 45th Reg't, N.C. Troops, aged 39 years. He leaves a wife and four children in Guilford County to mourn his loss. He was wounded at the battle of Gettysburg.

Died in the Hospital, at Orange Court House, Va., March 7th, 1864, **Corporal Hezekiah G. Reid**, of Company C, 45th Regt. N.C. Troops, aged 26 years and son of Buford Reid of Guilford County, N.C. He was in a skirmish with the Yankees near New Bern in March 1863.

—*Greensborough Patriot,* March 17, 1864

Died in the 2d Corps Hospital, Orange Court House, Va., April 4th, 1864, **George Stoves**, member of Company C, 45th Regt. N.C. Troops, aged 24 years. He was a brave and faithful soldier, and popular with his comrades. He was wounded in the head at Gettysburg and returned to his Regiment in late 1863. He leaves a wife and child living in the north part of Guilford County, N.C., who deserve the sympathy and kindness of the people of the community in which they live.

—*Greensborough Patriot,* April 21, 1864

Gen'l Junius Daniel was born in June 1824, in Halifax, N.C. and was the youngest son of Hon. J. R. J. Daniel. He was the only surviving child. He was the pupil for many years of J. M. Lovejoy, Esq. of Raleigh. He entered West Point in 1846, and left that renowned institution, having completed its curriculum, in 1859. He entered the army and was engaged for several years in active service upon the frontier, in Utah and in New Mexico. It was in this severe and arduous school that he acquired those habits and received that training which so admirably qualified him for the part he was to perform in this savage and long protracted war. He was in one fight with the Indians, perhaps more. At the beginning of hostilities with the North, he was residing upon his plantation on the Red River in Louisiana, but he promptly repaired to his native State, and at Raleigh tendered his services to the late Gov. Ellis. He was soon after elected Colonel of the 4th (now 14th) Reg't of N.C. Volunteers, which he commanded for one year. This regiment was one of the four that went to Virginia a few weeks after Sumter fell. Upon its re-organization he would have been unanimously chosen again as its leader, but having been previously elected Col. of both of the 43d and 45th Regt's, he thought it proper to accept the latter, having been twice chosen by that regiment although personally an entire stranger to the command. This regiment was besides organized for the war, and Gen'l Daniels had determined never to lay down his sword until freedom's day was sure.

Whilst Col. of the 14th he had no opportunity of distinction, but his desire to engage and free his country from the polluting tread of the enemy will be testified to by those who saw him return twice to the Peninsula to lead his old regiment. He rendered valuable service whilst Colonel of the 45th both in Virginia and North Carolina, although not in any regular battle. His soldierly qualities soon attracted the attention of his superiors, and he was made a Brigadier General even before he had afforded him an occasion for displaying his unquestioned capacity for command amid the smoke and din of battle. That the appointment was worthily and sagaciously bestowed his subsequent career amply confirms. Although not actively engaged around Richmond, his regiment was tried by being subjected to a severe shelling when there was no chance whatever to engage the enemy. But it was upon the bloody field of Gettysburg that he displayed those admirable characteristics of the true soldier which placed him at once among the foremost officers of his grade. He managed his brigade with great skill and displayed amid the havoc of that sanguinary struggle the lofty courage for which he was distinguished even when a schoolboy. Said one of his soldiers to me who saw him amid the smoke and carnage of that terrible fight: "Soldiers would be obliged to fight if all the Generals did as ours, for Gen Daniel was right up with us, cheering and encouraging us all the time." I regret that I have not by me a copy of the late numbers of the Richmond Dispatch which contained a full and no doubt accurate description of the Battle of Gettysburg. The writer, evidently a man of fairness and discrimination, awards high praise to Gen. Daniel and his command for their conspicuous gallantry.

His second battle was his last. On that bloody Thursday at Spotsylvania—a day to be ever memorable in yankee history—when our peerless Gen'l Lee and his magnificent army hurled back the whiskey maddened vandals as the surf-beaten rock dashes back the spray:—on that day, when it is said 20,000 heartless mercenaries were placed *hors du combat*, Gen. Junius Daniel fell, pierced through the body by a minnie ball, and the bright, gleaming falchion dropped from his nerveless hand. Upon the very ramparts of freedom he received his death wound, and was borne to the rear amid the loud roar of battle and the "fiery pang of shells." No more upright spirit—no more lofty manhood went down amid the terrors of that day. He lived for two days, and as I learn, "With no vain sigh or throb of craven fear," he passed away, the "light of battle" having faded from his eyes forever. He said he had fallen where he desired to fall, at the head of his brave men.

His funeral obsequies took place on the 21st inst., when his remains were deposited in the ancient burying ground of the town of Halifax. The delicate hand of woman had decorated the warrior's coffin with a beautiful Confederate flag made of flowers. He leaves a wife, to whom he was wedded since the war began, to mourn her irreparable loss. May God pity the young widow in her sad bereavement, and may the consolation of a Redeemer's love bring her solace and relief in her heart-anguish.

May 26, 1864

—T. B. K., *Fayetteville Observer*, June 9, 1864

We are deeply pained to announce the death of **Major Thomas McGehee Smith**. This gallant officer died in Richmond on Monday, May 30th, from a wound received in a fight with the enemy at Bethesda Church. Maj. Smith was attached to the 45th Regiment N.C. Troops in Daniel's Brigade, and was previously Captain of Company I. His remains are en route to Milton for interment.

—**Originally published in the *Milton Chronicle*, and reprinted in the *Fayetteville Observer*, June 9, 1864**

Died at Moore Hospital, Richmond, Va., June 6th, of wounds received in battle May 30th, **Pleasant D. Cardwell**, Co. D, 45th N.C.T. He was from Wake County and aged 19 years.

—*North Carolina Presbyterian*, July 6, 1864

Notwithstanding the exceedingly inclement weather, there was a very general turn-out of our citizens yesterday afternoon, to pay funeral honors to the soldier-brothers, **Major James J.** and **Capt. Campbell T. Iredell**. This demonstration was most proper, creditable and gratifying,—proper as a tribute of respect to the memory of two brave, young townsmen, who sealed with their blood their devotion to the cause of their State and section.

At the hour designated for the funeral, the Episcopal Church was crowded almost to its full capacity. The remains of the deceased brothers rested on a catafalque in front of the chancel, which fair and sympathizing hands had beautifully festooned with crosses and wreaths of flowers and evergreens. The solemn ritual was read by the Rev. Dr. Mason, when the cortege moved to the City Cemetery,—a number of ex-Confederate soldiers preceding the hearse, and a large portion of the community, of both sexes, following. The falling rain did not deter the young ladies from mingling in the procession, each provided with a floral offering, with which to strew the last resting places of the lamented dead—"nobly dying ere their prime."

James Johnston Iredell was major of the 45th Regiment of N.C. Troops, Daniel's Brigade. The writer of this was his College class-mate and knew him intimately up to that sad 10th day of May 1864, when he fell at his post on the field of Spotsylvania. Possessing a strict sense of personal honor, a gentle and charitable heart, remarkable regard for the feelings of others and for the high-toned amenities of life, and inheriting all the generous qualities of the stock from which he sprung, he was in the truest sense of that comprehensive word, a *gentleman*. Green be the turf above him.

—*Wilmington Journal*, November 15, 1866

46th Regiment North Carolina Troops

Nathan Raines, of the Randolph Rangers, Co. G, 46th Reg't N.C. State Troops, enlisted in March died of disease in Raleigh, May 14th. He was a farmer there.

—*Fayetteville Observer*, May 26, 1862

Died, in the 2d N.C. Hospital in Petersburg, Va., on Sunday the 27th July, of brain fever, **John H. Hasty**, a farmer, aged 19 years 8 months and 20 days. During the latter part of March he enlisted for the war. He leaves a father and mother. He was from Richmond County, and was a member *Capt. Colin Stewart's* (138) Company D, 46th Reg't., N.C.T.

—*Fayetteville Observer*, August 18, 1862

Died of typhoid fever at Petersburg, Va., on the 13th August, **Hector Smith**, aged 18 years, 8 months and 13 days, a member of Co. H, 46th Reg't. N.C.T. He was a son of Archibald C. Smith of Moore County.

—*Fayetteville Observer*, September 18, 1862

Sergeant Angus Medlin, of *Capt. Neill McNeill's* (139) Company H, 46th N.C.T., died of typhoid fever at the Hospital in Petersburg, on the 14th of July last, leaving a wife and one child. He was 31 and enlisted in Moore County, where he farmed, in March of this year. He was a member of Crain's Creek Lodge, No. 218.

—*Fayetteville Observer*, September 22, 1862

The following members of *Capt. Obed Carr Williams's* (140) Company G, 46th N.C.T., have died since entering the service and from the causes and at the times and places herein stated, viz:

Privates Nathan Raines, disease, Hospital, Raleigh, N.C. May 16th, 1862. **Daniel Raines**, disease, Hospital, Raleigh, N.C., May 17th, 1862. Both were from Randolph County.

Private J. H. Brock, of Jones County, disease, Hospital near Drury's Bluff, Va. July 7th, 1862.

Privates John A. Aldridge, disease, Hospital, Farmville, Va. August 6th, 1862. **Wiley R. Jackson,** disease, Hospital, Farmville, Va. September 14th, 1862. Both were from Randolph County.

Private Zebedee Kinley, Randolph County, probably killed at Sharpsburg, Md. Sept. 17th, 1862.

Private William T. Hill, Randolph County. Typhoid fever, Hospital, Richmond, Va. Sept. 20th, 1862.

Corporal Winburn H. Steed, Randolph County, disease, Hospital, Winchester, Va. Oct. 26th, 1862.

Private Annual Riddick, Randolph County, typhoid fever, Hospital, Staunton, Va. Oct. 29, 1862.

Private Thomas T. Nance, Randolph County, typhoid, Hospital, Gordonsville, Va. Nov. 10th, 1862.

Private James D. Ball, Randolph County, pneumonia, Hospital, Charlottesville, Va. Nov. 13th, 1862.

Private Jesse Vernon, wound, Fredericksburg, Va. Dec. 15th, 1862.

Private Squire Floyd, wounded in the leg at Sharpsburg, chronic diarrhea, Hospital, Richmond, Va. Dec. 22nd, 1862. **Fred Black**, pneumonia, Hospital, Richmond, Dec. 24th, 1862. Both Randolph County.

Private W. P. Steed, disease, home, Randolph County, N.C. Jan. 23rd, 1863.

Lieut. Robert Wiley Stinson, wounded in the arm at Sharpsburg, disease, home, Randolph County, Feb. 3rd, 1863.

Serg't. John Owen Bowden, Consumption, home, New Hanover County, N.C. May 19th, 1863.

Private Jesse A. Edwards, disease, home, Randolph County, N.C. Sept. 27th, 1863.

Private Eli Wright, disease, Hospital, Brandy Station, Va. Oct. 29th, 1863.

Private Peter F. Hoyle, wounded in face at Sharpsburg, wounded again Bristoe Station, Hospital, Richmond, Va. Oct. 21st, 1863, of wounds.

—*Greensborough Patriot,* **December 3, 1862**

Killed on Saturday the 13th inst., on the battle field before Fredericksburg, Va.: **Lieut. Samuel Park Weir** of Co. K, 46th Reg. N.C. Troops (son of Dr. D. P. Weir, of Greensboro), aged 23 years, 2 mos. and 1 day. Col. John A. Gilmer, of this place, the personal friend of Lieut. Weir and Colonel of the 27th N.C. Reg., had a little before received a leg wound, and was limping off the field with some difficulty and unaccompanied, when Lieut. Weir stepped forward, expressing his anxious and kind sympathy and proffered his assistance to call for an escort. The balls were flying thick and fast. He had come out from a place of comparative security, where he and his company were posted. In a moment after, he was shot through the head and fell dead without a struggle. His very last act and words were those of self-sacrifice and kindness. He had served as a private in Company B, 27th Regiment, before transferring to the 46th in April 1862. He was later wounded at Sharpsburg by a shell fragment. Lieut. Weir was a graduate of the University of this State. He was a candidate for the gospel ministry, having spent about a year at the Seminary when the war commenced, and afterwards acted as Chaplain for the Guilford Greys while in Fort Macon, to which company, as a private, he first belonged, until elected Lieutenant in Co. K., of the 46th Regiment.

—Pastor, *North Carolina Presbyterian,* **January 3, 1863**

Killed, on the battle field, near Fredericksburg, Va., February 13th, **James Franklin McNeill**, son of Simon P. and Mary J. McNeill, aged about 19 years, 2 months and 23 days. He was a member of the "Catawba Braves," Co. K, 46th Reg't N.C. Troops.

—*Fayetteville Observer,* January 12, 1863

We deeply regret to announce the death of this gallant young officer, at Scottsville, Va., on Tuesday last, of wounds received that morning in an encounter with deserters whom he was endeavoring to arrest. The following dispatch from Capt. Bost of the 46th, commanding the party to which Lieut. Mallett was attached, contains all that we yet know of the circumstances of his death.—

RICHMOND, Aug 26th—**Richardson Mallett** mortally wounded on Tuesday morning at 1 o'clock, at Bowling's Landing, Fluvanna County, Va., by a deserter. One deserter killed, one wounded, and ten captured and confined in Castle Thunder, Richmond; will be tried for their lives to-morrow. Adj't. Mallet died in Hospital, Scottsville, Va., 7½ o'clock yesterday. He was attended by Dr. Jeffries.

A. F. BOST, Capt. Comd'g.

Lieut. Mallett was a native of this town, son of Charles P. Mallett, Esq., and nearly 28 years of age. One of six brothers in the army, he had been in the service since the beginning of the war. He left the University to join the Orange Light Infantry (Co. D, 1st N.C. Volunteers, Capt. Richard J. Ashe), and served with that Company as 3d Lieutenant throughout the Peninsular campaign. He established a reputation there for gentlemanly and soldierly qualities of the highest order—such as drew from General Hill one of the most marked compliments we have ever read of any one. Since that Reg't was disbanded he had been 1st Lieut. and Adjutant of the 46th N.C. Troops, Col. Edward D. Hall.

[The Official N.C. Roster states his killers were hanged or shot September 5, 1863.—Ed.]

—*Fayetteville Observer,* August 31, 1863

"Tell Col. Hall I was doing my duty. God's will be done!" were the last words of Adjutant Richardson Mallett, the noble young officer who fell by the hands of a gang of deserters in Virginia on the 25th ult., and whose loss is deeply deplored by a large circle of devoted friends.

The following tribute to his memory was written by a Lady of Chapel Hill:—

Thursday August 27th was one of the saddest days in my hearts' calendar of mournful reminiscences. A telegram was received stating that Lieut. Richardson Mallett, son of our highly esteemed and venerable fellow-citizen, Chas. P. Mallett, Esq., had fallen "mortally wounded at Bowling's Landing, near Scottsville, Va., on Monday night the 24th inst., at one o'clock in the morning, while engaged in the attempt to capture a deserter, and that his remains would be brought home for interment.

I cannot tell what my feelings were when this announcement was made me, and if I felt sad, O! what must be the sorrow of his bereaved parents—of the father whose dearest hopes were centered in his son, of the mother whose heart he had lain underneath, of the fair young sister who almost idolized him.

On Friday evening the 28th when the streets of our village were draped in moonlight, and a "deep and exceeding peace" had gathered over hill and valley, there came borne on the still night air, a subdued sound as of measured footfalls, and then the semblance of something shadowy approaching,—slowly, sadly. The truth revealed itself. I understand it now. The old stagecoach, wont to bring back to us the familiar form of absent loved ones, has come, bearing a solitary passenger—its dark freight—"a vanished life." O, how pale, and cold, and still he is—that silent traveler—his voyage how endless—the travel of eternity! They press nearer; I can see distinctly now that column of soldier comrades, with arms reversed, and slow and solemn tread. Tenderly they have come to pillow that young head on the turf of the village green.

On the following morning the funeral rites were performed at the Episcopal Church, and a long concourse followed his remains to the "city of the silent"—the garden of the slumberers. The day was gloomy. The elements seemed to mourn his death; but just as his body was being committed to the grave a flood of sunlight enveloped the coffin—bright emblem of "the hope of the general resurrection in the last day and the life of the world to come through our Lord Jesus Christ, at whose second coming in glorious majesty to judge the world, the earth and the sea shall give up their dead."

For six year he had been a communicant member of the Episcopal Church. A noble and honorable death, in defense of the law of his country.
—*Fayetteville Observer,* **September 14, 1863**

Serg't. Nathan Spencer, aged 27 and a farmer, **Privates Frederick L. Yeates**, aged 26 and also a farmer, and **James M. Brower**, a farmer aged 26, members Company F, 46th N.C.T., died of wounds received at the battle of Bristoe Station, Virginia, October 14, 1863. All three were from Randolph County. Sergeant Spencer was shot in the chest and leg and died on the battlefield. Private Yeates was wounded in the hip and carried back to Richmond where he died on October 24th. Private Brower was wounded in the chest and died in the hospital at Gordonsville, October 25th.
—*Greensborough Patriot,* **December 24, 1863**

We are pained to hear from the *Salisbury Watchman*, that the report of the death of **Capt. Nathan N. Fleming,** of the 46th Regiment, Company B, is confirmed. He fell in the battle of the Wilderness, May 5th. He was also wounded at the Battle of Sharpsburg. He represented Rowan County in the General Assembly for several years, and was at the time of his death a member of the House of Commons. As soon after the commencement of the war as he could return from his legislative duties, he went home, and with others, organized a company for the war; and notwithstanding he has continuously been a member of the legislature since, he never gave up his position in the army longer than to attend to the duties of his constituents.—Whilst others sought Legislative honors, to free them from military service, Capt. Fleming merely regarded them as an additional duty imposed upon him by the people and performed both. His prominence in the Legislature elevated him to the position of Speaker of the House at a recent session. He was 36.
—**Originally published in the** *Goldsboro' State Journal* **and reprinted in the** *Wilmington Daily Journal,* **May 13, 1864.**

Mortally wounded in a skirmish near White Oak Swamp, Va., on the 15th June 1864, **Lt. Robert S. Small,** in his 23rd year. He was sent to a Richmond hospital where he died June 28th. When the National struggle commenced, Lt. Small was employed in State service, he, being a tutor in the Deaf and Dumb Asylum in Raleigh (which exempted him honorably from all military duty), but he was too noble and generous to allow his comrades to endure the privations and hardships of a soldier's life and he remain at home in luxury and ease, so he immediately volunteered his services to his country as a Private, and by deeds and untiring zeal to his country's cause, he was soon promoted to a Lieutenancy in Co. G, 46th N.C. Troops, which position he filled with alacrity up to the period of his death. For some time previous to the present campaign he acted Adjutant to his Regiment, and in this, like all other vocations, he acquitted himself with honor. He stood first at Trinity College, where he graduated. For ten years he was a consistent member of the M. E. Church. He leaves a father and brother.

—*Wilmington Daily Journal,* July 22, 1864.

Lieut. John Archibald Baxter Blue, of Co H, 46th N.C.T., was killed on the 5th May in the bloody battle of Wilderness, Va. He was a native of Moore County. At the outbreak of the war he assisted in raising a company in his native county, and was elected 2d Lieutenant, but had been promoted to the command of the company a short time before his death.

—Cousin, *Fayetteville Observer* August 29, 1864.

Died, at the Field Hospital on the morning of the 26th August, from wounds received in the memorable charge at Reams' Station, the evening of the 25th, **Serg't. Angus J. McPhaul**, Co D, 46th N.C. Troops. At the commencement of the war he entered the service as a private. After the enemy had been entirely routed at Reams's, when our forces were pursuing the fleeing hosts, he was foremost in the pursuit, and when he arrived at the railroad and mounted the banks thrown up there, he received a wound in the bowels. It was hoped for some time that he might recover, but early on the morning of the 26th, he breathed his last. Serg't. McPhaul was 24 years 9 months and 1 day old. He leaves an aged father and mother, four sisters and three brothers.

—Amicus, *Fayetteville Observer,* October 27, 1864.

Serg't. George A. Harmon, Company G, 46th N.C. Troops, was killed at Reams's Station, Va. Aug. 25th, 1864, aged 22 years. He entered service in the Spring of 1862. He had passed unharmed through many hard fought battles in Virginia and was always cheerful and full of life on the weariest march. On the evening of the 25th, just as Cooke's and McRae's Brigades had gloriously carried the enemy's works he received the fatal shot, and before the shouts of his victorious comrades had died away he yielded up his spirit to the God who gave it, and his gallant form now rests undisturbed beneath a few clods far away from the home he loved so much.

—*Fayetteville Observer,* December 1, 1864

Lt. George Horah, Company B, 46th N.C., was instantly killed by a ball in the head, in the battle of the Wilderness, May 5th, 1864, at the age of 23 years. The body was interred on the battle field, but has recently been brought home and re-interred among the graves of his kindred, in Salisbury. Lt. Horah was a brave and efficient officer and a devoted Christian, a member of the Presbyterian Church of Salisbury. He leaves a widow who was a bride of only a few weeks. Recently he made a public profession of religion and connected himself with the Presbyterian Church.

—Pastor, *North Carolina Presbyterian,* December 14, 1864.

IN TRENCHES, NEAR PETERSBURG, VA.,
The following soldiers in Company D, 46th Reg't N.C.T. have recently died:
James H. Stewart, of Richmond County, was killed at the Wilderness, May 5, 1864.
Starling Rachels of Richmond County, aged 42, was killed at the Wilderness, May 5, 1864.
Robert A. Hasty, aged 23, of Richmond County, was killed at the Wilderness, May 5, 1864.

John A. H. McLean of Robeson County, aged 19, was killed May 5, at the Wilderness.

Corporal James S. Watson, aged 22, Robeson County, killed May 10, 1864, at Spotsylvania Court House.

Henry A. Campbell, aged 21, Robeson County, had been wounded at Fredericksburg, December 13, 1862. He was wounded at Jack's Shops, June 15, 1864, and died at Richmond June 26th.

Sgt. John Kelly, of South Carolina, but living in Robeson County, aged 32, was killed at Reams' Station, Aug 25, 1864.

—**Fayetteville Observer, December 22, 1864**

NOTES

Introduction

1. Raymer, Jacob Nathaniel, ed. E. B. Munson. *Confederate Correspondent: The Civil War Reports of Jacob Nathaniel Raymer, Fourth North Carolina.* Jefferson, N.C.: McFarland, 2009.

1st Regiment North Carolina Troops

2. Manarin, Louis A., and Jordan, Weymouth T. Jr., comps. *North Carolina Troops, 1861–1865: A Roster.* [Hereafter referred to as *A Roster.*] Vol. 3, p. 13, Vol. 9, p. 134. **Private Richard N. Tiddy** was living in Mecklenburg County when the war began. In April he joined the 1st N.C. Infantry (6 Months, 1861) at age 26. At the expiration of his enlistment in November he was mustered out and later enlisted in the 33rd Regiment N.C. Troops. He was wounded at the battle of Spotsylvania Court House on May 12, 1864. Declared no longer fit for the field, he was assigned light duty at Charlotte and was paroled there May 6, 1865.

2nd Regiment North Carolina Troops

3. *A Roster.* Vol. 3, p. 421. **1st Lieutenant James M. Hobson** was a native of Rockingham County and was 21 when he joined on July 26, 1861. He was wounded at Chancellorsville on May 3, 1863, and was later captured at Spotsylvania Court House May 6, 1864. Sent first to Point Lookout in Maryland, he would pass through five prison camps before he was released from Fort Delaware, Delaware.

3rd Regiment North Carolina Troops

4. *A Roster.* Vol. 3, pp. 487, 501. **Captain Stephen D. Thurston** was appointed Captain of Company B in May 1861, and was promoted to Major of the regiment, July 1, 1862. He was promoted to Lieutenant Colonel in the spring of 1863 and a few months later wounded at Chancellorsville. In the fall of 1863 he was promoted to Colonel and was wounded at Spotsylvania Court House and again at Winchester, Virginia September 19, 1864. He returned from the hospital in January 1865 and in April 1865 declared no longer able to perform field duty.

5. *A Roster.* Vol. 3, p. 511. **Captain Henry W. Horne** was a resident of Cumberland County at the time of his enlistment in May 1861 at age 25. He rose through the ranks, becoming Captain of Company C in May 1862. He was wounded at the Battle of Sharpsburg, September 17, 1862. He was captured at Spotsylvania Court House, May 12, 1864. Sent first to Fort Delaware, Delaware, he would pass through four more prison camps before returning to Fort Delaware for release on June 16, 1865.

6. *A Roster.* Vol. 3, p. 511. **Captain Peter Mallett** became Captain of a company he raised in Cumberland County in 1861. He was later promoted to Major and in May 1862 became the Assistant Adjutant General to serve as Commandant of Conscripts in North Carolina.

4th Regiment North Carolina Troops

7. *A Roster.* Vol. 4, p. 67. **Captain Jesse S. Barnes** enlisted in 1861 at age 23. He was killed at the Battle of Seven Pines, May 31, 1862.

8. *A Roster.* Vol. 4, p. 25. **Captain James H. Wood** was living in Rowan County when he enlisted

at age 21 and was appointed Captain in May 1861. He was wounded at the Battle of Seven Pines and promoted to Major shortly afterwards. Later promoted to Colonel in 1864, he was killed at Snicker's Gap, Virginia, on July 18, 1864.

    9. *A Roster.* Vol. 4, pp. 9, 55. A resident of Moore County, **Captain David M. Carter** was appointed Captain at the time of his enlistment in May 1861. He was 31. He sustained a wound in his right arm at the Battle of Seven Pines, and a few weeks later was promoted to Lieutenant Colonel. He was forced to resign in December 1862 because of his Seven Pines wounding.

    10. *A Roster.* Vol. 4, p. 98. **Captain Edward Stanley Marsh** was 22 when he enlisted in Beaufort County in June 1861. He rose through the ranks to become Captain of Company I. At the Battle of Chancellorsville, he was wounded in the armpit and left lung. He was appointed Major in 1864, but had to resign in December because of his wounding at Chancellorsville.

5th Regiment North Carolina Troops

    11. *A. Roster.* Vol.4, pp. 127, 197. **Captain Thomas M. Garrett** was living in Bertie County and at age 30, he enlisted, becoming Captain of Company F. He was wounded in the arm at Williamsburg and in the leg at the Battle of Chancellorsville. He was appointed Colonel in January 1863 and was killed at Spotsylvania Court House.

    12. *A. Roster.* Vol. 4, p. 130. **Captain Benjamin Robinson** was living in Cumberland County at the time of enlistment at age 18. He rose through the ranks to a Captaincy. He was wounded during the Battle of Gettysburg and a second time at Spotsylvania Court House. He was retired to the Invalid Corps and sent back to North Carolina to perform light duty.

    13. *A Roster.* Vol. 4, p. 253. **John A. Rose,** also of Rowan County, was a farmer and enlisted at age 22.

    14. *A Roster.* Vol. 4, p. 233. **Captain John E. Bailey,** who resided in Chatham County, enlisted at age 30 in 1861. He rose through the ranks to the Captaincy of Company I. According to records, he resigned in November 1864 because of liver disease.

6th Regiment North Carolina Troops

    15. *A Roster.* Vol. 4, 267, 368. **Captain Richard Watt York,** a resident of Chatham County, enlisted at age 22 in May 1861 and was appointed to a Captaincy. He was wounded at the Battle of Gaines' Mill, Virginia. In July 1863 he was appointed Major of the Regiment. He was again wounded at the fight at Fisher's Hill, Virginia, September 1864.

    16. *A Roster.* Vol. 4, p. 282. **Captain William K. Parrish,** from Orange County, enlisted at age 30 in 1861, and was appointed 1st Lieutenant, then Captain of Company B. He sustained a head wound at Gaines' Mill, Virginia, and in November 1863, was captured at Rappahannock Station, Virginia. Held prisoner first at Johnson's Island, Ohio, he was later sent to Point Lookout, then to Fort Delaware, where he was released in June 1865.

    17. *A Roster.* Vol. 4, p. 344. **Captain James Alexander Craige** enlisted at age 20 and was appointed Captain of Company G in May 1861. He was from Rowan County. In July of 1862 he was elected Major of the 57th Regiment. He sustained a knee wound in the fight at Winchester, Va., July 1864. He received a parole at Salisbury, N.C., May 3, 1865.

7th Regiment North Carolina Troops

    18. *A. Roster.* Vol. 4, p. 483. **James G. Harris** was a native of Mecklenburg County and was farming in Cabarrus County when he joined the army at age at age 20. He was appointed Captain of Company H in May 1861. In the fighting at Jones' Farm, Va., September 1864, he was twice wounded. He was promoted to Major in November and received his parole at Greensborough May 1, 1865

    19. *A Roster.* Vol. 4, 405. A lawyer in Wake County, **Edward Graham Haywood** was 30 when he enlisted in May 1861. He was appointed Lieutenant Colonel and the following year was raised to full Colonel. He was wounded at Second Manassas August 1862 and again at Chancellorsville the next year. He resigned in July 1864 due to partial blindness caused by his wounding.

    20. *A Roster.* Vol. 4, pp. 405, 430. **Robert B. McRae** was a native of New Hanover County and was 28 when he enlisted in May 1861. He was appointed Captain of Company C. He was wounded in the fighting at Gaines' Mill, Va., in June 1862 and again at Ox Hill, Va., in September. He was promoted to Major in January 1863 and resigned the following month because of the neck wounding received at Ox Hill. He died in December 1864, and the place and cause were not reported.

21. *A Roster.* **Joshua Washington Vick** was a native of Nash County, N.C. and put aside his farming implements to enlist at age 18. As corporal, then sergeant, he was wounded at Winchester in December 1862 and released a few days later. He was 1st Lieutenant when he was wounded in the leg July 3, at Gettysburg. He was promoted to Captain of Company E in December 1863 and served until he received his parole at Greensborough May 1, 1863.

8th Regiment North Carolina Troops

22. *A Roster.* Vol. 4, p. 561. **Captain Luther R. Breece** was a farmer in his native county of Cumberland. He enlisted at age 20 in May 1861. He was captured at Roanoke Island in February 1862 during Burnside's invasion and released at Elizabeth City a few weeks later. He was captured again during the fight at Fort Harrison, Virginia in September 1864 and was held prisoner in Washington, D.C., until sent to Fort Delaware. He was released from there in June 1865.

9th Regiment North Carolina Troops (1st Regiment North Carolina Cavalry)

23. *A Roster.* Vol. 2, p. 8. **Colonel Laurence Simmons Baker**, a native of Gates County, was appointed Lieutenant Colonel in May 1861 and promoted to Colonel the following year. In 1863 he transferred out of the regiment when he was promoted to Brigadier General

24. *A Roster.* Vol. 2, p. 53. **Captain Rufus Barringer** was 39 when he was appointed to the Captaincy of Company F. In June 1863, he was wounded in action at Brandy Station and in August of the same year promoted to Major of the regiment.

25. *A Roster.* Vol. 2, 9. 80. **Captain William J. Houston** was appointed to rank in May 1861. He was captured in November 1862 at a place not given and released a few days later. In June 1863, he was killed in action at Upperville, Va.

10th Regiment North Carolina Troops (1st Regiment North Carolina Artillery)

26. *A Roster.* Vol. 1, p. 119. **Private Stephen B. Holland** farmed in Carteret County before enlisting at age 23 in Company G of the 10th Regiment. He was captured at Fort Macon in April 1862 during General Burnside's invasion of Eastern North Carolina. He was exchanged in August of the same year. Records account for him through February 1865. No further information.

27. *A Roster.* Vol. 1, p. 89, Vol. 15, p. 313. **Captain Alexander D. Moore,** of New Hanover County, resigned from the Academy at West Point at the outbreak of hostilities and came home. Governor Ellis appointed him to the rank of Captain of Company G. In August 1863 he resigned to take the position of Colonel of the 66th North Carolina Troops. In the Battle of Cold Harbor, Virginia, June 3, 1864, a sharpshooter's ball struck him in the neck and he died within minutes.

28. *A Roster.* Vol. 1, p. 150. In November 1863, **Thomas J. Southerland** transferred from the 2nd Regiment, N.C. Artillery [36th Regiment North Carolina Troops] to the 10th Regiment with the rank of Captain. During the attack on Fort Fisher in January 1865, he was wounded. He was paroled at Greensboro, North Carolina in May 1865.

11th Regiment North Carolina Troops

29. *A Roster.* Vol. 5, p. 20. **Captain Mark D. Armfield** first served his country in the First N.C. Infantry (6 months), as 2nd Lieutenant in Company G. At the expiration of his term, he was appointed Captain of Company B. During the fighting at Gettysburg he was captured either on the third or fourth day. He was held prisoner in Maryland and Delaware before being sent to Johnson's Island, Ohio, in July 1863, where he died December 3, 1863.

30. *A Roster.* Vol. 5, p. 49. **Captain John S. A. Nichols** was 28 when he became Captain of Company E in February 1862. He died on July 11, 1862, in Wilmington. There was no cause of death reported.

12th Regiment North Carolina Troops

31. *A Roster.* Vol. 5, p. 146. **Captain Thomas L. Jones** was living in Warren County and was a medical student before he was appointed to a Captaincy in May 1861. He was 21. He was promoted to Major the following May. He was later promoted to Lieutenant Colonel but was forced to resign in October 1862 because of disability.

32. *A Roster.* **Captain Henry Eaton Coleman** was farming in Granville County when he enlisted at age 24. He was appointed Captain in May 1861 but lost his bid for reelection when the regiment reorganized in 1862. He was later Lieutenant Colonel and then appointed Colonel of the regiment in 1863. He was wounded at Spotsylvania Court House May 12, 1864, and was absent wounded through December.

13th Regiment North Carolina Troops

33. *A Roster.* Vol. 5, p. 375. **Captain Giles P. Bailey** was a physician in Rockingham County and at age 36 enlisted in May 1861 in Company K and was elected Captain. While leading his company in a charge on the enemy at Williamsburg in May 1862, he was shot, stabbed, and captured. He was treated in hospitals at Williamsburg and Fortress Monroe, then sent to Fort Delaware. He was exchanged in August 1862, but had to resign in October because of his wounds.

14th Regiment North Carolina Troops

34. *A Roster.* Vol. 5, pp. 394, 396. **Captain William A. Johnston** was living in Halifax County when the war began. He was 26. He was elected Captain of Company A in March 1861. He was appointed Lieutenant Colonel the following year and was wounded in the arm at Chancellorsville and again in a skirmish with the enemy during the siege of Petersburg. His wounds put him permanently on the disabled list. He was paroled at Appomattox Court House, April 9, 1865.

35. *A Roster.* Vol. 5, 395. **Chaplain Needham Bryan Cobb** was preaching in Wake County when he was appointed Chaplain of the regiment in June 1861. He resigned a few months later with no reasons given.

36. *A Roster.* Vol. 5, p. 473. **Captain Jesse Hargrave** was a lawyer residing in Davidson County. He was 23 when he was elected Captain of Company I. When the regiment was reorganized in April 1862, he was no longer Captain. It is not known whether he declined reelection or was defeated in a bid for reelection.

37. *A Roster.* Vol. 5, pp. 394, 424. **Captain Edward Dixon** was a Cleveland County farmer before he enlisted at age 30. He was elected Captain of his company in April 1861, and in the following year elected Major of the regiment. He died of disease at Richmond, Va., on July 8, 1862.

38. *A Roster.* Vol. 5, p. 438. **William Henry Hamilton** was mustered in as Sergeant. He was wounded in the head and captured during the fighting at Williamsburg. His eyes were severely damaged. He was held prisoner at Fortress Monroe then released a month after the battle. He was absent wounded through August 1864.

39. *A Roster.* Vol. 5, p. 444. **Bailey M. Yarborough** enlisted in Wake County when he was 21 in May 1861. He died of typhoid pneumonia in a Richmond hospital in January 1863.

40. *A Roster.* Vol. 5, p. 444. **Captain James M. Gudger** was a Buncombe County farmer who enlisted at age 24 in May 1861. He rose through the ranks to a Captaincy. He was wounded at the battle of Seven Pines and a second time at Spotsylvania Court House, May 12, 1864. Records indicate he was absent wounded through February 1865.

15th Regiment North Carolina Troops

41. *A Roster.* Vol. 5, p. 576. A resident of Alamance County, **Captain John R. Stockard** joined in May 1861 at age 33. He was sick most of the time for the following year and was finally dropped from the rolls because of being away so much.

16th Regiment North Carolina Troops

42. *A Roster.* Vol. 6, p. 105. Vol. 16, pp. 285, 311. **Sergeant William Henry Moore** joined Company L with the rank of Sergeant in May 1861. He was living in Haywood County at the time. In October of the following year he was transferred to Company E, Infantry Regiment, Thomas's Legion. He later served in Company C.

43. *A Roster.* Vol. 6, pp. 10, 29. **Captain John S. McElroy**, a resident of Yancey County, was 26 when he joined Company C and was elected its Captain in May 1861. He was elected Lieutenant Colonel in April of the following year and three months later Colonel of the regiment. He was wounded in the fighting at Chancellorsville in May 1863 and resigned the following December.

44. *A Roster.* Vol. 6, pp. 46, 52–53. **Captain Elijah J. Kirksey** was living in Burke County when he joined Company E and was elected its Captain in May 1861. He was 36. He resigned his commission the following May. In January 1864 he returned and reenlisted for the war in his old company. He was captured at Hatcher's Run, Va., April 2, 1865, during the final days of the war. He was held prisoner at Point Lookout and released in June.

18th Regiment North Carolina Troops

45. *A Roster.* Vol. 6, P. 344. **Captain Morgan C. T. Lee** was a native of Robeson County and enlisted at 28 in May 1861. He rose through the ranks and was elected Captain the following year. He had sustained a left shoulder wound at the Battle of Cedar Mountain in August 1862. Paralysis of the left arm set in later and it forced him to resign in November 1862.
46. *A Roster.* **Colonel Robert H. Cowan** was a resident of New Hanover County when he joined the army. He was appointed Lieutenant Colonel of the 3rd Regiment North Carolina Troops and the following April was appointed Colonel of the 18th Regiment North Carolina Troops. Liver problems and chronic diarrhea led to his resignation in November 1862.
47. *A Roster.* Vol. 6, p. 322. **Captain Marcus W. Buie,** Company B, was a farmer in his native Bladen County before enlisting at age 23 in May 1861. At the Battle of Reams' Station, Va., in August 1864, he was wounded in the right foot and was absent because of it through February 1865.
48. *A Roster.* Vol. 6, P. 367. **Captain Charles Malloy**, a native of Cumberland County, enlisted at age 43 and was appointed Captain. He was a planter. When the regiment reorganized, he was defeated for reelection.

19th Regiment North Carolina Troops (2nd Regiment North Carolina Cavalry)

49. *A Roster.* Vol. 2, p. 139. At age 22 **John F. Owens** enlisted in the 2nd Cavalry for the war. Records show that he was accounted for through September 1864.
50. *A Roster.* Vol. 2, p. 129. **Captain James William Strange** was 43 when he enlisted in Cumberland County in June 1861. He resigned in March 1864 because he felt he had been wronged in not being promoted to the Majority. He felt the person who received the position had less experience and less time in service.
51. *A Roster.* Vol. 2, p. 104. **Colonel Samuel B. Spruill** from Bertie County was appointed Colonel of the regiment in June 1861, but later resigned a year later.
52. *A Roster.* Vol. 2, p. 170. **Captain Josiah Turner, Jr.,** of Orange County, received an appointment as Captain of Company K in September 1861. In the fight at Gillett's, N.C., in August 1862, he was wounded in the heart which brought about his resignation in November of the same year.

20th Regiment North Carolina Troops

53. *A Roster.* Vol. 6, p. 512. Vol. 17, p. 211. **Captain James A. Faison** was a resident of Sampson County and was 30 when he was elected Captain of Company I in June 1861. When the regiments reorganized the following April, he was defeated for reelection. He was later Captain of Company H, 1st Regiment N.C. Junior Reserves.
54. *A Roster.* Vol. 6, pp. 433, 465. **Captain John Franklin Ireland** held a number of responsible positions during the war. He served first as a 2nd Lieutenant in Company E, then became Adjutant of the Regiment. He was captured at Chancellorsville in May 1863, held prisoner in Washington, D.C., and released later in the same month. He became Captain of Company D in October 1863. He was wounded at Spotsylvania Court House on May 12, 1864, and on his return took command of Company K. He was captured at Fort Stedman, Virginia, near the close of the war and again held prisoner in Washington, D.C., before being sent to Fort Delaware. He was released from there in June 1865.
55. *A Roster.* Vol. 6, p. 457. **1st Lieutenant Arthur N. Jones** was a native of Virginia but resided in Columbus County, N.C., where he was an overseer. He was aged 24 at his enlistment. He was promoted to Lieutenant in April 1862, just two months before he was killed at Gaines' Mill.
56. *A Roster.* Vol. 6, p. 461. **Sergeant Calvin H. Meares** was farming in his home county of Columbus before he enlisted in 1861 at age 24. He received his promotion to Sergeant in April 1862, just two months before he was killed at Gaines' Mill.

21st Regiment North Carolina Troops

57. *A Roster.* Vol. 6, p. 538. **Colonel William Whedbee Kirkland**, an Orange County native, was a professional soldier before enlisting in the Confederate Army at age 28. He was elected Colonel in July 1861, but was defeated for reelection the following year. The newly appointed colonel, Thomas Settle, declined the position; this brought Kirkland back as acting Colonel. He sustained a thigh wound at Winchester, May 1862, and the following year was reappointed Colonel. In August 1863, he was promoted to Brigadier General.

58. *A Roster.* Vol. 6, p. 538. **Lieutenant Colonel James M. Leach** began his service as Captain of Company A before being promoted to Lieutenant Colonel in July 1861. He resigned in December of the same year but there is no information why he left the service.

59. *A Roster.* Vol. 6, pp. 538, 555. **Captain Bazillia Yancey Graves** was a Surry County native and joined the army at age 25. Elected Captain in May 1861, he was promoted to Major the following May. He sustained a leg wound near Richmond in the early summer of 1862 and upon his recovery was promoted to Lieutenant Colonel in August of the same year. The following month he was wounded in the right arm and shoulder in the fighting at Ox Hill, Virginia. These wounds brought about his resignation in February 1863.

60. *A Roster.* Vol. 6, p. 572. **Private William Sprinkle** enlisted in Forsyth County in February 1863. He was captured at Hatcher's Run, Va., near the end of the war, sent to Point Lookout, and released in June 1865, after taking the Oath of Allegiance.

22nd Regiment North Carolina Troops

61. *A Roster.* Vol. 7, p. 36. **Captain Harper Evans Charles** enlisted at age 26 in 1861 and was elected Captain of Company E in 1862. He was killed at Frayser's Farm, Va., June 30, 1862.

62. *A Roster.* Vol. 7, p. 112. **Private Josiah Luther** of Randolph County joined the army in March 1862. On the retreat from Gettysburg, he was captured July 1863 at Falling Waters, Md. and held prisoner at Point Lookout, Md. In August 1864 he was sent to the prison at Elmira, New York, and was later exchanged in March 1865.

63. *A Roster.* Vol. 7, p. 36. **Captain Joseph A. Hooper** from Guilford County was 26 when he joined the army in May 1861. He was wounded at Seven Pines, Va., in May 1862. He was promoted to Captain the following month, but disease forced his resignation in March 1863.

64. *A Roster.* Vol. 7, p. 67. **2nd Lieutenant Mason Tyler Mitchell**, Stokes County, joined the service in June 1861. He was 25. He was wounded at Seven Pines in May 1862. Returning to duty, he was wounded again at Gettysburg. In the fall of 1864 he was court-martialed, but no reason was given, and resigned in February 1865.

24th Regiment North Carolina Troops

65. *A Roster.* Vol. 7, pp. 251, 311. **Captain Thaddeus D. Love** of Robeson County was appointed Captain in June 1861 and the following year elected Major. He was captured at Fort Stedman, Virginia, May 25, 1865, held prisoner in Washington, D.C., then sent to Fort Delaware where he was eventually released.

66. *A Roster.* Vol. 7, pp. 251, 320. **Captain John L. Harris** entered service in June 1861 with the rank of Captain. In May the following year he was elected Lieutenant Colonel. He was wounded at Fredericksburg, December 13, 1862. He returned to duty about six months later and was wounded in the leg near Fort Stedman, Virginia, in March 1865. He was treated in a hospital at Petersburg and was captured there when Union forces broke through General Lee's lines in early April. He was held in several Federal hospitals then was sent to City Point, Virginia, in May 1865 for transfer.

67. *A Roster.* Vol. 7, p. 251. **Colonel William John Clark** aged 41 was appointed Colonel in July 1861. He was wounded in the fighting at Drury's Bluff in May 1864 and returned to duty about seven months later. He was captured at Dinwiddie Court House, Virginia, in February 1865, held a prisoner in Washington, D.C., then sent to Fort Delaware where he was released the following July.

68. *A Roster.* Vol. 7, p. 301. **Captain Charles H. Blocker** enlisted at 18 and was appointed Captain in July 1861. He was defeated for reelection the following year. He later served in the 36th Regiment North Carolina Troops (2nd North Carolina Cavalry).

69. *A Roster.* Vol. 7, p. 275. **Sergeant John D. Gulley** enlisted at age 20 with the rank of sergeant. He was promoted through the ranks to a Captaincy in 1863. He sustained a head wound and was captured during the fighting at Globe Tavern, Virginia, August 21, 1864, and died three days later.

25th Regiment North Carolina Troops

70. *A Roster.* Vol. 7, p. 398. **Captain Francis Withers Johnstone** was appointed Captain at age 46 in June 1861. He was defeated for reelection the following year.

71. *A Roster.* Vol. 7, p. 408. **Captain Thomas Isaac Lenoir** was appointed Captain in June 1861 at age 43. He declined reelection the following year.

72. *A Roster.* Vol. 7, p. 427. **Captain Thomas J. Young** was 26 when he joined the army as sergeant in July 1861. He was promoted to Captain in December 1862 and was with the regiment until it surrendered at Appomattox Court House.

73. *A Roster.* Vol. 7, p. 427. **Captain Fred Blake** was elected Captain in July 1861 at age 23. He was defeated for reelection the following year.

26th Regiment North Carolina Troops

74. *A Roster.* Vol. 7, p. 561. **Captain William Pinckney Martin** was 43 when he joined Company H and was elected its Captain in June 1861. At the Battle of New Bern, N.C., March 14, 1862, during the Burnside invasion, he was struck in the head by a ball and killed.

75. *A Roster.* Vol. 7, p. 561. **1st Lieutenant Clement Dowd** was 28 when he joined Company H and was elected its Lieutenant in June 1861 and the following year Captain. Illness forced his resignation later in the same year.

76. *A Roster.* Vol. 7, p. 563. **Private Enoch S. Cagle** of Moore County joined the army in June 1861. He was discharged in 1862 after providing A. McNeill, Sr., as substitute, which at the time he could legally do. McNeill, also of Moore County, was accounted for through October 1864.

77. *A Roster.* Vol. 7, p. 589. **Captain James C. Caraway** of Anson County joined Company C at age 36 and was elected its Captain in July 1861, but was defeated for reelection the following year.

78. *A Roster.* Vol. 7, 519. **Captain William Spearman Webster** from Chatham County was 48 when he joined Company E and was elected its Captain in May 1861, but was defeated for reelection the following year.

79. *A Roster.* Vol. 7, p. 507. **Captain Oscar R. Rand** joined Company D at age 28 and was elected its Captain in May 1861. He was captured at the Battle of New Bern March 14, 1862, and was held a prisoner of war at Fort Columbus on an island in New York Harbor. Even though he was still a prisoner when the regiment reorganized in 1862 and his name was put up, he was defeated for reelection. He was later sent to Johnson's Island, Ohio, and finally moved to Vicksburg, Mississippi, where he was declared an exchanged prisoner in November 1862.

80. *A Roster.* Vol. 7, p. 589. **Captain J. C. McLaughlin** joined Company K at age 28 was first elected a Lieutenant in July 1861 and then Captain the following year. He was wounded at Malvern Hill, July 1, 1862, and wounded later in the hand at Gettysburg. His thumb was amputated, disabling from further service. He resigned his commission in October 1862. **1st Sergeant Benjamin McLaughlin** joined Company K when he was 17 in July 1861. He died of typhoid fever in Kinston April 1862.

27th Regiment North Carolina Troops

81. *A Roster.* Vol. 8, p. 39. **Captain William T. Wooten** from Lenoir County was elected Captain in April 1861, but died the following February.

82. *A Roster.* Vol. 8, p. 11. **Captain Marshall D. Craton,** a native of Rutherford County, was elected Captain of Company A in April 1861. He was 31. The following November he was elected Lieutenant Colonel of the 35th Regiment. Vol. 9, p. 258. He retained this rank until April 11, 1862, when he was appointed Colonel of the 50th Regiment on April 15.

83. *A Roster.* Vol. 8, pp. 7, 8, 20. **Captain John A. Sloan** was 22 when he joined Company B as Sergeant. He moved up through the ranks until he was promoted to Captain in September 1862. He was wounded at the Wilderness in May 1864, returned in November, and was with the Regiment until its surrender at Appomattox Court House.

28th Regiment North Carolina Troops

84. *A Roster.* Vol. Vol. 8, pp. 206–207. **Captain William H. Asbury Speer** was appointed Captain of Company I at age 30 in 1861. He was captured at the Battle of Hanover Court House, Va., in May 1862. Sent first to Fortress Monroe, Va., he then went to an island prison camp in New York harbor,

and finally to Johnson's Island, Ohio. In September he reached Vicksburg where he was exchanged. Two months later he was promoted to Major and Lieutenant Colonel the following year. He was wounded at the Battle of Chancellorsville again at Gettysburg. He was promoted to Colonel in July 1864. He sustained a head wound at the Reams' Station August 25, 1864, and died four days later.

    85. *A Roster.* Vol. 8, p. 220. **Captain John A. Moody** was 33 when he was appointed Captain in September 1861. Chronic diarrhea and typhoid fever forced his resignation July 1, 1863.

    86. *A Roster.* Vol. 8, p. 185. **Captain George A. McCauley** joined Company G at the age of 29. He rose through the ranks to a Captaincy in July 1863. He was wounded and captured at Petersburg, Va., April 2, 1865, and released from a Washington, D.C., hospital in June 1865.

    87. *A Roster.* Vol. 8, p. 187. **Private James F. Craige** from Orange County joined in September 1861, age 25. He was captured at the Battle of Hanover Court House and later held prisoner at Fortress Monroe and then at Fort Columbus, New York Harbor. He was exchanged in August 1862. He was captured again at Spotsylvania Court House, May 12, 1864, and this time held at Point Lookout and then at Elmira, New York, later in the year. He was released in July 1865.

29th Regiment North Carolina Troops

    88. *A Roster.* Vol. 8, p. 306. **Captain Bacchus S. Profitt** joined Company K as a Sergeant and shortly afterwards was appointed Captain in September 1861. He was appointed Major in October 1863 and Lieutenant Colonel in 1864. He died in Alabama in March 1865.

    89. *A Roster.* Vol. 8, p. 255. **Private Samuel J. Westall** at age 33 joined Company B in July 1861. He was dropped from company rolls with no date or reason given.

    90. *A Roster.* Vol. 8, 292. **Captain Wiley F. Parker** enlisted at age 32 and was appointed 2nd Lieutenant in September 1861 and promoted to Captain the following year. He tendered his resignation in November 1862 because he was a minister and because of chronic diarrhea.

    91. *A Roster.* Vol. 8, p. 235. **Lieutenant Colonel William C. Walker** enlisted at age 40 and was appointed Captain in June 1861. Three months later he was promoted to Lieutenant Colonel. When the regiment reorganized the following year, he chose not to stand for reelection.

    92. *A Roster.* Vol. 8, 255–256. **Captain John W. Gudger** was 22 at the time of his enlistment. He was appointed 2nd Lieutenant in August 1861 and promoted to Captain the next year. He received his parole at Meridian, Mississippi, in May 1865.

30th Regiment North Carolina Troops

    93. *A Roster.* Vol. 8, p. 412. **Captain James T. Kell** was appointed Captain of Company K in September 1861 and then elected Major in the same month. The following year he was promoted Lieutenant Colonel and at the battle of Gaines' Mill, Va., in June 1862 he was wounded three times. He resigned in August 1863 because of his disabling wounds.

    94. *A Roster.* Vol. 8, p. 391. **Captain Jesse Johnson Wicker** of Moore County enlisted at age 22 and rose through the ranks until he was elected Captain in May 1862. He was wounded near Boonsboro, Maryland, September 14, 1862, and was later captured at Spotsylvania Court House, May 12, 1864. He was sent to Fort Delaware the same month and was released from there in June 1865.

31st Regiment North Carolina Troops

    95. *A Roster.* Vol. 8, p. 431. **Captain Condray Godwin** of Robeson County was 28 when he enlisted and was appointed Captain in September 1861. He was with the regiment until October 1862 when he resigned.

    96. *A Roster.* Vol. 8, 438. **Captain Charles B. Lindsay** of Anson County was 25 when he joined the army and was appointed 2nd Lieutenant of Company B in October 1861. He was captured at Roanoke Island in February 1862 during the Burnside invasion and was released at Elizabeth City, N.C., a few weeks later. He was promoted to Captain later in the year and resigned his commission in April 1863.

    97. *A Roster.* Vol. 8, p. 464. **Captain Jesse Miller** from Orange County enlisted at age 27 and was appointed Captain in October in 1861. He was one of the many captured at Roanoke Island and later set free. When the regiments reorganized later in 1862, he was defeated for reelection.

    98. *A Roster.* Vol. 8, p. 464. **Captain Julius F. Allison** from Orange County enlisted at age 27 in October 1861. He was captured at Roanoke Island in February 1862 and paroled later in the month. He was appointed Captain in September 1862. In June 1864 he was wounded by a gunshot and hospitalized

in Richmond, but the records do not record the place and date of the shooting. He was back on duty in January 1865 and was paroled in Greensboro in May 1865 at the end of hostilities.

32nd Regiment North Carolina Troops

99. *A Roster.* Vol. 9, p. 92. **Captain William Lord London** previously served as Captain in the 15th Regiment North Carolina Troops before his transfer to 2nd Company I of the 32nd. He was wounded at Gettysburg but returned to duty the following September. He later served as Assistant Adjutant General and Inspector General of Gen. Junius Daniel's brigade.

33rd Regiment North Carolina Troops

100. *A Roster.* Vol. 9, p. 196. **Captain Robert Wooten** was a native of Bladen County and was farming in Cumberland County when he enlisted. He was 46 and was appointed Captain in September 1861. He was at New Bern in March 1862 and resigned the following year because of heart trouble.

101. *A Roster.* Vol. 9, p. 220. Vol. 2, p. 696. At the age of 28 **George C. Stowe** enlisted in Company I and in July 1861, appointed its Captain. In the fighting at Culpepper, Va., a minie ball took off one of his thumbs. He returned to duty just before the battle at Fredericksburg December 13, 1862, and was captured, but released a few days later. His disabled hand brought about his resignation in July 1863. He later served as Captain of Company A, McRae's Battalion N.C. Cavalry, Major James. C. McRae commanding. When the battalion disbanded in 1864, Stowe became Lieutenant Colonel of the 5th Regiment N.C. Senior Reserves.

102. *A Roster.* Vol. 9, p. 196. **William J. Callais** served in a South Carolina regiment before he was appointed 2nd Lieutenant in Company G in August 1862. He was promoted to Captain in July 1863. The previous month he had been wounded at Chancellorsville but returned to duty by September. He was in the hospital at Richmond in May 1864, but returned to duty and was with his regiment until the surrender at Appomattox Court House, April 9, 1865.

103. *A Roster.* Vol. 9, pp. 203–204. **Private Roburtes C. Lineback** enlisted for the war at age 30, July 1862. He was killed the following year at Chancellorsville.

104. *A Roster.* Vol. 9, p. 199. **Private John G. Brock** was employed as a cooper before he enlisted at age 17 in September 1861. The following year he was captured during the New Bern battle in March 1862 and was paroled the following summer. He was killed at Chancellorsville.

105. *A Roster.* Vol. 9, p. 207. **Private H. Slater** enlisted at age 20 in July 1862. He was killed at Chancellorsville.

106. *A Roster.* Vol. 9, p. 234. **Lieutenant John G. Rencher** enlisted at age 24 and was appointed 1st Lieutenant in November 1863. He was wounded in the arm at the Wilderness, May 6, 1864. He returned to duty in December.

107. *A Roster.* Vol. 9, p. 147. **Captain John D. Fain** was a Private in the 12th Regiment North Carolina Troops before his appoint as a Lieutenant in Company C of the 33rd. He was wounded in the leg at the Wilderness, May 6, 1864. He was appointed Captain the following summer and was killed in a skirmish near Petersburg, April 1, 1865, just before the war ended.

34th Regiment North Carolina Troops

108. *A Roster.* Vol. 9, p. 342. **Captain Jesse S. Spencer** was a merchant in Montgomery County and also the Clerk of the Court of Pleas and Quarter Sessions. He was appointed Captain in October 1861 at age 26. He resigned the following year because of his health and duties as the Court's Clerk.

109. *A Roster.* Vol. 9, p. 315. **Captain William Raeford Myers** was a native of Anson County and had moved to Mecklenburg County to farm. When hostilities broke out he was 43. He was appointed Captain in September 1861 but was defeated for reelection when the regiment reorganized the following year.

110. *A Roster.* Vol. 9, p. 315. **Captain Joseph B. McGee** was farming in Mecklenburg County when the war began. He was 32 when he enlisted in September 1861 and was promoted to Captain in 1862. He was appointed Major in September 1862 but resigned the following December because of internal bleeding.

111. *A Roster.* Vol. 9, pp. 251, 285. **Captain William Lee J. Lowrance** was an Iredell County school teacher and was appointed 1st Lieutenant when he enlisted in September 1861. He was promoted to Captain the following month. He was 25. He was wounded at Gaines' Mill, Va., in June 1862, and on

his return he was appointed Colonel in September. He is accounted for from that date until October 1864.

 112. *A Roster.* Vol. 9, p. 286. **Lieutenant John P. Parks** was a native of Rowan County and was a merchant there when he enlisted at age 27.

 113. *A Roster.* Vol. 9, p. 285. **Lieutenant Robert T. Cowan** was also born in Rowan County and was farming there when he enlisted at age 22.

 114. *A Roster.* Vol. 9, p. 285. **Lieutenant Monroe Michael Gillon** was from Cabarrus County and was 20 years old when he enlisted as a Private in September 1861. He was appointed 1st Lieutenant in 1862 and sustained a shoulder wound in the fighting around Petersburg in July 1864. He was with the regiment from that point on until the surrender at Appomattox Court House.

 115. *A Roster.* Vol. 9, p. 323. **Captain Samuel A. Hoey** had been a Lieutenant in the 15th Regiment North Carolina Troops before he was transferred and appointed Captain of Company H in October 1861. He resigned his commission in 1863 but no reason was given.

35th Regiment North Carolina Troops

 116. *A Roster,* Vol. 9, pp. 437–438. **1st Sergeant Leander Query** at age 22 enlisted as a Corporal in September 1861 and was later promoted to 1st Sergeant. He sustained an arm wound in the fighting near Petersburg in June 1864 but was back on duty in January 1865. He was captured at Dinwiddie Court House April 1, 1865, just before the end of the war, and held prisoner on a New York Harbor island when he was released the following June.

36th Regiment North Carolina Troops (2nd Regiment North Carolina Artillery)

 117. *A Roster.* Vol. 1, p. 226. **Captain Kinchen J. Braddy** enlisted and was appointed 1st Lieutenant of his company in February 1862. He was 23. He was promoted to Captain during the following summer. He was captured in January 1865 at Fort Fisher, held prisoner at Fort Columbus in New York Harbor, and released in March.

37th Regiment North Carolina Troops

 118. *A Roster.* Vol. 9, pp. 497–498. **Captain James Monroe Potts** was farming in his native county of Mecklenburg at the state of the war. At the age of 21 he joined the 37th and was appointed a Captain in September 1861. He resigned the following year because of disease.

 119. *A Roster.* Vol. 9, p. 591. **Captain William M. Fetter** entered service at age 21 and was appointed 2nd Lieutenant in Company K in August 1862. Later that same month he was wounded at the Battle of Second Manassas. When he returned to duty in February 1863, he was promoted to 1st Lieutenant and the following month Captain. He was court-martialed in the summer of 1863 and resigned in October of the same year. No reason was given for the resignation.

 120. *A Roster.* Vol. 9, p. 468. **Lieutenant Colonel William M. Barbour** entered service as Captain of Company F in September 1861. He was 27. In November 1861 he was elected Lieutenant Colonel. The following June he was elected Colonel of the 37th. He was wounded at Fredericksburg, December 13, 1862. He returned to duty in March 1863 and was again wounded at Chancellorsville. He was back on duty by September. He was captured at Spotsylvania Court House May 12, 1864, and was held in several prisons before he was exchanged in August and returned to duty. He was wounded in the fighting at Jones' Farm, Virginia, in September 1864 and died October 3, 1864, at Petersburg.

 121. *A Roster.* Vol. 9, pp. 469, 524. **Adjutant (1st Lieutenant) William T. Nicholson** enlisted at 21 and was appointed Adjutant in November 1861. He was promoted to Captain in December 1862 and assigned to Company E. In May 1864 a gunshot wound put him in a Richmond hospital, but the where and when was not reported. He returned to duty in March 1865 and was killed at Five Forks, Virginia, on April 2, one week before the end of the war.

 122. *A Roster.* Vol. 9, pp. 469, 537. **Captain Charles N. Hickerson** was farming in Wilkes County before he enlisted as a Private at age 30, September 1861. He was elected Captain two months later and elected Major the following April. In June 1862 he was promoted to Lieutenant Colonel but resigned the next month because of disease.

 123. *A Roster.* Vol. 9, p. 476. **Private William J. Goss** was farming in his home county of Ashe before he enlisted in Company A at age 16 in December 1861. He was wounded at the Battle of Second

Manassas in August 1862 and captured at Warrenton, Va., in late fall. He received a parole from there in November and rejoined his company in January 1863. For his gallantry at Chancellorsville he was nominated for the Badge of Distinction and promoted to Corporal after the battle. He was captured at Gettysburg and held prisoner at Point Lookout. He was released from there February 2, 1864, after taking the Oath of Allegiance and joining the Union Army.

38th Regiment North Carolina Troops

124. *A Roster.* Vol. 10, pp. 8, 48. **Captain Oliver H. Dockery**, a Richmond County planter, enlisted at age 31 and was elected Captain in October 1861. He was elected Lieutenant Colonel the following January, but was defeated for reelection when the regiment reorganized in April.

125. *A Roster.* Vol. 10, p. 76. **Captain William Lindsey Thornburg** was farming in Randolph County when he enlisted as a Private at age 24, November 1861. He was elected Captain in April 1862 and wounded near Richmond during the following summer. He returned to duty in January 1863 and was so badly wounded in the face at the Battle of Gettysburg that he lost sight in his right eye. He was retired to the Invalid Corps in September 1864 and received his parole in Charlotte in May 1865.

126. *A Roster.* Vol. 10, pp. 10, 48. **Lt. Alfred W. Dockery** enlisted as a Private in Company E as a Private and in March 1862 was promoted to Ordnance Sergeant of the 38th. The following April he was elected 2nd Lieutenant of his company and went back. He was promoted to 1st Lieutenant in November. In May 1864 he was treated in a Richmond hospital for a gunshot wound but the place and date were not stated. He returned to duty in the fall of 1864 and resigned in December.

39th Regiment North Carolina Troops

127. *A Roster.* Vol. 10, pp. 129-130. **Captain Hugh Harvey Davidson** was county sheriff of Cherokee County. He was 47 and was elected Captain of Company C in September 1861. He was elected Lieutenant Colonel the next year but resigned in December because of chronic diarrhea. However he had not been notified of the acceptance of his papers by December 31, 1862. Fighting had broken out at Murfreesboro, Tennessee, and he sustained an arm wound. He was captured near there, sent to Louisville, Kentucky, then to Camp Chase, Ohio, and finally to Fort Delaware. He was exchanged in May 1863 and later retired. For his gallantry in the fight at Murfreesboro, he was nominated for the Badge of Distinction.

128. *A Roster.* Vol. 10, p. 120. **Captain Alfred W. Bell** was a Macon County dentist and druggist before enlisting at age 32. He was elected Captain in October 1861. He resigned in March 1865 because of chronic rheumatism.

40th Regiment (3rd Regiment North Carolina Artillery)

129. *A Roster.* Vol. 1, pp. 417-418. **Captain Malcom H. McBryde** at age 25 enlisted as 1st Sergeant in August 1861. When the company reorganized in 1862, he was elected Captain. He was captured at Fort Fisher, January 15, 1865, and held prisoner at a fort on an island in New York Harbor. He was paroled and exchanged in March 1865.

41st Regiment (3rd Regiment North Carolina Cavalry)

130. *A Roster.* Vol. 2, p. 205. **Captain Alexander Murchison** of Harnett County enlisted at age 57 in March 1862. He resigned in 1863 of the hardships of service on his constitution.

43rd Regiment North Carolina Troops

131. *A Roster.* Vol. 10, p. 359. **Captain John H. Coppedge** was an Anson County farmer and enlisted at age 33. He was elected Captain in March 1862 but resigned the following summer because of bad health.

132. *A Roster.* Vol. 10, p. 294. There were two Chaplains attached to the 43rd. **Joseph W. Murphy** was with the regiment until he was transferred to the 32nd in August 1862. Since this particular Chaplain was writing the information in August/September 1863, I believe him to be **Eugene W. Thompson,** a resident of Lincoln County. He enlisted in October 1862 at age 30 and was with the 43rd until he surrendered at Appomattox Court House.

133. *A Roster.* Vol. 10, p. 369. **Captain Robert T. Hall** was Captain of Company C, 14th Regiment

when he was appointed Captain of this company in February 1862. He was wounded at the Battle of Winchester, September 19, 1864, during Union General Sheridan's Valley Campaign, and was absent because of wounds through February 1865.

44th Regiment North Carolina Troops

134. *A Roster.* Vol. 10, p. 467. **Captain William D. Moffitt** was a Montgomery County merchant at the time of his enlistment. He was 28 and was appointed Captain in March 1862. He resigned the following summer because of ill health.

135. *A Roster.* Vol. 10, p. 478. **Corporal Louis J. B. Edwards** was from Pitt County and was farming there when he enlisted at age 24.

136. *A Roster.* Vol. 10, p. 448. **Private William H. Heathcock**, a Montgomery County farmer, enlisted at age 23.

137. *A Roster.* Vol. 10, 445. **Captain David D. DeBerry** enlisted at age 34 in March 1862. He died of disease at a ferry crossing on the Yadkin River about a month later.

46th Regiment North Carolina Troops

138. *A Roster.* Vol. 11, p. 169. **Captain Colin Stewart** was born in Richmond County and farmed there. He was 20 and was appointed Captain in February 1862. He was wounded at Cold Harbor, Va., in June 1864 and returned to duty later in the summer. He received his parole at Greensboro in May 1865.

139. *A Roster.* Vol. 11, pp. 134, 208. **Captain Neil McKay McNeill** was a native of Moore County and a farmer. He enlisted at age 36 and was elected Captain in March 1862. He served in that capacity until he was appointed Major in March 1864. Two months later he received a knee wound during the fighting in the Wilderness, returned to duty in early fall, and surrendered at Appomattox Court House.

140. *A Roster.* Vol. 11, p. 198. A native of Duplin County, **Captain Obed William Carr** was a professor at Trinity College in Randolph County when he joined the army at age 28. He was elected Captain in March 1862 but illness forced his resignation in November of the following year.

BIBLIOGRAPHY

Farrell, James J. *Inventing the American Way of Death, 1830–1920*. Philadelphia: Temple University Press, 1980.

Landerman, Gary. *The Sacred Remains: American Attitudes Toward Death, 1799–1883*. New Haven, CT: Yale University Press, 1996.

Manarin, Louis A., and Weymouth T. Jordan, Jr., comps., *North Carolina Troops, 1861–1865: A Roster*. Raleigh, N.C.: Division of Archives and History, Department of Cultural Resources, 1966–. Cited as *A Roster*.

Myer, Robert G. *Embalming: History, Theory, and Practice*. Norwalk, CT: Appleton and Lange, 1990.

Raymer, Jacob Nathaniel. *Confederate Correspondent: The Civil War Reports of Jacob Nathaniel Raymer, Fourth North Carolina*. Edited by E. B. Munson. Jefferson, N.C.: McFarland, 2008.

Steiner, Peter E. *Disease in the Civil War: Natural Biological Warfare, 1861–1865*. Springfield, IL: C.C. Thomas, 1968.

Index

Adams, Mrs. Sarah 142
Adams, Peter 142
Adams, William 142
Albright, George Nicholas 39
Alderman, Louis Thomas 94
Alderman, Owen 90
Alderman, William H. 90
Aldred, Absalom 206
Aldridge, John A. 211
Alexander, Dr. John Brevard 184
Alexander, Julius J. 201
Alexander (Lowry), Mrs. Annie 184
Allen, W.H. 88
Allison, John Q. 38
Allison, Julius 161, 224
Allsbrook, Marcus 7
Alvin Lodge No. 762, A.F. & A.M.—Alvin, Texas 39
Amis, William J. 116
Ammons, Thos. H. 192
Anderson, General George Burgwyn 23–24, 25, 27, 79, 193
Anderson (Cameron), Mrs. Rebecca 193
Anderson, Robert Walker 193
Anderson, Colonel W.E. 23
Anderson, Walker E. 23, 24
Anderson, William Tillinghurst 31–32
Andrews, C.M. 23
Andrews, Clinton N. 97–98
Andrews, John Barr 23
Andrews, William H. 70
Andrews, William Murphy 70–71
Anson Guard 75, 76
Armfield, Mark 56, 219
Armstrong, Thomas E. 18–19
Arnett, Goodman 166
Arrington, Samuel L. 7
Arrington, William T. 154
Ashe, Richard J. 212
Asheville Spectator (newspaper) 75
Ashley, John P. 104

Ashley, W.H. 104
Atkinson, John A. 20
Atkinson, Jonas Johnston 20–21
Atkinson, Mrs. Esther 20
Atkinson, R.W. 21
Atwater, John Wilbur 12
Avery, Clark Moulton 167, 168–169
Avery, E. 26
Avery, Henry Harrison 7
Avery, James 7
Avery, W.W. 139

Badge of Distinction 86, 117
Badge of Honor and Merit 30
Bailey, Giles P. 71, 220
Bailey, John E. 30, 218
Bailey's Factory Hospital—Richmond, VA 183
Baity, William T. 31
Baker, Jesse J. 107
Baker, John C. 97
Baker, Laurence Simmons 48, 219
Baker, Miss Martha J. 107
Baker, Thomas W. 198
Baker, Thomas Wilson 201
Baldree, Arnold T. 20
Balfour Lodge, No. 188—Asheboro, NC 97
Ball, Henry 71
Ball, James D. 211
Baptist Church—Bethlehem, NC 133
Baptist Church—Holly Springs, NC 130, 131
Baptist Church—Magnolia, NC 17
Baptist Church—Mill's River, NC 85
Baptist Church—Mount Gilead, NC 18, 106
Baptist Church—Shady Grove, NC 34
Barber, George 200
Barber, George W. 159
Barbour, William M. 180, 226
Barger, John 22

Barger, Paul 22–23
Barker, John W. 8
Barker, Lemuel G. 8
Barnes, Jesse S. 20, 217
Barringer, David M. 45
Barringer, Rufus 49, 50, 219
Barrow, James F. 141
Battle, Junius C. 182, 183–184
Battle, R.H., Jr. 183
Battle, Wesley Lewis 182, 183–184
Battle, Hon. Wm. H. 182
Beaman, John A. 106
Beaver, William Hampton 39
Beckwith, Daniel G. 130–131
Beckwith, Green 130
Belcher, G.A. 100
Belcher, William Augustus 100
Bell, Alfred 191, 227
Bell, John A. 181
Bell, T.W. 188
Belmont Lodge, No. 108—Duplin County 100
Bennett, Mrs. John T. 80
Bennett, Judge Risden Tyler 78–80
Best, John A.J. 84
Betts, the Rev. A.D. 156
Betts, Andrew W. 158
Beveridge, J.T. 55
Beverly, Hampton 202
Bingham, S.M. 187
Bird, James C. 159
Black, Duncan A. 186–187
Black, Fred 211
Blackman, William B. 99
Blackmer Lodge A.Y. M., No. 127—Mt. Gilead, NC 115
Blacknall, Charles C. 120
Bladen Guards 93
Bladen Rifles 19
Blades, W.B. 55
Blake, Fred 126, 223
Blakeley, John B. 180
Blakeley, W.F. M. 181
Blalock, Jesse 160
Blalock, William H. 160
Blocker, Charles H. 122, 222

Index

Bloody Angle, Spotsylvania Court House, Battle of 80
Bloody Lane, Sharpsburg, Battle of 24, 25, 79
Blount, Hosea 40
Blue, John Archibald Baxter 214
Blue, William P. 137
Boggan, William W. 198
Boggan, William Willington 201
Boggs, Mrs. J.W. 71
Bond, John F. 53
Boney, Catherine 106
Boney, Mrs. Linda 106
Boney, Wright 106
Bost, A.F. 212
Bostick, Annie J. 186
Bostick, James T. 186
Botick, Sallie L. 186
Bowden, John Owen 211
Boyd, John H. 107
Boyett, Ezekiel M. 188
Boykin, Loftin 105
Boykin, Miss Mary A. 105
Boykin, Mrs. Haywood 105
Brabble, Edmund Carey 165
Bracy, W.J. 192
Braddy, Josephus 83
Braddy, K.J. 177, 226
Branch, General L. O'B. 43, 131
Brandon, David Calvin 22
Brandon, Matthew H. 22
Brandon, Mrs. Elizabeth H. 22
Branson, E.B. 82
Branson, Eli B., Jr. 82–83
Branson, Mrs. L. 82
Breece, L.R. 45, 219
Brett, Aurelius 87
Brewer, Nathan 138
Bridgers, Newitt D. 30
Briggs, James 21
Briley, James 199
Brinn, Seth 21
Britt, Benjamin E. 7
Britt, M.C. 199
Broadhurst, Charles S. 107
Broadhurst, David J. 106–107
Broadhurst, Edgar 107
Broadhurst, F.K. 107
Broadhurst, Hugh H. 107
Broadhurst, J.J. 107
Broadhurst, R.S. 107
Brock, J.H. 210
Brock, John 167, 225
Brooke, Robert D. 164
Brooks, R.H. 120
Broughton, William H. 127
Brower, James M. 213
Brown, Alexander 22
Brown, Capt. Owen N. 180
Brown, Maj. Owen N. 182
Brown, R.D. 143
Brown, Samuel S. 75
Brown, Stephan A. 22

Brown, W.H. 40
Brown, William C. 74–75
Brunswick Guards 99
Bryan, Geo. Pettigrew 98
Bryan, General Henry 145
Bryan, James Devereux 145
Bryan, Hon. John H. 98
Buchanan, James Calvin 94
Buchanan, Mr. _____ 14
Buchanan, William 94
Buckingham Female Collegiate Institute—Buckingham County, VA 120
Buffalo Lodge, No. 172, F. & A.M. 156
Buie, Archibald 195
Buie, David Calvin 195
Buie, Duncan Alexander 195
Buie, Kate 195
Buie, M.W. 92, 221
Buie, Mrs. Flora McInnis 195
Buie (McGeachy), Mrs. Kate 195
Bullard, Thomas 43
Buncombe Rangers 48
Burgess, Calvin 191
Burgess, Zephaniah W. 178, 193
Burgin, Charles H. 111
Burgwyn, Henry King, Jr. 2, 131–133
Burke Rifles 7
Burnside, General Ambrose 131
Burton, Dixon 177
Butler, Joshua H. 67
Byers, Charles R.P. 75

Cagle, Enoch S. 127, 223
Caldwell, the Rev. J.L. 184
Callais, John Dudley 167
Callais, William J. 167, 225
Cameron, James L. 174
Cameron, P.C. 193
Camp, David Clark 196
Camp Lookout, Maryland 27
Camp Ruffin, U.C.V.—Burlington, NC 151
Campbell, H. McL. 187
Campbell, Henry A. 215
Campbell, John C. 123
Campbell, John L. 187
Campbell, Joseph A. 123
Campbell, Kenneth A. 174
Campbell, Reuben P. 41, 42, 131
Canady, John 144
Candler, Charles Z. 75
Cane Creek Riflemen 126
Cape, Buck 71
Cape, Henry Harrison 71
Cape, Mattie 71
Cape, Mrs. Bettie 71
Cape, Samuel 71
Cape Fear Light Artillery 177
Cape Fear Riflemen 15
Caraway, J.C. 197, 223

Cardwell, Pleasant D. 209
Carlisle, James S. 158
Carmichael, A. 131
Carmichael, Abner Bryan 129, 131
Carmichael, Thomas Clay 141
Carolina Boys 185, 187, 189
Carpenter, John A. 86–87
Carpenter, Pinkney D. 86
Carr, Obed 153
Carr, William G. 167
Carroll, Stephen S. 19
Carter, D.M. 21, 217
Carter, N.H. 188
Carter, P.W. 188
Carter, Thomas 40
Carthage Lodge, No. 181, A.Y.M.—Carthage, NC 174
Case, James O. 191–192
Casper, Simeon 206
Catawba Braves 212
Center, Charles 157
Central Military Academy—Selma, AL 202
Chadwick, Barnabas 56
Chadwick, Mrs. Mary A. 56
Chadwick, Mrs. Walter 56
Chadwick, Winfield Scott 56
Chambers, Peyton 69
Chance, Henry T.C. 193–194
Chance, Richard 193
Chance, Terrell 189
Chaplain, 43rd North Carolina Regiment 198, 227
Charles, Harper Evans 111, 222
Chatham Boys 127, 130, 133, 135
Chatham Rifles 82, 163
Cheek, William H. 51–52
Cherokee Lodge, No. 197, A.Y.M. 207
Chimborazo Hospital—Richmond, VA 8, 14, 72, 74, 76, 90, 92, 100, 137, 156, 161, 182, 200, 204
Chrisman, Thomas P. 76
Chrisman, Thomas P., Jr. 76
Christenbury, Thomas C. 3
Christian, Edmund J. 115
Christian Advocate (newspaper)—Richmond, VA 120
Christian Church 34
Christie, Daniel Harvey 118–120
Christie (Norfleet), Mrs. Lizzie A. 118, 119
Christie, Robert W. 118
Christmas, Charles R. 11
Christmas, John R. 11
Church Graveyard at Friendship, NC 97
Church of Christ—Six Runs—Sampson County, NC 188
Church of the Advent (Episcopal)—Williamston, NC 88
Church of the Holy Innocents,

Henderson—Vance County, NC 51
Churchyard at Hawfields 35
Clarendon Guards 8
Clark, George 151
Clark, George M. 172
Clark, the Rev. J.D. 11
Clark, John 151
Clark, John B. 8
Clark, Neil A. 121
Clark, Nevin 151
Clark, Stephen L. 161-162
Clark, W.J. 122, 222
Clayton, George M. 126-127
Clegg, Thomas D. 163-164
Cleveland Blues 77
Clinton Cemetery—Clinton, NC 106
Clinton Hotel—Clinton, NC 105
Clodfelter, John 187
Cobb, Dr. Gaston B. 48
Cobb, the Rev. J.H. 122
Cobb, James G. 122
Cobb, Chaplain the Rev. Needham Bryan Cobb 71, 220
Coble, Alfred F. 143
Coble, Robert S. 143
Coggin, George W. 172
Coggins, Matthew A. 205
Coker, John C. 7
Cole, Andrew 156
Cole, Christopher Columbus 110, 113
Cole, James A. 97
Cole, Solomon N. 176
Coleman, Andrew A. 85
Coleman, Charles 220
Coleman, David 192
Coleman, Levi Parkinson 201
Coletrane, John W. 34
Collins, J.B. 40
Collins, John D. 141
Collins, S.P. 2, 133
Collins, Samuel P. 161
Colson, J.J. 78
Columbus Lodge No. 102—Pittsborough, NC 81, 82
Concord Female College—Statesville, NC 23
Confederate Greys 100
Confederate Hospital—Petersburg, VA 196
Congleton, Owen 54
Connollee, Mrs. L.G. 32
Conoley, Daniel A. 121
Conoley, William C. 121
Conrad, James Dallas 150
Conrad, Joseph 150
Conrad, Mrs. Elizabeth 150
Cook, Anderson 156
Cook, William D. 140-141
Cooley, Thomas L. 36-37
Coppedge, John H. 197, 228

Corbett, C.C. 106
Corbett, James 195-197
Cotton, General R.C. 146
Courtney, Andrew H. 140
Cowan, James P. 26
Cowan, Robert H. 90, 221
Cowan, Robert T. 171, 226
Cowan, Thomas 18
Cox, Calvin 158
Cox, Charles, Jr. 174
Cox, Wiley E. 21
Craige, Cicero H. 20
Craige, James Alexander 38, 218
Craige, James F. 150, 224
Crain Creek Lodge, No. 213—Moore County, NC 97, 155, 176, 210
Cranford, John Milton 77
Cranford, N.H. 187
Craton, Marshall 145, 223
Crider, Henry 144
Crisco, C.L. 187
Cross Roads Church—Alamance County, NC 38
Crouch, John 185
Crow Hospital—Richmond, VA 123
Crowson, E.M. 146
Crumpler, Thomas Newton 48-49
Crutchfield, William H. 136
Culberson, William 85
Culbreth, James L. 122
Culbreth, Malcom 193
Culbreth, Mrs. B.L. 195
Cumberland Cavalry 96
Cumberland Plough Boys 122
Current, Francis M. 21
Currie, Archibald B. 121
Currie, James A. 121
Currie, Lauchlin A. 137
Currie, Mrs. Jannette 121
Curtis, Benjamin F. 125
Custis, Dr. Peter Barton 159
Cutts, Joseph F. 158
Cutts, Mrs. Martha 158
Cutts, William 158

Dalton, Euel 68
Dalton, John D. 191
Dalton, John S. 207
Dalton, Mrs. Sarah 68
Dalton, Nicholas H. 68
Daniel, Hon. J.R.J. 208
Daniel, Junius 208-209
Dart, Josiah T. 138
Davenport, John W. 170
Davidson, Hugh Harvey 191, 227
Davis, Archibald J. 163
Davis, Champion Thomas Neal 84
Davis, Daniel M. 125
Davis, E. 117

Davis, George W. 154
Davis, Dr. J.Z. 146
Davis, James H. 104
Davis, Mrs. Ann 117
Davis, Roderick Cotton 146
Davis, Wiley P. 117
Davis, William Henry Harrison 130
Davis, William P. Oliver 170
Deaton, James 23
Deaton, Thomas C. 23
DeBerry, D.D. 205, 228
DeBerry, James N. 162
Deboard, James R. 72
Deems, Charles F. 26
Deems, the Rev. Dr. _____ 29
Deems, Theodore DeSausure 29
DeLoatch, the Rev. B.F. 190
DeSoto Camp, No. 220, U.C.V.—Hernando, MS 191
Dewar, A.H. 162
Dewar, John P. 162
Dickey, Allen S. 70
Dickey, James A. 70
Dickey, (Maydard), Mrs. Permelia 70
Dismukes, Henry A. 204-205
Dixon, Caleb 161
Dixon, Edward 72, 220
Dixon, John A. 38
Dobson, Joseph A. 21
Dockery, Alfred W. 191, 227
Dockery, Oliver H. 185, 227
Dorsett, A.M. 187
Douglas, John H. 160
Douglas, Samuel T. 171
Douglas, William J. 83
Dowd, Clement C. 127, 128, 193, 223
Draughon, G.W. 155
Draughon, George H. 155
Draughon, Walter 106
Draughon, William Avery 101
Drumwright, William H. 121
Drysdale, Robert H. 15, 17
Dumas, Franklin Wall 115
Dunlap, William Pines 117
Dunn, Andrew Jackson 154
Dunn, J.A. 153
Dunn, Nathaniel A. 52
Dunn, Samuel W. Thomas 153
Duplin Rifles 202
Duplin Turpentine Boys 153
Dupree, Joseph W. 66

Eagle Lodge, No. 71, F. & A.M. 148
Early, General Jubal A. 27, 80
Earnhardt, George R. 149
Eaton, Charles R. 73
Edgecombe Guards 87
Edwards, Alpheus 120
Edwards, James M. 143

Edwards, Jesse A. 211
Edwards, Julius A. 86
Edwards, Louis J.B. 203, 228
Edwards, the Rev. P.W. 86
Edwards, Pinkney L. 86
Edwards, Thomas 153
Egerton, Rufus E. 163
Ellerbee, Stephen W. 201
Ellis, James N. 136, 138
Ellis, Joseph G. 137-138
Ellis, William B. 138
Ellis Anson Rifles 117
Ellis Artillery 52
Emack, George 42
Emack, James W. 42
Enfield Blues 7
Enloe, Thomas G. 85
Episcopal Graveyard—Upperville, VA 187
Erwin, Thomas M. 43
Evangelical Lutheran Church—Luther's Chapel, Rowan County, NC 22
Evans, Dr. Augustine C. 54
Evans, Junius G. 99
Evans, Oren S. 130
Evans, Orpheus Harris 130
Evans, Richard Washington 54
Everett, James H.M. 90
Everett, Troy 128

Fain, John D. 169, 225
Fair Grounds Hospital—Petersburg, VA 29
Fairlee, John Paisley 123
Fairlee, Mrs. Jennet 123
Fairlee, Neill 123
Fairmount Cemetery 95
Faison, Franklin J. 100
Faison, James A. 99, 221
Falkland Masonic Lodge, No. 196 83
Farrior, Mrs. John 107
Faucett, Albert F. 98-99
Faucette, Levi 37
Faucette, Mrs. Ann 149
Faucette, R.C.P. 149
Faucette, Thomas D. 149
Faulkner, John 161
Fayetteville Independent Light Infantry 7, 177
Ferguson Hospital—Lynchburg, VA 108
Ferrell, Francis B. 196
Ferrell, J.A. 106
Ferrell, James P. 159
Ferrell, Simeon D. 75
Fetter, William M. 179, 226
Fidler, David H. 180
First Baptist Church 43
1st Georgia Hospital 181
First N.C. Hospital—Petersburg, VA 207
Fisher, Charles F. 32-33, 34

Fisher, Freeman J. 21
Fisher Light Infantry 197
Flat River Guards 33, 34
Fleming, Bithel 206
Fleming, C.E. 206
Fleming, Edward P. 206
Fleming, J.E. 206
Fleming, John W. 115
Fleming, Nathan N. 213
Flemming, Tom 111
Flowers, Thomas J. 189-190
Floyd, Squire 211
Fonville, James R. 37
Foote, J.H. 10
Forsyth Rifles 109
Fort Caswell Hospital—Smithville, NC 192
Fort Delaware, Delaware 32
Fort Johnson 22
Forte, John F. 162
44th Georgia 190
45th North Carolina Regiment of Militia 35
Foster, James J. 70
Foster, Nathaniel 137
Foust, Mrs. John M. 84
Fowler, Henry Barksdale 68
Fraley, Ashbel S. 24
Fraley, Jacob L. 27
Fraley, John T. 14-15
Fraley, Milas J. 14
Franklin, L.M. 3
Franklin Rifles 163
Frazier, John R. 113
Freeland, William Johnson 34
Freeman, Eli 77
Freeman, Eli P. 203
Freeman, Noah R. 172
Freeman, R.W. 172
Friedberg Moravian Church 83
Frink, John O'Neill 95
Fry, Johnston 52
Fulton, Saunders F. 108, 110
Furr, John B. 54

Gaines, James L. 205
Gaines, John C. 205
Gainesville Camp, No. 12, U.C.V. 185
Gainor, William T. 53
Gaither, Ephraim 25
Gaither, Mrs. S.H. 25
Gaither, William Henry 25
Gales, Thomas L 200-201
Gardner, James 167
Gardner, Thomas F. 153
Garmon, Marcus D.L. 153
Garrett, Henry B. 135-136
Garrett, the Rev. Jacob 135
Garrett, John F. 16
Garrett, Mrs. Anna 135
Garrett, Thomas 185
Garrett, Capt. Thomas M. 28, 218

Garrett, Thos. 116
Garrett, William A. 135-136
Garriss, Francis D. 92
Gaskill, J.W. 56
Gaskill, Washington 56
Gaskill, William 56
Gay, George G. 199
Geddie, Mrs. Agnes 189
Geddie, William 189
Geddie, William McP. 189
Gee, George W. 177
Gee, William H. 135
General D.H. Hill's Military School—Charlotte, NC 54
General Hospital—Goldsboro,' NC 149, 160
General Hospital—Raleigh, NC 53
General Hospital—Richmond, VA 136
General Hospital No. 1—Richmond, VA 146
General Hospital No. 24—Richmond, VA 196
General Military Hospital—Wilson, NC 175
Gibson, Dempsey 168
Gibson, the Rev. J. 10
Gibson, James J. 181
Gibson, James T.S. 168
Gibson, Thomas 194
Gibson, Virgil A. 168
Gibson, William H. 168
Gilbreth, George R. 179
Giles, Matthew M. 99
Giles, Ryon 99
Gillett's Farm—Onslow County 96
Gillon, Monroe M. 171, 225
Gilmer, John A. 211
Glenn, Chalmers 67-68
Glenn, Mollie 126
Glenn, Napoleon L. 126
Glenn, W.L. 191
Globe Hospital—Richmond, VA 117
Godwin, C. 158
Godwin, Condray 157, 224
Goff, J.M., 5th Alabama Regiment 26
Goforth, John P. 112
Goldsboro' Rifles 145, 146
Goldstone, Robert Wm. 127
Goodman, James C. 30-31
Gore, William K. 91
Gorrell, Henry Clay 12-13
Goss, Wm. 182, 226-227
Grace Church Hospital—Alexandria, VA 50
Grady, William S. 126
Graham, Daniel B. 185
Granville Stars 115, 117
Granville Targeteers 115
Graves, Bazillia Yancey 107, 222

Gray, the Rev. Henry 194
Gray, Robert M. 21
Green (Meares), Mrs. Frances Iredell 194
Green, Dr. W.H. 194
Greenlee, James Logan 111–112
Greensborough Lodge, No. 76, A.Y. M.—Greensborough, NC 142
Greenwood Hospital, VA 34
Gregory, Major D. 165
Gregory, Eddie 165
Gregory, Frank 165
Gregory, Howard 165
Gregory, Miss Bessie 165
Gregory, Richard 165
Gregory, Wilson G. 40
Griffin, W.B. 40
Griffith, A.J. 79
Grimes, Col. Bryan 22, 26
Ground Squirrel Church, VA 98
Grove Academy—Kenansville—NC 202
Gudger, Hugh L. 152–153
Gudger, James M. 72, 75, 220
Gudger, John W. 153, 224
Gudger, Mrs. Mary 152
Gudger, Robert L. 152
Guilford Grays 140, 141, 142, 144, 147, 148, 211
Guilford Light Infantry 206
Gulley, John D. 123, 222
Gulley, William Bryant 122–123
Gunter, Asa J. 175
Guthrie, George Clayton 12
Guthrie, William F. 167–168

Hackney, Samuel C. 29
Haigh, Charles T. 183
Hailey, Hiram H. 116
Haizlip, Vincent W. 110
Hall, Edward D. 212
Hall, Hugh A. 143
Hall, James 94
Hall, James A. 17
Hall, Lucian H. 96
Hall, R.T. 199, 227–228
Hall, Robert A. 21
Hall, Washington 94
Hall, William H. 172
Hamilton, Floreida 56
Hamilton, William Henry 72, 220
Hammond, H.B. 200
Hammond, Joseph M. 200
Hammond General Hospital—Point Lookout, MD 26
Hancock, Elisha 30
Hancock, J.N. 162
Hancock, Mrs. Anna 30
Hancock, Thomas J. 30
Harden, Mrs. Jas. P. 12
Hardister, Agrippa S. 190

Hardister, Ashberry 190
Hardister, Levi P. 112
Hardister, Mrs. Cynthia 190
Hargrave, Jesse 71, 72, 220
Harmon, George A. 214
Harpers Ferry, VA 46
Harrell, James G. 40, 218
Harrell, John R. 40
Harrington, Philip H., Jr. 192–193
Harris, Brantley 117
Harris, Claiborne 204
Harris, J.G. 40
Harris, John L. 121, 222
Harris, Mrs. Abigail 117
Harris, Parsons 117
Hart, William Speight McLean 67
Hartin, Rufus James 183
Hartman, George C. 107
Haskell, J.C. 194
Hasty, John H. 210
Hasty, Robert A. 214
Hatcher, Charles L. 187
Hawley, John 104
Hawley, Ransom G. 104
Haynes, Lewis F. 186
Haywood, Duncan Cameron 41
Haywood, Edward Graham 41, 218
Haywood, William H. 43–44
Haywood, Hon. Wm. H. 41, 43
Heartsfield, John Wesley 9, 10
Heartsfield, Dr. W. 9
Heathcock, William H. 203, 228
Hellen, John F. 88
Henderson, Archibald 46
Henderson, David Long 102
Henderson, J.A. 86
Henderson, Leonard A. 45–47
Henderson, Mrs. Mary Steel 46
Henderson, Mrs. S.P. 86
Henderson, Robert 182
Henderson, William Adolphus 86
Henderson, William Augustus 181–182
Henderson, William F. 181
Henley, E.J. 187
Henley, Mrs. Joliette 84
Hensley, William Malcombe 152
Herbin, James Monroe 67
Herring, Henderson 70
Herring, James 90
Herring, John 90
Herring, Leonidas 141
Herring, Mrs. Line 148
Herring, Robert D. 107
Herring, William H. 102–103
Hertford Light Infantry 87
Hester, John A. 107
Hickerson, C.N. 181, 226
Hicks, Solon S. 116

Highland Boys 121, 123, 124, 125
Highland Rangers 194, 195
Highsmith, James T. 89
Hill, General D.H. 24, 79, 80, 132
Hill, Hugh Alex 166
Hill, Junius L. 42, 43
Hill, W.L. 187
Hill, William T. 211
Hillsboro Military Academy 38
Hinson, George W. 101
Hobbs, Judson 157
Hobson, James M. 12
Hodge, Marshall 174–175
Hodges, John H. 196
Hoey, S.A. 171, 226
Hoke, Wm. J. 187
Holden, W.W. 139
Holeman, Edwin 33
Holeman, Silas J. 33
Holland, Henry B. 81
Holland, P. 14
Holland, Stephen B. 52, 219
Holleman, W.J. 81
Hollingsworth, David T. 18
Holmes, the Rev. Geo. W. 84
Holmes, James A. 98
Holmes, General T.H. 17, 131
Holmes Riflemen 103
Hominy Creek Division, No. 289, Son of Temperance 85
Hood, George Washington 136
Hooper, F. Marion 112
Hooper, J.A. 112, 222
Hooper, Nelson P. 21
Horah, George 214
Horne, Henry W. 17, 217
Hornet's Nest Riflemen 7
Hospital at Fortress Monroe, VA 149
Hospital No. 9—Richmond, VA 145
Houston, W.J. 50, 219
Howard, James E.M. 27
Howard, William 86
Howard's Grove Hospital—Richmond, VA 101, 116, 123, 150, 162, 199
Hoyle, Alfred E. 115
Hoyle, Peter F. 211
Hughes, Doctor 156
Hughes, Nicholas Collin 14
Humphrey, John 191
Hundley, Daniel Turner 199
Hunt, Jabez 96–97
Hunter, the Rev. Mr. _____ 15
Hunter, Samuel A. 141
Hunter, William F. 144
Huntley, Edmund P. 128
Huske, Henry D. 28–29
Hutcheson, John 37

Icehower, Hugh Franklin 179
Independent Blues 99, 101

Ingold, Monroe 207
Iredell, Campbell T. 209–210
Iredell, James Johnston 209–210
Iredell Blues 24
Ireland, Frank 100, 221
Ireland, John Rich 69
Ireland, Mrs. Julia E. 69
Irvin, Andrew M. 207
Irvin, William C. 207
Iverson, General Alfred 101–102

Jackson, Randol R. 190
Jackson, Thomas J. 132
Jackson, William H. 99
James, Isaac 195
James, Samuel C. 109
Jeff Davis Camp, No. 117, U.C.V.—Goldthwaite, Texas 71
Jerusalem Church—Davis, NC 29
John A. Wharton Camp No. 286, U.C.V.—Alvin Texas 39
Johnson, A.F. 106, 195
Johnson, Amos, Neil 193–194
Johnson, Archibald 175
Johnson, Dr. Charles E. 150
Johnson, Dr. Chas. E. 23
Johnson, David George 81
Johnson, David W. 158
Johnson, E.N. 195
Johnson, Edward N. 89
Johnson, Geo. M. 154
Johnson, George 99
Johnson, George W. 99
Johnson, Isaac N. 131
Johnson, J.D. 195
Johnson, J.S. 195
Johnson, James 119
Johnson, John A. 44
Johnson, John A.G. 175
Johnson, Joseph A. 7
Johnson, Josiah 153
Johnson, Milton H. 16–17
Johnson, Mrs. Ann 194
Johnson, Mrs. Anna 99
Johnson (Herring), Mrs. Ellen 195
Johnson, Mrs. J.D. 105
Johnson, Mrs. Nancy 44
Johnson, R.C. 16
Johnson, Samuel 194
Johnson, T.O. 158
Johnson's Island, Ohio 37
Johnston, George 149
Johnston, George Burgwyn 150–151
Johnston, Jonas 20
Johnston, Mrs. L.F. 84
Johnston (Johnson), Mrs. Nannie Taylor 150
Johnston, the Rev. Samuel I. 150
Johnston, William A. 71, 78, 220

Johnston, Dr. William L. 207
Johnstone, Francis 125, 223
Jolly, Frederick 40
Jones, Arthur N. 100, 221
Jones, Charles R. 21
Jones, Daniel McLean 162
Jones, Edward S. 136
Jones, Elder W.C. 71
Jones, Hardy 125
Jones, Dr. J.B. 136
Jones, John 16
Jones, John G. 175–176
Jones, John Thomas 136
Jones, the Rev. Jos. 118
Jones, Miss Alice 51
Jones, Mrs. Martha A. 125
Jones, Mrs. Mary M. 162
Jones, Nat. G. 162
Jones, Owen D. 125
Jones, Samuel A. 21
Jones, Thomas 28
Jones, Thomas L. 61, 219
Jones, William T. 177
Jordan, John W. 160
Jordan, Joseph P. 173
Joyner, Jason P. 141–142
Jump, John W. 141
Justice, Alex 131

Kallam, David 207
Kearns, Whitson O. 187
Keith, Hugh 128
Kell, James 153, 224
Kellam, William H. 206
Kelly, Eban N. 185
Kelly, George 185
Kelly, John 215
Kelly, John McDonald 174
Kelly, Michael 129–130
Kelly, Neill A. 195
Kelly, Neill R. 175
Kelly, Dr. Thomas J. 19
Kelly, Wm. John 195
Kenan, Thomas Stephen 202–203
Kennedy, Levi B. 53
Kenyon, Mrs. J.T. 195
Kerns, Joseph A. 180
Kerr, Nathaniel R. 66–67
Kerr, William J. 39
Kilby, Wilbur P. 119
Killett, James Cedric 105
Killian, Miles 85
Kilpatrick, William A. 172–173
Kimbrough, Lewis W. 166
Kincey, James W. 192
King, James 26–27
King, William E. 69
King's School House, VA 130
Kinley, Zebedee 211
Kirby, William H. 78
Kirkland, William 107, 222
Kirkman, Dr. George 133
Kirkman, George E. Badger 134

Kirkman, Henry Clay Bascom 134
Kirkman, Wiley Prentiss 134
Kirkman, William Preston 133–134
Kirksey, Elijah J. 86, 220
Kistler, Theo. J.H. 173
Kite, Stephen 40
Knight, James Richard 117
Knight, James S. 116–117
Knotts, Thomas C. 128
Koonce, Miss Sally J. 55
Koonce, Mrs. Daisy 55
Kornegay, Ashley S. 200
Ku Klux Klan 39

Lack, Jno. P. 10
Lafayette Light Infantry Company 87
Lamb, Isaac 8
Lamb, John C. 88
Lamb, Orren 83
Lance, James P. 126
Lane, General James 151
Langley, John L.R. 174
Lanier, William Waddell 76
Lasater, Hardy 176
Latham's Battery 56, 178, 193, 194, 203
Latimer, Wm. J. 87
Laurel Hill Church 94
Lawrence, Andrew 161
Lawrence, Thos. R. 15
Lawson, Thomas T. 69
Lawson, William 53
Lawson Ball Camp, U.C.V. 32
Leach, James M. 107, 222
Leak, Mrs. John 80
Leasburg Grays 66, 67
Leathers, John B. 33
Leathers, Joseph Armstrong 33
Leathers, Mrs. Parthenia 33
Lee, Charles Cochrane 179–180
Lee, Lemon H. 99
Lee, Morgan C.T. 89, 221
Lee, Mrs. Elmira 28
Lee, Stephen 180
Lee, the Rev. T.M. 106, 157
Lee, William Henry 110
Leffers, Isaiah C. 55
Leffers, Robert 55
Leinback, Philemon J. 108–109
Leith, James E. 88
Lenoir, Thomas 126, 223
Lenoir Braves 192
Leverett, Thomas 72
Lewis, Camden 94
Lewis, Claton S. 187–188
Lewis, Geo. T. 72
Lewis, Jacob H. 190
Lewis, Mrs. Aubine 106
Lexington Wild Cats 71
Liddon, David S. 55

Index

Ligon Hospital—Richmond, VA 34
Liles, James A. 161
Liles, Junius A. 161
Lillington Rifle Guards 8
Lindsay, Charles B. 160, 224
Lineback, R.C. 167, 225
Linwood Cemetery—Graham, NC 105
Little, Mrs. Eugene 80
Little, William Calvin 77
Livengood, Henderson E. 14
Lloyd, Lucian 150
London, William 163, 225
Long, William A. 77
Lord, W.C. 193
Love, T.D. 121, 222
Lovejoy, J.M. 208
Lowrance, William 170, 225
Lowry, Mrs. Mary Johnston 184
Lowry, Samuel 184
Luckey, T.S. 180
Lumber Bridge Presbyterian Church—Robeson County, NC 48
Luria, Alfred M. 115
Luther, Josiah 112
Luther, Martin 112
Luther, Mrs. Sarah 112
Luther, Whit J. 112
Lyon, Zack E. 120-121

Mabrey, Baker W. 204
Macon, Henry Allston 201
Macon, William R. 171
Mallett, Charles P. 212
Mallett, Peter 17, 217
Mallett, Richardson 212-213
Malloy, Charles 92, 221
Malloy, Duncan 122
Malloy, James H. 122
Malloy, Mrs. Isabella 122
Manassas 2
Mangum, Hon. W.P. 33
Mangum, William Preston, Jr. 33
March, A.B. 127
Marine Hospital—Wilmington, NC 159
Marsh, Edward Stanley. 27, 218
Marsh, William T. 25, 27
Martin, Amos 194
Martin, G.W. 162
Martin, John A. 162-163
Martin, John B. 134
Martin, John P. 167
Martin, Mrs. Susan 162
Martin, Samuel 194
Martin, William P. 127
Martin, William Pinckney 74, 223
Martin, Wm. P. 130
Martindale, Bryant B. 70
Masonic Fraternity, Mingo Lodge, No. 206—Dunn, Harnett County, NC 99, 101, 103
Masonic Lodge—Graham, NC 37
Masonic Lodge No. 134—Mocksville, NC 75
Massey, Adolomus 159
Massey, William H. 170
Mat 67-68
Matlock, Columbus C. 191
Matthews, Isaiah 96
Matthews, John E. 127
Matthews, William H. 28
May, William R. 208
Maynard, R.C. 82
McAlister, James D. 124
McArthur, J.A. 106
McArthur, O. P. 106
McArthur, V.J. 106
McArthur, Vann J. 106
McArthur, W.O. 106
McAulay, Hugh W. 149
McAuley, Hugh E. 180
McBryde, M.H. 192, 227
McCauley, George 149, 224
McClellan, Albert B. 41
McConnell, Daniel W. 147
McCray Primitive Baptist Church Cemetery—Burlington, NC 71
McDaniel, James W. 136
McDonald, Allen E. 174
McDonald, Archibald 92
McDonald, John D. 92
McDonald, Mrs. Sarah 92
McDonald, Neill 134-135
McDougald, Duncan 155
McDougald, Hugh W.W. 123
McDougald, William 155
McDuffie, Daniel 188
McElroy, J.S. 85, 220
McGee, Joseph B. 170
McGoogan, Hugh 178
McGregor, Archibald W. 92-93
McInnis, Allen M. 172
McInnis, John M. 172
McIntire, David 100
McIntire, Mrs. Sarah P. 100
McIntire, Thomas Tate 100
McIntyre, the Rev. John 123
McIver, D.D. 156
McIver, Edward 155
McIver, Kenneth H. 156
McIver, Murdock A. 154
McKay, Alexander 185
McKeithan, Frederick J. 89
McKeithan, John W.I. 53
McKenzie, Bethune B. 117
McKenzie, Colon R.C. 185
McKenzie, Kenneth 117
McKenzie, M. Stokes 22
McKenzie, Dr. William M. 22
McKethan, James 45
McKethan, James K. 45
McKinney, Robert M. 81
McKinnon, Andrew W. 48
McKinnon, Archibald P. 124
McKinnon, Martin A. 130
McKnight, John H. 144
McLauchlin, Benjamin 127-128, 223
McLauchlin, Duncan (Cumberland County) 127, 129
McLauchlin, Duncan (Richmond County) 90
McLauchlin, J.A. 188
McLauchlin, J.C. 129, 131
McLauchlin, William A. 129
McLauchlin, William John 177
McLaughlin (McKay), Mrs. Cornelia 191
McLaughlin, Murdock 185
McLaughlin, Murdock McRae 190-191
McLean, Daniel H. 125
McLean, Hector 177
McLean, John A.H. 215
McLean, Dr. John H. 125
McLean, Samuel 146
McLean, William H. 143
McLellan, Neil 122
McLeod, James A.N. 134
McLeod, K.J. 206
McLeod, Mudoch D. 205-206
McLeod, N.C. 206
McLeod, Nevin C. 173
McLeod, Norman J. 172
McManning, Wm. E. 34-35
McMillan, A. 189
McMillan, Alexander C. 41-42
McMillan, Daniel 189
McMillan, Daniel L. 203-204
McNair, John G. 123
McNair, Malcolm 195
McNatt, John 166
McNeely, James Brown 36
McNeill, Angus 124
McNeill, Jesse Franklin 212
McNeill, John J. 124
McNeill, John McIntyre 123-124
McNeill, Lauchlin 123
McNeill, Malcom A. 176
McNeill, Mrs. Mary J. 212
McNeill, Mrs. Mary P. 123
McNeill, Neill 210, 228
McNeill, Simon P. 212
McPhaul, Angus J. 214
McPhaul, Daniel A. 187
McQuay, Seaborn 56
McRae, Archibald 196
McRae, John 196
McRae, Mrs. Catharine A. 196
McRae, R.B. 43, 218
McRee, James F., Jr., Surgeon 19
McRee, Robert Cowan 19-20
McRimmon, Joseph 91-92

M.E. Church, South—Eleazer, Randolph County 30
Means, George W. 170
Means, Wm. 170
Meares, Calvin H. 100, 221
Meares, Gaston 16
Meares, Wm. B. 16
Mecklenburg Farmers 173
Medlin, Angus 210
Meece, Mathias 86
Meece, Peter 86
Melvin, Love 96
Merrill, B.W. 126
Merrill, Henry C. 125–126
Merritt, Benajah C. 50
Merritt, Leonidas J., Company M 82
Merritt, Leonidas, J., 2nd Company I 163
Methodist Episcopal Church 10, 25, 34
Methodist Episcopal Church, South—Newton Grove, NC 149
Midyett, J.C. 40
Miller, Carlos W. 107
Miller, Evan L. 8
Miller, Jesse 161, 224
Miller's Battery 53
Mills, Francis M. 27
Mingo Lodge 206—Sampson County, NC 190
Mitchell, Anderson 24
Mitchell, M.T. 113, 222
Mitchell, Mrs. P.A. 37
Mocksville Masonic Lodge No. 134—Mocksville, NC 75
Modlin, A. 40
Moffitt, William 203, 228
Moneghan, Edward, Jr. 28
Monroe, Daniel A. 188–189
Monroe, Daniel Melvin 91
Monroe, John 175
Montague, James 9–10
Montague, P. 9
Montgomery, Dr. J.H. 204
Montgomery, John C. 204
Montgomery Grays 150
Montgomery Volunteers 115
Moody, John A. 149, 224
Moore, A.D. 16, 53, 219
Moore, Alexander Duncan 89
Moore, Chas. 85
Moore, David Swain 85–86
Moore, George W.J. 192
Moore, John 89
Moore, Mrs. Lucinda 85
Moore, Samuel P. 66
Moore, W.H. 84, 220
Moore, Walter R. 72
Moore, William, Jr. 89
Moore, Wilson D. 207
Moore County Independents 127, 130

Moore County Rifles 154, 155
Moore Hospital—Richmond, VA 94, 209
Moore's Creek Rifle Guards 89, 91, 94
Moose, Edmund 150
Moran, John A.J. 135
Moran, Mrs. Elizabeth 135
Moran, William 135
Morehead, John Henry 207
Morgan, Henry C. 185
Morris, Baxter B. 149
Morris, Joseph T. 33
Morris, L. 26
Morris, Nathaniel 175
Morrison, Earnest A. 21
Morrow, Daniel Foust 151
Morrow, Elijah Graham 150
Morrow, R. Alexander 149
Mosley, Elisha 153
Mt. Olivet Lodge, No. 164 204
Mull, Jackson R. 84
Munn, Ollin 92
Murchison, Alexander 195, 227
Murchison, John Reed 47–48
Murchison, William G. 140
Murphy, Mrs. John 105
Muse, Ashly F. 133
Muse, Jesse 133
Myers, William R. 170, 225

Nance, Thomas T. 211
Nantz, Clement R. 180
Nash, Frederick 95
Nash, the Rev. Frederick K. 92
Nash, Henry Potter 92
Neal, John Q. 128
Neely, James W. 25
Neuse River Bridge, Battle of 44
New-Hope Church—Gaston County, NC 8
New Providence Christian Church—Alamance County, NC 71, 114
New Salem Lodge, No. 209 114
Newel, Gideon 98
Newell, Harris 104–105
Newell, Hope 104–105
Newell, Mrs. Elizabeth 104
Newell, Warren 104–105
Newell, Warren W. 100–101
Newkirk, A.J. 90
Newton Academy Burying Ground—Asheville, NC 73
Nichols, John S.A. 56, 219
Nichols, Leander C. 112
Nicholson, Malcolm C. 115
Nicholson, Wm. T. 180, 226
Nixon, N.N. 84
Nolley, the Rev. George W. 120
Norman, James S. 55
North Carolina Soldiers' Home—Raleigh, NC 120, 152
Norwood, Joseph B. 117

Nunn, Benjamin Franklin 143
Nunn, James, Sr. 143
Nunn, Jesse Isler 143

Oak City Guards 72, 73, 75, 76
Oak Grove Cemetery—Randolph County 112
Oakdale Cemetery—Wilmington, NC 16, 89
Oakland Guards 170, 173
Oakmont Cemetery—Raleigh, NC 203
O'Brien, Dr. John 49
O'Brien, Marcemas 49
O'Brien, Mrs. Elizabeth 49
O'Bryan, Elijah 205
Ochiltree, Alexander 177
Officers' Hospital—Petersburg, VA 88
O.K. Boys 158, 159, 163
Orange Light Infantry 150, 213
Orrell, Joseph N. 120
Osborne, E. 126
Osborne, Roland C. 126
Oscar R. Rand Camp, No. 1278 U.C.V. 166
Ousby, William Clark 201
Overcash, Joel J. 170
Owen, Chaplain the Rev. W. Burton, 17th Mississippi 182
Owens, John F. 96, 221

Paisley, James 146
Paisley, William M. 146–147
Palmer, John C. 22
Palmer, John H. 113
Palmyra Masonic Lodge 147—Dunn, NC 81
Parker, Allen B. 160
Parker, Charles 141
Parker, Hardy W. 28
Parker, Ica 82
Parker, James H. 145–146
Parker, James R. 145
Parker, Wiley 152, 224
Parker, William Thomas 158
Parks, John P. 170–171, 226
Parnell, Benjamin 160
Parrish, Allen C. 36
Parrish, William K. 33, 35, 218
Patterson, J.R. 152
Patterson, James W. 152
Patterson, John A. 175
Patterson, Mrs. Nancy 152
Patterson, Neill A. 176
Patterson, Robert B. 72
Patton, George 56
Patton, John 56
Paul, Thomas P. 11
Paul, William C. 11
Peace Institute Hospital—Raleigh, NC 207
Pearce, Obediah W. 124
Pearsall, Leonidas 189

Peck, the Rev. _____ 75
Pee Dee Guards 116, 117
Pee Dee Wildcats 128
Peel, Wm., Jr. 66
Peeler, Moses 54
Perkinson, John B. 74
Perry, Hezekiah D. 114
Perry, Thomas L. 21
Perry, Willie, Jr. 82
Persons, William M. 134
Pescud, P.F. 76
Pescud's Drug Store—Raleigh, NC 76
Pettigrew Hospital—Raleigh, NC 197
Petty, Robert 176
Pfohl, William J. 109–110
Pharr, John M. 49–50
Philips, Owen C. 13
Phillips, Edmund M. 160
Phillips, Robert L. 113
Phillips, William J. 115
Philpot, W.A. 40
Pine Hill Cemetery—Burlington, NC 37
Pinkston, Julius C. 200
Pisgah Guards 125
Pittman, Benjamin F. 157
Pleasant Grove—Anson County, NC 78
Plesants, Albert 8–9
Plesants, Robert 8
Pool, Hartwell S. 76
Pool, John S. 76
Pool, Mrs. Nancy 76
Pool, Thomas 156
Pope, Abner C. 160
Porterfield, James H. 160
Porterfield, John W. 160
Porterfield, Joseph W. 162
Potter, Mr. J., and Mrs. 99
Potts, James M. 179, 226
Potts, William Marcellus 50
Powe, Hugh Torrence 29
Powell, P.M. 118
Powell, Thomas F. 118
Powers, David 72
Powers, Lewis H. 72
Presbyterian Church—Alamance County, NC 144
Presbyterian Church—Chapel Hill, NC 149
Presbyterian Church—Cypress, NC 175
Presbyterian Church—Euphronia, NC 174
Presbyterian Church—Galatia, NC 186
Presbyterian Church—Graham, NC 37
Presbyterian Church—Hawfields, NC 37
Presbyterian Church—Little River, NC 36

Presbyterian Church—Lumber Bridge, NC 122
Presbyterian Church—Poplar Tent, Cabarrus County, NC 51
Presbyterian Church—St. Pauls, NC 123
Presbyterian Church—Salisbury, NC 214
Presbyterian Church—Sandy Grove, NC 188
Presbyterian Church—Smyrna, NC 167
Presbyterian Church, Bethesda—Caswell County, NC. 67
Presbyterian Churchyard—Strasburg, VA 110
Presbyterian Grave Yard—Asheville, NC 75
Presnell, Josiah 112–113
Price, E. 178
Price, T.A. 207
Pridgen, Hugh Francis 25–26
Primitive Baptist Church—Carteret County, NC 56
Prior, John N. 87
Prior, Mrs. Louisa McIntyre 87
Prior, Warren 87
Prisoners of war 40, 53–54
Pritchard, Calvin 166
Pritchard (Ward), Mrs. Maria 166
Profitt, Bacchus 152, 224
Profitt, Wm. H. 11
Protestant Episcopal Church 15

Query, James Patrick 42
Query, Leander 174, 226
Quinn, John A. 145

Rachels, Starling 214
Ragan, Robert F. 182
Raines, Nathan 210
Rainey, William W. 69
Raleigh General Hospital No. 7—Raleigh, NC 205
Raleigh Rifles 72, 73, 74
Raleigh Typographical Society—Raleigh, NC 123
Ramseur, General Stephen D. 80
Rand, Oscar R. 129, 130, 223
Randall, J.P. 77
Randlesburg Riflemen 67
Randolph, Ansel 85
Randolph, John E. 148
Randolph, Mrs. Patsa 85
Randolph, Wm. 85
Randolph Rangers 210
Raney, George H. 13–14
Raney, Thomas H. 13
Rankin, Joseph W. 144
Ransom, Robert 51

Rawls Mill, Battle of—Martin County, NC 131, 132
Ray, Archibald 152
Ray, George M. 160
Ray, Lauchlin 187
Ray, Malcom, Jr. 175
Ray, Silas M. 152
Ray, William G. 35–36
Raymer, Nat 2, 217
Record, John J. 138
Red House Presbyterian Church—Semora, Caswell County, NC 69
Reed, Andrew J. 185
Reese, Randall H. 97
Reeves, H.R. 26
Reid, Buford 208
Reid, Hezekiah G. 208
Rencher, John G. 169, 225
Rex Hospital—Raleigh, NC 151
Reynolds, Daniel W. 109
Rhew, Allen 201
Rhew, David W. 160
Rich, William A. 114
Richards, Henry 148
Richards, Mrs. Eliza 148
Richards, Roscoe 148
Richmond Boys 185, 186
Rickets, Alexander 128
Rickman, Caleb A. 85
Rickman, Marquis Lafayette 85
Rickman, Marvin 85
Rickman, Mrs. Sarah 85
Riddick, Annual 211
Riddick, Elbert Thomas 143
Riddick, Joseph 143
Riddick, Richard H. 171
Rimmer, Merrell 124
Ripley's Brigade 16, 18
Roach, William S. 54
Roanoke Minute Men 71, 78
Robbins, Isaiah S. 114
Roberson, Harrison 54
Roberson, M. 40
Roberson, Stanton 40
Roberts, Charles Chalmers 137
Roberts, David 159
Roberts, Joshua 73
Roberts, Mrs. Lucinda 73
Roberts, Philetus W. 73, 74
Robertson, Charles W. 72
Robertson, Wiley P. 66
Robeson, Milton B. 143
Robeson, Mrs. A.C. 88
Robeson, W.B. 88
Robeson, William 88
Robeson Rifle Guards 89
Robinson, Capt. Benjamin 28
Robinson, James R. 154
Rockbridge Alum Springs 35
Rocky River Lodge, No. 159 138
Rocky River Presbyterian Church—Cabarrus County, NC 40, 41, 42, 43, 49

Rodes, General R.E. 79
Rogers, Jacob M. 73
Rogers, James W. 73
Rogers, Mrs. Mary Adeline 73
Rogerson, D. 40
Rollins, Harrison H. 114
Roney, Daniel M. 66
Roper, John W. 150
Rosborough, James T. 38–39
Rose, Allen 29
Rose, John A. 29, 218
Rose, Rufus Allen 29
Rose, Samuel 191
Ross, Alpheus Adolphus 110
Rough and Ready Guards 72, 75
Roundtree Masonic Lodge—Pitt County, NC 54
Rowan, George W. 98
Rowan Artillery 54
Rowan Rifle Guard 22, 25, 27
Royal, Mrs. Joe 148
Rudisill, Dr. J.C. 8
Rudisill, Jonas Gallant 8
Rudisill, Mrs. C.A. 8
Rudisill (Simonton), Mrs. J.O. 8
Ruffin, Samuel 20
Ruffin, Thos. 50
Runciman, John W. 15
Ruscoe, Jno. 197
Russell, N.E. 188
Russell, Sterling H. 180
Russell, Wilbern 30

Sadler, Julius 7
St. Charles Hospital—Richmond, VA 17, 84, 112, 170, 174
St. John's Episcopal Church—Pitt County, NC 54
Salem Church 23
Sample, William Leroy 181
Sanders, B.F. 55
Sanders, Dr. John W. 55–56
Sanders, S.J. 55
Sanders, Samuel T. 128
Sapp, Alpheus F. 111
Sasser, Edward Ballard 146
Savage, James M. 87
Scarlott, J.M. 188
Schuyler Sutton Camp of the Mountain Remnant Brigade, U.C.V. 95
Scotch Boys 90, 92
Scott, Edward M. 8, 11
Scott, John 34
Scott, John B. 40
Scott, Thomas 34
Scott, William R. 34
Seabrook Hospital—Richmond, VA 172, 175
Seagraves, Mrs. W.A. 166
Seagroves, Pascal 128–129
Sechler, John F. 170
2nd Corps Hospital—Orange Court House, VA 208

Second N.C. Hospital—Petersburg, VA 206, 210
Sedberry, William B. 189
Shaw, Angus 185–186, 187
Shaw, Dr. Daniel M. 127
Shaw, Henry M. 45
Shaw, Wesley, P. 35
Shearin, Elbert J. 71
Shenandoah Valley 27
Shepherd, Miss Kate 80
Sheppard, Hon. A.H. 35
Sheppard, Jacob 35
Sherman's Battery, Manassas, Battle of 32, 33
Shine, John D. 100
Shinn, Dr. James W. 25
Shipp, Ephraim S. 190
Shipp, John S. 118
Shipp, Mrs. H.M. 118
Shipp, W.M. 85
Shipp, Wm. T. 118
Short, Alexander P. 128
Sibley, Jeremiah B. 76
Sidbury, James M. 90
Sidbury, Mrs. Nancy 90
Sidbury, Woodman 90
Sikes, B.F. 198
Sikes, Mrs. J.B. 198
Sikes, S. Thomas 198–199
Siler, Jesse W. 49
Siler, Samuel 130
Siler, Samuel W.C. 130
Siler, Wesley C. 113–114
Sillers, William W. 156
Simmons, David W. 196
Simmons, Manuel 91
Simons, Thomas D. 75
Simonton, Capt. _____ 24
Simpson, J.W. 26
Simpson, Thomas M. 89–90
Singer, Arthur L. 197–198
Singletary, George Badger 203
Skinner, Benjamin S. 147
Skinner, Tristram Lowther 9
Slater, H. 167, 225
Sloan, George J. 141
Sloan, James 141
Sloan, John A. 147, 223
Sloan, Joseph Junius 171–172
Sloop, Nehemiah John 22
Small, Robert S. 213–214
Smedes, Edward S. 31
Smedes, Ives 31, 42
Smedes, the Rev. Dr._____ 42
Smiley, Matilda C. 120
Smith, Archibald C. 210
Smith, Hector 210
Smith, Hugh James 42–43
Smith, James K. 159–160
Smith, John Calvin 122
Smith, John Henry 125
Smith, John Kerr 181
Smith, the Rev. Leland I. 56
Smith, Marion 74

Smith, Mrs. _____ 118
Smith, Mrs. A.M. 181
Smith, Mrs. Julia 157
Smith, Mrs. Mary 159
Smith, Neill, T. 135
Smith, the Rev. P. 181
Smith, Dr. R.C. 32
Smith, R. Leyton 143
Smith, Richard A. 159
Smith, Samuel A. 159
Smith, Thomas McGehee 209
Smith, W.E. 159
Smith, William Henry 99, 100
Smith, William L. 30
Snead, E.D. 102
Snead, James A. 187
Snead, Nathan 101–102
Sockwell, John T. 144
Sorrell, Sidney J. 40
South Carolina Hospital—Petersburg, VA 206
Southerland, Charles Cornelius 53
Southerland, T.J. 53, 219
Southern Graveyard—Winchester, VA 36
Sparta Band 153
Speer, William H.A. 149, 223
Speight, Abner 17
Speight, Arthur (Arch) W. 17–18
Spencer, Jesse 170, 225
Spencer, Nathan 213
Sprinkle, Wm. 109, 222
Spruill, Samuel B. 98, 221
Sprunt, the Rev. James 202
Squires, Mrs. Reesie 71
Stallings, Dr. Cornelius Haywood 80–81
Stallings, Slade R. 54
Starnes, Henry Roland 29
Starr's Light Battery 177
Stedman, David B. 156
Steed, A.C. 188
Steed, W.P. 211
Steed, Wilburn H. 211
Steel, Andrew F. 154
Steele, General John 46
Steele, Mrs. Elizabeth 46
Stephen 111–112
Stephenson, James R. 155
Stevens, John B. 195
Stevens, Milton 188
Stewart, Colin 210, 228
Stewart, James H. 214
Stewart, John Walter 93
Stewart, the Rev. Mr. _____ 73
Stinson, Robert Wiley 211
Stirewalt, John R. 51
Stockard, John R. 84, 220
Stokes, Montfort Sidney Stokes 9
Stokes, General Montfort Stokes 9

Stone, Carney P. 176
Stone, John Crausbey 176
Stonewall Cemetery—Winchester, VA 119
Story, Julius 2056
Stoves, George 208
Stowe, George C. 166, 225
Strange, James William 96, 221
Strayhorn, Thomas J. 147
Stringfield, David J. 94
Sturdivant, C.H. 198
Sturdivant, Caswell 201–202
Styron, the Rev. W. 56
Sudderth, G.H. 136
Sudderth, Joseph G. 136–137
Suggs, Nathaniel S. 170
Sutton, John W. 141
Sutton, Noah 197
Swain, David 40
Swann, Robert Lee 68
Swindall, Chester 93
Sykes, Henry 205
Sykes, Mrs. Eliza 205
Sykes, Richard A. 205

Tait's Bladen Artillery Guards 192
Talent, Richard T. 198
Tarpley, J.H. 38
Tart, Mrs. Whitfield 106
Taylor, Samuel 206
Taylor, Sylvester 14
Teal, John C. 114–115
Teal, William H. 128
Tedder, Sidney 154
Terrell, Thomas T. 83
Tesh, Solomon 83
Tetterton, Samuel 40
Tew, William Roberson 101
Thaggard, Joseph G. 178
Thomas, Robert D. 115
Thomas, Thos. 54
Thompson, George W. 73
Thompson, Mrs. Nancy Ann 192
Thompson, the Rev. Robert B. 118
Thompson, Samuel 192
Thompson, William Anderson 14
Thompson, William Marcellus 73–74
Thompson, Wm. B.B. 192
Thornburg, W.L. 188, 227
Threadgill, Benjamin K. 78
Thurston, Stephen D. 16, 217
Tice, George W 199–200
Tiddy, Richard 7, 217
Tinnen, Joseph A. 160
Torrence, Hugh L. 183
Tranter's Creek 203
Treadaway, James A. 199
Trimble, General J.R. 108
Triplett, Mrs. Dorcia 181
Triplett, Pickens Lewis 181

Triplett, Thomas 181
Triplett, William T. 181
Tucker, John Randolph 80
Turnage, Benjamin W. 87
Turnage, Luke 128
Turner, John 164–165
Turner, John F. 127
Turner, John McLeod 44
Turner, Josiah, Jr. 98, 221
Turner, Dr. Vines E. 119
Turner, Wm. D. 127
Turrentine, Michael H. 178
Tutor, William O. 158
20th Michigan 118
Tyler, H.W. 73
Tyler, J.R. 26
Tyson, H. 40
Tyson, Joel 88
Tyson, William Thomas 188

Underwood, William W. 143
Universalist Church—Red Springs, NC 106
Upchurch, J.H. 36
Upchurch, Sims 36
Utley, James M. 197

Van Bokkelen, John F.S. 19
Vance (Espy), Mrs. Harriet 140
Vance (Martin), Mrs. Florence 140
Vance, Zebulon Baird 73, 129, 138–140
Varner, John L. 179
Vernon, Jesse 211
Vick, Bushrod W. 44
Vick, Joshua Washington 44, 219
Videl, Mrs. Dr. _____ 105
Vincent, G.D. 38
Vincent, John T. 38
Vincent, Thomas 206

Wade, Edwin P. 149
Wake Guards 127
Walker, Edwin 52
Walker, L.P., Secretary of War, Confederate 132
Walker, William 152, 224
Walker's Brigade 16, 18
Wallace, Charles S. 180
Wallace, J.O. 101
Wallace, William 53
Wallace, William H. 101
Warren, Benjamin F. 125
Warsham, Alexander 180
Washington Light Infantry 88
Watkins, James M. 78
Watkins, Willis 115
Watson, Giles H. 103–104
Watson, James S. 215
Watson, James Thomas 103–104
Watson, William H. 10
Watts, William H. 141

Weathersbee, Frank J. 179
Weatherspoon, Hiram 40
Weaver, J.C. Fulton 74
Weaver, the Rev. M.M. 74
Weaver, Mrs. Jane 74
Webb, D.D. 167
Webster, James 81
Webster, James Gallatin 81
Webster, William 128, 223
Wedding, John T. 34
Weddon, Henry A. 66
Weeks, Mrs. J.W. 148
Weeks, Rufus 157
Weir, Andrew 177–178
Weir, Dr. D.P. 211
Weir, Samuel Park 211
Welborn, Lynson M. 12
Wemyss, Davis 8
Wemyss, Ellen 8
Wemyss, James 7–8
West Hospital—Baltimore, MD 29
Westall, Samuel J. 152, 224
Westbrook, A.T. 148
Westbrook, J.F. 148
Westbrook, J.L. 148
Westbrook, Joseph T. 148–149
Westbrook, Julius 178
Westbrook (Elderidge), Mrs. Phoebe 148
Westbrook, Mrs. Saby 178
Westbrook, Uriah 178
Wexler, Chaplain E.C. 153
White, Benjamin 206
White, Daniel Cornelius 40
White, Franklin D. 101
White, James Amzi 173–174
White, Jas. I. 37
White, John 48
White, John E. 150
White, Jonathan Berry 48
White, Marshall Lindley 49
White, Mrs. Margaret 206
White, N.T. 40
White, Thomas Graham 37
White, William Cummins 206
White, William R. 101
White, Wm. 101
White Oak Swamp, VA 98
Whitehurst, James 40
White's Tavern, VA 98
Whitley, John B. 159
Wicker, J.J. 154, 156, 224
Wicker, Louis M. 156
Wilcox, General Cadmus W. 44
Wilcox, Harmon H. 133
Wilder, John W. 33
Wilkes, Neill A. 97
Wilkinson, James G. 109
Wilkinson, Neill 109
Willett, Joseph J. 207
Williams, C.R. 180
Williams, Franklin C. 180
Williams, Henry G. 164

Williams, Hiram 196
Williams, Hugh 171
Williams, Joel 19
Williams, John T. 19
Williams, Joseph A. 144
Williams, Lewis A. 149
Williams, M.D. 36
Williams, Marshall 196
Williams, Miss Delia 36
Williams, Mrs. Nancy 29
Williams, Mrs. O.C. 106
Williams, Mrs. Pearcy 19
Williams, N.C. 29
Williams, Obed Carr 210, 228
Williams, Richard 29
Williams, Samuel M. 108
Williams, Sol 96
Williams, William T. 164
Williamson, Mrs. A.D. 106
Williamson, Ruth 106
Willing, the Rev. Mr. _____ 182
Willis, Alexander 161
Willis, Mrs. Lucy 55
Willis, Mrs. Maude 55
Wilmington Artillery 52
Wilmington Light Infantry 18
Wilson, David L. 101
Wilson, Francis C. 103
Wilson, John 35
Wilson, John J. 102, 103
Wilson, Mrs. Jeanette 35

Wilson, Philo D. 35
Wilson, Thomas C. 180
Wilson, William P. 144
Wilson, Willis J.J. 159
Wimbish, John 203
Winder Hospital—Richmond, VA 72, 73, 75, 77, 83, 96, 105, 130, 154
Winfield, John P. 131
Winfree, Eli P. 197
Winkleman, Mrs. Lila B. 107
Winningham, Eli H. 111
Winters, George S. 21
Witherspoon, John G. 154, 157
Wolf, Thomas D. 156
Womack, David G. 71
Womble, Jesse C. 128
Wood, J.H. 21, 22, 217
Wood, Jasper N. 84
Wood, Lemuel S. 15
Wood, Miss Daisy 84
Woodall, Marion J. 134
Woolen, George H. 148
Wooley, Calvin W. 204
Wooley, Preston H. 204
Wooster, W.A. 16
Wooster, William Augustus 89
Wooten, Robert 166, 225
Wooten, William T. 145, 223
Wootten, William P. 27–28

Worley, Henry C. 85
Worth, Shubal G. 97
Wright, Eli 211
Wright, Isaac 105
Wright, James Allen 9
Wright, James W. 105–106
Wright, John 105
Wright, John C. 105
Wright, Mrs. M.G. 165
Wright, Thomas Charles 183
Wright, Dr. Thomas H. 9
Wright, Dr. Thomas M. 183
Wright, Thos. L. 105
Wynn's Mill 163

Yanceyville Greys 66
Yarborough, Bailey 72, 220
Yarborough, Samuel 76
Yates, John Watson 111
Yeates, Frederick L. 213
York, Richard Watt 33, 218
York Hospital—Winchester, VA 30
Young, Ephraim 125
Young, Samuel 143
Young, Thomas 126, 223
Younger, James Jefferson 37

Zeb Vance Camp, No. 681, U.C.V. 127
Zeta Phi Fraternity 142

www.ingramcontent.com/pod-product-compliance
Lightning Source LLC
Chambersburg PA
CBHW081550300426

44116CB00015B/2830